ISBN 978-1-333-90460-9
PIBN 10641110

1 MONTH OF
FREE
READING

at

www.ForgottenBooks.com

By purchasing this book you are eligible for one month membership to ForgottenBooks.com, giving you unlimited access to our entire collection of over 700,000 titles via our web site and mobile apps.

To claim your free month visit:

www.forgottenbooks.com/free641110

English
Français
Deutsche
Italiano
Español
Português

www.forgottenbooks.com

Mythology Photography **Fiction**
Fishing Christianity **Art** Cooking
Essays Buddhism Freemasonry
Medicine **Biology** Music **Ancient**
Egypt Evolution Carpentry Physics
Dance Geology **Mathematics** Fitness
Shakespeare **Folklore** Yoga Marketing
Confidence Immortality Biographies
Poetry **Psychology** Witchcraft
Electronics Chemistry History **Law**
Accounting **Philosophy** Anthropology
Alchemy Drama Quantum Mechanics
Atheism Sexual Health **Ancient History**
Entrepreneurship Languages Sport
Paleontology Needlework Islam
Metaphysics Investment Archaeology
Parenting Statistics Criminology
Motivational

A

THEORETICAL AND PRACTICAL

GRAMMAR

OF THE

FRENCH TONGUE.

A

THEORETICAL AND PRACTICAL

GRAMMAR

OF THE

French Tongue;

IN WHICH

THE PRESENT USAGE IS DISPLAYED,

AND

ALL THE PRINCIPAL DIFFICULTIES EXPLAINED

AGREEABLY TO THE DECISIONS

OF THE FRENCH ACADEMY.

TO WHICH ARE ADDED

SOME SELECT FAMILIAR PHRASES

On the principal Difficulties and Niceties of the French Language,

By M. DE LEVIZAC.

THE THIRD FRENCH EDITION,

Revised, carefully corrected, and improved by the addition
of a Treatise on French Versification,

By G. HAMONIÈRE.

~~~~~~~

PARIS:

PRINTED FOR THEOPHILUS BARROIS, JUNIOR, FOREIGN
BOOKSELLER, QUAI VOLTAIRE, N°. 11.

~~~~~~~

1819.

AVIS DU LIBRAIRE.

La Grammaire de M. DE LÉVIZAC, revue et augmentée par M. HAMO-NIÈRE, est la première qui ait été publiée en France. Les changemens et les augmentations considérables qu'elle renferme en forment un ouvrage nouveau. Je préviens donc que j'ai déposé les exemplaires voulus par la Loi, et que je poursuivrai avec la plus grande rigueur tout contrefacteur et débitant d'édition contrefaite.

Printed by J. SMITH, rue Montmorency, no. 16.

ADVERTISEMENT.

~~~~~~~~~~~~~

A Grammar, written by an author so advantageously known as M. de Lévizac, could not fail of being favourably received by the public; and many considerable editions, published in England, have had a rapid sale. All the principles contained in it are sanctioned by the authority of the French Academy and of the excellent Grammarians who for a century past have laboured to give fixed rules to the French language. This advantage, joined to another, which is, that all the phrases given as examples, or exercises, are extracted from the Dictionary of the French Academy, or the works of the best authors, gives it a decided superiority over all the French Grammars hitherto published for the use of Englishmen. We have made no alteration in

M. de Lévizac's work as to the plan ; we have only made a few corrections which appeared to us to be necessary ; and in order to render it as complete as possible, we have added a Treatise on French Versification. We have bestowed also the greatest care in correcting the text, that this edition may give perfect satisfaction, and prove far superior to all those that have preceded it, in that so important a part of an elementary work.

FRENCH GRAMMAR.

GRAMMAR, in general, is the art of *speaking* and *writing* correctly.

To speak—is to convey our thoughts by means of articulated sounds.

To write—is to render those thoughts permanently visible by means of certain Signs, or Characters, called *Letters*, and their number disposed in order constitutes what is called the ALPHABET.

FRENCH ALPHABET.

ROMAN LETTERS.		ITALIC LETTERS.		OLD PRO-NUNCIAT:	NEW PRO-NUNCIAT:
A —	a —	*A* —	*a* —	*ah* ——	*ah*
B. .	b. .	*B.* .	*b.* .	*bay* * .	*be* *
C. .	c. .	*C.* .	*c.* .	*say.* .	*ke*
D. .	d. .	*D.* .	*d.* .	*day.* .	*de*
E —	e —	*E* —	*e* —	*a* ——	*a*
F. .	f. .	*F.* .	*f.* .	*eff.* . .	*fe*
G. .	g. .	*G.* .	*g.* .	*jay* † . .	*ghe*
H. .	h. .	*H.* .	*h.* .	*ahsh.* .	*he*
I —	i —	*I* —	*i* —	*e* ——	*e*
J. .	j. .	*J.* .	*j.* .	*jee* † . .	*je* †
K. .	k. .	*K.* .	*k.* .	*kah.* .	*ke*
L. .	l. .	*L.* .	*l.* .	*ell.* . .	*le*
M. .	m. .	*M.* .	*m.* .	*emm.* .	*me*
N. .	n. .	*N.* .	*n.* .	*enn.* .	*ne*
O —	o —	*O* —	*o* —	*o* ——	*o*
P. .	p. .	*P.* .	*p.* .	*pay.* .	*pe*
Q. .	q. .	*Q.* .	*q.* .	*k u.*	*ke*
R. .	r. .	*R.* .	*r.* .	*heir.* .	*re*
S. .	s. .	*S.* .	*s.* .	*ess* . . .	*se*
T. .	t. .	*T.* .	*t.* .	*tay* . .	*te*
U —	u —	*U* —	*u* —	*u* ‡ ——	*u* ‡
V. .	v. .	*V.* .	*v.* .	*vay.* .	*ve*
X. .	x. .	*X.* .	*x.* .	*eeks.* .	*kse*
Y —	y —	*Y* —	*y* —	*e grec* —	*e grec*
Z. .	z. .	*Z.* .	*z.* .	*zed.* . .	*ze*

* Here both the old pronunciation and the new are expressed by English sounds, and in the new the letter *e* after each consonant is sounded as in the English word *battery*.

† The two consonants *g* and *j* are sounded in the Alphabet like *s* in *pleasure*, or *z* in *azure*.   ‡ See the second note, page 4.

GENERAL OBSERVATIONS.

The French ALPHABET contains, it is seen, *twenty-five letters*, which are divided into *Vowels* and *Consonants*.

A *vowel* is the simple emission of the *voice* forming an articulate sound by itself.

A *consonant*, on the contrary, cannot be articulated without the assistance of a *vowel*.

The *vowels* are *a, e, i, o, u*, and *y*, which sometimes has the sound of *one i*, and sometimes of *two*.

The nineteen remaining letters, *b, c, d, f, g, h, j, k, l, m, n, p, q, r, s, t, v, x, z,* are consonants.

THE VOWELS.

N. B. { The French language comprehends more distinct simple sounds than are here represented by the above five vowels; for, according as these are pronounced close or broad, short or long, with the appropriate accentuation, they furnish—*ten simple sounds.*

Add to these—*three* other *simple sounds,* each represented by the combination of two vowels, and

Lastly — *four nasal simple sounds,* which again, for want of more appropriate signs, are represented by the coalition of *n* or *m* with the above vowels, and they complete the number of } *seventeen simple sounds.* — See TABLE I. p. 4.

The vowels are either long or short;
The long vowels require more, the short vowels less time in pronouncing, thus :

a	is long in	pâte...	tough	and short in	patte....	paw
e	———	tempête	storm	———	trompette	trumpet
i	———	gîte....	abode	———	petite ...	little
o	———	hôte...	host..	———	hotte....	wicker basket
u	———	flûte...	flute .	———	hutte....	hut

Besides the *simple* there are also the *compound* sounds, in which two vowels are distinctly heard by a single emission of the voice; these are the *diphthongs.*—See Table III. p. 6 and 7.

The sound of one or more letters, pronounced with a single emission of the voice, is called a syllable; one or more syllables make a word.

ACCENTUATION AND PUNCTUATION.

In reading, due attention should be paid to the *accents* and *cedilla,* to the *apostrophe, diœresis, hyphen,* etc. the two former of which are peculiar to the French language.

There are *three accents,* the

acute....(') never placed but on *e,* as in *bonté.*

grave....(`) —placed over *a, e, u,* as in *voilà, procès, où.*

circumflex(^) employed over any long vowel, as *plâtre, rêve, épître, apôtre, bûche.*

The *cedilla* is a kind of comma placed under *c,* giving it the sound of *s* before *a, o, u,* as in *façade, façon, reçu*

The *apostrophe* (') marks the suppression of a *vowel* before another *vowel,* or *h* mute, as in *l'église, l'oiseau, l'homme, s'il vient,* for *la église, le oiseau, le homme, si il vient.*

The *diœresis* (¨) is placed over the vowels *e, i, u,* to intimate that they are to be pronounced distinctly from the vowels by which they are accompanied.

The *hyphen* (-) is particularly used in connecting compound words, as in *Belles - lettres, tout - puissant, chefs-d'œuvre, arc-en-ciel,* etc.

All the other distinctive marks, as the *comma, semi-colon, colon, period, interrogation, note of admiration,* and *exclamation, parenthesis,* etc. etc. are the same in the French as in the English language.

TABLE I.

THE SEVENTEEN SIMPLE SOUNDS OF THE FRENCH TONGUE.

	SOUND.	EXAMPLES.		SOUNDED AS	
1.	a *short*...	ami...	*friend*....	a in	*amateur*
2.	â *long*. ..	bas...	*stockings*..	a	*bark*
3.	e........	tenir..	*to hold*...	e	*battery*
4.	é........	été....	*summer*...	a	*paper*
5.	è........	modèle	*model*....	e	*met*
6.	ê (1).....	téte...	*head*.....	e	*there*
7.	i........	imiter.	*to imitate*.	i	*timid*
8.	o *short*...	école..	*school*....	o	*scholar*
9.	ô *long*....	côte...	*rib*.......	o	*note*
10.	u........	vertu..	*virtue*....	(2)	——
11.	eu *short*..	jeune..	*young*....	u	*shun*
12.	eû *long*...	jeûne..	*fast*......	(2)	——
13	ou......	soupe .	*soup*.....	ou	*soup*
14.	an ⎫	ange..	*angel*.....	en	*encore*
15.	in ⎬ (2)	lin....	*flax*......	en	*length*
16.	on ⎪	long...	*long*.....	on	*long*
17.	un ⎭	brun..	*brown*....	un	——

(1) Besides these four sorts of *e*, there is one entirely mute at the end of many words, as in the above *modèle, téte, école, côte;* and sometimes in the beginning and middle, as in *cependant, javeline, Roquefort, l'empereur,* etc.

(2) The sound of the French *u*, to which there is no similar, nor even approximate sound in English, must be heard from the master, and it may be necessary to add, that, though we have attempted to exhibit the French sounds by English letters, yet they can only be correctly learnt by hearing them from the lips of a native. In particular, the nasal sounds cannot be conveyed by any combination of English letters.

N. B.—The figures in the following tables relate to the above seventeen simple sounds.

TABLE II.

COALITION OF LETTERS REPRESENTING SEVERAL OF THE SEVENTEEN SIMPLE SOUNDS.

SIMPLE SOUNDS REPRESENTED BY EXAMPLES.			
1.	a.	ea	il gagea	*he betted*
4.	é.	ai	aigu	*sharp*
		eai	geai	*jay*
		ée	année	*year*
		œ	œsophage	*œsophagus*
5.	è.	ai	aide	*aid*
		aie	baie	*bay*
		ei	baleine	*whale*
		eoi	je nageois	*I did swim*
		oi	foïble	*weak*
		oie	monnoie	*money*
6.	ê.	ai	aîné	*eldest*
		oi	paroître	*to appear*
7.	i.	ie	folie	*folly*
8.	o.	au	aurore	*dawn*
		eo	flageolet	*flagelet*
9.	ô.	au	auteur	*author*
		eau	marteau	*hammer*
		eo	geole	*gaol*
10.	u.	eu	gageure	*wager*
		eue	eue f.	*had*
		ue	laitue	*lettuce*
11.	eu.	œu	sœur	*sister*
12.	eû.	œu	nœud	*knot*
		eue	queue	*tail*
13.	ou	oue	il joue	*he plays*
		aoû	Aoît	*August*
14.	an	am	jambe	*leg*
		ean	affligeant	*afflicting*
		em	membre	*member*
		en	entendre	*to hear*
15.	in	aim	essaim	*swarm*
		ain	crainte	*fear*
		ein	peinture	*picture*
		im	impoli	*impolite*
		ym	symbole	*symbol*
		yn	syntaxe	*syntax*
16.	on	eou	pigeon	*pigeon*
		om	ombre	*shade*
17.	un	eun	à jeun	*fasting*
		um	parfum	*perfume*

THE SOUNDS
TABLE III.
DIPHTHONGS.

COMPOUND SOUNDS REPRESENTED BY EXAMPLES.				
7..... 1 or 2..	*i.* *a.*}	ia {	fiacre..... galimatias.	*hackney-coach* *nonsense*
7..... 4.....	*i.* *é.*}	iai........... ie....... iez	je défiai... amitié..... vous riez..	*I challenged* *friendship* *you laugh*
7..... 5.....	*i.* *è.*}	iai........... iè....... ie........... ioi.........	biais...... bière...... ciel....... je purifiois.	*bias* *beer* *heaven* *I purified*
7..... 8 or 9.	*i.* *o.*}	io iau.	violon .... miauler ...	*violin* *to mew*
7..... 10.....	*i..* *u.*}	iu	reliure	*binding*
7..... 11 or 12	*i..* *eu*}	ieu {	relieur. mieux.....	*bookbinder* *better*
7..... 13.....	*i..* *ou.*}	iou	chiourme..	*crew of a galley*
7..... 14.....	*i..* *an.*}	ian .... ien	viande.... audience...	*meat* *audience*
7..... 15.....	*i..* *in.*}	ien	chrétien...	*christian*
7..... 16.....	*i..* *on.*}	ion	passion....	*passion*
8..... 2.....	*o..* *â.*}	oi .... oî.......... oie.........	bois....... boîte...... foie.......	*wood* *box* *liver*
8..... 6.....	*o..* *é..*}	oe .... oi .... eoi.........	moelle.... voisin..... nageoire...	*marrow* *neighbour* *fin*
8..... 15.....	*o..* *in.*}	oin	besoin.....	*want*
10..... 1.....	*u..* *a..*}	ua	nuage.....	*cloud*
10..... 4.....	*u..* *é..*}	uai .... ue .... ué .... uée	je remuai.. éternuer.. dénué..... nuée.......	*I moved* *to sneeze* *stript* *cloud*

TABLE III.

DIPHTHONGS CONTINUED.

COMPOUND SOUNDS REPRESENTED BY EXAMPLES.				
10..... 5.....	*u..* *è..* }	ue......... uoi........	menu*et*..... il suo*it*.....	*minuet* *he perspired*
10..... 7.....	*u..* *i..* }	ui......... uie........	bu*isson*..... parapl*uie*...	*bush* *umbrella*
10..... 8.....	*u..* *o..* }	uo	impét*uo*sité..	*impetuosity*
10..... 11.....	*u..* *eu.* }	ueu	l*ueu*r.......	*glimmering*
10..... 12.....	*u..* *eŭ.* }	ueu	majest*ueux*..	*majestic*
10..... 14.....	*u..* *an.* }	uan........ uen........	n*uan*ce..... infl*uen*ce...	*shade* *influence*
10..... 15.....	*u..* *in.* }	uin	J*uin*.......	*June*
10..... 16.....	*u..* *on.* }	uon	t*uon*s......	*let us kill*
13..... 1.....	*ou.* *a..* }	oua	r*oua*ge.....	*wheel-work*
13..... 4.....	*ou.* *é..* {	oue........ oué........ ouée....... ouai.......	dén*oue*r.... déj*oué*...... fille enj*ouée*. je j*ouai*.....	*to untie* *frustrated* *cheerful girl* *I played*
13..... 5.....	*ou.* *è..* }	oue........ ouoi.......	f*oue*tter.... je dén*ouois*..	*to whip* *I untied*
13..... 7.....	*ou.* *i..* }	oui......... ouie........	camb*ouis*... l'*ouie*......	*cart grease* *hearing*
13..... 11.....	*ou.* *eu.* }	oueu	b*oueu*r.....	*scavenger*
13..... 12.....	*ou.* *eŭ.* }	oueu	n*oueux*.....	*knotty*
13..... 14.....	*ou.* *an.* }	ouan....... ouen.......	l*ouan*ge.... R*ouen*......	*praise* *Rouen, a city*
13..... 15.....	*ou.* *in.* }	ouin	bab*ouin*....	*baboon*
13..... 16.....	*ou.* *on.* }	ouon	j*ouon*s.....	*let us play*

OBSERVATIONS

Upon the two first Tables.

Am, an, do not take the nasal sound when *m* or *n* are doubled, as in *constamment, année. Am* is not nasal at the end of some foreign names, as *Abraham, Roboam,* etc.; except *Adam,* which has the nasal sound..

Em and *en* are articulated as in the English words *hem* and *men :*

1. In words taken from foreign languages; as *Jerusalem, item, hymen,* etc. and also in *décemvirat, décemvirs, étrenner, ennemi, moyennant, penne, pennage,* and in the second syllable of the compound word *empenné.*

2. In some persons and tenses of the verbs, *tenir, venir, prendre,* and their compounds, as *que je vienne, que tu soutiennes, qu'il comprenne,* etc. in the pronouns feminine, *la mienne, la tienne, les siennes,* in many other words, as *antienne, magicienne, Vienne en Autriche,* etc.

3. In many nouns and persons of verbs ending in *ène, ème,* as in *arène, ébène,* je me *promène,* il *égrène,* il *sème,* where however the *e* is somewhat more open.

Aen has the sound of the French nasal *an* in *Caen* a town of Normandy.

And *aon* has the same sound in *Laon,* another town of France, in *faon* a fawn, and in *paon* a peacock; but these letters have the sound of *on* in *taon* an oxfly.

N in the monosyllable *en* both when a preposition and when a pronoun, in *on, mon, ton, son* pronouns, and in *bon, bien,* and *rien,* ceases to be nasal when these words are immediately followed by a vowel or an *h* mute, as *en Italie, on en aura, mon ami, c'est un bon homme, on a bien essayé, je suis bien aise qu'il n'ait rien oublié.* But *en* and *on* remain nasal, when placed after the verbs to which they belong; as *donnez-en à votre sœur. A-t-on essayé ? va-t'en au logis.*

Im and *in* are not nasal :

1. In the word *intérim*, and in proper names taken from foreign languages, as *Sélim*, *Éphraïm*, *Ibrahim*. However the nasal sound is preserved in *Benjamin*, *Joachim*.

2. In the beginning and middle of words, when *m* or *n* is followed by a vowel or an *h* mute, as *inanimé*, *inimaginables*, *unanimité*, etc.

3. Whenever *m* or *n* is doubled, as *immoler*, *immersion*, *innover*, *inné*, *innocent*, though in this latter word only one *n* is sounded.

Un has the sound of *u* close in *une*, *unième*, *unanime*, and of *eun* in *jeune homme*, when followed by a word beginning with a vowel or an *h* mute, as *un homme*, *un esprit*, *aucun ami*, *commun accord*.

Um is pronounced *omm* in some words adopted from the Latin, as *centumvirs*, *album*, *quinquennium*, *ladanum*, *laudanum*, *géranium*.

U after the consonants *q* and *g* is generally silent, as in *quatre*, *guerre*, etc. See those letters.

OF THE Y.

This letter, when alone, or when preceded, or followed by a consonant, is pronounced as simple *i*, except in *pays*, *paysan*, *paysage*, and *abbaye*, which are pronounced *pé-is*, *pé-isan*, *pé-isage*, *abé-ie*. *Y* between two vowels is pronounced *ii*, and when preceded by *a*, it gives to this letter the sound of *ai*, and when by *o* or *u*, it gives to them the sound of the diphthongs *oi* or *ui*. The vowel which follows the *y* is pronounced like one of the diphthongs *ia*, *ie*, etc. for which reason we have deferred speaking of the *y* till after the diphthongs.

ab-ba-ye	*Abbey*	nous é-ga-yons	*we enliven*
a-bo-yer	*to bark*	es-su-yer	*to wipe*
ap-pu-yer	*to support*	mo-yen	*means*
ba-la-yer	*to sweep*	net-to-yer	*to clean*
bé-ga-yer	*to stammer*	je pa-yois	*I was paying*
cra-yon	*pencil*	je ra-ye-rois	*I would streak*
cro-ya-ble	*credible*	ro-yau-me	*kingdom*
é-cu-yer	*esquire*	vo-ya-ge	*voyage*
il ef-fra-ya	*he frightened*	vo-ya-geur	*traveller*

EXERCISES
ON MONOSYLLABLES, OR WORDS OF ONE SYLLABLE.

Gras	*fat*	il rend	*he returns*
ma	*my*	il sent	*he smells, feels*
ta	*thy*	je vends	*I sell*
sa	*his, her, its*	je	*I*
la	*the, her, it*	me	*me*
las	*tired*	ne	*not*
pas	*step*	te	*thee*
un plat	*a dish*	ce	*this, that*
bac	*ferry-boat*	se	*himself, etc.*
sac	*sack, bag*	le	*the, him, it*
arc	*arch, bow*	de	*of*
parc	*park*	lé	*breadth*
bal	*ball*	né	*born*
cap	*cape*	mais	*but*
car	*for*	mes	*my,* pl.
par	*by, through*	tes	*thy,* pl.
part	*share*	ses	*his, her, its* pl
art	*art*	les	*the, them*
char	*chariot*	pré	*meadow*
dard	*dart*	près	*near*
lard	*bacon*	prêt	*ready*
tard	*late*	ver	*worm*
quand	*when*	vers	*towards*
rang	*rank*	vert	*green*
blanc	*white*	il perd	*he loses*
sans	*without*	il sert	*he serves*
dans	*in*	peur	*fear*
gland	*acorn*	il meurt	*he dies*
pan	*skirt of a coat*	pleurs	*tears*
cran	*notch*	leur	*their*
plant	*plantation*	sel	*salt*
plan	*plan*	tel	*such*
flanc	*flank*	quel	*which*
grand	*great*	sec	*dry*
en	*in*	bec	*beak*
il fend	*he splits*	chef	*chief*
gens	*people*	bref	*short*
lent	*slow*	neuf	*new*
main	*hand*	Est	*East*
il ment	*he lies*	vingt	*twenty*
il pend	*he hangs*	crin	*horse-hair*
il prend	*he takes*	lin	*flax*
ceint	*girt*	brin	*sprig*
cinq	*five*	pain	*bread*
sain	*wholesome*	pin	*pine*
sein	*bosom*	vin	*wine*
saint	*holy*	fi	*fy*
seing	*signature*	fils	*son*

rit	*fried*	rond	*round*
lis	*lily*	bloud	*light (hair)*
pris	*taken*	pont	*bridge*
prix	*price*	long	*long*
ris	*laugh*	fond	*bottom*
riz	*rice*	ils font	*they do*
ni	*neither, nor*	jonc	*rush*
nid	*nest*	uon	*no*
si	*if*	goud	*hinge*
il fit	*he did*	nom	*name*
mis	*put*	plomb	*lead*
plis	*folds*	nu	*naked*
fil	*thread*	du	*of the*, sing. m.
vil	*vile*	il dut	*he owed*
vif	*lively*	bru	*daughter-in-law*
sot	*fool*	brut	*rough*
tôt	*soon*	il but	*he drank*
clos	*shut up*	cru	*raw*
nos	*our*	il crut	*he believed*
vos	*your*	je fus	*I was*
gros	*big*	jus	*juice*
trop	*too much*	lu	*read*
trot	*trot*	il lut	*he read*
croc	*hook*	plus	*more*
or	*gold*	tu	*thou*
bord	*edge*	vu	*seen*
fort	*strong*	flux	*flux*
tort	*wrong*	glu	*bird-lime*
je sors	*I go out*	duc	*duke*
sort	*fate*	suc	*juice*
port	*port*	sur	*upon*
il mord	*he bites*	mur	*wall*
vol	*theft*	nul	*no, none*
choc	*shock*	bout	*end*
roc	*rock*	joug	*yoke*
bloc	*block*	nous	*we, us*
troc	*exchange*	vous	*you*
dot	*dowry*	clou	*nail*
ou	*one, people, they*	cou	*neck*
bon	*good*	coup	*blow, stroke*
bond	*bound*	trou	*hole*
ton	*thy*	mou	*soft*
son	*his, her, its*	tout	*all*
ils sont	*they are*	toux	*cough*
mon	*my*	pou	*louse*
don	*gift*	cour	*yard*
dont	*of which*, etc.	il pleut	*it rains*
donc	*therefore*	peu	*little, few*
front	*forehead*	il veut	*he is willing*

ON DISSYLLABLES,

OR WORDS OF TWO SYLLABLES.

A-bus	abuse	clé-ment	clement
a-chat	purchase	cli-mat	climate
ac-teur	actor	cloi-son	partition
â-ge	age	co-hue	throng
ai-greur	acidity	com-mun	common
â-me	soul	com-pas	compasses
an-neau	ring	com-te	earl
ar-deur	ardour	con-gé	holiday
ar-gent	money	cou-te'	tale
as-tre	star	co-quin	rogue
au-cun	none	cor-deau	line
a-veu	confession	cô-té	side
a-vis	advice	cou-ple	couple
au-tre	other	cou-reur	runner
bal-con	balcony	cous-sin	cushion
ban-que	bank	cou-vent	convent
bar-que	a bark	crè-me	cream
ba-teau	boat	cri-me	crime
bâ-ton	stick	crot-te	dirt
beau-té	beauty	crou-te	crust
bè-gue	stammerer	da-me	lady
bê-te	beast	dan-seur	dancer
beur-re	butter	dé-bit	sale
bi-ble	bible	de-bout	erect
blâ-me	blame	de-mi	half
bon-heur	happiness	dé-pôt	deposit
bon-té	goodness	dé-sert	wilderness
bos-quet	grove	des-sert	dessert
bou-quet	nosegay	dis-cours	speech
bour-geon	bud	dou-leur	pain
bour-ru	surly	é-cu	crown
bras-seur	brewer	en-clin	inclined
bri-gand	robber	en-fant	child
brus-que	abrupt	é-poux	spouse
bru-te	brute	es-poir	hope
buf-fet	cupboard	é-tain	pewter
bu-reau	office	ex-cès	excess
bus-te	bust	fes-tin	feast
ca-deau	present	tê-te	festival
ca-fé	coffee	fi-lou	pickpocket
ca-hot	jolt	fla-con	decanter
ca-non	cannon	flam-beau	flambeau
ca-ve	cellar	flû-te	flute
cau-se	cause	fo-rêt	forest
cer-cle	circle	fou-dre	thunderbolt
ci-seau	chissel	four-mi	ant

fri-pon	knave	mons-tre	monster
fu-reur	fury	mou-le	mould
gaie-té	cheerfulness	mou-lin	mill
gar-çon	boy	ni-gaud	silly fellow
gâ-teau	cake	nou-veau	new
ga-zon	turf	œu-vre	work
gen-dre	son-in-law	on-guent	ointment
gen-re	gender	or-dre	order
gi-got	leg of mutton	ou-bli	oblivion
gla-çon	piece of ice	pa-rent	relation
goû-ter	luncheon	par-rain	godfather
gout-te	drop	pâ-te	dough
grâ-ce	favour	pâ-té	pie
gron-deur	grumbler	pat-te	paw
gru-au	oatmeal	pê-che	fishing
guè-re	little	pé-ché	sin
guer-re	war	pê-cheur	fisherman
gueu-le	mouth of a beast	pé-cheur	sinner
gui-de	guide	pei-ne	trouble
'hai-ne	hatred	pein-tre	painter
'hal-le	market-hall	pè-re	father
'har-pe	harp	peu-ple	people
'hâ-te	haste	peu-reux	fearful
'hau-teur	height	pin-te	pint
'ha-sard	chance	plu-me	feather
'hê-tre	beech	por-trait	picture
hom-me	man	pour-pre	purple
hon-neur	honour	prin-ce	prince
'hon-te	shame	pru-neau	prune
hor-reur	horror	ra-goût	ragout
hô-te	landlord	rè-gle	rule
hu-main	human	rè-gne	reign
im-pie	impious	rei-ne	queen
ju-ge	judge	ren-te	annuity
jour-née	day	rê-ve	dream
lai-teux	milky	ri-re	laughing
la-quais	footman	rou-te	road
lar-cin	theft	ru-se	trick
lar-geur	breadth	sa-bre	sabre
li-queur	liquor	sa-lut	salute
lo-gis	dwelling	sa-tin	satin
lon-gueur	length	sau-ce	sauce
mar-bre	marble	sau-teur	tumbler
mar-chand	tradesman	sé-jour	residence
ma-ri	husband	si-gnal	signal
mè-re	mother	si-gne	sign
meu-ble	furniture	som-bre	dark
mon-de	world	sou-hait	wish

sou-pe	*soup*	tou-pie	*top*
sou-ris	*smile*	tonr-neur	*turner*
su-cre	*sugar*	trai-neau	*sledge*
sus-pect	*suspicious*	trô-ne	*throne*
ta-che	*spot*	trou-peau	*flock*
tâ-che	*task*	veu-ve	*widow*
tam-bour	*drum*	vi-gne	*vine*
tom-beau	*grave*	zè-le	*zeal*
to-me	*volume*	zé-lé	*zealous*

WORDS OF THREE SYLLABLES.

a-bî-me	*abyss*	cham-pi-gnon	*mushroom*
a-bré-gé	*abridgement*	cha-pel-le	*chapel*
a-bri-cot	*apricot*	cha-pi-tre	*chapter*
ab-so-lu	*absolute*	char-la-tan	*quack*
ab-sur-de	*absurd*	char-ret-te	*cart*
ac-tri-ce	*actress*	châ-ti-ment	*chastisement*
am-pou-le	*blister*	chau-de-ment	*warmly*
â-pre-té	*asperity*	chauf-fa-ge	*fuel*
a-rai-gnée	*spider*	ci-vi-ère	*hand-barrow*
ar-moi-re	*cabinet*	cla-ve-cin	*harpsichord*
a-tro-ce	*atrocious*	clo-a-que	*sewer*
au-ber-ge	*inn*	col-li-ne	*hill*
a-voi-ne	*oats*	co-lon-ne	*column*
aus-tè-re	*austere*	co-lo-ris	*colouring*
ba-bio-le	*bawble*	co-mé-die	*comedy*
bas-ses-se	*baseness*	com-mer-çant	*merchant*
bâ-ti-ment	*building*	com-pa-gnie	*company*
bê-le-ment	*bleating*	com-pa-gnon	*companion*
ber-gè-re	*shepherdess*	con-dui-te	*behaviour*
bê-ti-se	*stupidity*	con-quê-te	*conquest*
bien-fai-sant	*benevolent*	con-ti-gu	*contiguous*
blan-châ-tre	*whitish*	cor-don-nier	*shoemaker*
bor-du-re	*edging*	co-ri-ace	*tough*
bou-lan-ger	*baker*	cor-ni-chon	*girkin*
bou-ti-que	*shop*	cou-ron-ne	*crown*
bra-vou-re	*valour*	cou-te-las	*hanger*
breu-va-ge	*drink*	cou-tu-re	*seam*
brou-et-te	*wheelbarrow*	cra-moi-si	*crimson*
brû-lu-re	*burning*	cru-au-té	*cruelty*
brus-que-ment	*bluntly*	cui-si-ne	*kitchen*
ca-de-nas	*padlock*	cul-bu-te	*tumble*
cam-pa-gne	*country*	dé-com-bres	*rubbish*
ca-rê-me	*lent*	dé-jeu-ner	*breakfast*
cein-tu-re	*girdle*	de-meu-re	*abode*
ce-pen-dant	*however*	dés-hon-neur	*dishonour*

dis-ci-ple	*pupil*	gué-ri-son	*healing*
dis-grâ-ce	*disgrace*	gui-mau-ve	*marsh-mallow*
dro-guis-te	*druggist*	ha-lei-ne	*breath*
droi-tu-re	*uprightness*	' har-di-ment	*boldly*
é-cha-faud	*scaffold*	' ha-ri-cot	*French bean*
é-chel-le	*ladder*	hor-lo-ge	*clock*
é-che-veau	*skein*	hor-ri-ble	*horrid*
é-cu-me	*froth*	hô-tes-se	*landlady*
em-pe-reur	*emperor*	i-gno-rant	*ignorant*
em-plâ-tre	*plaster*	im-men-se	*immense*
em-plet-te	*purchase*	im-pu-ni	*unpunished*
en-clu-me	*anvil*	in-cen-die	*conflagration*
en-ga-geant	*engaging*	in-con-nu	*unknown*
en-ne-mi	*enemy*	in-gé-nu	*ingenuous*
en-sei-gne	*sign*	in-hu-main	*inhuman*
é-pa-gneul	*spaniel*	in-sec-te	*insect*
é-pi-ce	*spice*	ins-truc-tif	*instructive*
é-pi-cier	*grocer*	i-voi-re	*ivory*
é-pou-se	*wife*	i-vro-gne	*drunkard*
es-ca-lier	*staircase*	ja-quet-te	*jacket*
es-pa-ce	*space*	jour-na-lier	*journeyman*
es-pè-ce	*kind*	lai-tiè-re	*milk-woman*
es-quis-se	*sketch*	lan-gou-reux	*languishing*
es-tra-gon	*stragon*	len-til-le	*lentil*
é-tei-gnoir	*extinguisher*	li-ma-çon	*snail*
é-tour-di	*thoughtless*	ma-ga-sin	*warehouse*
é-vê-ché	*bishoprick*	mal-a-droit	*awkward*
é-veil-lé	*awake*	ma-nœu-vre	*manœuvre*
ex-ces-sif	*immoderate*	mar-mi-ton	*scullion*
ex-em-ple	*example*	mas-cu-lin	*masculine*
fa-bu-leux	*fabulous*	mé-con-tent	*discontented*
fa-ça-de	*front*	mé-moi-re	*memory*
fa-ïen-ce	*delft-ware*	mé-na-ger	*thrifty*
fa-ri-neux	*mealy*	men-son-ge	*falsehood*
fa-rou-che	*fierce*	mé-pri-se	*mistake*
fi-las-se	*flax*	mé-tho-de	*method*
fleu-ris-te	*florist*	mo-des-tie	*modesty*
foi-bles-se	*weakness*	mon-ta-gnard	*highlander*
fo-lâ-tre	*playful*	mou-tar-de	*mustard*
fou-droy-ant	*thundering*	mur-mu-re	*murmur*
four-bis-seur	*sword-cutler*	na-tu-rel	*natural*
four-ru-re	*fur*	nau-fra-ge	*shipwreck*
fram-boi-se	*raspberry*	né-an-moins	*nevertheless*
fri-su-re	*curling*	no-bles-se	*nobility*
frois-su-re	*bruising*	noi-râ-tre	*blackish*
gi-ro-fle	*cloves*	o-bli-geant	*obliging*
go-be-let	*tumbler, goblet*	om-bra-ge	*shade*
gou-lu-ment	*greedily*	op-pro-bre	*disgrace*

C 2

o-ra-geux	*stormy*	symp-tô-me	*symptom*
or-fè-vre	*goldsmith*	tein-tu-re	*dying*
or-phe-lin	*orphan*	ten-dres-se	*tenderness*
pa-moi-son	*fainting-fit*	té-né-breux	*dark*
pan-tou-fle	*slipper*	thé-â-tre	*theatre*
pa-pe-tier	*stationer*	thé-i-ère	*tea-pot*
pa-que-bot	*packet-boat*	toi-let-te	*toilet*
pa-ren-te	*kinswoman*	tour-ne-vis	*screwdriver*
pa-rois-se	*parish*	tou-te-fois	*nevertheless*
pas-sa-ble	*tolerable*	tri-che-rie	*cheat*
pois-sar-de	*fishwoman*	tri-om-phe	*triumph*
poi-tri-ne	*breast*	trom-pet-te	*trumpet*
por-tiè-re	*coach-door*	tu-mul-te	*tumult*
pos-tu-re	*posture*	va-can-ces	*holidays*
po-ta-ge	*porridge*	ver-get-te	*brush*
pous-siè-re	*dust*	ver-mis-seau	*small worm*
pré-tex-te	*pretence*	vic-toi-re	*victory*
prin-ces-se	*princess*	vi-gou-reux	*vigorous*
pro-mes-se	*promise*	vil-la-geois	*countryman*
pro-tec-teur	*protector*	voi-tu-re	*carriage*
pu-é-ril	*childish*	af-fai-re	*business*
puis-san-ce	*power*	ap-pé-tit	*appetite*
que-rel-le	*quarrel*	ar-tis-te	*artist*
ra-piè-re	*rapier*	as-si-du	*assiduous*
ra-tiè-re	*rat-trap*	bien-sé-ant	*becoming*
ré-col-te	*crop*	bien-ve-nu	*welcome*
ré-ser-vé	*reserved*	bles-su-re	*wound*
res-sour-ce	*resource*	boi-se-rie	*wainscoat*
re-trai-te	*retirement*	bou-ta-dé	*whim*
rê-ve-rie,	*meditation*	bras-se-rie	*brewhouse*
rou-geâ-tre	*reddish*	bro-de-rie	*embroidery*
rus-ti-que	*rural*	car-ros-se	*coach*
scan-da-leux	*scandalous*	cha-pe-lier	*hatter*
scru-pu-leux	*scrupulous*	chau-de-ment	*warmly*
sé-an-ce	*sitting*	chau-diè-re	*copper*
ser-ru-ré	*lock*	chaus-su-re	*shoes, stockings*
sif-fle-ment	*whistling*	co-li-que	*colick*
sim-ple-ment	*plainly*	col-lé-ge	*college*
so-bri-quet	*nick-name*	co-mé-dien	*comedian*
so-len-nel	*solemn*	con-qué-rant	*conqueror*
son-net-te	*little bell*	cons-tam-ment	*constantly*
so-no-re	*sonorous*	cou-chet-te	*couch*
sou-cou-pe	*saucer*	cou-te-lier	*cutler*
soup-çon-neux	*suspicious*	cré-du-le	*credulous*
spec-ta-cle	*sight*	cri-ti-que	*critic*
splen-di-de	*splendid*	cu-re-dent	*tooth-picker*
suc-ces-seur	*successor*	dé-goû-tant	*disgusting*
su-prê-me	*supreme*	des-po-te	*despot*

OF CONSONANTS.

B, b, this letter has the same sound as in English.

Bal	*ball*	bo-bi-ne	*bobbin*
Ba-bel	*Babel*	bar-ba-ris-me	*barbarism*
ba-bil	*prating*	bi-bli-o-thè-que	*library*
ba-bouin	*baboon*	bur-les-que	*burlesque*

B is always pronounced in the middle of words, as *ab-di-quer, sub-ve-nir, ob-vi-er;* and at the end of proper names, as *Job, Caleb, Moab;* also in the words, *radoub,* the refitting of a ship, *rumb,* point of the compass; but it is never sounded in *plomb,* lead.

When double, as in *abbé,* abbot; *rabbin,* rabbin; *sabbat,* sabbath; and their derivatives, only one of these letters is sounded.

C, c, has the sound of
{
  k, or English *c* in *cart,* before *a, o, u, l, n, r,* but of
  s, or *c* in *cedar, cider,* before *e, i,* and *y.*
}

C sounded as *k.*		C sounded as *s.*	
Cal-cul	*calculation*	ce-ci	*this*
ca-co-pho-nie	*cacophony*	cé-ci-té	*blindness*
clé-ri-cal	*clerical*	cé-ta-cée	*cetaceous*
Cra-co-vie	*Cracow*	cer-ceau	*hoop*
co-que-li-cot	*wild-poppy*	Cir-cé	*Circe*
cro-co-di-le	*crocodile*	ci-li-ce	*hair-cloth*
cris-tal	*crystal*	cy-ni-que	*cynic*
cu-cur-bi-te	*cucurbite*	cy-près	*cypress*

C is not sounded in the middle of words before *q, ca, co, cu, cl, cr,* as *socque, acquérir, accabler, acclimater, acclamation, accomplir, accoutrer, accréditer, ecclésiastique,* which are pronounced *so-que, a-quérir,*

c 3

ac-cabler, etc. except, however, in the words, *pec-cable, pec-cant, pec-cadille, pec-cavi, sac-cho-lactique,* in which the sound of the double *c* is distinctly heard. — It has the sound of *k* before *ce* and *ci,* as in *suc-cès, ac-cident, vac-cine,* etc. and takes the sound of *s* before *a, o, u,* when there is a cedilla under it, as in *façade, façon, reçu.*

C is sounded as *g* hard in *second* and its derivatives, and by many in *Claude,* and *Reine-Claude,* and even by some, but improperly, in *secret.*

C, at the end of words, is usually pronounced *k,* as in *cognac, lac* (a lake), *avec, bec, pic, syndic, roc, froc, estoc, duc, aquéduc, agaric, arc, zinc,* etc. and in the singular of *échec;* but it is not sounded in *croc, ac-croc, arc-boutant, banc, broc, clerc, marc d'argent, cric, esto-mac, flanc, jonc, lacs* (toils), *tabac, tronc, échecs,* nor in *donc* before a consonant; but

It is always sounded in *croc-en-jambe, franc étourdi, du blanc au noir,* and in both syllables of *mic-mac, tric-trac, cric-crac, ric-à-ric,* and *porc-épic.*

In words ending in *ct,* both consonants are generally sounded, as in *tact, contact, intact, exact, inexact, abject, correct, direct, infect, strict, succinct;* but neither of them in *aspect, suspect, circonspect, amict, instinct, distinct;* and only *c* in *respect,* though both letters are always heard in *suspecte, circonspecte, respecte, distincte,* as well as in the middle of other similar words, as *recteur, vecteur, séducteur, rédacteur, humecter, injecter, dactyle, ductile, tactique,* etc.

Ch has two sounds { one, which is most general like *sh,* in *she, shake;* the other, which very rarely occurs, is that of *k* in *chimera.*

Examples of *sh.*

Chat	*cat*	ar-chi-tra-ve	*architravi*
che-val	*horse*	chou-et-te	*screech-ou*
cher-cher	*to seek*	chu-te	*fall*
chi-che	*stingy*	chu-cho-ter	*to whisper*
ar-chi-tec-te	*architect*	chy-le, etc. etc.	*chyle*

and in many proper names, as *Achille,* *Joachim,* *Zachée,* etc.

Examples of *ch* as *k.*

Ach-ab	Cham	Ma-chi-a-vel	Cal-chas
A-ché-lo-üs	Cha-na-au	Mi-chel-Ange	Bac-chus
An-ti-o-chus	Chi-o	Pul-ché-rie	Cha-ron
A-cha-ie	Cho-rè-be	Ti-cho-Bra-hé	Ci-vi-ta-Vec-
A-na-char-sis	Chos-ro-ès	Dyr-ra-chi-um	chia
a-na-cho-rète	Chal-da-ï-que	chi-ro-man-cie	Zu-rich
arch-an-ge	Chal-dée	chœur	é-cho
Arch-an-gel	cha-os	cho-ris-te	scho-li-e
ar-ché-type	ché-li-doi-ne	or-ches-tre	cha-li-bé
ar-chon-tes	Cher-so-nè-se	i-cho-reux	chon-dril-le
ar-chi-é-pis-co-	Chi-li-ar-que	cho-rè-ge	chi-ra-gre
pal	chal-co-gra-phi-e	Na-bu-cho-do-	ar-cha-ïs-me
Chal-cé-doi-ne	ca-té-chu-mè-ne	no-sor	
eu-cha-ris-tie	Za-cha-rie		

Examples of *cht* as *k.*

Yacht, U trecht, Maes-tricht } are pronounced { Yak, Utrek, Mastrik } without sounding the *t.*

Ch takes the sound of hard *g* in *drachme,* and is dropped in *almanach;* and on account of their Italian origin in *vermicelle* and *violoncelle,* *c,* without *h,* takes the sound of the English *sh.*

Ch has uniformly the sound of *k,* in all words where it is followed by a consonant, as *Christ, chrétien, Chloris, chronique, isochrone, chronomètre, Arachné, ichneumon, technique,* etc.

D, d, has the same sound as in English.

Dé-da-le	*labyrinth*	Dry-ade	*Dryad*
do-du	*plump*	dro-ma-dai-re	*dromedary*
din-don	*turkey*	dé-di-ca-toi-re	*dedicatory*

D is always sounded in the middle of words, as *adjectif, adverbe, admirable.*

It is likewise heard at the end of proper names,

as in *David, Obed, Gad, Alfred,* etc. and in some other words, as *Cid, Sud, Sund, Talmud, éphod, lamed.* At the end of many words before a vowel, or *h* mute, *d* takes the sound of *t*, as *quand il viendra; un grand homme; vend-il?* etc. however it is never sounded in *bond, gond, fond, nid, nœud, muid,* and *pied;* except in *de fond en comble, de pied en cap, tenir pied-à-boule, avoir un pied-à-terre,* where it is sounded as *t.*

D is sounded double in some few words derived from the Latin, as in *ad-dition, ad-ducteur, red-dition.*

F, f, is sounded like the same letter in English.

Examples.

Far-fa-det	*hobgoblin*	fé-bri-fuge	*febrifuge*
fau-fi-ler	*to baste (in sewing)*	fruc-ti-fi-er	*to fructify*
fet-fa	*edict of the Mufti*	fi-fre	*fifer*
fan-fa-ron	*boaster*	for-fait	*crime*

Final *f* is sounded in all words ending in *if*, which amount to nearly 260, most adjectives, and in *raf, bref, brief, chef, fief, nef, nerf, grief, serf, relief, méchef, Azof, lof, tof, tuf, ouf, pouf, œuf, veuf, bœuf,* and *neuf* (new); but not in *clef, cerf, éteuf, chef-d'œuvre, œuf frais,* nor in the plural of *nerf, œuf, bœuf,* and *neuf* (new). In *neuf* (nine), when alone, or when it terminates the sentence, *f* is distinctly sounded. but it takes the sound of *v* before a vowel, and is silent before a consonant.

When it is doubled, only one of these letters is sounded; however, in some few words, as *effusion, af-fadir, effraction,* it seems more proper to sound both.

G, g, has { before *a, o, u,* the hard sound of *g* in the English word *go,* and before *e, i, y,* the soft sound of *s* in *pleasure.*

Examples of *g* hard.

Gan-grè-ne	*gangrene*	gut-tu-ral	*guttural*
Gro-nin-gue	*Groningen*	gom-me	*gum*
gai	*cheerful*	gla-ce	*looking-glass*
go-gue-nard	*joker*	Gor-go-ne	*Gorgon*

Examples of *g* soft.

Geai	*jay*	gé-né-ral	*general*
gé-or-gi-ques	*georgics*	gens	*people*
gen-re	*gender*	gin-gem-bre	*ginger*
gé-mir	*to groan*	gym-ni-que	*gymnastic*

G final has the hard sound in *joug*, and in proper names, as *Agag, Doeg,* but it takes the sound of *k* in *rang, sang,* and *long* masculine before a vowel; and also in *bourg.* It is silent in *faubourg, Luxembourg,* etc. and in *Bourg-l'abbé, Bourg-la-Reine,* etc.; and likewise in *sang-sue, de sang froid, sang-de-dragon,* in *rang, sang, long,* before a consonant, and always in *doigt, legs, poing, vieux-oing, hareng, étang, seing,* and *vingt.*

Bourg-mestre is pronounced *bourgue-mestre,* and by some persons it is now, and not improperly, written in this latter manner.

Gu forms a distinct syllable in the inflections of the verb *ar-gu-er;* is strongly sounded in *aiguë, suraiguë, ciguë, ambiguë, contiguë, exiguë,* and *bésaiguë;* has a mixed sound with the following *i* in *aiguille, aiguillade, aiguillonner, aiguiser,* and derivatives, and in the proper names, *d'Aiguillon, de Guise, le Guide.* But the *u* in the inflections of more than forty verbs ending in *guer,* and in many other words, where it stands before *e* and *i,* being intended only to give *g* the hard sound, is entirely silent, as in *bague, bègue, figue, dogue, fougue, fugue, onguent, langue, longue, nargue, vergue, morgue, distingue, gué, gui, guérir, guinder, guise, languir, guinguette,* etc.

Gua takes the mixt sound of the diphthong *goua* in some few words, as *lingual, paraguante, Guadeloupe, Guadalquivir, Guatimala, Guastalla.*

When *g* is doubled, only one is sounded, except before *e* and *i*, then the first *g* retains the *hard*, and the second adopts the *soft* sound, as in *suggérer, suggestion.*

G before *h*, and before several consonants in the middle of words, retains its hard sound, as in *Berghen, Enghien, église, énigme, segment, amygdales.* Before *l* there are two exceptions, in the words *imbroglio* and *de Broglio*, where it is sounded liquid, as in *seraglio*, and these words are generally pronounced as if written *imbroille, de Broille.*

Gn has two sounds { one hard, as in the English word *ignorant*, and the other liquid, as in the last syllable of *onion.*

Examples of the hard sound.

Gni-de	gua-pha-li-um	ag-na-ti-que	rég-ni-cole
Gno-me	gnos-ti-que	cog-na-ti-que	mag-né-sie
guo-mi-de	ag-nat	ag-nus	stag-nant
gno-mi-que	ag-na-ti-on	ig-née	stag-na-ti-on
gno-mou	cog-nat	ig-ni-cole	di-ag-nos-ti-que
gno-mo-ni-que	cog-na-ti-on	ig-ni-ti-on	mag-nats

G is silent in *signet* and *Regnard*, a French writer of comedies, pronounced *sinet, Renard.*

H, h, when aspirated, is sounded with a strong guttural impulse, and when mute, it has no power but that of showing etymology.

H *is aspirated in*		H *is mute in*	
'Ha bler	*to romance*	ha-bit	*coat*
'ha-che	*axe*	her-be	*grass*
'ha-ïr	*to hate*	heu-re	*hour*
'har-pe	*harp*	heu-reux	*happy*
'haut	*high*	hé-ro-ïne*	*heroine*
'hé-ros*	*hero*	hé ro-ï-que*	*heroic*
'hé-ris-son	*hedge-hog*	hé-ro-ïs-me*	*heroism*
'hi-deux	*hideous*	his-toi-re	*history*
'hon-te	*shame*	hi-ver	*winter*
'hur-ler	*to howl*	hor-reur	*horror*
and about 160 more words.		and about 135 other cases.	

All generally noted in my Pocket Dictionary.

* Observe that *h* is aspirated in '*héros*, but not in its derivatives.

H is never aspirated in the middle of a word, except when that word is the compound of another beginning with an *h* aspirated, as in *s'aheurter*, *déhaler*, *déhanché*, *déharnacher*, *enharnacher*, *s'enhardir*, *dehors*.

N. B. Though there is no aspirated *h* before *onze*, *onzième*, and *oui*, we pronounce and write more generally *le onze*, *le onzième*, than *l'onze*, *l'onzième*, and say always *le oui et le non* without elision, and final *s* in *mes*, *tes*, *ses*, *nos*, *vos*, *leurs*, *ces*, and *les*, is never sounded when placed before any of these words, as *tous vos oui et vos non ; sur les onze heures*, and even before *un* in *sur les une heure.*

For what concerns *h* placed after *c* or *g*, see the remarks on those two letters, p. 18 and 22.

H, after *r* or *t*, is always silent, as *rhéteur*, *Rhône*, *rhubarbe*, *thé*, *Thomas*, *thym*.

J, j, has constantly the sound of *z* in *azure*, or *s* in *pleasure.*

Examples.

jus	*gravy*	jou-jou	*toy*
ja-mais	*never*	ju-ju-be	*jujube*
jo-vi-al	*jovial*	jeu-nes-se	*youth*

K, k, has always a hard sound, as in the English word *king.*

This letter can hardly be considered as belonging to the French alphabet, as it is found only in some few words borrowed from foreign languages, as

Kan-gu-rou	*kanguroo*	ki-os-que	*Turkish pavilion*
ker-mès	*cochineal*	ky-ri-elle	*tedious enumeration*

L, l, has two sounds, the
{
first, is precisely the same as *l* in the English words *lily, law,* etc.

second (liquid), resembles that of *ll* in *brilliant.*
}

Examples of the First.

La–té–ral	*lateral*	li–las	*lilach*
lé–gis–la–teur	*legislator*	lo–cal	*local*
li–bel–le	*libel*	lu–ni–so–lai–re	*lunisolar*

Examples of the Second.

Bail	*lease*	cail–lou–tage	*pebble-work*
som–meil	*sleep*	mer–veil–leux	*wonderful*
œil	*eye*	œil–lade	*glance*
é–cu–reuil	*squirrel*	Guil–lau–me	*William*
or–gueil*	*pride*	or–gueil–leux*	*proud*
fe–nouil	*fennel*	gri–bouil–lette	*scramble*
tail–le	*shape*	ga–zouil–le–ment	*warbling*
tail–la	*he did cut*	bar–bouil–lage	*scrawl*
tail–lé	*cut*	cha–mail–lis	*squabble*
tail–lis	*copse*	o–reil–le	*ear*
tail–lons	*let us cut*	pé–ril	*danger*
tail–leur	*tailor*	pé–ril–leux	*dangerous*
tail–lu–re	*kind of embroidery*	oil–le	*olio*
Neuil–ly	*Neully*	im–broil–le	*intricacy*

As the pronunciation of this letter is attended with some difficulty, observe that the final syllables, *ail, eil, œil, euil, ueil,* and *ouil,* are always *liquid;* so are in any situation *aill, eill, œill, euill, ueill,* and *ouill,* followed by a vowel, as is seen in the list of examples just given.

* There is a perceptible difference between the vowel sound of the second syllable of *orgueil* and *orgueilleux;* the former is pronounced like *œil,* the latter like the second syllable of *sommeil.*

L final, preceded simply by *i,* is liquid in some few words, of which the following is nearly a list; *avril, babil, Brésil, cil, gril, grésil, péril,* and *gentil,* when before a vowel, though in some even of these the *l* is occasionally dropped in familiar conversation; in other words of this termination, the *l* is usually suppressed, as in *fusil, outil*, etc. pronounced *fusi, outi*

In *fils*, a son, or sons, the *l* is mute; but in *fil, fils* thread, threads, it is always heard, but is not liquid! The same remark applies to *poil*, pronounced *poél*, the hair of an animal, and to *il* the personal pronoun; in the plural of this latter *ils* the *l* is sometimes rejected and sometimes pronounced, though the first mode is preferable.

Observe that *Milhaut, Pardalhac*, and *Sully*, proper names, are pronounced *liquid*, contrary to the established rule, and that the two latter are nearly the only known instances of an *l* or *ll* sounded *liquid*, without being immediately preceded by the vowel *i*.

Ill, in the middle of a word, is generally liquid, there being no exceptions to this rule, but those words which begin immediately by *ill*, as *illégal, illuminer*, etc. and the following *distiller, instiller, osciller, scintiller, titiller, vaciller, fritillaire, imbécille, mille, tranquille*, with their derivatives and inflections when verbs, and *ville* with its compounds, as also *Achille, campanille, codicille, fibrille, Gille, maxillaire, pupille, la Sybille*, and *sille*.

In most of these exceptions *ll* are both sounded, as well as in several other words, in which these letters are preceded by other vowels, as *allégorie, allusion, appellatif, appellation, belligérant, belliqueux, collation de bénéfices, follicule, malléole, velléité, collusion, constellation, constellé, ébullition, Gallican, Gallicisme, intellect*, etc. *malléable, médullaire, palliatif, pellicule, équipoller, hellénisme*, and in proper names, as *Apollon, Bellone, Dolabella, Pallas, Sylla*, etc.

M, m, corresponds in sound with the same letter in English.

Examples.

Mar-me-la-de	*marmalade*	mo-mie	*mummy*
mar-mot-te	*marmot*	mo-ment	*moment*
mé-mo-ra-ble	*memorable*	Mu-sul-man	*Musulman*
mir-mi-don	*myrmidon*	mur-mu-re	*murmur*
mi-mi-que	*mimic*	mys-tè-re	*mystery*

M, though usually sounded in the middle of words before *n*, as in *amnistie, calomnie, hymne, insomnie, somnambule, automnal,* is yet mute in *damner* and its derivatives, and in the substantive *automne*.

. When double, only one of these letters is usually sounded, except, 1st. in proper names, as *Em-manuel;* 2dly, in words beginning with *imm*, as *im-mortel*.

In words in which *em* is followed by *m*, as *emmencher,* it is pronounced like *an*, with the nasal sound.

When this letter is final, see tables first and second, (p. 4 et 5), and the accompanying observations, (p. 8 et 9), where we necessarily, in part, discussed the nature of this letter.

N, n, has the same sound as in English.

Examples.

A-na-nas	*pine-apple*	non-ne	*nun*
Né-nu-far .	*Nenuphar*	non-ob-stant	*notwithstanding*
na-ti-o-nal	*national*	Ni-ni-ve	*Niniveh*
no-mi-nal	*nominal*	noc-tur-ne .	*nocturnal*
no-na-gé-nai-re	*a man of ninety*	nym-phe	*nymph*

When *n* follows the letter *g*, see *gn*, (p. 22).

N is often nasal, see TABLE I. (p. 4) and TABLE II. (p. 5), and our observations, (p. 8 et 9.)

N takes the sound of *s* in *monsieur*, pronounced *mossieu.*

N after *e* before *t* final in the third person plural of any French verb is constantly silent, and the *e* is mute, as *ils consentent au marché, ils aimoient à rire, ils lurent un chapitre;* here the final *t* is only sounded before a vowel.

When *n* is double, one only is generally pronounced, except in *an-nexe, an-nal, an-nuel, an-notation, an-nuler, in-né, in-nové, in-novation,* and a few other cases.

P, p, is sounded as in English.

Examples.

Pa-pil-lon	*butter-fly*	pou-pée	*doll*
pé-pin	*pippin* .	po-pu-lai-re	*popular*
pied-plat	*mean fellow*	pour-pre	*purple*
prin-ci-pe	*principle*	pur-pu-rin	*purplish*
pro-pos	*discourse*	py-ra-mi-de	*pyramid*

P followed by *h* has the sound of *f,* as *philosophe, phosphore, physique.*

P preserves its sound in the middle of a word, as in *adapter, adopter, capter, captieux, baptismal, aptitude, exception, exemption, inepte, contempteur, gypse, Septembre, Septuagésime, corruption, rupture, apsides, rapsodies, symptôme.*

But it is not heard in *baptéme, baptiser, baptistaire, Baptiste, exempt, exempter, sculpter, sculpteur, sculpture, je romps, il corrompt, sept, septième, temps,* and *printemps,* nor in *prompt,* and its derivatives.

Final *p* is always sounded in *Alep, cap, Gap, jalap* and *julep;* it is also heard in *trop, beaucoup,* and *coup,* when before a vowel, but never in *champ, camp, drap, loup, sirop,* and *galop.*

In *laps, relaps,* and *rapt,* both the final consonants are pronounced, but neither in *ceps de vigne.*

When *p* is doubled, only one is generally sounded; however, in such words as *lippitude, hippocentaure, hippopotame, Hippomène, Agrippa, Agrippine, Philippiques,* and *Hippias,* both are distinctly heard.

Q, q, has generally the hard sound of *k* in *king.*

As this letter is constantly followed by the vowel *u,* except in *cinq* and *coq,* we shall simply remark, that

Qu has three sounds, that of

- *k* by far the most general before any vowel
- *kou* before *a* in some particular words.
- *ku* before *e,* or *i* in some others.

Examples of *k.*

Quai	*wharf*	ques-tion	*question*
qua-li-té	*quality*	sé-ques-tre	*sequestration*
quel-que	*some*	queue	*tail*
qui-con-que	*whosoever*	a-queux	*watery*
qui-pro-quo	*blunder*	a-qué-duc	*aqueduct*
quo-li-bet	*pun*	é-qui-vo-que	*ambiguity*
quin-qui-na	*Peruvian bark*	se re-quin-quer	*{ to trick one-self out*
que-nouil-le	*distaff*		

etc. etc. etc

Examples of *kou*.

A-qua-ti-que	aquatic	qua-ter-ne	quaternion
é-qua-teur	equator	qua-dra-gé-⎫ naire ⎬	a man of forty
é-qua-tion	equation		
qua-cre	quaker	qua-dra-gé-⎫ si-mal ⎬	quadragesimal
qua-dra-ture	quadrature		
qua-dri-ge	{ ancient cha- riot with four horses	a-qua-ti-le	aquatil
		a-qua-rél-le	aquatinta
		li-qha-tion	liquation
qua-dru-pè-de	quadruped	in-quar-to	quarto size
qua-dru-ple	quadruple	lo-qua-ci-té	loquacity

Examples of *ku*.

E-ques-tre	equestrian	é-qui mul-tip-le	equimultiple
li-qué-fac-tion	liquefaction	é-qui-ta-tion	horsemanship
ques-teur	questor	quin-tu-ple	quintuple
ques-tu-re	questura	quin-tile	quintile
quin-quen-⎫ nium ⎬	quinquennium	quin-quen-nal	quinquennial
		quin-dé-cem-⎫ virs ⎬	quindecemviri
équi-la-tè-re⎬	of equal dimen- sions	quin-qué-rème	ancient galley
é-qui-la-té-ral	equilateral		{ a term of the
é-qui-an-gle	equiangular	quin-quer-ce {	ancient gym-
é-qui-dis-tant	equidistant		nasium.

In *quinquagénaire*, a man of fifty, and *quinquagésime*, quinquagesima, the first syllable corresponds with the sound of *qu* in *équestre*, and the second corresponds with the sound of *qu* in *aquatique*. This letter is never doubled.

R, r, is sounded as in English, but much stronger.

Examples.

Ra-re-té	scarcity	rhyth-me	rhythm
ras-su-rer	to hearten	sour-dre	to spring
ra-bou-gri	stunted	cour-roux	wrath
re-brous-ser	to recoil	il cour-ra	he will run
ri-gou-reux	rigorous	cor-ro-de-ra	it will corrode
rom-pre	to break	cor-ro-bo-re-ra	{ it will corro- borate
rou-vrir	to open again		
ru-gir	to roar	ir-ra-dia-ti-on	irradiation
ru-ral	ru-ral	ir-ro-ra-ti-on	irrigation
rus-tre	a boor	tor-ré-fac-ti-on	torrefaction

R is always sounded at the end of words after the

vowels, *a, i, o, u,* except in *Monsieur,* pronounced as we have said, *Mos-sieu.*

Er, in the following adjectives and substantives, constantly rhymes with *air,* which is pronounced alike in both languages.

Examples.

Cher	*dear*	bel-vé-der	*belvidere*
fer	*iron*	Lu-ci-fer	*Lucifer*
ver	*worm*	Pa-ter	*{ the Lord's prayer*
mer	*sea*		
fier	*haughty*		*{ ignorant medical practitioner*
gas–ter	*stomach*	frater	
hi-er	*yesterday*		
hi-ver	*winter*	ma-gis-ter	*{ a village schoolmaster*
a·mer	*bitter*		
can-cer	*cancer*	Stat-hou–der	*Stadtholder*
en–fer	*hell*	Ju-pi-ter	*Jupiter*
é-ther	*ether*	Al-ger	*Algiers*
a-vant-hier	*{ the day before yesterday*	Gess–ner	*Gessner*
		Ni–ger	*Niger, a river*
ou–tre-mer	*ultramarine*		

In all other substantives, ending in *er,* the *r* is silent, and the *e* pronounced *close* and *short* as in *clarté.*

When the following adjectives and a few others precede immediately a substantive which they qualify, if this begins with a vowel, the *r* is pronounced, but in no other case.

R sounded	Le premier acte	*the first act*
	son dernier ouvrage	*his last work*
	un singulier évènement	*a singular event*
	un entier abandon	*an entire cession*
	un léger obstacle	*a slight obstacle*

R not sounded
{ Il est le *premier* à vous promettre et le *dernier* à vous tenir parole.—*He is the first to promise and the last to keep his word.*
C'est un homme *léger* et inconstant, *entier* en tout ce qu'il veut, et *singulier* en tout ce qu'il fait.—*He is a light versatile character, positive in all he undertakes, and singular in all he does.*

Final *r* in the present of the infinitive of all the verbs of the first conjugation, is always pronounced when immediately followed by a word beginning with a vowel, when the style is dignified; but in conversation this distinction is seldom observed.

When this letter is doubled, only one is pronounced, except, 1st. in *aberration, abhorrer, horreur, errer, torréfier,* and their derivatives ; 2dly, in words beginning with *irr,* as *irrévocable, irrégulier, irruption,* etc.; 3dly, in the future and conditional of the verbs *acquérir, courir, mourir,* and their derivatives—*j'acquerrai, je mour-rois, nous cour-ri-ons,* etc.

Rh. See *h,* (p. 23)

S, *s,* has two | *hard,* as in the English word *sister.*
sounds, the | *soft,* as in *rose* and *please.*

In the following list of words the first *s* has the *hard,* and the second the *soft sound.*

Examples of both sounds.

Sai-son	*season*	sour-noi-se	*a sullen woman*
sai-sie	*seizure*	sup-po-sez	*suppose*
sé-sa-me	*sesamum*	sé-dui-sant	*alluring*
si-se	*situate*	Su-se	*Susa*
Sou-bi-se	*Soubise*	su-sin	*quarter-deck*
sot-ti-se	*silly action*	Sy-ra-cu-se	*Syracuse*
sous-en-ten-te	{ *mental reservation*	Syn-thè-se	*Synthesis.*

S has uniformly the *hard* sound at the beginning of words, except in *Sbire, Svelte, Sganarelle* and *Sdili,* for *Délos,* where it has the *soft* sound; and in familiar conversation *aller à Sedan; il est le second de sa classe,* are pronounced as if these words were written *azdan, le zgon.* Before *ch, s* is mute, as in *Schall, Schaffouse, Schelling, Schiste, Schorl.*

Sh in *shérif,* a sheriff, is sounded as in English.

When *s* is followed by *ce, ci, cy,* the sound of only one of these consonants is heard, as in *Scène,* science, Scythie, etc. except, however, in *efferves-cence, efflores-cence, turges-cence, incandes-cence, réminis-cence, résipis-cence, mis-cible, res-cinder, sus-ception, sus-citer, sus-citation, vis-cère, vis-céral, transcendance,* and a few others, where *s* cannot be rescinded without altering the pronunciation. In all other combinations, *sc* yield the sound of *sk,* as *scapulaire, scolie, sclérotique, scribe, esclave, scrupule,* etc.

S preserves the *hard* sound in the middle of a word, when preceded or followed by a consonant, as in *transe, transir, Transylvanie, convulsion, valse, espace, ustensile, statistique,* etc. etc. However it takes the *soft* sound, or that of *z* in *Alsace, Arsace, Asdrubal, asbeste, balsamine, balsamique, bisbille, Israël, Israélite, Esdras, Thisbé, presbitère, transaction, transiger, transitoire, intransitif, transalpin, Lesbos, Isboseth, Brisgaw, Ryswick, Louisbourg, Augsbourg, Presbourg, Philipsbourg,* and some few others.

S takes the *soft* sound when between two vowels, as in *base, Thèse, bise, rose, ruse,* etc. Except in compound words, where it preserves the *hard* sound of the *initial s* of its root; as in *désuétude, entresol, monosyllabe, polysyllabe, parasol, tournesol, préséance, présupposer, resaisir, resaluer, vraisemblable,* and some derivatives.

St final, see final *t,* (p. 33.)

Final *s* is always heard in *as, atlas, argus, bibus, blocus, bolus, agnus, fœtus, calus, sinus, Phébus, les us, virus, en sus, aloés, bis, jadis, iris, gratis, lapis, le lis, la Lys* (a river), *maïs, métis, vis, tournevis, Amadis, Adonis, Paris* (the shepherd), *pathos, Athos, Lesbos, Minos, Délos, Paros, Brutus, Vénus, Régulus, Protésilas, Blas, Gil Blas, Las Casas,* and many more foreign proper names.

In almost all other cases final *s* is silent when the next word begins with a consonant, as *au moins vous ne pouvez pas dire, que je vous répète toujours les mêmes chos-s;* but it generally takes the *soft* sound of *z* before another word, begining with a vowel or *h* mute, as *aurez-vous au moins alors assez de patience, pour,* etc.

Though there is no *s* in *quatre,* yet, before *yeux,* it is, in conversation, pronounced as if ending in that letter.

Finally, *ss* have generally the sound of a single *s*

pronounced *hard*, as in *je ressassasse, assassinasse, Mississippi*, etc.; except in some few words, where both are heard, *assation, assonance, dissonance, accessible, inaccessible, admissible, inadmissible, missive, scissile, scission, scissure, fissure, fissipède, assentiment, asservir*. Thus there is a difference in pronunciation between these phrases: *C'est un homme à* SENTIMENS; *il aime à* SERVIR *ses amis;* and *il faut son* ASSENTIMENT; *cet ambitieux voudroit* ASSERVIR *l'univers;* and again between *l'alun de plume est* SCISSILE and *LA* SICILE *est une île triangulaire,* etc. the double *ss* must be distinctly heard.

T, t, has two sounds, the

first, *hard,* as in the English word *tit,*
second, *soft,* like *c* in *cedar* and *civil.*

First Sound.

Examples of *t hard* before vowels and diphthongs.

Tac-ti-que	*tactics*	ti-are	*tiara*
tes-ta-teur	*testator*	bas-ti-on	*bastion*
thé-à-tre	*theatre*	ques-ti-on	*question*
to-ta-li-té	*totality*	mix-ti-on	*mixture*
tour-te-rel-le	*turtle*	com-bus-ti-on	*combustion*
ti-tu-lai-re	*titulary*	bi-jou-tier	*jeweller*
ti-thy-ma-le	*tithymal*	Ma-thi-as	*Mathias*
chré-tien	*christian*	Pon-thieu	*Ponthieu*
dy-nas-tie	*dynasty*	tu sou-tiens,	*thou supportest*
le tien	*thine*	etc. etc. etc.	

Second Sound.

T is *soft* before *i*, connected with some other following vowel or vowels, in some particular words, that are given as exceptions to the *first sound* of *t.*

Examples.

Par-ti-al	*partial*	ac-ti-on	*action*
par-ti-a-li-té	*partiality*	bal-bu-ti-er	*to stammer*
par-ti-el	*partial*	in-i-ti-er	*to initiate*
pa-ti-ence	*patience*	bal-bu-tia	*he stuttered*
im-pa-ti-ence	*impatience*	bal-bu-tie-ment	*stammering*
quo-ti-ent	*quotient*	in-i-ti-é	*initiated*
cap-ti-eux	*captious*	in-i-ti-a-ti-on	*initiation*
ar-gu-tie	*cavil*	Vé-ni-ti-en	*Venitian*
cau-ti-on-ne-ment	*bail*	se pré-cau-ti-on-ner	*to be cautious*

Sti, xti, thi, preserve invariably the *first sound* of *t* before any letter.

To complete this second list, observe that *t* always takes the sound of *c* —1st. In all adjectives ending in *-tial, -tiel, -tient, -tieux,* and their derivatives;—2dly, in all the inflections of the two verbs quoted, *balbutier* and *initier ;*—3dly, in several hundred words ending in *tion,* when *tion* is not immediately preceded by an, *s,* or an *x ;* and finally, in the following additional list of words, ending in *-tie* and *-tien,* viz. the substantives *calvitie, facétie, impéritie, inertie, minutie, péripétie, primatie, prophétie, suprématie, aristocratie, démocratie, théocratie ;* in the names of countries, as *Béotie, Croatie, Dalmatie, Galatie ;* and of nations, or persons, as *Béotien, Egyptien, Capétien, Dioclétien, Domitien, Gratien, Le Titien,* and some few others.

T final is always sounded in *apt, rapt, fat, malt, mat, pat, opiat, exeat, transeat, vivat, spalt, spath, Goliath, net, fret, tacet, Thibet, aconit, déficit, granit, introït, pré-térit, transit, subit, dot, Astaroth, azimut, brut, comput, chut, bismuth, indult, luth, lut, occiput, sinciput,* and both *s* and *t* are articulated in *Le Christ, l'est,* (east), *l'ouest, Brest, lest, test, Pest, toast,* and *entre le zist et le zest ;* but neither of these letters is heard in *Jésus Christ,* which is pronounced *Jésu Cri.*

T final is likewise generally heard, when the following word begins with a vowel or *h* mute, as *c'est un petit homme,* etc. etc.; however, there are many words in which it always remains silent, as *mort, tort, goût, court,, bât, mât, lit, respect, instinct, navet, assassinat,* *artichaut, défaut, debout, brulôt, statut,* etc. so that a person would almost be regarded with astonishment who should affectedly sound it in these sentences: *L'assaut* *a été terrible.—Le contrat est signé et le dépôt est chez* *moi.—Le gigot est cuit et le ragoût aussi.—Avant de* *pêcher mettez l'appât à la ligne.—J'ai fait un bon marché;* *voyez, l'achat est là;* such a pronunciation would be barbarous and óften equivocal.

T is always silent in the conjunction *et,* pronounced *é,* therefore to avoid what is called *hiatus* in French verse, this word is never placed before a vowel.

For words ending in *ct,* see page 18.

When this letter is doubled, only one is heard, except in *atticisme, attique, Atticus, battologie, guttural,* and *pittoresque.*

V, v, has the same sound in French as in English.

Examples.

Val-ve	*valve*	vi-vre	*to live*
vál-vu-le	*valvule*	vi-vo-ter	*to live poorly*
vau-de-vil-le	*ballad*	vi-re-vol-te	*quick irregular walk*
ver-ve	*poetic fire*	vi-re-veau	*windlass*
vi-va-ce	*vivacious*	veu-ve	*widow*
vis-à-vis	*opposite*	veu-va-ge	*widowhood*

This letter, when doubled, is represented by the character *w,* which is met with in some foreign words, and is always pronounced as a simple *v,* as in *Wigh, Wolfram, Warwick, Windsor, Walcourt, Wallon, Warsovie, Westphalie, Wirtemberg, Wolga, Weser, Wendover, Ryswick,* etc. except in *wist* and *wiski,* where it has the English sound; but in *Newton,* the first syllable *new* is pronounced as *neu* in *neu*tralité.

X, *x*, has the five dif-
ferent sounds of
{
ks, in *axe, expense*
gz, in *exhibit, exhale*
k, in *excellent, exsiccative,*
ss, in *bliss, mossy*
z, in *Xenophon.*

Examples of the First Sound, *ks.*

axe	*axis*	A-lex-an-dre	*Alexander*
sexe	*sex*	Xan-tip-pe	*Xantippe*
ri-xe	*altercation*	ox-y-gè-ne	*oxygen*
box-er	*to box*	pa-ra-do-xe	*paradox*
lu-xe	*luxury*	flu-xi-on	*defluxion*

Examples of the Second Sound, *gz.*

Xa-vi-er	*Xaverius*	ex-a-men	*examination*
Xénophon	*Xenophon*	ex-au-cer	*{ to hear fa-vourably*
ex-il	*exile*	ex-haus-ser	*to raise*
ex-or-de	*exordium*	ex-hi-ber	*to produce*
ex-ubé-ran-ce	*exuberance*	ex-hu-mer	*to disinter*

Examples of the Third Sound, *k.*

ex-cé-der	*to exceed*	ex-sic-ca-ti-on	*exsiccation*
ex-cel-ler	*to excel*	ex-suc-ci-on	*exsuction*
ex-cès	*excess*	ex-su-da-ti-on	*exsudation*
ex-cep-ter	*to except*	ex-su-der	*exsude*
ex-ci-se	*excise*	ex-ci-per	*{ to plead an exception*

Examples of the Fourth Sound, *ss.*

Aix	*Aix*	Soixante	*Sixty*
Aix-la-Chapelle	*Aix-la-Chapelle*	Bruxelles	*Brussels*
Auxerre	*Auxerre*	Luxeuil	*Luxeuil*
Auxonne	*Auxonne*	and some few more.	

Examples of the Fifth Sound, s.

Deuxième	second	dix écus	ten crowns
sixième	sixth	dix hommes	ten men
dixième	tenth	deux aunes	two ells
dix-huit	eighteen	beaux yeux	fine eyes
dix-neuf	nineteen	etc. etc.	

The first sound of this letter *ks* is by far the most general.

The second sound *gz* takes place in all words beginning with *x* or *ex*, followed by a vowel, or the letter *h*, as *le Xanthe, Xénocrates, Ximénès, exorable*, and several others with those already mentioned in the second exemplification.

The third sound *k* is limited to words beginning with *exce, exci,* and *exs.*

The fourth sound *ss* is only found in the above quotations, and in *six* and *dix* when unaccompanied by substantives, as in *de seize ôtez six, reste dix*, where *six* and *dix* are pronounced with the hissing sound of *ss* in the English word *bliss.*

Final *x* is generally pronounced as *s*, when the next word begins with a vowel or *h* mute, otherwise it is silent, as *Il est heureux auprès de vous, et malheureux loin de vous; le flux et reflux de la mer*, etc. except in the following words, where it has always the sound of *ks. Ajax, Astianax, borax, storax, Halifax, Hipponax, Dax, climax, thorax, Pertinax, Syphax, index, perplex, Béatrix, Erix, Félix, préfix, phénix, Fox, Palafox, Coysevox, lynx, sphinx, larynx, syrinx, onyx, Styx,* and *Pollux.*

N. B. X takes the sound of *sh* only in *Don Quixote,* generally pronounced *Don Kishot,* or rather *ghishot.*

Z, z, is generally pronounced as *z* in *zone,* or *s* in *rose.*

Examples.

Zi-za-nie	tare	zig-zag	zigzag
zé-nith	zenith	zin-zo-lin	reddish purple
zo-ne	zone	Zuy-der-zée	Zuyderzee

Except some few words, as *assez, chez, nez, sonnez,* (two sixes), and some proper names, as *Alvarez, Suarez, Metz, Senez, Rhodez,* etc. *z final* is the distinctive mark of almost all the second persons plural in the French verbs, where it is generally heard, when followed by a word beginning with a vowel, or *h* mute; otherwise it is only sounded in the proper names already mentioned.

Z is doubled in a few words taken from the Italian language, as *lazzi* (dumb show), *mezzanine, mezzoterminé, mezzo-tinto,* and in some names of towns or provinces, as *Arezzo, l'Abruzze,* etc.

OF GENDER.

Gender in all languages marks the distinction of sex, and as there are only two of these, the French agreeably to this view have but two genders, the masculine and feminine: the neuter they do not admit.

The masculine gender expresses the male kind, as *un homme,* a man ; *un lion,* a lion.

The feminine gender denotes the female kind, as *une femme,* a woman; *une lionne,* a lioness.

The gender of nouns, in inanimate objects, is generally expressed by their termination; thus, final *e* mute is the distinctive mark of the *feminine gender,* every other final letter is the sign of the *masculine.* This would be an excellent rule, were it universal; but foreigners, who wish to be thoroughly acquainted with the French language, experience great difficulty from the number of exceptions to this general principle. It is with the intention of throwing some light on this obscure and intricate subject, and of affording the learner a tolerable clew, that some few concise rules will be here laid down, the knowledge of which will prove very useful.

B

A TABLE OF SUBSTANTIVES

THAT ARE MASCULINE IN ONE SIGNIFICATION, AND FEMININE IN ANOTHER.

Masculine.		Feminine.
Assistant, helper	AIDE	Aid, help, support
eagle; a great genius	AIGLE	a Roman standard
au angel	ANGE	a kind of thornback
an alder-tree	AUNE	an ell, a sort of measure
barb, a Barbary horse	BARBE	beard
bard, a poet	BARDE	a slice of bacon · horse-armour
red-breast	BERCE	cow-parsnip
a sort of privateer	CAPRE	caper, an acid pickle
a scroll, or ornament in painting	CARTOUCHE	cartouch, cartridge
a caravan, a hoy	COCHE	a notch; a sow
cornet, a standard-bearer	CORNETTE	a woman's head-dress when in dishabille
a couple, a man and wife	COUPLE	a brace, a pair, two of a sort
Croat, a Croatian soldier	CRAVATE	a cravat; a neckcloth
an echo, the return of sound	ÉCHO	Echo, a nymph
ensign, an officer who carries a flag	ENSEIGNE	a sign post
example, model, instance	EXEMPLE	a copy for writing
a drill, a piercer	FORÊT	a wood, a forest
un foudre de guerre, foudre d'éloquence	FOUDRE	lightning, thunderbolt
keeper, warden	GARDE	watch; hilt; nurse
hoar-frost	GIVRE	a snake, or serpent (in heraldry)
the rolls, a register	GREFFE	a graft
gules in heraldry	GUEULE	the mouth of beasts
guide, director	GUIDE	rein, for governing a horse
heliotrope, sunflower	HÉLIOTROPE	heliotrope; jaspar
iris, the rainbow; iris of the eye	IRIS	sprig-crystal; a proper name
a book	LIVRE	a pound
a hat of otter's hair	LOUTRE	an otter

N. B. Of this table it is to be remarked, that the French word stands in the middle column, and its signification on the right handand on the left. When it has the meaning which stands on the left, it is the masculine; when that which stands to the right is feminine.

Masculine.		Feminine.
handle of a tool	MANCHE	a sleeve, English channel
a labourer	MANŒUVRE	the working of a ship
memoir; a bill	MÉMOIRE	memory
thanks	MERCI	pity, mercy
mood; mode	MODE	fashion
a pier, or mound	MÔLE	mole, moon-calf
mould, cast, form	MOULE	muscle, a shell fish
a ship-boy	MOUSSE	moss, a plant
the philosopher's stone	ŒUVRE	action; an author's works
office, business; prayers	OFFICE	pantry, larder, buttery
ombre, a game at cards	OMBRE	shade, shadow
page of a prince, etc.	PAGE	page in a book
a hand's breadth	PALME	the branch of a palm-tree; victory
easter, easter-day	PAQUE	the passover
a comparison	PARALLÈLE	a parallel line
pendulum	PENDULE	a clock
le Perche, in France	PERCHE	pole; perch, a fish
summit, highest pitch	PÉRIODE	period, epocha
spade, at cards	PIQUE	a pike
gnatsnapper, a bird	PIVOINE	peony, a flower
a plane-tree	PLANE	plane, an instrument
a stove; a canopy	POÊLE	a frying-pan
post; a military station	POSTE	the post for letters
punto at cards	PONTE	the laying of eggs
purple colour; purples (a distemper)	POURPRE	purple fish; purple die
quadril at cards	QUADRILLE	party of horse in a tourney
the calling back a hawk	RÉCLAME	a catch-word (in printing)
rest, relaxation	RELACHE	harbour
a glass coach	REMISE	a coach-house; a delay
a sort of pear-tree	SANS-PEAU	a sort of pear
satyr, a sylvan god	SATYRE	a satire, a lampoon
serpentaria	SERPENTAIRE	snake-root, dragon's wort
nap, slumber	SOMME	sum; load; name of a river
a smile	SOURIS	a mouse
a tour; turn; trick	TOUR	tower; rook at chess
triumph	TRIOMPHE	a trump
trumpeter	TROMPETTE	trumpet
the airy plains	VAGUE	a wave, surge

B 2

Masculine.		Feminine.
a váse, vessel	VASE	{ the slime in ponds, lakes, etc.
a hat of vigon's wool	VIGOGNE	a vigou, or llama
a veil	VOILE	a sail

SUBSTANTIVES DENOTING SPECIES,

WHICH HAVE A FIXED GENDER INDEPENDENTLY OF TERMINATION.

1 { God, his angels, cherubim and seraphim, are of the masculine gender.

2 { *All* terms seeming to constitute an appellation, and all *proper names* of men and women are of the gender of the sex to which they respectively belong, as are likewise all names of animals, when the male is distinguished from the female by a different denomination; but when the same name is used for both male and female, as *un éléphant, un zèbre, une panthère, un vautour, un cygne, une caille, une perdrix, un barbeau, une truite, un congre*, its gender must then, like that of any inanimate object, be determined by its termination. Here the only difficulty respects substanstives ending in *e* mute, all the rest being of the masculine gender, with such exceptions as will be seen page 45.

3 { All *diminutives of animals*, when there is but one common denomination for both sexes, are of the masculine gender, whatever may be the gender of the original form from which they are derived, as *un lionceau, un souriceau, un perdreau, un cornillas, un carpillon, un couleuvreau, un vipereau, un bécasseau*, etc. except *une bécassine ;* but these two latter, although derived from the word *bécasse*, and belonging to the genus, are not of the same *species*. In other cases, the diminutives follow the gender their sex indicates, as *un poulain, une pouliche, un cochet, une poulette*.

{ Diminutives of inanimate objects generally follow the gender of their roots, as *batelet, maisonnette, globule;* from *bateau, maison, globe,* etc. except, however, *corbillon, soliveau, cruchon, savonnette, trousseau,* from *corbeille, solive, cruche, savon,* and *trousse,* and more than thirty others.

4

{ All the names of the days, months, and seasons of the year, are of the *masculine gender*, except *automne,* which is of both genders; when, however, the diminutive *mi* (half) is prefixed to the name of a month, the compound word then takes the feminine gender, as *la mi-mai, la mi-août;* etc. except also *la mi-carême* and saint-days, as *la Saint-Jean, la Toussaint,* etc.

5

6 All names
{
of *trees,* except *yeuse,* a sort of oak,
of *shrubs,* with some exceptions,
of *metals,* without excepting *platine,* formerly feminine,
of *minerals,* a few excepted,
of *colours,* without excepting *l'Isabelle, le Feuille-morte,* etc. though they have a feminine termination,
} are masculine.

6 All names
{
of *mountains,* except those chains which have no singular,
of *winds,* except *la bise, la tramontane, la brise,* and *les moussons,*
of *towns,* except those which necessarily take the article *la* before them, as *la Rochelle, la Ferté-sur-Aube,* etc. and some others,
} are masculine.

8 { Ordinal, distributive, and proportional numbers, adjectives and infinitives of verbs, prepositions and adverbs, all these, when used substantively, are masculine, as *le tiers, le quart, un cinquième, le quadruple, le beau, le sublime, le boire, le manger, le mieux, le pour, le contre, un parallèle* (a comparison), etc. except *la moitié*, and the elliptical forms of speech, *une courbe, une tangente, une perpendiculaire, une parallèle, une antique*, used for *une ligne courbe, une ligne tangente*, etc. *Antique* is feminine, for the same reason ; the word *médaille*, or *statue* appearing to be understood.

9 { All names of *virtues* are of the feminine gender, except *courage, mérite*.

GENDERS OF NOUNS MOSTLY DEPENDING ON THEIR

TERMINATION.

10 { It will be recollected that final *e* mute constitutes the feminine gender, and every other final letter the masculine.

11 { *All names of states, empires, kingdoms*, and *provinces*, are of the gender which their terminations indicate; except *le Bengale, le Mexique, le Péloponèse, le Maine, le Perche, le Rouergue, le Bigorre, le Vallage, la Franche-comté*, and perhaps a few more.

12 { The names of fruits, grain, plants, and flowers, follow pretty generally the gender of their terminations, but there are too many exceptions to be introduced here.

TABLE.

SHEWING THE GENDER OF ALL WORDS THAT DO NOT END 1
e MUTE.

MASCULINE		FEMININE	
0 0	-tié	amitié, moitié, pi- tié, inimitié......	4
11 { Aparté, arrêté, bé- nédicité, comté, côté, été, pâté, traité, té, thé, Léthé .... }	-té	absurdité, beauté, charité, cité, dig- nité, fidélité, gé- nérosité, etc. etc...	500
40 { alibi, biribi, lundi, gui, grand merci, etc. .... }	-i	Fourmi, merci, gagui, après-midi	4
15 convoi, effroi, etc.	-oi	foi, loi, paroi......	3
30 { ergo, vertigo, in- digo, etc......... }	-o	albugo, virago....	2
10 { fichu, cru, écu, tissu, etc........ }	-u	bru, glu, tribu, vertu	4
200 { aloyau, anneau, etc. etc........... }	-au	eau, peau, sur- peau, sans-peau...	4
5 { bref, chef, fief, grief, relief....... }	-ef	clef, nef, soif.....	3
2 daim, essaim......	-aim	faim, malefaim...	2
100 { an, ban, cran, é- cran, pan, etc. }	-an	maman..........	1
200 { bain, gain, frein, basin, bassin, etc. }	-in	fin, main, non- nain...........	5
4 { scion, bastion, bes- tion, Ixion..... }	-cion -sion -tion -gion -nion -xion	succion, cession, friction, gestion, région, opinion, réflexion, flu- xion, etc., etc., etc..........	1100
30 { gabion, taudion, million, lion, cami- on, lampion, sep- tentrion, brimbori- on, gavion, etc.... }	-bion -dion -lion -mion -pion -rion -vion	rébellion, dent- de-lion.........	2

MASCULINE.				FEMININE.
8	alcyon, clayon, crayon, rayon, sayou, trayon, lamproyon, Amphictyous	-yon	....	o
o	....	-aison	cargaison, etc. etc.	3o
11	peson, bison, grison, groison, . horizon, sison, tison, oison, poison, contrepoison, buson	-eson -ison -uson	garnison, guérison, prison, trahison, cloison, foison, pamoison, toison, camuson	11
15	basson, caisson, cavesson, taisson, poisson, cosson, buisson, frisson, hérisson, maudisson, nourrisson, palisson, polisson, unisson, saucisson......	i- -sson	paisson, boisson, moisson, cuisson, salisson, mousson.........	6
4	arcanson, échanson, tenson, pinson	-nson	chanson	1
20	charançon, caveçon, pinçon, suçon, etc.............	-çon	façon, contrefaçon, malfaçon, leçon, rançon....	5
3o	bridou, guéridon, etc...............	-don	doudon..........	1
150	tendron, jeune tendron, baron, etc...	-lon -ron	laideron, souillon, tatillon..........	3
70	abattis, appentis, iris, etc..........	-is	brebis, souris, chauve-souris, vis, iris.........	5
15	bois, mois, carquois, harnois, etc.	-ois	fois.............	1
12	cure-dent, occident, trident, etc..	-dent -gent	dent, surdent, gent.	3
7oo	acharnement, assortiment, etc.....	-ment	jument..........	1
250	ballet, billet, bosquet, minuit, conduit, réduit, etc, billot, brûlot, complot, etc. bout, goût, ragoût, etc..........	-et -uit -ot -out	forêt, nuit, dot, glout.............	4

	MASCULINE.		FEMININE.	
15	faix, choix, cruci-fix, prix, etc. taux, houx, courroux, époux, etc.	-ix -aux -oux	paix, croix, noix, poix, voix, per-drix, chaux, faux, toux	8
20	art, départ, cham-part, rempart, ef-fort, port, fort, tort, etc.	-art -ort	hart, part, mort, malemort	4
40	fer, ver, hiver, etc. air, éclair, etc. tour, contour, four, etc.	-er -air -our	cuiller, mer, chair, cour, tour,	5
900	bonheur, malheur, labeur, honneur, déshonneur, cœur, chœur, choufleur, pleurs, équateur, secteur, etc. etc. etc.	-eur	aigreur, am-pleur, ardeur, blancheur, can-deur, chaleur, chandeleur, cla-meur, couleur, douceur, dou-	72

leur, épaisseur, erreur, fadeur, défaveur, ferveur, fleur, passe-fleur, sans-fleur, fraîcheur, frayeur, froideur, fureur, grandeur, grosseur, hauteur, horreur, humeur, laideur, langueur, largeur, lenteur, liqueur, longueur, lourdeur, lueur, maigreur, moiteur, noirceur, odeur, pâleur, pésanteur, peur, primeur, profondeur, puanteur, pudeur, impudeur, rigueur, roideur, rondeur, rou-geur, rousseur, rumeur, saveur, senteur, sœur, souleur, splendeur, sueur, teneur, terreur, tiédeur, torpeur, tumeur, valeur, non-valeur, vapeur, verdeur, vigueur, and mœurs.

There are a great many proper names of females, which, though they may not have the feminine termination, are of that gender, as the learner, from their nature, will easily comprehend : such are, among the heathens, *Pallas, Céres, Thétis, Vénus, Junon, Didon*, etc.; among christian names, *Sara, Débora, Elizabeth, Agnès*, etc. and many of these are contractions, as *Fanchon, Louison, Manon, Jeanneton, Madelon, Margot, Babet*, etc. [*See Article 2 page 40.*]

As this list of exceptions will be found pretty accurate, all other nouns that belong to this termination, must be strictly considered as being of the masculine gender, since they are not enumerated in this Table.

EXPLANATION

OF THE

ABBREVIATIONS USED IN THE EXERCISES.

m.	stands for	masculine.
f.	....	feminine.
pl.	....	plural.
s. *or* sing.	......	singular.
h m.	....	*h* mute.
h asp.	....	*h* aspirated.
pr.	....	preposition.
art.	....	article.
pr-art.	....	article contracted.
pron.	....	pronoun.
inf-1	....	present of the infinitive.
inf-2	....	the past.
inf-3	....	participle present.
inf-4	....	participle past.
ind-1	....	present of the indicative.
ind-2	....	imperfect.
ind-3	....	preterit definite.
ind-4	....	preterit indefinite.
ind-5	....	preterit anterior.
ind-6	....	pluperfect.
ind-7	....	future absolute.
ind-8	....	future anterior.
cond-1	....	present of the conditional.
cond-2	....	first conditional past.
cond-3	....	second conditional past.
imp.	....	imperative.
subj-1	....	present of the subjunctive.
subj-2	....	imperfect.
subj-3	....	preterit.
subj-4	....	pluperfect.

* in the exercises denotes that the word under which it is placed, is not expressed in French.

— denotes that the English word (see page 50) is spelt alike in French, or at least the part under which this sign is placed.

· = denotes that the French word differs from the English only by its termination, as directed page 51.

Those French words which are followed by the above signs, are to take the form which they point out.

Iu the *Third Part*, the * is uo longer placed under the word, but after it.

In filling the exercises, the order of the figures placed sometimes in the phrases after the French words, is to be observed.

In the exercises, when several English words are included between a parenthesis they must be translated by the only words placed under.

INTRODUCTION

TO THE

EXERCISES.

OF THE APOSTROPHE AND ELISION IN THE FRENCH LANGUAGE.

(SEE PAGE 3, FOR WHAT CONCERNS ACCENTUATION AND PUNCTUATION.)

The *Apostrophe* (') marks, we have said, the suppression of a *vowel* before another *vowel*, or *h* mute, as in *l'église* for *la église*, etc.

This suppression is called ELISION: *a, e, i,* are the only vowels liable thus to be cut off, and even of the suppression of the last of these, only two instances occur, viz. in the conjunction *si* before the pronoun singular and plural, *il, ils.*

The *a* is suppressed only in *la* feminine, both when an article and pronoun.

But the ELISION of *e* occurs, not only in the masculine article and pronoun *le,* but also in many other monosyllables, such as *je, me, te, se, de, ce, ne, que,* and in the compound of *que,* such as *parceque, quoique, puisque, jusque, vûque,* etc.

EXAMPLES.

of	in		for		
la	in	l'amitié		la amitié	the friendship
la	—	l'herbe		la herbe	the grass
le	—	l'oiseau		le oiseau	the bird
le	—	l'honneur		le honneur	the honour
je	—	j'ai		je ai	I have
me	—	il m'oublie		il me oublie	he forgets me
te	—	je t'aime		je te aime	I love thee
se	—	il s'habille		il se habille	he dresses himself
le	—	vous l'aidez		vous le aidez	you help him
la	—	vous l'obligez		vous la obligez	you oblige her
ce	—	c'est vrai		ce est vrai	it is true
de	—	un coup d'œil		un coup de œil	a glance
ne	—	n'oubliez pas		ne oubliez pas	do not forget
que	—	qu'attendez-vous?		que atten-dez-vous?	what do you expect?
si	—	s'il arrivoit		si il arrivoit	if it happened
si	—	s'ils pouvoient		si ils pouvoient	if they could
parceque	—	parcequ'il faut		parceque il faut	because it is requisite
quoique	—	quoiqu'il fasse		quoique il fasse	whatever he may do
puisque	—	puisqu'on vous dit		puisque on vous dit	since they tell you
jusque	—	jusqu'à de-main		jusque à de-main	till to-morrow
vû-que	—	vû qu'il ob-tiendra		vû que il ob-tiendra	since he will obtain
dèsque	—	dèsqu'on saura		dèsque on saura	as soon as it will be known
quelque	—	quelqu'un vient		quelque un vient	somebody comes

It is allowable either to retrench or retain the final *e* of the preposition *entre*, between, among, when it is placed before the pronouns *eux, elles,* and *autres;* but it is always rescinded in the following compound words:

Entr'acte	an interlude		entre-acte
s'entr'aider	to help one another	for	se entre-aider
entr'ouïr	to hear imperfectly		entre-ouïr
entr'ouvrir	to half open		entre-ouvrir

And a few others; but it is indifferent to say:

entre eux		entr'eux	between them
entre elles	or	entr'elles	between them
entre autres choses		eutr'autres choses	among other things

EXERCISE.

The soul; *the* heroine; *the* mind; he loves *him*; she
âme f.   heroïne f.   esprit m.   il aime 2 le 1;   elle
loves *her;*   I love this man;   you do not understand
  2   la 1   je aime   homme m. vous *   ne entendez 2 pas 3
me;   he esteems *thee;*   he goes away;   *it* was *the* golden age;
me 1;   il estime 2 te 1;   se en-va   ce étoit de   or 2 âge 1;
do *not* go   there;   *if* he comes;   *if* they please;   *what* has he
* ne allez pas là   si   vient   ils veulent;   que a-t-il
said?   *till*   night;   *though* he says;   *since* he knows;
dit?   jusque au soir m.   quoique   dise;   puisque   sait;
when   he saw;   *between* them;   somebody is come.
lorsque '   vit;   entre   eux;   quelque un est venu.

N. B. In the following French negative modes of speech,
which answer to the accompanying English translation,
the *caret* points out the place which the French verb must
occupy, whenever it is not in the infinitive mood.

Not	ne ^ pas		jene *suis* pas, etc.	I am not, etc.
	ne ⌄ point		nous n'*avons* point	we have not
never	ne ^ jamais		il ne *joue* jamais	he never plays
nothing	ne ⌄ rien		vous ne *dites* rien	you say nothing
nobody	ne ^ personne	as	je ne *vois* per-sonne	I see nobody
not a jot	ne ^ goutte		je ne *vois* goutte	I do not see, or I see not in the least
no where	ne ^ nulle part		je ne *vais* nulle part	I go no where

But in compound tenses, it is the auxiliary verb that parts
the negative *ne* from the *pas* or *point,* etc. that accompany
it, as nous n'*avons* point parlé, *we have not spoken;* on
n'*auroit* jamais cru, *one could never have believed.*

N. B. The addition of *pas,* or *point,* to the negative particle *ne,* must
not be considered as a second negation; but only as a complementary
part of it. For in such cases, *pas, point, goutte,* are mere restrictive
terms, nearly resembling the English words, *jot, bit, tittle,* sometimes
added to not, with this difference, that *pas* and *point* in French have
nothing trivial in them.

F

EXERCISE.

I do *not* say;   I have *not* said;   I have *never* seen;   I *never*
  *   *dis*   *ai*   *dit*   *ai*   *vu*
(tell a falsehood);   I do *nothing;* I have done *nothing;*   is he
  mens   *fais*   *fait*   *est-il*
not arrived? does *not* he come? I see *nothing;* has he *never* seen?
  arrivé   *   2 vient 1 vois*   *a-t*   *vu*
he *never* loses his time;   that (is worth) *nothing.*   I met *nobody.*
    perd   temps m. *cela   vaut*   *rencontrai*

There are many words which are alike in both languages, and others which differ only in their termination.

The expressions, which are perfectly alike, are particularly those that have the following terminations:

-al	as	animal, cardinal, fatal, général, local, moral, natal, original, principal, etc.
–ble	— —	capable, fable, etc. bible, éligible, etc. noble, double, soluble, insoluble, etc.
–ace	— —	face, grimace, grace, place, préface, race, surface, trace, etc.
–ance	— —	chance, complaisance, extravagance, ignorance, lance, tempérance, etc.
–ence	— —	abstinence, conférence, continence, diligence, éloquence, patience, etc.
–ice	— —	artifice, auspices, édifice, justice, injustice, office, orifice, précipice, solstice, etc.
–acle	— —	miracle, oracle, obstacle, réceptacle, tabernacle, spectacle, etc.
-ade	— —	ambuscade, cavalcade, brigade, esplanade, sérénade, rétrograde, etc.
–age	— —	âge, adage, bandage, cage, cordage, image, page, plumage, rage, etc.
–ege	— —	collége, privilége, sacrilége, siége, sortilége, etc.
–ge	— —	vestige, doge, barge, charge, orange, forge, rouge, refuge, déluge, etc.
–ule	— —	globule, ridicule, animalcule, corpuscule, formule, module, mule, pustule, valvule, etc.
–ile	— —	bile, débile, agile, docile, ductile, facile, fragile, nubile, reptile, versatile, etc.
–ine	— —	carabine, fascine, doctrine, héroïne, machine, marine, famine, mine, rapine, etc.
–ion	— —	action, fraction, légion, nation, opinion, passion, question, religion, etc.

| -ant | as | arrogant, constant, élégant, éléphant, pétu-lant, piquant, poignant, vigilant, etc. |
| -ent | —— | absent, accident, compliment, augment, con-tent, élément, fréquent, serpent, etc. |

Many other English words require only the change of termination, in the following manner:

-ary	into	-aire	as	*military*	militaire
-ory	——	-oire	—	*glory*	gloire
-cy	——	-ce	—	*clemency*	clémence
-ty	——	-té	—	*beauty*	beauté
-ous	——	-eux	—	*dangerous*	dangereux
-our	——	-eur	—	*favour*	faveur
-or	——	-eur	—	*error*	erreur
-ine	——	-in	—	*clandestine*	clandestin
-ive	——	-if	—	*expressive*	expressif
-ry	——	-rie	—	*fury*	furie

N. B. Adjectives in $\left\{\begin{array}{l}\text{-eux}\\\text{-if}\\\text{-in}\end{array}\right\}$ make their feminine in $\left\{\begin{array}{l}\text{-euse}\\\text{-ive}\\\text{-ine}\end{array}\right.$

EXERCISE.

The beauty of that fable; the horror of vice; the utility
   f.   f.   f. *h* m.   m.   f.
of science; the atrocity of this action; the violence of his
art. f.   f.   f.   f.
passions; the simplicity of that machine; an audacious
pl.   f.   f.   2
conspirator; the absurdity of that opinion; the military
m. 1.   f.   f.   pl. 2
evolutions; an industrious nation; an important victory; an
pl. 1.   2   f. 1   2   f. 1
alimentary pension; a dangerous animal; a figurative
    2   f. 1   2   m. 1   2
expression; a famous general; his constant generosity; he is
f. 1   m.   , 2   f. 1   *il est*
incapable of attention; his impudence is visible; his fidelity
                son   f.
is indubitable; she is very attentive; your clemency is
             elle   *très-* f.   f.
admirable; the destruction of his fortune was the consequence
        f.   f. *fut*   f.

of his temerity; she is very scrupulous; his condition is horrible;
f.   *très-*   f.   f.
his parents are very miserable; this history is incontestable;
.pl.   *sont très-*   pl.   f.
your facility is prodigious; his perfidy is odious; it was an hor-
f.   f.   f.   *ce étoit*
rible famine; the sublimity of his sentiments is still preferable to
f.   f.   m.   *encore*
the energy of his expressions; it was a decisive action ;   the
f.   f. 2   f. 1
carnage was terrible;   that obstacle is invincible;   this
m.   *fut*   *cet*   m.
instrument is not harmonious; the prosperity of the wicked is
m.   -   f.   *méchans* pl.
not durable; your insidious presents are not acceptable;   his
2   pl. 1 *sont*   pl.
memory is truly extraordinary; that is his principal occupation;
f.   *vraiment*   *ce est*   f.   f.
a central position; his extravagance is visible; these argu-
f. 2 f. 1   *son*   f.   *ces*   m.
ments are insoluble.
pl.

PART I.

OF WORDS CONSIDERED IN THEIR NATURE AND INFLECTIONS.

There are, in French, nine sorts of words, or parts of speech, namely,

1. Substantive, or Noun,   4. Pronoun,   7. Preposition,
2. Article   5. Verb,   8. Conjunction,
3. Adjective,   6. Adverb,   9. Interjection.

CHAP. I.

OF THE SUBSTANTIVE, OR NOUN.

The substantive is a word, which serves to name a person, or thing, as *Pierre*, Peter; *livre*, book, etc.

There are two sorts of substantives, the *substantive pro-*

per, or *proper name*, and the *substantive common*, also called *appellative*.

The *proper name* is that which is applied to a particular person, or thing, as *César*, Cesar; *la Tamise*, the Thames.

The *substantive common* is that which belongs to a whole class of objects. The word *homme*, man, is a substantive common, as it is applicable to any individual, as *Peter, Paul, John*, etc.

Of these nouns, some are *collective*, and others *abstract*.

Collectives express either a whole mass, as *une armée*, an army; *une forêt*, a forest; or a partial assemblage, as *une quantité de*, etc. a certain quantity of; *la plupart*, most part, etc.

Abstract nouns are the names of qualities abstracted from their subjects, as *surface, rondeur, science, sagesse;* surface, roundness, knowledge, wisdom, etc.

In substantives are to be considered *Gender* and *Number*.

OF GENDER.

There are *only* two genders, the *masculine* and *feminine*.

The masculine belongs to the male kind, as *un homme*, a man; *un lion*, a lion, etc.

The feminine belongs to the female kind, as *une femme*, a woman; *une lionne*, a lioness, etc.

This distinction has, through imitation, been extended to all substantives, as *un livre*, a book, is masculine; *une table*, a table, is feminine, etc. (see p. 37, 40, etc.)

OF NUMBER.

There are two numbers; the *singular* and the *plural*.

The *singular* expresses *one single* object, as *un homme*, *un livre*.

The *plural* announces *more* objects *than one,* as *des hommes, des livres.*

Proper names have no plural, as *Londres, Paris, Milton,* etc.

OF THE FORMATION OF THE PLURAL OF FRENCH SUBSTANTIVES.

GENERAL RULE.

	Singular.		Plural.	
The singular is generally changed into a plural, by adding an *s.* as	*le roi*	the king	*les rois*	the kings
	la reine	the queen	*les reines*	the queens

EXCEPTIONS.

FIRST EXCEPTION.

Sing.		Plural	Singular.		Plural.	
-*s*	remain un-	-*s*	*le fils,*	*the son ;*	les fils,	*the sons.*
-*x*	alterable.	-*x* as	*la voix*	*the voice;*	les voix,	*the voices.*
-*z*		-*z*	*le nez,*	*the nose,*	les nez,	*the noses.*

SECOND EXCEPTION.

Sing.		Plural.	Singular.		Plural.	
-*au*	take an *x*	-*aux*	*bateau,*	*boat;*	bateaux,	*boats.*
-*eu*	and make	-*eux* as	*feu,*	*fire ;*	feux,	*fires.*
-*ou**		-*oux*	*bijou,*	*jewel ;*	bijoux,	*jewels.*

THIRD EXCEPTION.

Sing.		Plural.	Singular.		Plural.	
-*al†*	are changed	-*aux*	*cheval,*	*horse ;*	chevaux,	*horses.*
-*ail‡*	into	-*aux* as	*travail,*	*work ;*	travaux,	*works.*

---

* Those in -*ou,* that take *x* in their plural, are *chou, caillou, bijou, genou, hibou, joujou, pou ;* the others now follow the general rule and take *s,* as *clou, clous; verrou, verrous,* etc.

† Several nouns in -*al.* as *bal, cal, pal, régal, carnaval, local.* etc. follow however the general rule, simply taking *s.*

‡ Those in -*ail,* making their plural in *aux,* are particularly *bail, sous-bail, corail, émail, soupirail, travail, vantail, ventail ;* the rest, as *attirail, détail, éventail, gouvernail, portail, sérail,* etc. follow the general rule.

FOURTH EXCEPTION.

Sing.	Plural.	Singular.		Plural.	
-ant*⎫now drop their ⎰ -ans ⎱ as -ent*⎭in polysyllables⎱ -ens ⎰		enfant, moment,	child; moment;	enfans, momens,	children. moments.

	Singular.		Plural.	
These six are irregular	⎧ ail ⎪ bétail ⎨ aïeul ⎪ ciel ⎪ œil ⎩ bercail	garlick cattle grandfather heaven eye sheepfold	aulx bestiaux aïeux cieux yeux has no plural	heads of garlick cattle ancestors heavens eyes

EXERCISE.

The flowers of the gardens; the niceties of the languages;
fleur   jardin   délicatesse   langue
the palaces of the kings; the woods of those countries;
palais-   roi   bois   pays
the walnuts of their orchards; the pictures of those painters;
noix   verger   tableau   peintre
the feathers of these birds; the melody of their voices; the
plume   oiseau   =f. s.   voix
gods of the pagans; the jewels of my sisters; the cabbages
dieu   païen   bijou   sœur   chou
of our gardens; these charming places; the horses of my
jardin   charmans 2 lieu 1   cheval
stables; the fans of these ladies; the (front gates) of those
écurie   éventail   dame   portail
churches; the actions of my ancestors; the evils of this
église   —   aïeul   mal
life, the victories of those generals; the works of those
vie   =   —   travail
architects; the corals of those seas; the (learned men) of
—tecte   corail   mer   savant
those times; the presents of my parents; the teeth of your
temps-là   —   —   dent
combs; the playthings of our children; the heads of these
peigne   joujou   enfant   tête
nails.
clou.

---

* Only polysyllables in -nt drop the t, but monosyllables retain
it, as *chant, chants; gant, gants; dent, dents;* etc. except, however,
gent, gens.

CHAP. II.

OF THE ARTICLE.

The *Article* is a small word prefixed to substantives, to determine the extent of their siguification.

The French article is { le before a masc. substantive / la before a femin., substantive } the plural is *les* for both genders.

EXAMPLE.

Sing. { *le* jour | *the day* / *la* nuit | *the night* } plur. { *les* jours | *the days* / *les* nuits | *the nights*

EXERCISE.

The sun, *the* moon, and *the* stars, are *the* glory of
soleil m. lune f. étoile f. pl. *sont* = f.
nature. *The* king, *the* queen, and *the* princes are well
art. —f. .roi m. reine f. — m. pl. très-
pleased. *The* rose, *the* violet, *the* tulip, *the* narcissus,
satisfaits. . — f. violette f. tulipe f. narcisse m.
the hyacinth, *the* gilliflower, *the* jasmine, *the* lily, *the*
jacinthe f. giroflée f. jasmin m. lis m.
honeysuckle, *the* rauunculus, are *the* delight of *the* sight.
chèvre-feuille m. renoncule f. délices f. pl. vue f.
Poetry, painting, and music, are (sister arts.) *The*
art. poésie f. art. peinture f. art. musique f. sœur f. pl.
day and *the* night are equally necessary.
jour m. nuit f. également nécessaires.

The article is subject to elision and contraction. (*See* p. 47 and 48.)

Elision of the article is the omitting of the *e* in *le*, or the *a* in *la*, when these articles precede a noun beginning with a vowel, or *h* mute.

EXAMPLE.

l'argent / l'histoire } instead of { le argent / . la histoire | *the money* / *the history*

But in this case the place of the letter thus omitted is supplied by an apostrophe.

EXERCISE.

The soul of man   without cultivation is like a
 âme f. art. *homme* m. *sans culture* f. *est comme*
diamond (in the rough). *The* history of Spain is sometimes
diamant m. *brut* = h m. *Espagne quelquefois*
very interesting. (Look at) *the* amaranth and *the* anemone;
très-intéressante. *Considérez amaranthe* f. — f.
what beauty! Self-love and pride are always the
quelle = f. art. *amour-propre* art. *orgueil toujours*
offspring of a weak mind. . Honesty,   inno-
partage m. *foible* 2 *esprit* m. 1. art. *Honnêteté, h.* m. art.
cence, honour, and *the* love of virtue are (very
— art. *honneur, h* m. *amour* art. *vertu* f. *très-*
much) esteemed. Summer, autumn, and winter,
 estimés art. *été* art. *automne* art. *hiver, h.* m.
are very changeable. France is separated from Italy by the
 variables art. — *séparée de* art. *Italie par*
Alps, and from Spain by the Pyrenees.
Alpes, pl. art. —pl.

Contraction in grammar is the reducing of two syllables
into one, and takes place when the preposition *a* or *de*
precedes the article; in which case, instead of putting
de le before a masculine singular, beginning with a consonant, or *h* aspirated, *du* must be employed; instead of *à le,*
au must be used; and before the plural substantives of
both genders, *de les* is changed into *des,* and *à les* into
aux.

		is instead of		
Thus	Du roi	————	*de le* roi	*of the king*
	du héros	————	*de le* héros	*of the hero*
	au roi	——⸺	*à le* roi	*to the king*
	au héros	————	*à le* héros	*to the hero*
	des rois	————	*de les* rois	*of the kings*
	des reines	————	*de les* reines	*of the queens*
	aux rois	————	*à les* rois	*to the kings*
	aux reines	————	*à les* reines	*to the queens*

EXERCISE.

The top *of the* mountains, and the bottom *of the* vallies
 sommet m. *montagne* *fond* m. *vallée*
are equally agreeable. Silk is soft . *to the* touch. The
 également agréables. art. *soie* f. *douce* *toucher* m.
happiness of a feeling man is to relieve *the* wants *of the*
bonheur m. *sensible* 2 1 *de subvenir à* *besoin*

poor. A man given *to* pleasure was never a great man.
pauvre m. s. *livré* art. *plaisir* m. *fut grand*
He obeyed *the* orders *of the* king. The warbling *of* birds,
Il obéit à ordres gazouillement m. art. *oiseau*
the murmuring *of* streams, the enamel *of* meadows, the
—*re* m. art. *ruisseau émail* m. art. *prairie*
coolness *of* woods, the fragrance *of* flowers, and the sweet
fraîcheur f. art. *bois parfum* m. art. *fleur • douce*
smell *of* plants, contribute greatly *to the* pleasure of the
odeur f. art. *plantes contribuent beaucoup*
mind and to the health *of the* body.
esprit santé f. *corps* m.

De and à are never contracted with *la.*

De la reine of the queen | *à la reine* to the queen

Nor are *de* and *à* contracted with *le,* before a masculine
substantive singular, beginning with a vowel or *h* mute.

De l'esprit of the mind | *de l'homme* of man
A l'esprit to the mind | *à l'homme* to man

Contraction likewise does not take place, when the
adjective *tout,* all, every, intervenes between *de,* or *à,* and
the article.

De tout le monde,	of every body.
De tous les hommes,	. of all men.
A tout le monde,	to every body.
A tous les hommes,	to all men.
De toutes les vertus,	of all virtues.
A toutes les maisons,	to all houses.

The hope *of* success strengthened the cause *of*
espérance f. art. *réussite* f. *fortifia* —f.
virtue, and weakened the audaciousness *of* rebellion.
art. *vertu* f. *affoiblit audace* f. art —f.
Fire *of* imagination, strength *of* mind, and
art. *Feu* m. art. —f. art. *force* f. art. *esprit* art.
firmness *of* soul, are gifts *of* nature. We saw
fermeté f. art. *âme des dons* m. pl. art. —f. *Nous vîmes*

with horror that man given up *to* avarice and vo-
avec = *livré* * art. — *à* art. *vo-*
luptuousness. Good cultivation is that which contributes
lupté f. art. *bonne culture* f. *ce qui contribue*
most *to the* fertility *of the* soil. More or less pain
le plus = *terre* f. *Plus ou moins de peine*
is the lot *of* every body. The history of man under
partage m. *tout* art. *monde* m. = art. *sous*
all the circumstances *of* life, is the study of the
toutes art. *circonstance* f. art. *vie* f. *étude*
wise. Playfulness does not become all ages
sage m. art. *Enjouement* m. * *ne sied ni à* art.—m. pl.
nor all characters.
ni à art. *caractère* m. pl.

I. GENERAL RULE. In French, the article always agrees
in gender and number with the substantive to which it
relates.

Le *livre que je cherche*,	The book which I am looking for.
La *femme que je vois*,	The woman whom I see.
Les *hommes qui étudient*,	The men that study.

The father, mother, brothers, sisters,
père m. art. *mère* f. art. *frère* m. pl. art. *sœurs* f. pl.
uncles, aunts, and several other relations
art. *oncles* m. pl. art. *tante* f. pl. *plusieurs autres parent* m. pl.
were present. What we value is health, frugality,
étoient présens. Ce que nous estimons c'est art. *santé* f. art. = f.
liberty, vigour of mind and body; it is the love of
art. = f. art. *vigueur* f. art. art. *corps* m. *ce amour* m.
virtue, reverence for the gods, fidelity to all
art. f. art. *crainte* f. *de dieu* m. pl. art. = f. *envers*
mankind, moderation in prosperity, for-
art. *monde* m. art. — f. *dans* art. = f. art. *for-*
titude in adversity, courage, good morals, and the
ce f. art. = f. art. — m. art. *bonnes mœurs* f. pl.
abhorrence of flattery.
horreur f. *h* m. art. = f.

II. GENERAL RULE. The article and the prepositions
à and *de*, whether contracted or not, are invariably to be
repeated before every substantive.

EXAMPLES.

L'*esprit*, les *grâces*, et la *beauté* nous *captivent.*	Wit, grace, and beauty, captivate us.
Je *vis hier* le *roi*, la *reine*, *et* les *princes.*	I saw yesterday the king, queen, and princes.
L'*ignorance est la mère de* l'*erreur*, de l'*admiration, et des préventions de toute espèce.*	Ignorance is the mother of error, admiration, and prejudices of every kind.

EXERCISE.

Innocence   of manners,   sincerity,   obedience,
art. — f.   art. *mœurs*, pl. art.   = f.   art. *obéissance* f.
and   abhorrence of   vice,   inhabit this happy region.
art. *horreur, h* m.   art. — m.   *habitent*   . *heureuse* — f.
The plants of the gardens, the animals of the forests, the minerals
    plante   *jardin* m.   —   *forêt* f.   —
of the earth,   the meteors of the sky,   must   all   concur
    terre f.   *météore*   *ciel* m. *doivent tous concourir*
to store   the mind with an inexhaustible variety. Neither
à enrichir   *par*   *inépuisable* 2 = f. 1   *
    suffering,   punishment nor   kindness   make   any
art. *peine* f. art. *châtiment* m. * art. *caresse* f. pl. *ne font nulle*
impression on those minds.   The lily is the emblem   *of*
—   *sur*   *âme* pl.   *lis* m.   *symbole* m.
    virginity,   candour,   innocence and
art. = f.   *de* art. = f.   *de* art.   — f.   *de* art.
purity.
pureté f.

     Du, de la, de l', des, answering to the English partitive *some* expressed, or understood, have by way of ellipsis passed into habitual use.

EXAMPLES.

Je *mange* du *pain.*	I eat bread.
Il *prend* de la *peine.*	He takes some trouble.
Nous *mangeons* du *hachis.*	We eat some hash.
Elle *conçoit* de la *haine.*	She conceives a hatred.
Vous *avez* de l'*amitié.*	You have some friendship
Vous *prenez* de l'*humeur.*	You go into an ill humour
Nous *cueillons* des *pommes.*	We gather apples.
Ils *vendent* des *oranges.*	They sell oranges.

EXERCISE.

Give me   *some* bread and   butter.   Offer him *some*
Donnez-moi   *pain* m. pr. art. *beurre* m.   *Offrez-lui*

meat.   Take *some* salt.   (There is)   musta?d. `   We
viande f. *Prenez*   *sel* m.   *Voilà* pr. art. *moutarde* f.   *Nous*
have *some* girkins.   Shall I offer you *some* fowl?   Shall
avons   *cornichons* pl. *Vous offrirai-je*   *poulet* m. *Vous*
I help you to *some* fruit?   I will take (with pleasure) *some*
servirai-je *   — m.   *Je prendrai*   *volontiers*
broth.   Bring me   *some* bread.   Pour me   out *some* beer.
bouillon m. *Apportez-moi*   *Versez-moi* *   *bière* f.
Drink *some* wine.   Take   *some* tea.   Put (in it) *some* sugar
Buvez   *vin* m.   *Prenez*   *thé* m. *Mettez-y*   *sucre* m.
and   milk.   I hear *some* noise.   There falls *some* hail.
    pr. art. *lait* m. *J'entends*   *bruit* m.   *Il tombe*   *grêle* f. s.
She has *some* pride.   Have you   any   ink   and
Elle a   *orgueil* m.   *Avez-vous* pr. art. *encre* f.   pr. art.
pens?   Put *some* oil   and   vinegar   to the sallad.
plumes pl. *Mettez*   *huile*, h m. pr. art. *vinaigre* m. *dans salade* f.
Eat   *some* lobster.   He has received *some* gold and
Mangez pr. art. *homard* m. h. asp. *Il a*   *reçu*   *or* m.
    silver.
pr. art. *argent* m.

. CHAP. III.

OF THE ADJECTIVE.

The adjective is a word which is added to a substantive
to express its quality, as

bon père	*good father*	bonne mère	*good mother*
beau livre	*fine book*	belle image	*fine image*

These words *bon, bonne, beau, belle,* are adjectives, as
they express the qualities of *père, mère, livre, image.*

A word is known to be an adjective, when it can be properly joined with the word *personne,* or the word *chose.*
Thus, *habile,* skilful, and *agréable,* agreeable, are adjectives, because we can say *personne habile,* skilful person;
chose agréable, agreeable thing.

In French the adjective takes the *gender* and *number* of
the substantive to which it relates.   This difference of *gender* and *number* is generally marked by the termination.

OF THE FORMATION OF THE FEMININE OF FRENCH
ADJECTIVES.

Rule I. *All* adjectives ending in the singular in *e* mute,
are of *both* genders.

EXAMPLES.

Un homme aimable ;	An amiable man.
Une femme aimable ,	An amiable woman.

Rule II. *Whenever* the adjective does not end in *e* mute,
the *e* mute is added to form its feminine.

EXAMPLES.

m.	*f.*	
prudent	prudente	*prudent*
sensé	sensée	*sensible*
poli	polie	*polite*
tortu	tortue	*crooked*
instruit	instruite	*informed*

Rule III. Adjectives in *-el, -eil, -ien, -on,* and *-et,* to
form their feminine. double their last consonant and take
e mute.

EXAMPLES.

m.	*f.*			
cruel	cruel*le*	*cruel*	= 50	
pareil	pareil*le*	*like*	= 3	
ancien	ancien*ne*	*ancient*	= 80	of each termination.
bon	bon*ne*	*good*	= 18	
net*	net*te*	*clean*	= 34	

Rule IV. Adjectives ending in *f*, change this letter into
v, and take *e* mute.

EXAMPLES.

m	*f.*	
bre*f*	brève	*short*
acti*f*	active	*active*
naï*f*	naïve	*ingenuous*
neu*f*	neuve	*new*

Rule V. Adjectives ending in *-x* change *-x* into *s,* and
take *e* mute.

EXAMPLES.

m.	*f*	
honteu*x*	honteuse	*ashamed*
vertueu*x*	vertueuse	*virtuous*
jalou*x*	jalouse	*jealous*

RULE VI. Adjectives, or rather *substantives*, ending in -*eur*, derived from verbs, *generally* change the *r* into *s*, and take *e* mute; but several, mostly of Latin origin, require -*eur* to be changed into -*rice*; in others -*eur* is transformed into -*eresse*, and about twelve, as *antérieur*, *citérieur*, *extérieur*, *intérieur*, *inférieur*, *meilleur*, *mineur*, *majeur*, *postérieur*, *supérieur*, *ultérieur*, *prieur*, take only an *e* mute, and follow the *Second Rule*.

EXAMPLES.

m.		f.		
	trompeu*r*		trompeu*se*	*deceitful*
m.	menteu*r*	f.	menteu*se*	*lying*
	parleu*r*		parleu*se*	*talkative*
	acteur		act*rice*	*actor, actress*.
m.	accusa*teur*	f.	accusa*trice*	*accuser*
	admira*teur*		admira*trice*	*admirer*
	enchan*teur*		enchan*teresse*	*enchanting*
m.	pécheur	f.	pécher*esse*	*sinful*
	ven*geur*		ven*geresse*	*avenging*

EXERCISE.

She is *decent*. This house is well *situated*. This pear
Elle — Cette maison f. bien *situé* poire f.
is too *ripe*. She is *tall* and well *formed*. This story is
trop mûr grand bien fait histoire f.
very *entertaining*. This person is very *volatile*. This moun-
très-amusant personne f. bien léger mon-
tain is *steep*. This road is not very *safe*. The door is not
tagne f. escarpé route f. sûr porte f.
open. This room is *dark*. This street is too *narrow*. It is
ouvert chambre f. obscur rue f. étroit Ce
an *ancient* custom. She has carnation lips. His
. coutume f. a art. vermeil 2 lèvre f. pl. 1 Sa
memory will be *immortal*. His manners are *natural*. The
= f. sera — tel. Ses manières f. pl. naïf.
engagement was *warm*. (That is) an *original* thought. This
action f. fut vif voilà neuf 2 pensée f. 1.
cloth. is the *best* of all. They are *delusive* pro-
étoffe f. meilleur f. pl. Ce des trompeur 2 promises. He seduces by his *fawning* manners. The
messe f. pl. 1. séduit par flatteur 2 manières f. pl. 1.
delightful valley of Tempe is in Thessaly.
délicieux vallée f. Tempé dans art. = f.

EXCEPTIONS TO THE SECOND RULE.

The following adjectives double the last consonant in forming the feminine.

m.	f.		m.	f.	
bas	basse	*low*	épais	épaisse	*thick*
gras	grasse	*fat*	métis	métisse	*mongrel*
las	lasse	*tired*	gros	grosse	*big*
exprès	expresse	*express*	sot	sotte	*silly*
profès	professe	*professed* { monk or nun }	vieillot	vieillotte	*oldish*
			nul	nulle	*no*
			gentil	gentille	*genteel*

OTHER EXCEPTIONS TO THE SECOND AND FIFTH RULES.

The following adjectives form their feminine by doubling the *l* in the masculine before a vowel.

m.	f.		m.	f.	
beau, bel	} belle	*fine*	fou, fol	} folle	*mad*
nouveau, nouvel	} nouvelle	*new*	mou, mol	} molle	*soft*
vieux, vieil	} vieille	*old*			

The following are entirely irregular.

m.	f.		m.	f.	
blanc	blanche	*white*	faux	fausse	*false*
franc	franche	*frank*	roux	rousse	*red*
frais	fraîche	*fresh*	doux	douce	*sweet*
Grec	Grecque	*Greek*	aigre-doux	aigre-douce	*tartish sweet*
public	publique	*public*	tiers	tierce	*third,* etc.
caduc	caduque	*frail*	tors	{ torse, or torte }	*twisted*
Turc	Turque	*Turkish*			
long	longue	*long*	coi	coite	*still, snug*
beuin	benigne	*benign*	favori	favorite	*favorite*
malin	maligne	*malignant*	jumeau	jumelle	*twin*
			traître	traîtresse	*traitor*

m.		f.	
concret		concrète	following the second
discret		discrète	rule, except in the
indiscret		indiscrète	*additional accent,*
N. B. { inquiet	} make	inquiète }	and diff-ring from
complet		complète	the numerous ter-
incomplet		incomplète	minations in -*et*,*
replet		replète	of the THIRD RULE.
suret		surète	
prêt		prête	

Préfix m. makes *préfixe f.* and is the only adjective in -*x*,
which preserves this letter and follows the SECOND RULE.

Some adjectives have no feminine, as *bisché, dispos, fat,*
paillet, etc.; others have no masculine, as *blette,* etc.

EXERCISE.

The grass is very *thick*.　That soup is very *good*, but too *fat*.
herbe f.　　　　　　*soupe* f.　　　　*mais trop*
It is a *foolish* undertaking.　There is *no* truth in all that.
sot entreprise f.　*Il n'y a nul vérité* f. *dans tout cela*
This water is not *clean*.　It is a very *silly* history.　It is in the
eau f.　*net*.　　*Ce 2 fol 3 = f. 1*　　　*à*
newest fashion.　It is a *fine* statue. The law is *express* upon
nouveau mode f.　*beau = f.*　*loi* f.　　*sur*
that point.　He lives in a state of *luxurious* idleness.　This wax
*— m. Il vit dans * * mou oisiveté.*　*cire* f.
is not very *white*.　She is as *fresh* as a rose.　The paint
*　　　　　comme — f.*　　*peinture* f.
on that wainscot is not *dry*.　His answer is a *mere* evasion.
de lambris m.　　*réponse* f.　　*franc défaite* f.
The thing is *public*.　That plant possesses a *pernicious*
chose f.　　　*herba* f. *à malin 2*
property.　She is of a *benevolent* character.　The *avenging*.
qualité f. 1　*a * benin 2 humeur* f.　*vengeur 2*
thunderbolt smote that impious wretch.　He extended to
foudre f. 1 *frappa impie* m. *tendit 2 **
us a *protecting* hand.　This woman is jealous and *deceit-*
nous 1 —teur 2 main f. 1.　*femme* f. *jaloux faux*
ful.　His temper is *mild*.　This colour is too *red*.　These *old*
Son humeur f. *doux couleur* f. *trop roux*
clothes are *good* for nothing.
hardes f. pl. *ne d' rien*.

OF THE FORMATION OF THE PLURAL FRENCH ADJECTIVES.

GENERAL RULE. Every adjective forms its plural by the
simple addition of *s*, as *bon, bons, bonne, bonnes, poli, polis,*
polie, polies.　This rule is without exception as it regards
the feminine termination; but the masculine has the four
following exceptions.

G 3

EXCEPTIONS.

1. Adjectives ending in -*s*, or -*x*, do not change their termination in the plural, as *gros*, *gras*, *hideux*.

2. Those ending in -*au*, take *x* in the plural, as *beau*, *beaux*, *nouveau*, *nouveaux*.

3. Some adjectives in -*al*, change this termination into *aux*, as *égal*, equal, *égaux* ; *général*, *généraux* ; but most of these have no plural masculine, as *amical*, *austral*, *boréal*, *canonial*, *conjugal*, *diamétral*, *fatal*, *filial*, *final*, *frugal*, *jovial*, *lustral*, *matinal*, *naval*, *pastoral*, *pectoral*, *spécial*, *vénal*, and some others.

4. Polysyllables ending in -*nt*, according to the most general practice, drop the *t* in the plural, as *excellent*, *excellens*; but monosyllables retain it, as *lent*, slow, *lents*. The adjective *tout*, all, makes *tous*.

EXERCISE.

They are *envious* and *jealous*.   Those fowls   are *big* and
Ils   =   *poulet* m. pl.
fat.   Owls   are   *frightful* birds.   (There
art. *hibou* m. pl.   *des*   *hideux* 2 *oiseau* m. pl. 1.   *Voilà*
are) some *beautiful* jewels.   The two *new*   operas
de   *beau*   *bijou* m. pl.   *deux nouveau* — m. pl.
have succeeded.   Men are only   equal in the
ont   *réussi*   art.   2   *ne* 1 *que* 4   3   *par*
infirmities of   nature.   The *general* officers   are
=   art. — f.   — 2   *officiers* m. pl. 1
assembled. This fruit   is *excellent*.   His proficiency
— *blé*   — m. pl. *sont* —   *Ses progrès* m. pl.
is *slow*, but solid. *All* his friends   have been very *glad* to
sont   *solide*   *ami* m. pl.   *ont été bien aise de*
see   him.   Those ladies   are tired with walking.   You
voir 2 *le* 1   *dame* f. pl.   *las*   *de*   *marcher*   *Vous*
have   powerful enemies,   but their efforts   will be vain
avez · de   *ennemi* m. pl. *mais leurs* — m. pl. *seront* —
and useless. The four   cardinal points   are the east,
inutile   *quatre*   *point* m. pl. 1.   *orient* m.
west,   south, and   north.
art. *occident* m. art. *midi* m.   art. *nord* m.

OF THE DEGREES OF SIGNIFICATION OF THE ADJECTIVE.

Grammarians commonly reckon *three* degrees of comparison; the *positive,* the *comparative,* and the *superlative.*

The *positive* is the adjective expressing the quality of an object, without any increase or diminution, as *beau, belle.*

EXERCISE.

A child   *gentle, amiable,* and *docile,* is beloved by every
  enfant m. *doux, aimable*   —   *aimé de tout*
body.   An *ingenuous* candour, an *amiable* simplicity and a
le monde.   —*nu* 2   = f. 1   = f.
lively   artlessness are the charm   of   youth.   The
piquant 2   *naiveté* f. 1   *charme* m. art. *jeunesse* f.
sight of an *agreeable* landscape is a *varied* and rapid source
vue f.   *agréable paysage* m.   *varié* 2   *rapide* 3 — f. 1
of *delightful* sensations.
délicieux 2 — f. pl. 1.

The *comparative* is so called, because it draws a comparison between two or many objects. When two things are compared, the one is either superior, inferior, or equal to the other; hence three sorts of comparison, that of *superiority, inferiority,* and *equality.*

N.B. The adverbs *plus, moins,* and *aussi,* which mark these three kinds of comparison, are to be repeated before every adjective, when several are joined to the same substantive, and are followed by the conjunction *que,* rendered in English by *than,* or *as.*

The *comparative of superiority* is formed by putting *plus,* more, before the adjective, and *que,* than, after it.

EXAMPLE.

La rose est plus belle que la violette,	The rose is more beautiful than the violet.

EXERCISE.

The republic of Athens was *more illustrious* than that
  république f. Athènes a été illustre celle
of Lacedemon. Homer was, perhaps, a *greater* genius
  Lacédémone. Homère étoit peut-être grand génie m.
than Virgil; but Virgil had a *more delicate* and *more refined*
  Virgile mais a eu fin 2 délicat 3
taste than Homer. Milton appears (to me) *more sublime*
  goût m. 1 h m. paroît 2 me 1 ——
than all the other epic poets.
  autre 1 épique 3 poète m. pl. 2.

The *comparative of inferiority* is formed by prefixing
moins, less, to the adjective, and adding *que*, than, after it.

EXAMPLE.

La violette est moins belle que la rose,	The violet is less beautiful than the rose.

EXERCISE.

Shipwreck and death are *less fatal* than the pleasures
art. *naufrage* m. art. *mort* f. *funestes* pl. m.
which attack virtue. The violet is *less brilliant* to the
  qui attaquent art. f. f. *brillant.*
eye than the lily, a true emblem of modesty
m. pl. *lis* m. * *véritable* 2 *emblème* m. 1 art. = f.
and of pride. Autumn is *less varied* than
  de art. *orgueil* m. art. *automne* f. *varié* art.
spring, but it is richer.
  printemps m. *elle* *riche*.

The *comparative of equality* is formed by placing *aussi*,
as, before the adjective, and *que*, as, after it.

EXAMPLE.

La tulipe est aussi belle que la rose,	The tulip is as beautiful as the rose.

EXERCISE.

Pope's images are *as perfect* as his style is har-
de *Pope* 2 art. — f. pl. 1 *parfait* son — m.
monious. Delicacy of taste is a gift of na-
  = art. *délicatesse* f. art. *goût* m. don m. art.

re *as scarce* as   true genius. The love of our neighbour
th f.   *rare*   art. *vrai génie* m.   *amour du* * *prochain*
as *necessary* in   society for the happiness of   life,
    =   *dans* art. = f. *pour   bonheur* m.   art. *vie* f.
in   christianity for   eternal salvation. It is *as easy*
    art. *—nisme* m.   art. *—nel* a   *salut* m. 1   *aisé*
do   good   as to do   evil.
faire art. *bien* m. *de*   art. *mal* m.

The three following adjectives, *meilleur*, better, *pire*,
worse, *moindre*, less, are comparatives in themselves.

N. B. As most beginners are apt to confound these comparative adjectives with the comparative adverbs, MIEUX,
PIS, and MOINS, because they are generally rendered by the
same English words *better, worse*, and *less*, it may be
advisable to subjoin here these comparative adverbs with
their positives, that the difference of meaning may serve as
a distinction.

Adjectives. {
Meilleur, better, is the comparative of *bon*, good, and
is used instead of *plus bon*, which is never said.
Pire signifies *plus mauvais*, worse, or more wicked,
and is used instead of this.
Moindre means *plus petit*, less, or smaller, and is
used instead of these terms.
}

Adverbs. {
Mieux*, better, is the comparative of *bien*, well, and
is used instead of *plus bien*, more well, which is said in
neither language.
Pis* is the comparative of *mal*, badly, and is used for
plus mal, worse. which is likewise employed.
Moins is the comparative of *peu*, little, and is used
for *plus peu*, which is never heard.
}

EXAMPLES.

Ce fruit-là est bon, mais celui-ci est meilleur,	*That fruit is good, but this is better.*
Sa condition est mauvaise, mais elle a été pire,	*His condition is bad, but it has been worse.*
Ma dépense est petite, mais la vôtre est moindre,	*My expense is small, but yours is smaller.*

* There are some instances of *pis* and *mieux* used adjectively, but this is not the place to notice them.

Il se conduit bien, mais elle se conduit encore mieux,	*He behaves well, but she behaves still better.*
Il se portoit mal, mais il est pis que jamais,	*He was badly, but he is worse than ever.*
Je parle peu, vous parlez encore moins,	*I speak little, you speak still less.*

EXERCISE.

His reasoning   is not *better* than yours.   Your style is
Son raisonnement m.   *le vôtre   Votre* m.
(a great deal) *better* than that of his brother.   The thickness   of
de beaucoup   celui   son   épaisseur f.
this wall is less than that of the next   wall.   This column
  mur m.   *celle   voisin* 2   1   *colonne* f.
is *less* than the other in height and   thickness.   The remedy
          autre en hauteur f. *en grosseur* f.   *remède* m.
is *worse* than the disease.   Your horse is *worse* than mine.
          mal m.   *cheval* m.   *le mien.*

The adjective is in the *superlative* degree, when it expresses the quality in a very high, or in its highest state: hence there are two sorts of superlatives, the *absolute* and the *relative.*

The *superlative absolute* is formed by putting *très, fort, bien,* very, before the adjective; it is called *absolute,* because it does not express any relation to other objects.

EXAMPLE.

Londres est une très-belle ville, | London is a very fine city.

REMARK. The adverbs *extrémement,* extremely, *infiniment,* infinitely, are likewise marks of the superlative absolute.

EXAMPLES.

Cet homme est extrémement savant,	That man is extremely learned.
Dieu est infiniment heureux,	God is infinitely blessed.

EXERCISE.

That landscape is *very diversified, very extensive,* and *infi-*
          paysage m.   *varié   étendu*
nitely agreeable on every side.   The Alps are *very high* and
  agréable de tout côté m.   f. pl.   *haut*

very steep. The style of Fenelon is *very rich,* and *very*
    escarpé.   — m.   —
harmonious, but it is sometimes prolix; that of Bossuet is
     =   *il*   *quelquefois prolixe; celui*
extremely sublime, but it is sometimes harsh and unpolished.
    élevé   *dur*   *rude*

The *superlative relative* is formed by prefixing the article
le to the comparatives *meilleur, moindre, pire,* and to the
adverbs *plus* and *moins;* it is called *relative,* as it expresses
a relation to other objects.

EXAMPLES.

Londres est la plus belle des villes,	London is the finest of cities.
Je préfère une maison de campagne au plus beau palais,	I prefer a country-house to the finest palace.

Plus and *moins* with the article are repeated before
every adjective.

EXERCISE.

The most beautiful comparison   that there is perhaps in
          comparaison f. *que il y ait peut-être dans*
any language, is that which Pope has drawn from the Alps,
aucun langue f. *celle que*   *tiré* f. *de*
in his Essay on Criticism. *The most able* men are
dans son Essai sur art. *Critique* f.   *habile gens* m. pl.
not always *the most virtuous. The most ancient* and *most*
    toujours   *vertueux*   f.
general of all kinds of idolatry, was the worship ren-
   f.   art. *espèce* f. pl.   =   *étoit*   *culte* m. rendered to the sun. *The least excusable* of all errors is
du   *soleil* m.   —   art. = f.
that which is wilful.
celle qui volontaire.

AGREEMENT OF THE ADJECTIVE WITH THE SUBSTANTIVE.

RULE I. The adjective always agrees in gender and number with the substantive to which it relates.

EXAMPLES:

Le bon père,	The good father.
La bonne mère,	The good mother.
De beaux jardins,	Fine gardens.
De belles promenades,	Fine walks.

Bon is masculine singular, because *père* is masculine, and in the singular; *bonne* is feminine singular, because *mère* is feminine, and in the singular; *beaux* is in the masculine plural, because *jardins* is masculine, and plural, etc.

These hills   are *covered* with trees   *loaded* with
    coteau m. pl.   *couvert de arbre* m. pl. *chargé de*
fruit   already *ripe.* A *pure* stream   rolls its *limpid*
— m. pl. *déjà mûr*   *clair ruisseau* m. *roule son limpide* 2
water   through the midst of meadows   *enamelled* with
cristal m. 1   *à*   *milieu* m.   *prairie* f. pl. *émaillé de*
flowers.   (Every thing) interests the heart in this abode
fleur f. pl.   *tout*   *intéresse*   *cœur* m.   *séjour* m.
which is *full* of charms.   Fly,   *inconsiderate* youth,
 *   *plein attrait* m. pl. *Fuyez,*   —*déré* 2 *jeunesse* f. 1
fly from the *enchanting* allurements of a *vain* world:
   *   —*teur* 2   *attrait* 1   — 2 *monde* m. 1
its *perfidious* sweets   . are a *slow* poison which (would
ses — *de* 2 *douceur* f. pl. 1   *lent* 2 —m.   *qui dé-*
destroy) in your soul the *noble* enthusiasm   of   goodness,
truiroit dans   *âme*   —   *enthousiasme* m. art. *bien* m.
and the *precious* seeds   of   *sublime* virtues.
    =   *germe* m. art. — 2 *vertu* 1.

. **RULE II.** When the adjective relates to two substantives singular of the same gender, it must be put in the plural, and agree with them in gender.

Le roi et le berger sont égaux | The king and the shepherd are
après la mort,   equal after death.

     Uprightness and   piety are much *esteemed,* even by
art. *droiture* f.   art. *piété* f.   *très estimé même de*
the wicked.   A   man in the most elevated
méchant pl. * art.   *dans*   *élevé* 2 art. *état* 1
and a   man in the most obscure   situation, are equally
   * art.   *obscur* 2 art. *état* m 1   *également*
precious in the eyes of God. Pilpay and Confucius are very
 =   *à*   m. pl. *Dieu*   —   —

celebrated among the nations .of Asia. ·
célèbre parmi peuple m. pl. art.

RULE III. When the two substantives, to which the adjective relates, are of different genders, the adjective is to be put in the masculine plural.

EXAMPLE.

Mon père et ma mère sont contens,	My father and mother are contented.

EXERCISE.

His probity and disinterestedness are *known* (every where).
=f. son désintéressement m. connu partout
The love of life, and the fear of death, are
amour m. art. *vie* f. *crainte* art. *mort* f.
natural to man. Ignorance and self-love are
—*rel* art. art. —f. art. *amour-propre* m.
equally *presumptuous*. My sister and brother were very
présomptueux f. *mon* m. *ont été*
attentive to the instructions of their masters.
= — *maître* m. pl.

NOUNS AND ADJECTIVES OF NUMBER.

Numbers are divided into five classes, viz. *cardinal, ordinal, collective, distributive,* and *proportional.*

	CARDINAL NUMBER.	ORDINAL NUMBER.		NUMERICAL COLLECTIVE NOUNS.	
1	un, une	*premier*	*first*	unité	*unit*
2	deux	deuxième second	2d	couple, paire	*couple*
3	trois	troisième	3rd	trio	
4	quatre	quatrième	4th	deux couples	*two couples*
5	cinq	cinquième	5th		
6	six	sixième	6th	demi-douzaine	*half a dozen*
7	sept	septième	7th		
8	huit	huitième	8th	huitaine	*week*
9	neuf	neuvième	9th	neuvaine	*nine days of prayer*

H

CARDINAL NUMBER.	ORDINAL NUMBER.		NUMERICAL COLLECTIVE NOUNS.	
10 dix	dix*ième*	10th	dizaine	*half a score*
11 ouze	onz*ième*	11th		
12 douze	douz*ième*	12th	douzaine	*dozen*
13 treize	treiz*ième*	13th		
14 quatorze	quatorz*ième*	14th		
15 quinze	quinz*ième*	15th	quinzaine	{ *fortnight,* etc.
16 seize	seiz*ième*	16th		
17 dix-sept	dix-sept-*ième*	} 17th		
18 dix-huit	dix-huit-*ième*	} 18th		
19 dix-neuf	dix-neu-*vième*	} 19th		
20 vingt	viugt*ième*	20th	vingtaine	*a score*
21 vingt-et-un	vingt-et-un*ième*	} 21st		
22 vingt-deux	vingt-deux*ième,* etc.	} 22d		
30 trente	trent*ième*	30th	trentaine	{ *a score and a half*
31 trente-et-un, etc.	trente-un*ième*	} 31st		
40 quarante	quarant-*ième*	} 40th	quarantaine	*two score*
41 quarante-et-un	quarante-un*ième*	} 41st		
50 cinquante	cinquant-*ième*	} 50th	cinquan-taine	{ *two score and a half*
51 cinquante-et-un	cinquante-un*ième*	} 51st		
60 soixante	soixant*ième*	60th	soixantaine	*three score*
61 soixante-et-un	soixante-un*ième*	} 61st		
70 soixaute-dix	soixante-dix*ième*	} 70th		
71 soixante-ouze	soixante-onz*ième*	} 71st		
72 soixante-douze, etc.	soixante-douz*ième*	} 72d		
80 quatre-vingts	quatre-vingt*ième*	} 80th	......	*four score*

CARDINAL NUMBER.	ORDINAL NUMBER.		NUMERICAL COLLEC-TIVE NOUNS.	
81 { quatre vingt-un, etc.	{ quatre-vingt-*unième*	81st		
90 { quatre-vingt-dix	{ quatre-vingt-*dixième*	90th		
91 { quatre vingt-onz*e*	{ quatre-vingt-onz*ième*	91st		
100 cent	cent*ième*	100th	1 centaine	1 *hundred*
101 { cent-un, etc.	{ cent-un-*ième*, etc.	101st		
200 { deux cent*s*	{ deux-cent-*ième*	200th	2 centaines	2 *hundred*
1,000 { mill*e*	mill*ième*	1,000th	1 millier	1 *thousand*
2,000 { deux mill*e*, etc.	{ deux-mil-*lième*, etc.	2,000th	2 milliers	2 *thousand*
10,000 { dix mille	dix-mill*ième*	10,000th	1 myriade	1 *myriad*
1,000,000 { mille fois mille	{ million-*ième*	millionth	1 million	1 *million*

Un milliard, or *billion*, a thousand millions, *un trillion*, etc.
The formation of the ordinal number from the cardinal does not require any explanation, except that -*unième* is only found in compound numbers, where *premier* and *second* are inadmissible.

When mentioning the days of the month, the French make use of the cardinal instead of the ordinal number, and say, *le onze d'avril*, not *le onzième*, etc. *le vingt-cinq du mois prochain*, and not *le vingt-cinquième*, etc. except however, that instead of *l'un du mois*, they say, *le premier*, the first day of, etc. and sometimes *le second*, though not so well, for *le deux*; but this proceeds no farther.

Mille never takes *s* in the plural; thus *vingt mille* is twenty thousand, and not *vingt milles*, which would mean twenty miles; and when mentioning the christian æra, it is customary to curtail this word into *mil*, and to write, for example, *l'an mil huit cent dix-huit*, and never *l'an mille*, etc.

There are many other numerical expressions used in poetry, music, games, etc. as *distique, tercet, quatrain, sixain, huitain*, etc. *solo, duo, trio, quatuor, quinque, quinte, octave*, etc. *beset, sonnez*, etc.

Un millier is very often employed for one thousand *weight*, but *quintal* is never used except in the sense of one hundred weight.

The distributive numbers are those which express the different parts of a whole; as *la moitié*, the half; *le quart*, the quarter; *un cinquième*, a fifth, etc.

The proportional denote the progressive increase of things; as *le double*, the double; *le triple*, the treble; *le centuple*, a hundred-fold, etc.

CHAP. IV.

OF THE PRONOUN.

A *pronoun* is a word substituted in the place of a noun. There are several kinds of pronouns, as the *personal, possessive, relative, absolute, demonstrative*, and *indefinite.*

§ 1.

OF THE PERSONAL PRONOUNS.

Personal pronouns are used for the names of persons, or things.

There are three *persons:* the first who speaks; the second who is spoken to; and the third is the person or thing spoken of.

PRONOUNS OF THE FIRST PERSON.

Singular.

Subject. je	....	*I*	je loue Dieu	*I praise God*
me	à moi *to me*	il me donne	*he gives me*
me	moi *me*	il me blesse :	*he hurts me*
moi	à moi *to me*	donnez-moi	*give me*
moi	moi *me*	aidez-moi	*help me*

(Object ... for)

Plural.

Subj. nous	....	*we*	nous louons Dieu	*we praise God*
Obj. {neus} {nous} for {à nous *to us*} {nous *us*}			il nous donne	*he gives us*
			il nous blesse	*he hurts us*

They are both masculine and feminine, that is, of the same gender as the person or persons they represent.

In general, *je* and *me* are put before the verb; *moi* after it; and *nous* before, but sometimes likewise after it.

EXERCISE.

I cast my eyes upon the objects which surrounded *me,*
portai vue f. s. sur objet qui environnoient me
and saw with pleasure that all was calm and tranquil. Do
je vis avec que étoit calme tranquille *
you not see in all the features of my father that he is
3 1 4 voyez 2 dans trait m. pl. que
satisfied with *me?* *We* have told the truth. What were
content de moi avons dit vérité f. Que *
they saying of *us?* If *we* desire to be happy, we must
on 2 disoit 1 Si désirons de devons 2
not deviate from the path of virtue.
1 5 nous écarter de sentier m. art.

PRONOUNS OF THE SECOND PERSON.

Singular.

Subj. tu	......	*thou*	tu crains Dieu	*thou fearest God*
te	à toi *to thee*	il te parle	*he speaks to thee*
te	toi *thee*	il te voit	*he sees thee*
toi	à toi *to thee*	donne-toi la peine	*give thyself the trouble*
toi	toi *thee*	habille-toi	*dress thyself*

(Obj ... for)

H 3

Plural.

| Subj. | vous | | | | | | {ye, or / you} | vous louez Dieu | {you praise / God |
| Obj. | {vous / vous} | for | {à vous / vous} | | {to you / you} | il vous parle | il vous respecte | {he speaks to / you | {he respects you |

In general *tu* and *te* are put before the verb, *toi* after, and *vous* before, but sometimes after it.

REMARK. Politeness has led to the use of the plural *vous*, instead of the singular *tu;* as *vous êtes bien bon*, you are very good, for *tu es bien bon*.

Thou art greater than I; and from *thee* I have (at once)
es · moi toi ai en même
learnt humility and wisdom. I (was telling)
temps 2 appris 1 art. = f. art. sagesse f. disois
thee that dancing is to the body what taste is to the mind.
te que art. danse f. m. ce que art. m.
You have shown us great talents; when (will *you* show)
avez 2 montré 3 1 de —m. quand montrerez-vous 2
us great virtues? How amiable *you* are! How good *you* are
1 de f. pl. Que 3 1 êtes 2 3 1 2
to have thought of us! (It was said) of *you* the other day,
de vous être occupé On disoit autre jour m.
that *you* intended to spend a winter in London (in order to)
vous vous proposiez de passer m. à —dres pour
see every thing curious which that city presents.
voir tout ce = 6 que 1 cette 2 ville 3 offre 4 de 5.

PRONOUNS OF THE THIRD PERSON.

Singular.

| Sub. | {il m. / elle f.} | | | | {he / she} | {il perd son temps / elle travaille toujours} | {he loses his time / she is always at work} |
| Obj. | {lui m. / lui f.} | for | {à lui / à elle} | {to him / to her} | | {dites-lui que je lui parlerai / dites-lui que vous lui donnerez} | {tell him that I will speak to him / tell her that you will give her} |

Singular.

Obj.						
	lui *m.*	*for*	le	*him*	je ne connois que *lui* de capable	*I know but him capable*
	le *m.* la *f.*	*or* —	lui elle	*him her*	je *le* méprise je *la* respecte	*I despise him I respect her*
	elle *f.*		elle	*her*	Il ne connoît qu'*elle*	*he knows but her*
	le *m.*	*for*	cela	*it*	je ne *le* savois pas	*I did not know it.*

Plural.

Subject.	ils *m.*	—	—	*they*	*ils* chantent	*they sing (gentlemen)*
	elles *f.*	—	—	*they*	*elles* rient	*they laugh (ladies)*
Object.	leur *m.*	*for*	à eux	*to them*	payez-*leur* ce que vous *leur* devez	*pay them what you owe to them (to men)*
	leur *f.*	*for*	à elles	*to them*	dites-*leur* que je désire *leur* parler	*tell them that I wish to speak to them (to ladies)*
	les *m.*	*or*	eux	*them*	vous *les* trouverez	*you will find them (men)*
	les *f.*	*or*	elles	*them*	il *les* admire	*he admires them (ladies)*
	eux *m.*	—	—	*them*	je ne vois qu'*eux*	*I see but them (gentlemen)*
	elles *f.*	—	—	*them*	il ne connoît qu'*elles*	*he knows but them (ladies)*

All the personal pronouns *je, tu, il, nous, vous, ils,* and *elle, elles,* when subjects, are put after the verb in interrogations, as,

Singular.

Subject.				
	je	*I*	*dois*-je payer?	*must I pay?*
	tu	*thou*	as-tu dit?	*hast thou said?*
	il	*he*	chante-t–*il* bien?	*does he sing well?*
	elle	*she*	travaille-t–*elle?*	*does she work?*

Plural.

Subject.				
	nous	*we*	irons-*nous?*	*shall we go?*
	vous	*you*	viendrez-*vous?*	*will you come?*
	ils *m.*	*they*	chantent-*ils?*	*do they sing?*
	elles *f.*	*they*	travaillent-*elles?*	*do they work?*

Il, le, ils, eux, are always masculine; *elle, la, elles,* feminine; and *les, leur,* of both genders, as well as *lui,* when meaning *to him,* or *to her;* in other cases, *lui* exclusively belongs to the masculine.

All personal pronouns, when subjects, are placed before their verbs, except in interrogative sentences, and most of them likewise, when objects precede them, except in the imperative affirmative. But the objective *eux, elles, lui* for *le,* and *moi, toi, soi,* with one exception of this last, in *soi-disant,* styling himself, are invariably placed after the verbs by which they are governed.

EXERCISE.

He loved *them,* because *they* were mild, attentive, and
    aimoit m. *parce que*   *doux* =
grateful. *He* (was saying) (to *them*), do you not know
reconnoissant.   *disoit*   *   3   1 4 *savez* 2
that the property of   merit   is to excite   envy?   *She*
que   *propre* m. art. *mérite* m. *de exciter* art. *envie* f.
often   exhorted me to the study the most useful, that of
souvent 2 *exhortoit* 1   *étude* f.   *utile*   *celle*
the human heart. *They* make us love   virtue, more by
    2   m. 1   *font*   *aimer* art.   f.   *par*
their examples than by their words.   What   has been
leurs exemple pl.   *parole* f. pl. *Que* 1 *on* 3 *a-t-2* *
said of *them?* Did they speak of *them?* Do you not see
dit   *eux*   *   *on* 2 *parloit* 1 *elle*   *   4   1 5 *voyez* 3
her? With what pleasure *she* plays!
   2   *quel*   *joue!*

REFLECTED AND RECIPROCAL PRONOUNS OF THE THIRD
PERSON.

			Singular.	EXAMPLES.
Object.	soi	with a *preposition*	chacun tire *à soi*	*every one draws* to himself
	soi	governed by the *verb*	l'égoïsme fait qu'on ne voit que *soi*	*egotism makes a person see none but* himself
Object.	se *for*	*à soi, à lui-même*	il *se* donne des louanges	*he gives* himself *praises*
		à elle-même	elle *se* fait illusion	*she imposes* on herself
		soi, or *lui-même*	il *se* perd	*he ruins* himself
		soi, or *elle-même*	elle *se* flatte	*she flatters* herself

		Plural.	EXAMPLES.
Object.	se *for*	*à eux-mêmes*	ils *s'*attribuent la gloire de, etc.	*they attribute* to themselves the glory of, etc.
		à elles-mêmes	elles *se* prescrivent pour règle de, etc.	*they prescribe* to themselves *as a rule to*, etc.
		l'un à l'autre	ils *s'*entredonnent, ou *se* font des cadeaux	*they exchange gifts*
		eux-mêmes	ils *se* sont déshonorés	*they have disgraced themselves*
		elles-mêmes	elles *se* sont flattées	*they have flattered* themselves
		l'un l'autre	ils *s'*entr'aident	*they help* one another
		les uns les autres	les rats, dit-on, *s'*entre-dévorent	*rats, it is said, eat* each other

REMARK. *Se* is placed before a verb, and *soi* after a
preposition, and sometimes after a verb.

EXERCISE.

In a thousand instances we do not watch sufficiently over
  * *mille*   *occasion* f. *on* *   *veille assez*   *sur*
ourselves. The glory of the world (passes away) in an instant.
soi   = f.   *monde* m. *s'évanouit en*   — m.
He gives *himself* (a great deal) of trouble. She tires *herself*.
  donne se   *beaucoup*   *peine* f.   *lasse se*
People should (very seldom) speak of *themselves*. Virtue is
On   *doit*   *rarement*   *parler   soi*   art. f.
amiable in *itself*. We must take   upon *ourselves* the care
      de soi   *On doit prendre sur   soi*   *soin* m.
of our own   affairs.
  ses propre affaire f. pl.

OF THE PRONOUN RELATIVE *en*.

EN *for*				
	de lui	*of him*	cet homme vous plait, vous *en* parlez souvent	*that man pleases you, you speak of him often*
	d'elle	*of her*	je ne crois pas cette femme sincère, je m'*en* méfie	*I do not believe that woman sincere, I distrust her*
	d'eux	*of them*	ces fruits paroissent bons, j'*en* mangerois volontiers	*these fruits look good, I should like to eat some of them*
	d'elles	*of them*	voilà de belles oranges, voulez-vous m'*en* donner?	*these are beautiful oranges, will you give me some?*
	de cela	*of that*	on ne m'a pas trompé, j'*en* suis sûr	*I have not been imposed upon, I am sure of it*
	d'ici	*hence*	il arriva ici, comme j'*en* partois	*he arrived here, as I was setting off from hence*
	de là	*thence*	vous allez à Paris, et monsieur *en* vient	*you are going to Paris, this gentleman comes from thence*

OF THE RELATIVE PRONOUN, OR ADVERB, *y*.

	à lui	*to him*	c'est un honnête homme, fiez-vous-*y*	*he is an honest man, trust to him*
	à elle	*to her*	cette raison est solide, je m'*y* rends	*that reason is good, I yield to it*
	à eux	*to them*	ces argumens sont pressans, je n'*y* vois point de réplique	*these arguments are cogent, I see no reply to them*
Y *for*	à elles	*to them*	accablé de vos civilités, je ne sais comment *y* répondre	*loaded with your civilities, I do not know how to acknowledge them.*
	à cela	*to it*	j'ai éprouvé cette perte quand j'*y* pensois le moins	*I experienced that loss, when I least thought of it*
	ici	*here*	nous partons de Londres, quand vous *y* venez	*we set off from London, when you come hither*
	là	*there*	c'est un endroit charmant, je compte m'*y* fixer	*It is a fine place, I intend to settle there*

REMARK. *Y* and *en* are always put before the verb, except with the imperative affirmative.

EXERCISE.

They speak (a great deal) *of it*. You like French
On parle beaucoup *aimez* art. *François* 2
authors, you are always speaking *of them*. That is a delicate
auteur 1 * 2 *parlez* 1 *Ce délicat* 2
affair; the success *of it* is doubtful. See them; I consent
= f. 1 *succès* m. *douteux*. *Voyez* 1 *consens* 3
to it, but do not trust them. That is a fine appoint-
2 * 1 5 *vous* 2 *fiez* 4 *y* 3. *Ce charge*
ment: he had long aspired *to it*. He has done
f. * *depuis long-temps* 3 — *roit* 2 1 *a fait*
it; but he will get nothing *by it*.
ne 1 *gagnera* 3 *rien* 4 *y* 2.

§ II.

OF POSSESSIVE PRONOUNS.

These pronouns are adjectives, which denote the possession of things. When we say, *mon habit*, my coat; *votre maison*, your house; *son jardin*, his, or her garden; it is the same as saying *l'habit qui est à moi*, the coat which belongs to me; *la maison qui est à vous*, the house which belongs to you; *le jardin qui est à lui*, or *à elle*, the garden which belongs to him, or to her.

Of these pronominal adjectives, *some* always agree with a noun *expressed*, and *the others* with a noun *understood;* hence there are *two sorts* of possessive pronouns.

Of those that always agree with a noun *expressed*, some relate to *one* person, and others to *several*.

PRONOMINAL ADJECTIVES RELATING TO ONE PERSON.

PERSON.	Singular.		Plural.	
for the 1st	mon, *m.*	ma, *f.*	mes, *m. f.*	*my*
2d	ton, *m.*	ta, *f.*	tes, *m. f.*	*thy*
3d	son, *m.*	sa, *f.*	ses, *m. f.*	*his, her, its*

PRONOMINAL ADJECTIVES RELATING TO MANY PERSONS.

PERSON.	Singular.	Plural.	
for the 1st	notre, *m. f.*	nos, *m. f.*	*our*
2d	votre, *m. f.*	vos, *m. f.*	*your*
3d	leur, *m. f.*	leurs, *m. f.*	*their*

N. B. These possessive pronouns in French always agree in gender and number with the object *possessed*, and not with the *possessor*, as in English, for which reason they must be repeated before every noun.

EXAMPLES.

Mon *père*, ma *mère et* mes *frères sont à la campagne avec* vos *amis et* leurs *enfans.*

My father, mother, and brothers are in the country, with your friends and their children.

Mon *cousin est allé consoler* sa *sœur, qui a perdu* son *fils.*

My cousin is gone to visit and console his sister, who has lost her son.

Mon, ton, son, are also used before a noun feminine, when beginning with a vowel, or *h* mute; thus, *mon âme,* my soul; *ton humeur,* thy humour; *son amitié,* his friendship; must be said instead of *ma âme, ta humeur, sa amitié.*

EXERCISE.

My principles, *my* love of retirement, *my* taste
  —*pe* *goût* m. *pour* art. *retraite* f. *amour* m.
for (every thing) that (is connected) with learning, and
 tout *ce qui* *tient* *à* art. *instruction*
my detestation of all spirit of party, (every thing) has
 haine f. *h.* asp. *pour* *esprit* *parti* *tout* *a*
induced me to prefer a life passed in the closet, to the
porté *préférer* * art. *vie* f. * de* * *cabinet*
active life of the world. Do not think, *my* daughter, that *thy*
= *a* f. *i* *m.* * pense* *que*
candour, *thy* ingenuousness, *thy* taste, so delicate and so
= f. *ingénuité* f. *m.* —*cat*
refined, and even *thy* graces, can shelter thee from
fin *même* — *puissent. mettre à l'abri de*
censure. *His* wit, *his* talents, *his* honesty,
art. — f. *esprit* m. — m. *honnêteté* f. *h.* m.
and even *his* (good nature) make him beloved by every body.
 même *bonhomie* f. *font* *aimer* *de tout le monde*
Our constancy and *our* efforts will (at last) surmount all
= f. — m. * enfin a surmonteront i*
 obstacles.' I see nothing that can (be cen-
art. —m. pl. *vois a ne i rien 3 que on puisse* re-
sured) in *your* conduct. *Their* taste for the fantastical, the
prendre dans conduite f. *pour bizarre,* m.
monstrous, and the marvellous, gives to all *their* compo-
monstrueux, m. *merveilleux,* m. *donne* —
sitions, although very fine in themselves, an air of deformity,
 f. *quoique* *en elles-mêmes,* —m. *difformité,* f.
which shocks at first sight.
qui choque à art. *coup-d'œil.*

Of the pronouns, which always agree with nouns *understood,* some relate to one person, and others to several persons.

Those which relate only to one person are:

	m. Sing.	f. Sing.	m. Plur.	f. Plur.	
1st.	*Le mien,*	*la mienne,*	*les miens,*	*les miennes,*	mine
2d.	*Le tien,*	*la tienne,*	*les tiens,*	*les tiennes,*	thine
3d.	*Le sien,*	*la sienne,*	*les siens*	*les siennes,*	his, her, its

I

Those which relate to several persons are :

	m. Sing.	f. Sing.	Pl. of both Gen.	
1st.	Le nôtre	la nôtre,	les nôtres,	ours
2d.	Le vôtre	la vôtre,	les vôtres	yours
3d.	Le leur	la leur,	les leurs,	theirs

N. B. The real use of these pronouns is to spare the repetition of the nouns, which have been expressed a little before.

EXAMPLE.

Avez-vous toujours votre *che-val? je n'ai plus* le mien,	Have you still your horse? I have disposed of mine.

EXERCISE.

Is it your temper   or *hers*, that hinders you from living well
   ce   humeur f.   qui empêche   de   vivre
together? If it be *yours*, it is easy   for you to   remedy
ensemble   ce est   il 2 aisé 3   *   1 de porter remède
it, by mastering (your temper); if it be *hers*, redouble   your
y en prenant sur vous-même   ce   redoublez de *
complaisance, attention, and   good behaviour ;   it is
   —   de   —   de   procédé m. pl. il
very seldom that this method   (proves unsuccessful).   If my
très-rare   ce   moyen ne   réussisse pas   Si
friends had   served me with the same zeal .   as *yours*, it
   avoient servi   même zèle m. que   il
is very certain that I (should have) succeeded : but *yours* have
   très sûr   aurois réussi   ont
been all fire, and *mine* all   ice. All the pictures   which we
été   de   de glace /   tableau m. que
expected from Rome are arrived : there are some that are a
attendions   arrivés il y en a qui
little damaged;   but *yours, his,* and *mine*, are in good
peu endommagés   en
condition. We know   perfec   well what are your
état m.   savons parfaitement   *   quels
amusements in   town, and I assure you   we are   very
  —   à art. ville f.   —   que sommes bien
far   from envying you them ; but if you knew
éloigné pl.   envier 3 1   2   connoissiez quels
   ours in the country,   it (is most likely)   you
sont   à   campagne f. . il y a toute apparence que
(would not be long) in giving them the preference.   You
  ne tarderiez pas   à donner leur   —f.
have opened your heart to me with that noble frankness
avez ouvert   — franchise f.

which so well becomes an honest man : this confidence well
qui si 2   3   sied 1 à   honnête.   confiance f. 2
deserves *mine.*
mérite 1

REMARK. When through politeness *vous* is used for *tu,*
then *votre, vos,* must take the place of *ton, ta, tes,* and *le
vôtre, la vôtre, les vôtres,* be used for *le tien, la tienne, les
tiens, les tiennes.*

EXAMPLES.

Que vous ressemblez peu à vos *ancêtres !*	How little you resemble your ancestors !
Quand vous aurez entendu nos *raisons, nous écouterons les* vôtres,	When you have heard our reasons, we will listen to yours.

§ III.

OF THE RELATIVE PRONOUNS.

Relative pronouns are those which relate to a preceding
noun, or pronoun, called *the antecedent.* In the phrase,
l'homme qui joue, the man who plays; *qui* relates to the
substantive *homme ; l'homme* is then the *antecedent* to the
pronoun relative *qui.*

Qui	who	*Dieu* qui *voit tout*	God *who* sees every thing
	which	*les chevaux* qui *courent*	the horses *which* are running
Que	whom	*l'homme* que *vous cherchez*	the man *whom* you seek
	which	*les lois* que *nous observons*	the laws *which* we observe
Dont or de qui	of which	*l'insulte* dont *vous vous plaignez*	the insult *of which* you complain
	whose	*la nature* dont *nous ignorons les secrets*	nature *whose* secrets are unknown to us
	of whom	*les gens* de qui *vous parlez*	the people *of whom* you speak
Lequel, Laquelle	which	*c'est une condition sans* laquelle *il ne veut rien faire*	it is a condition, without *which* he will do nothing

Lequel, *Laquelle* } whom	{ *ceux* auxquels *il s'est* *adressé, ont refusé* *de le défendre*	{ those to *whom* he ap- plied, refused to protect him.
Quoi { which	{ *ce sont des choses* à quoi *vous ne pensez pas*	{ these are things of *which* you do not think
{ why	{ *la cause* pourquoi *on l'a arrété, est* *connue.*	{ the reason *why* he was arrested, is known

Qui, que, and *dont,* are of both genders and both numbers.

Lequel is a compound of *quel,* and the article *le, la, les,* with which it coalesces in the following manner:

Singular.   Plural.

lequel	*laquelle*	*lesquels*	*lesquelles*	which
duquel	de laquelle	desquels	desquelles	of which
auquel	à laquelle	auxquels	auxquelles	to which

This pronoun always agrees in gender and number with its antecedent. *Quoi,* which sometimes supplies its place, is always governed by a preposition.

§ IV.

OF PRONOUNS ABSOLUTE.

Pronouns absolute are those which have no relation to an antecedent. They are the five following:

Qui { who	{ *je vous dirai* qui *l'a fait*	{ I will tell you *who* has done it
{ whom	{ *vous pouvez consulter* qui *vous voudrez*	{ you may consult *whom* you please
{ whom	{ qui *consulterez- vous?*	{ *whom* will you con- sult?
Que { what	{ *il ne sait* que *ré- soudre*	{ he does not know on *what* to determine
{ what		que *ferez-vous?*		*what* will you do?
Quoi	what	{ en quoi *puis-je vous servir?*	{ in *what* can I serve you?

Quoi	what	{ *il y a là je ne sais quoi d'obscur*	{ there is in it I do not know *what* obscurity
Quel	what	{ quelle *instabilité dans les choses humaines!*	} *what* instability in human affairs!
	what	{ *il ne sait* quel *parti prendre*	{ he does not know *what* resolution to take
Lequel	which	{ lequel *aimez-vous le mieux de ces ta-bleaux?*	{ *which* do you prefer of those pictures?
	which	{ *je sais bien* lequel *je choisirois*	{ I know well *which* I would choose

Qui applies only to persons. *Que* and *quoi* to things.

Quel, masc. *quelle*, fem. sing. *quels*, m. *quelles* f. pl. always precede a substantive, the gender and number of which they take.

Lequel, duquel, auquel, etc. are used to mark a distinction between several objects.

§ V.

OF DEMONSTRATIVE PRONOUNS, etc.

Demonstrative pronouns are those which point, as it were, to the objects spoken of. These are,

Singular.			Plural.		
masc.	fem.		masc.	fem.	
ce, cet*	cette	*this*, or *that*	ces	ces	*these*, or *those*
celui	cette	*this*, or *that*	ceux	celles	*these*, or *those*
celui-ci	celle-ci	*this*	ceux-ci	celles-ci	*these*
celui-là	celle-là	*that*	ceux-là	celles-là	*those*
ceci	......	*this* } these have no plural.			
cela	......	*that* }			

---

* m.	{ CE	before a consonant	CE *livre*	*this book*
	CE	before an *h* aspirated	CE *héros*	*that hero*
	CET	before a vowel	CET *enfant*	*this child*
	CET	before an *h* mute	CET *homme*	*that man*
f.	CETTE	before any feminine noun	CETTE *femme*	*that woman*

I 3

CE { when without a noun, / intimates a person or thing spoken of } as { *qui est-ce?* *ce que je vous dis* est vrai } { who is it? what 1 tell you is true. }

EXERCISE.

Nothing is so opposite to *that* true   eloquence, the office
ne 2   *rien* 1   *opposé*   *véritable*   —f.   *fonc-*
(of which) is to   ennoble   (every thing), as the use
-tion f. 2   1   *de* 1 *ennoblir* 3 *tout* 2   *   *que*   *emploi* m.
of *those* refined thoughts, and .   hunting   after *those* light,
    fin 2   *pensée* f. 1   art. *recherche* f. *de*   *léger* 2
airy,   unsolid   ideas,   which, like   a leaf   of
délié 3 *sans consistance* 4 *idée* f. 1   *comme*   *feuille* f.
beaten   metal,   acquire   brightness only by losing
battu 2   —m. *ne prennent de* art. *éclat* m. *que en perdant*
part of their   solidity.   *This* man has nothing in common
 *   * art. =f.   *h* m.   *de commun*
with *that* hero. *This* long   restrained hatred   broke,
 -    *h* asp.   1 *long-temps* 3 *contenu* 4 *haine* f. 2 *éclata*
and was the unhappy   source of *those* dreadful events.
 fut   *malheureux*   —f.   *terrible* *événe-*
It is a great pleasure to me.   *It* was a great
ment m. pl. *Ce*   *plaisir* m. *   *fut*
pain   to us.
déplaisir m. * *nous*

§ VI.

OF INDEFINITE PRONOUNS.

Indefinite pronouns are those which are of a vague and indeterminate nature.

They are of four sorts.

~~~~~~

FIRST CLASS.

Those that are never joined to a substantive.

ON { one a man } { *on aime à se flatter* *on n'est pas toujours maître de soi* } { *one* is apt to flatter one's self. *a man* is not always master of his own temper }

on			
	a woman	on *n'est pas toujours maîtresse d'aller où* l'on veut*	it is not always in the power of a *woman* to go where *she* wishes
	somebody	on *frappe à la porte*	*somebody* knocks at the door
	people	on *pense et* l'on dit tout haut*	*people* think and say openly
	they	on *raconte diversement cette histoire*	*they* relate that story differently
	we	on *acquiert l'expérience à ses dépens*	*we* acquire experience at our own expense
	you	on *trouve partout des importuns*	*you* will find troublesome people every where
	I	on *prévient qu'on n'a point eu l'intention de*, etc.	I beg to observe, that I had no intention to, etc.
	I	*Quand* on *vous dit que * l'on compte sur vous*	when I tell you that I depend upon you
	they	*si * l'on vous blâme et si * on le loue,* on *a tort*	if *they* blame you and praise him, *they* are wrong

Quelqu'un	one somebody some one	*quelqu'un m'a dit,* somebody told me.
Quiconque	whoever whosoever	*quiconque connoît les hommes, apprend à s'en défier,* whoever knows mankind, learns to distrust them.
Chacun	each every one	*chacun s'en plaint,* every one complains of him.

* Instead of	et on ou on si on	it is better for euphony to part these words with an *l*	thus	et l'on ou l'on si l'on	when the next word does not begin with an *l*, as is seen by the examples
and * Instead of	les habitudes *qu'on contracte* ce après *quoi on court* *quoiqu'on* croie un homme à *qui on* reproche		say rather	les habitudes que *l'on* contracte ce après quoi *l'on* court bien que *l'on* croie un homme à qui *l'on* reproche	

Autrui	other people / others	*n'enviez pas le bien d'autrui*, do not covet the property of others. *ne faites pas à autrui ce que vous ne voudriez pas qu'on vous fît*, do not do to others what you would not have done to you.
Personne	nobody / no one	*la fierté ne convient à personne*, pride becomes nobody.
Rien	nothing / not any thing / any thing	*rien ne lui plait*, nothing pleases him. *y a-t-il rien qui puisse lui plaire?* is there any thing that can please him?

EXERCISE.

If you (behave yourself) (in that manner), what will *people*
      vous conduisez   *ainsi*   *   *on* a
say   of you? *It* (is thought) that this *news*   is true.
dira-t- ı   *On   croit   —   nouvelle* f.
They write me word from Ispahan that thou hast left
      écrit   *   —   as   quitté* art.
Persia, and   art now   at Paris. *One* cannot read
Perse f.   *que tu es actuellement à*   *ne peut lire*
Telemachus, without becoming better: *we* there find (every
Télémaque m. *sans   devenir   meilleur*, *on   y   trouve par-*
where) a mild philosophy,   noble and elevated sentiments : *we*
tout,   doux   = f.   *des —* 2   *élevé* 3   *—* ı
there find in every line the effusions   of a noble soul, and *we*
y voit à chaque ligne   épanchement m. *beau.* f.
admire   precepts   calculated to effect the happiness of
      des précepte pl. *propre   faire   bonheur* m.
the world.
      monde m.

SECOND CLASS.

Those which are always joined to a substantive.

Quelque	some	*si cela étoit vrai, quelque historien en auroit parlé*, if that were true, some historian would have mentioned it.
Chaque	each, every	*à chaque jour suffit sa peine*, the trouble of each day is sufficient of itself.
Quelconque	whoever / whatever	*il n'y a raison quelconque qui puisse l'y obliger*, no reason whatever can oblige him to it.

| Certain | certain
some | *certain homme,* a certain man ;
certaines nouvelles, some news. |
| Un | a, an | *j'ai vu un homme,* I saw a man ;
prenez une orange, take an
orange. |

THIRD CLASS.

*Those which are sometimes joined to a substantive,
and sometimes not.*

Nul	no, none	*nulle raison ne peut le convaincre,* no reason can convince him ; *nul d'eux ne l'a rencontré,* not one of them has met him.
Pas un	no, not one	*il n'y a pas une erreur dans cet ouvrage,* there is no error in that work ; *pas un ne le dit,* not one says so.
Aucun	no, none	*je ne connois aucun de vos juges,* I know none of your judges ; *il n'a fait aucune difficulté,* he has made no difficulty.
Autre	other	*servez-vous d'une autre expression,* make use of another expression ; *je vous prenois pour un autre,* I took you for another.
Même	same	*c'est le même homme que je vis hier,* he is the same man I saw yesterday ; *cet homme n'est plus le même,* that man is no longer the same.
Tel	such like	*il tint à peu près un tel discours,* he delivered nearly such a discourse ; *je ne vis jamais rien de tel,* I never saw any thing like it.
Plusieurs	several many	*il est arrivé plusieurs vaisseaux,* several vessels are arrived ; *il ne faut pas que plusieurs pâtissent pour un seul,* many must not suffer for one.
Tout	all every every thing	*tous les êtres créés,* all created beings ; *tout disparoît devant Dieu,* every thing vanishes before God.

FOURTH CLASS.

Of those which are followed by QUE.

Qui que	whoever	qui que tu sois, whoever thou mayest be; qui que ce soit, whoever it may be.
Quoi que	whatever	quoi que ce soit, whatever it may be; quoi que vous disiez, whatever you may say.
Quel que	whoever whatever	quel que soit cet homme, whoever that man may be; quel que soit votre courage, whatever your courage may be.
Tel que	such as	cette étoffe est telle que vous voulez, this stuff is such as you wish for.
Quelque — que	whatever however	quelque raison que vous donniez, whatever reason you may give; quelque puissant que vous soyez, however powerful you may be.
Tout — que	however	tout savant qu'il est, however learned he may be.

CHAP. V.

OF THE VERB.

The *Verb* is a word, the chief use of which is to express affirmation; it has persons, moods, and tenses.

In the phrase, *la vertu est aimable,* virtue is amiable, it is affirmed, that the quality *aimable,* belongs to *la vertu;* likewise in this sentence, *le vice n'est pas aimable,* vice is not amiable, it is affirmed that the quality *aimable* does not belong to *le vice;* the word *est* expresses this affirmation.

That concerning which we affirm or deny a thing, is called the *subject,* and what is affirmed or denied, is called its *attribute.* In the two preceding sentences *vertu* and *vice* are subjects of the verb *est,* and *aimable* is the attribute affirmed respecting the one, and denied with respect to the other.

There are in verbs *two numbers,* the singular and plural, and in each number *three persons.*

1 { The first person is that who speaks; it is designated by *je,* I, in the singular, and by *nous,* we, in the plural; as *je pense,* I think; *nous pensons,* we think.

2 { The second is the person spoken to, expressed by *tu,* thou, in the singular, and by *vous,* you, in the plural; as *tu penses,* thou thinkest; *vous pensez,* you think.

3 { The third is the person spoken of, known by *il,* he, or *elle,* she, in the singular, and by *ils,* or *elles,* they, in the plural; as *il,* or *elle pense,* he, *or* she thinks; *ils,* or *elles pensent,* they think.

All substantives, either common or proper, are of the third person, when not addressed, or spoken to.

REM. { A word is known to be a *verb,* when it admits the personal pronouns : thus, *finir,* to finish, is a verb, because we can say, *je finis, tu finis, il,* or *elle finit,* etc.

There are *five moods,* or modes of conjugating verbs.

1 { The *infinitive mood* affirms, in an indefinite manner, without either number or person; as *aimer,* to love; *avoir aimé,* to have loved.

2 { The *indicative* simply indicates and asserts a thing in a direct manner; as *j'aime,* I love; *il aima,* he loved.

3 { The *conditional* affirms a thing with a condition, as *j'aimerois, si,* etc. I should love, if, etc.

4 { The *imperative* is used for commanding, exhorting, requesting, or reproving; as *aime,* love (thou); *aimons,* let us love.

5 { The *subjunctive* subjects a thing to what precedes; as *vous voulez qu'il aime ,* you wish that he may love; *que nous aimions,* that we may love.

There are three tenses; the *present*, which declares a thing now existing, or doing, as *je lis*, I read; the *past* or *preterit*, denoting that the thing has been done, as *j'ai lu*, I have read; the *future*, denoting that the thing will be done, as *je lirai*, I shall read. But these are subdivided, so that there are several preterit, and two future tenses.

There are five kinds of verbs, the *active, passive, neuter, pronominal*, and *impersonal*.

The *verb active* is that which expresses an action, the object of which is either declared or understood. *Aimer*, to love, is a verb active, as it expresses an action, the object of which may be *quelqu'un*, some person, or *quelque chose*, something; as *aimer Dieu*, to love God; *aimer l'étude*, to love study. The object of this action is called the *regimen*, or *government* of the verb active.

N. B. { A simple question will show this *regimen*, as *qu'est-ce que j'aime?* what do I love? answer, *Dieu*, God. *Dieu* is then the regimen of the verb *j'aime*.

In the French language the *passive verbs* are supplied by the verb *être*, as they are in English by the verb *to be*, and the participle past of the verb active followed by the preposition *de*, or *par*, the subject and regimen of the verb active being reversed. Thus to change the verbs from active to passive in these sentences, *mon père m'aime*, my father loves me; *le milan a enlevé le canari*, the kite has carried off the canary; they must be reversed in this way, *je suis aimé de mon père*, I am loved by my father; *le canari a été enlevé par le milan*, the canary has been carried off by the kite.

The *verb neuter*, is that which has no direct regimen, as the verb active has. *Aller*, to go; *marcher*, to walk, are verbs neuter, because we cannot say, *aller quelqu'un*, to go somebody; *marcher quelque chose*, to walk something. *Plaire*, to please, is likewise a verb neuter, as we cannot say in French *plaire quelqu'un*, to please somebody, but *plaire à quelqu'un*.

The pronominal verbs are those in which each person is conjugated through all the tenses, with a double personal pronoun.

as

	je me	I myself	nous nous	we ourselves
	tu te	thou thyself	vous vous	you yourselves or, ye yourselves
	il se	he himself	ils se	they themselves
	elle se	she herself	elles se	

There are four sorts of *pronominal verbs.*

1. The *pronominal verb active,* when the action of the verb falls upon the subject, as *je me flatte,* I flatter myself; *il se loue,* he praises himself. Almost all the active verbs are susceptible of being *reflected.*

2. The *pronominal verb neuter,* which indicates only a state, a disposition of the subject, as *se repentir,* to repent; *se désister,* to debist; *s'enfuir,* to run away.

3. The *reciprocal verb* expresses a reciprocity of action between two or more subjects, and consequently has no singular; such are *s'entr'aider,* to help one another; *s'entredonner,* to give each other.

4. The *pronominal verb impersonal,* is only used in the third person singular. Active verbs frequently assume this form, in a passive sense, for the sake of brevity and energy; as *il se bâtit,* there is building; *il se faisoit,* there was doing; *il se conclut,* there was concluded; *il s'est dit,* it has been said; *il se donnera une grande bataille,* a great battle will be fought.

The *impersonal verb* is only used in the third person singular, with the pronoun il, and has no relation to any person or thing. *Neiger,* to snow, is an impersonal verb, as it cannot be applied to any person, or thing; *il neige,* it snows: *il neigeoit,* it did snow.

K

.: Though the greatest part of the French verbs are regular, there are, however, as in other languages, some that are *irregular*, and others that are *defective*. Regular verbs are those which are congugated conformably to a general standard. Irregular verbs are those which do not conform to the verb employed as a model; and defective verbs are those which, in certain tenses or persons, are not used.

OF CONJUGATIONS.

To conjugate a verb is to rehearse it with all its different inflections.

. The French have four conjugations, which are easily distinguished by the termination of the present of the infinitive.

FIRST		-*er*	as, par*ler*, ai*mer*, chan*ter*, don*ner*, etc.
SECOND		-*ir*	as, fin*ir*, sen*tir*, ouvr*ir*, ten*ir*, etc.
THIRD		-*oir*	as, re*cevoir*, aperce*voir*, de*voir*, etc.
FOURTH		-*re*	as, ren*dre*, pla*ire*, paro*itre*, rédu*ire*, join*dre*, etc.

The French, like most modern nations, not having a sufficient number of inflections in their verbs to represent the great variety of their tenses, supply this deficiency with two auxiliary verbs, *avoir* and *être*, to have and to be.

Those tenses in a verb, whose inflections are derived pure and unmixed from the parent stock, are called *simple tenses*, and are always in French expressed by a *single word*. But the tenses, which are formed by the union of those of the verbs *avoir*, or *être*, with a participle past, are called *compound*, and necessarily consist of not less than two or three words. Thus, *avoir*, *j'ai*, *j'avois*, *j'eus*, etc. *parler*, *je parle*, *je parlois*, etc. are simple tenses; but *avoir eu*, *j'ai eu*, *j'eus eu*, *j'avois eu*, or *avoir parlé*, *j'ai parlé*, *j'eus parlé*, *j'ai eu parlé*, etc. are compound tenses.

CONJUGATION OF THE AUXILIARY VERB *Avoir,* TO HAVE.

INFINITIVE.

SIMPLE TENSES.		COMPOUND TENSES.	
PRESENT.		**PAST.**	
avoir	to have	avoir eu	to have had.

PARTICIPLES.

PRESENT.			
ayant	having		
PAST.		**PAST.**	
eu, *m.* eue, *f.*	had	ayant eu	having had

INDICATIVE.

PRESENT.		PRETERIT INDEFINITE, or *compound of the present.*	
j'ai	*I have*	j'ai	*I have*
tu as	*thou hast*	tu as	*thou hast*
il, *or* elle a	*he,* or *she has*	il a	*he has*
nous avons	*we have*	nous avons	*we have*
vous avez	*you have*	vous avez	*you have*
ils, *or* elles ont	*they have*	ils ont	*they have.*

(eu) (had)

EXERCISE.

REM. { In the following exercises, the substantive being taken in a partitive sense, it will be necessary to use the article, according to the direction given, page 60.

PRESENT. I have books. Thou hast friends. He has honesty.
livre   ami   honnêteté f. *h* m.

She has sweetness. We have credit. You have
douceur f.   — m.

riches. They have virtues. They have modesty.
richesse pl. m.   vertu f.   = f.

PRETERIT INDEFINITE. I have had pleasure. Thou hast had
plaisir m.

gold. He has had patience. She has had beauty. We have
or m.   — f.   = f.

had honours. You have had friendship. They have had
honneur   amitié f. m.

sentiments. They have had sensibility.
—   f.   = f.

IMPERFECT. I had ambition. Thou hadst wealth. He had
— f.   bien m.

K 2

SIMPLE TENSES.		COMPOUND TENSES.	
IMPERFECT.		**PLUPERFECT**, or *compound of the imperfect.*	
j'avois	I had, or *did* have	j'avois	I had
tu avois	thou hadst, or *didst* have	tu avois	thou hadst
il avoit	he had, or *did* have	il avoit	he had
nous avions	we had, or *did* have	nous avions	we had
vous aviez	you had, or *did* have	vous aviez	you had
ils avoient	they had, or *did* have	ils avoient	they had

(eu ... had)

PRETERIT DEFINITE.		**PRETERIT ANTERIOR**, or *compound of the preterit.*	
j'eus	I had	j'eus	I had
tu eus	thou hadst	tu eus	thou hadst
il eut	he had	il eut	he had
nous eûmes	we had	nous eûmes	we had
vous eûtes	you had	vous eûtes	you had
ils eurent	they had	ils eurent	they had

(eu ... had)

---

sincerity. She had graces. We had oranges. You had pears.
= f.   *poire*

They had apples. They had lemons.
m.   *pomme* f.   *citron*

PLUPERFECT I had had apricots. Thou hadst had nectarines.
                           abricot   *brugnon*

He had had walnuts. She had had hazel-nuts. We had had
    noix   *noisette*

chesnuts. You had had figs. They had had medlars. They
châtaigne.   *figue* m.   *nèfle.*   f.
had had filberts.
    aveline

PRETERIT DEFINITE. I had plumbs. Thou hadst cherries.
                             prune   *cerise*

He had strawberries. She had pine-apples. We had almonds.
    fraise   *ananas*   *amande*

You had currants. They had raspberries. They had grapes,
groseille m.   *framboise* f.   *raisin* m. pl.

SIMPLE TENSES.		COMPOUND TENSES
FUTURE ABSOLUTE.		**FUTURE ANTERIOR, or** *compound of the future.*
j'aurai	I shall, or *will* have	j'aurai	I shall, or will have
tu auras	thou shalt, or wilt have	tu auras	thou wilt have
il aura	he will have	il aura	he will have
nous aurons	we shall have	nous aurons	we shall have
vous aurez	you will have	vous aurez	you will have
ils auront	they will have	ils auront	they will have

REM. { In the following exercises, the addition of an adjective, after the substantive, will make no change in the remark on the preceding exercise.

PRETERIT ANTERIOR. I had had very black ink. Thou
fort 2 noir 3 encre f. 1
hadst had honest proceedings. She had had uncommon
honnête 2 procédé *rare 2*
graces. We had had very ripe rapes. You had had exquisite
1 *2 mûr 3 § 1* *exquis 2*
melons. They had had ready money.
— m. 1 *comptant 2 argent* m. 1

FUTURE ABSOLUTE. I shall have studious pupils. They
appliqué 2 élève m. 1
wilt have horrid pains. He will have ridiculous ideas.
horrible 2 peine f. 1 *ridicule 2 idée* f. 1
We shall have useless cares. You will have true and real
inutile 2 soin m. 1 *2 réel 3*
pleasures. They will have poignant griefs.
m. 1. *cuisant 2 chagrin* m. 1.

REM. { But if the adjective precedes the substantive, then *de*, or *d'*, only is to be used.

FUTURE ANTERIOR. I shall have had good paper. Thou
papier m.
wilt have had excellent fruit. She will have had charming
m. pl. *charmant*
flowers. We shall have had good pens. You will have had
fleurs f. *plume* f.

K 3

CONDITIONAL.

SIMPLE TENSES.		COMPOUND TENSES.	
PRESENT.		**PAST, or** *compound of the conditional.*	
j'aurois	I should, could, or *would have*	j'aurois	I should have
tu aurois	*thou should'st have*	tu aurois	thou should'st have
il auroit	*he should have*	il auroit	he should have
nous aurions	*we should have*	nous aurions	we should have
vous auriez	*you should have*	vous auriez	you should have
ils auroient	*they should have*	ils auroient	they should have

(eu ... had)

large buildings.　They will have had fine　clothes.
grand bâtiment m.　　　　　　　　*superbe habit* m.

PRESENT OF THE CONDITIONAL.　I should have fine engrav-
　　　　　　　　　　　　　　　　　　　　　　　　gravure
ings.　Thou should'st have pretty playthings,　He should
f.　　　　　　　　　　　*joli joujou* m.
have immense treasures.　We should have beautiful pictures.
　　　trésor m.　　　　　　　　　　　　*tableau* m,
You would have pretty houses.　They should have long con-
　　　　　　　　　　　　f.
versations.
f.

REM. { The preceding remark holds good likewise after a word expressing quantity, such as *beaucoup*, a great deal, great many ; *peu*, little, few ; *plus*, more ; *moins*, less ; *trop*, too much, too many, etc. except *bien*, much, many, which requires *du, de la, de l', des.*

CONDITIONAL PAST. I should have had a great deal of
trouble.　Thou would'st have had *more*　pleasure.　He would
peine f.　　　　　　　　　　　*de*
have had (*a vast deal*) of knowledge.　We should have had
　　　infiniment　connoisance f. pl.
more　opportunities of succeeding.　You would certainly
de occasion f. pl.　　*réussir*　　　　　　*certainement*

N. B. { *J'eusse eu, tu eusses eu, il eût eu, nous eussions eu, vous eussiez eu, ils eussent eu,* I should have had, etc. is also used for the conditional past.

IMPERATIVE.

Aie	*Have (thou)*
Qu'il ait	*Let him have*
Ayons,	*Let us have*
Ayez	*Have.(ye)*
Qu'ils aient	*Let them have*

---

have had *many* advantages over him. They would have
1   *beaucoup de avantage   sur lui*
had *many* enemies.
bien   ennemi.

Observe that, when the verb is followed by several substantives, the proper article and preposition must be repeated before each.

IMPERATIVE. Have complaisance, attention, and
— f.   *égard* m. pl.
politeness. Let him have modesty, and more correct ideas.
politesse f.   — f.   2 *juste* 3   1.
Let her have more decency. Let us have courage and firmness.
décence   — m.   *fermeté* f.
Have gravy soup,   nice roast-beef, and a pudding. Let
un gras 2 *soupe* f. 1 *un bon rosbif* m.   *pouding* m.
them have ale,   rum, and punch. Let them have manners in
m.   *aile* f. *rum* m.   *ponche* m.   f.   *mœurs* f. pl.
and conduct.
conduite f.

SUBJUNCTIVE.

PRESENT. That I may have many   friends. That thou
beaucoup
may'st have good reasons to give   him. That he may have
donner   lui
elevated sentiments. That we may have courage and mag-
élevé 2   — m. 1.   *bravoure* f.
nanimity. That you may have delightful   landscapes,   and
= f.   *délicieux* 2   *paysage* m. pl. 1.
beautiful sea-pieces. That they may have more condescension
marine f. pl.   —*dance*
and more prepossessing manners.
2 *prévenant* 3   *manière* f. pl. 1.
PRETERIT. That I may have had wine,   beer,   and cider.
vin m. *bière* f.   *cidre* m.

SUBJUNCTIVE.

SIMPLE TENSES.	COMPOUND TENSES.

PRESENT.	PRETERIT, or *compound of the present.*		
Que *	*That*	Que *	*That*
j'aie	*I may have*	j'aie	*I may have*
tu aies	*thou may'st have*	tu aies	*thou may'st have*
il ait	*he may have*	il ait	*he may have*
nous ayons	*we may have*	nous ayons	*we may have*
vous ayez	*you may have*	vous ayez	*you may have*
ils aient	*they may have*	ils aient	*they may have*

(eu) ... had

That thou may'st have had a good horse,   and a fine dog.
                    cheval m.   *chien* m.
That he may have had enlightened judges. That we may have
                éclairé 2   *juge* m. 1
had snow,   rain,   and wind. That you may have had a great
   neige f. *pluie* f.   *vent* m.
dining-room,   a beautiful drawing-room,   a pretty
salle à manger f.   *superbe* *salon de compagnie* m.   *joli*
dressing-room,   and a charming bed-room.   That
cabinet de toilette m.   —*mant chambre à coucher* f.
they may have had vast possessions, fine meadows, and de-
                vaste   — f.   *prairie* f.   *dé-*
lightful   groves.
licieux 2 *bois* m. 1.

   IMPERFECT. That I might have a sword, a musket, and
                         épée f.   *fusil* m.
pistols.   That thou might'st have a knife,   a spoon, and a
pistolet m.   *couteau* m. *cuillère* f.
fork.   That we might have a penknife, pencils, and good
fourchette f.   *canif* m. *pinceau* m.
copies.   That he might have a coach,   a good house, and
modèle m.   *carrosse* m.   f.

* REM. { The subjunctive, in French, is always preceded by the conjunctive *que*, that, which is often sup-pressed in English.

SIMPLE TENSES.		COMPOUND TENSES.	
IMPERFECT.		**PLUPERFECT,** or *compound of the imperfect.*	
Que	*That*	Que	*That*
j'eusse	*I had,* or *might have*	j'eusse	*I.. might have*
tu eusses	*thou might'st have*	tu eusses	*thou might-est have*
il eût	*he might have*	il eût	*he might have*
nous eussions	*we might have*	nous eus-sions	*we might have*
vous eussiez	*you might have*	vous eus-siez	*you might have*
ils eussent	*they might have*	ils eussent	*they might have*

(Compound column grouped with: eu } had)

furniture, simple but elegant. That you might have
meuble, m. pl. — *mais* —
health and great respect. That they might have fruitful
santé f. *un considération* f. *fertile* 2
lands.
terre f. 1.

PLUPERFECT. That I might have had friendship. That thou
amitié f.
might'st have had gloves, boots, and horses. That he
gant m. *botte* f. *cheval* m.
might have had zealous and faithful servants. That we
zélé 2 *fidèle* 3 *domestique* m. 1.
might have had fine clothes, precious jewels, and magnificent
= 2 *bijou* m. 1. *magnifique* 2
furniture. That you might have had warm friends. That
1 *chaud* 2 1
they might have had greatness of soul and pity.
grandeur f. *pitié* f.

N. B. { The verb *avoir,* serves not only as an auxiliary to conjugate its own compound tenses, but likewise the compound tenses of the verb *être,* and those of the active, the impersonal, and almost all the neuter verbs.

SENTENCES ON THE SAME VERB, WITH A NEGATIVE.

In the following sentences, the preposition *de*, or *d'*, is put before the substantive, according as it begins with a consonant or a vowel; *ne* between the personal pronoun and the verb, and *pas*, or *point*, after the verb in the simple tenses, and between the verb and the participle in the compound tenses; as,

Je n'ai pas de livres,	*I have no books.*
Tu n'avois pas de bien,	*Thou hadst no wealth.*
Elle n'eut pas d'honnêteté,	*She had no honesty.*
Nous n'avons pas eu d'amitié,	*We have had no friendship.*
Vous n'aviez pas eu de puissans amis,	*You had not had powerful friends.*
Ils n'auront pas d'ennemis redoutables,	*They will not have formidable enemies.*

EXERCISE.

INDICATIVE. PRESENT. I have no precious medals.
= 2 *médaille* f. 1

We have had no useless things. PRETERITE INDEFINITE.
inutile 2 *chose* f. 1

I have had no constancy. We have had no generosity.
— f. = f.

IMPERFECT. Thou hadst not a beautiful park. You had no
parc m.

good cucumbers. PLUPERFECT. He had had no fine houses.
concombre m. f.

They had had no money. PRETERITE DEFINITE. He had not
argent m.

a skilful gardener. They had no carpets. PRETERIT AN-
habile jardinier m. *tapis* m,

TERIOR. Thou hadst had no complaisance. You had had no
— f.

great talents. FUTURE ABSOLUTE. I shall have no great bu-
— m. *af-*

siness. We shall not have uncommon prints. FUTURE
faire f. pl *rare* 2 *estampe* f. 1

ANTERIOR. Thou shalt have had no consolation. You shall not
— f.

have had quiet days.
tranquille 2 m. 1.

CONDITIONAL. PRESENT. He should not have bad
mauvais

pictures. They should have no leisure. PAST. I should have
tableau m.   loisir m.
had no griefs.   We should have had no troubles.
    chagrin m. pl.   peine f. pl.

IMPERATIVE. Have no impatience. Let him not have
        sing.   —

absurd ideas. Let us not have dangerous connexions. Have
absurde 2 f. pl. 1.   = 2   liaison f. 1.
no such whims. Let them not have so whimsical a project.
    tel caprice m.   bizarre 2   projet m. 1.

SUBJUNCTIVE. PRESENT. That I may have no protectors.
                                = m.

That we may have no success. PRETERIT. That he may have
        succès m.
had no perseverance. That they may have had no valour.
    — f.   bravoure f.

IMPERFECT. That thou might'st have no principles of taste.
                    principe m. goût m.
That you might not have a just reward. PLUPERFECT.
        juste récompense f.
That I might have had no good advice. That we might
        avis m. pl.
have had no news.
    nouvelle f. pl.

THE VERB *Avoir*, INTERROGATIVELY AND AFFIRMATIVELY.

In interrogations, the personal pronoun, accompanied
by a hyphen (-), is placed after the verb in the simple
tenses, and between the verb and the participle in the
compound tenses, and, when the third person singular
of the verb ends with a vowel, for euphony a *t* is added
between it and the pronoun, preceded and followed by
a hyphen, thus (-*t*-). See likewise the remarks, page 99.

Ai-je des livres?	*Have I books?*
Avois-tu du bien?	*Hadst thou wealth?*
Eut-elle de l'honnêteté?	*Had she honesty?*
Avons-nous eu de bons conseils?	*Have we had good counsels?*
Aviez-vous eu de la prudence?	*Had you had prudence?*
Aura-t-il de l'argent?	*Will he have money?*
Aura-t-elle eu des protecteurs?	*Will she have had protectors?*

EXERCISE.

INDICATIVE. PRESENT. Hast thou needles? Have you
　　　　　　　　　　　　　　aiguille f.
coloured maps? PRETERIT INDEFINITE. Have I had pens?
enluminé 2 carte f. 2　　　　　　　　　　　　　　plume f.
Have we had convenient houses? IMPERFECT. Had she silk?
commode 2 f. 1.　　　　　　　　　　　　　soie f.
Had they large buildings? PLUPERFECT. Had she pins?
grand bâtiment m.　　　　　　　　　　　épingle f.
Had they had extensive fields? PRETERIT DEFINITE. Had
spacieux 3 champ m. 1.
he good shoes? Had they looking-glasses? PRETERIT ANTE-
soulier m.　　　f.　miroir m.
RIOR. Hadst thou had lace? Had you had odoriferous
　　　　　　　　　dentelle f.　　　　odoriférant 2
shrubs. FUTURE ABSOLUTE. Shall I have gold, silver,
arbuste m. 1.　　　　　　　　　　　m. argent m.
and platina. Shall we have (good luck)? FUTURE ANTERIOR.
platine m.　　　　bonheur m.
Will she have had joy? Will they have had company?
joie?　　　　　　　compagnie f.

CONDITIONAL. PRESENT. Should'st thou have happy
　　　　　　　　　　　　　　heureux
moments? Should you have good wine and nice cordials?
— m.　　　　　　　　　　vin m.　fin 2 liqueur f. 1.
PAST. Should he have had uncommon fruits? Should they
　　　　　　　　　　rare 2　　m. 1.
have had rich clothes?

THE SAME VERB INTERROGATIVELY AND NEGATIVELY.

In sentences of this form, observe the different rules
that are prefixed to the exercises on the verb, and in
sentences simply interrogative, always place ne at the
beginning of sentences, and pas, or point, after the personal pronoun, whether in the simple or compound tenses.

N'ai-je pas des livres?	*Have I no books?*
N'avois-tu pas des amis?	*Hadst thou no friends?*
N'a-t-elle pas beaucoup d'es-	*Has she not a great deal of*
prit?	*wit?*
N'avons-nous pas eu de bons	*Have we not maintained a good*
procédés?	*conduct?*

N'aviez-vous pas eu de nouvelles robes?	*Had you not had new gowns?*
N'aura-t-il pas des ressources?	*Will he have no resources?*
N'auront-elles pas eu des consolations?	*Will they have had no consolations?*

EXERCISE.

INDICATIVE. PRESENT. Hast thou no diamonds? Have
           diamant m.
you no indulgent parents? PRETERIT INDEFINITE. Hast thou
  — 2 — m. 1.
not had contempt, and even hatred,   for that man? Have
  mépris m. *même haine* f. *h.* asp. *pour cet*
you not had better examples? IMPERFECT. Had he not a
  meilleur exemple m.
rigid censor? Had they not inattentive children?
sévère 2 *censeur* m. 1.   = 2 *enfant* m. 1.
PLUPERFECT. Had I not had other views? Had we not had
        autre vue? f. pl.
amethysts, rubies, and topazes? PRETERIT DEFINITE. Had
améthyste f. *rubis* m. *topaze* f.
I no great wrongs? Had we not perfidious friends? PRETERIT
  tort m.   *perfide* 2 1
ANTERIOR. Had he not had too studied expressions? Had
     2 *recherché* 3 — f. 1.
they not had excellent models? FUTURE ABSOLUTE. Wilt thou
  — *modèle* m.
not have a more regular conduct? Will you not have
  plus 2 *réglé* 3 *conduite* f. 1.
fashionable gowns? FUTURE ANTERIOR. Shall I have had no
à la mode 2 *robe* f. 1.
sweetmeats? Shall we not have had a good preacher?
confitures f.   *prédicateur* m.

CONDITIONAL. PRESENT. Should she not have clear
           clair 2
and just ideas? Would they not have more extensive know-
 3 f. 1.   2 *étendu* 3 con-
ledge?   PAST. Should she have had no patience?
noissances f. pl. 1.   — f.
Should they have had no rectitude?
  f.   *droiture* f.

CONJUGATION OF THE AUXILIARY VERB
Être, to be.
INFINITIVE.

SIMPLE TENSES.		COMPOUND TENSES.	
PRESENT.		**PAST.**	
Être	to be	Avoir été	to have been

PARTICIPLES.

	PRESENT.		**PAST.**
Étant	being		
	PAST.	ayant été	having been
été	been		

INDICATIVE.

PRESENT.		PRETERIT INDEFINITE.	
je suis	I am	j'ai	I have
tu es	thou art	tu as	thou hast
il, *or* elle est	he, or she is	il a	he has
nous sommes	we are	nous avons été	we have been
vous êtes	you are	vous avez	you have
ils elles } sont	they are	ils ont	they have

EXERCISES.

As interrogative and negative sentences will now be promiscuously intermixed, the scholar will observe, that the adverb, in the following exercises, is to be placed before the adjective; and that whenever in interrogative sentences a substantive is the subject, it is to be placed at the head of the sentence, adding a pronoun for the interrogation immediately after the verb; as *mon frère est-il venu?* is my brother come?

PRESENT. I am very glad to see you. Art not thou pleased
aise de voir *satisfait*
with that book? Is she really amiable? We are
de *véritablement*
happy. Are not you too condescending? Are your friends
heureux *complaisant*
still in London?
encore à Londres
PRETERIT INDEFINITE. Have not I been constant? Hast

SIMPLE TENSES.		COMPOUND TENSES.		
IMPERFECT.		**PLUPERFECT.**		
j'étois	I was	j'avois	I had	
tu étois	thou wast	tu avois	thou hadst	
il étoit	he was	il avoit	he had	been
nous étions	we were	nous avions été	we had	
vous étiez	you were	vous aviez	you had	
ils étoient	they were	ils avoient	they had	
PRETERIT DEFINITE.		**PRETERIT ANTERIOR.** *		
je fus	I was	j'eus	I had	
tu fus	thou wast	tu eus	thou hadst	
il fut	he was	il eut	he had	been
nous fûmes	we were	nous eûmes été	we had	
vous fûtes	you were	vous eûtes	you had	
ils furent	they were	ils eurent	they had	

thou always been steady?   She has been faithful.   Have we
         posé   *fidèle*
been firm and courageous?   You have been charitable.   Have
ferme   =   —
those men always been good and benevolent?
                     bienfaisant

IMPERFECT. I was too busy to   see   you. Wast not thou
                 occupé pour recevoir
troublesome? Was this girl idle?   Were we not too untractable?
importun   *fille paresseux*   *indocile*
You were not quiet   enough.   They were vain, light, and
          tranquille 2 *assez* 1   f.   — *frivole*
coquettish.
coquette

PLUPERFECT. I had hitherto been very indifferent. Hadst
           jusqu'alors   *insouciant*
not thou been too imprudent? Had his wife been sufficiently
        —   *épouse*   *assez*
modest and   reserved?   We had not yet   been sufficiently
   assez réservé .   *encore*

Rem. { PRET. ANT.—Exercises upon this tense would be as yet too complicated, as may be seen by this sentence; à peine y eus-je été cinq ou six minutes, qu'il arriva, I had scarce been there five or six minutes, when he arrived.

SIMPLE TENSES.		COMPOUND TENSES.	
FUTURE ABSOLUTE.		**FUTURE ANTERIOR.**	
je serai	*I shall, or will be*	j'aurai	*I shall or will have*
tu seras	*thou wilt be*	tu auras	*thou wilt have*
il sera	*he will be*	il aura	*he will have*
nous serons	*we shall be*	nous aurons	*we shall have*
vous serez	*you shall be*	vous aurez	*you will have*
ils seront	*they shall be*	ils auront	*they will have*

été ... *been*

attentive.   Had you been envious and jealous?   They had not
appliqué   =   *jaloux*
been grateful.
     reconnoissant.

    PRETERIT DEFINITE.   Perhaps   I was not sufficiently
                   Peut-être que   *assez*
prudent.   Wast thou discreet enough on that occasion?   Was
    —   *discret*   1   *en*   —f.
not that princess too proud?   We were very unhappy.   Were
     —*cesse*   *fier*
not you too hasty?   They were not much satisfied.
       prompt   *fort satisfait*

    FUTURE ABSOLUTE.   To-morrow I shall be at home   till
                   Demain   *chez moi jusqu'à*
(twelve o'clock).   Wilt thou always be restless, brutal, and
      midi   *inquiet bourru*
sour?   Will   your father be at   home this evening?
chagrin   *Monsieur*   *chez lui*   *soir* m.
Shall not we be more diligent?   You will always   then   be
          —   5   *donc* 2   1
capricious, obstinate, and particular.   Will not your scholars be
quinteux   *opiniâtre*   *pointilleux*   *écolier*
troublesome?
incommode

    FUTURE ANTERIOR.   Shall not I have been too severe?   Thou
                             —
wilt have been too distrustful.   Will not his sister have been
            défiant   *sœur*
whimsical and capricious?   Shall not we have been eager
fantasque   =   *empressé* 2

CONDITIONAL.

SIMPLE TENSES.		COMPOUND TENSES.	
PRESENT.		**PAST.**	
je serois	*I should, would, or could be*	j'aurois	*I should have*
tu serois	*thou would'st be*	tu aurois	*thou would'st have*
il seroit	*he would be*	il auroit	*he would have*
nous serions	*we should be*	nous aurions	été *we should have* been
vous seriez	*you would be*	vous auriez	*you would have*
ils seroient	*they would be*	ils auroient	*they would have*

The conditional past, *J'eusse été, tu eusses été, il eût été, nous eussions été, vous eussiez été, ils eussentété*, is also used.

---

enough? Will not you have been inconsiderate? Will not the
indiscret
judges have been just?
juge

CONDITIONAL PRESENT. I would not be so rash.
téméraire
Would'st thou be as consistent in thy behaviour as in thy lan-
conséquent dans conduite f. pro-
guage? Would not his son be ready in time? Should we be
pos m. pl. fils prêt à
always incorrigible? You would not be disinterested enough.
désintéressé 2 1
Would not those ladies be always virtuous?
dame vertueux

PAST. (Had it not been for) your instructions, I should have
sans conseil m. pl.
been proud and haughty. Would'st not thou have been
dédaigneux hautain
malicious and sarcastic? Would that man have been so
malin ricaneur tellement
destitute of common sense? Certainly we should not have been
dépourvu bon sens
so ridiculous. Would not you have been more kind and
si ridicule doux plus
indulgent? They would not have been so ungenteel.
complaisant malhonnête

L 3

IMPERATIVE.

Sois	*Be (thou)*
Qu'il soit	*Let him be*
Soyons	*Let us be*
Soyez	*Be (ye)*
Qu'ils soient	*Let them be*

SUBJUNCTIVE.

SIMPLE TENSES.		COMPOUND TENSES.	
PRESENT.		**PRETERIT.**	
que	*that*	que	*that*
je sois	*I may, can, or should be*	j'aie	*I may, can, or should have*
tu sois	*thou may'st be*	tu aies	*thou may'st have*
il soit	*he may be*	il ait	*he may have*
nous soyons	*we may be*	nous ayons	*we may have*
vous soyez	*you may be*	vous ayez	*you may have*
ils soient	*they may be*	ils aient	*they may have*

(compound tenses: été ... been)

Be liberal, but with discretion.   Do not be so lavish.   Let
sing.   —   *avec*   —   sing. *prodigue*
us be equitable, humane and prudent.   Let us not be greedy.
  —   *humain*   —   *avide*
Be economical and temperate.   Do not be thoughtless.
pl. *économe*   *sobre*   pl. *léger*

As the *third person* singular and plural of the imperative
mood belong rather to the subjunctive, they are there exemplified.

It has already been observed, that before the *subjunctive*
can form complete sense, it must be preceded by another
verb. For the sake of brevity, therefore, complete sentences will only be given on the present tense. This remark applies alike to the four conjugations.

SIMPLE TENSES. *		COMPOUND TENSES.	
IMPERFECT.		**PLUPERFECT.**	
que	*that*	que	*that*
je fusse	*I might,* or *could be*	j'eusse	*I might,* or *could*
tu fusses	*thou might'st be*	tu eusses	*thou might'st*
il fût	*he might be*	il eût	*he might*
nous fus-sions	*we might be*	nous eus-sions	*we might*
vous fussiez	*you might be*	vous eussiez	*you might*
ils fussent	*they might be*	ils eussent	*they might*

(Compound tenses bracketed with été *... have been)*

PRESENT. Is it possible I can be so credulous? They wish
     —   *   *— le*   *On désire*
thou may'st be more modest. Is it possible she can be so
     modeste   *
obstinate? They wish we may be more assiduous. It is not
entêté   *assidu*   *On* *
expected you should be timid. It is feared they may
s'attend   *timide.*   *On* * *craint*   *ne*
be guilty.
coupable.

PRETERIT. That I may have been so hasty and impatient.
                        emporté   *si* *—.*
Thou may'st have been so bloated with pride. That she may
              bouffi de
have been so fickle. That we may have been so headstrong.
   volage   *têtu*
That you may have been so covetous. That they may have
          avare
been so unreasonable.
     deraisonable.

Observe, the verb *être* serves as an auxiliary to conjugate the
passive verbs through all their tenses, the compound tenses of
the pronominal verbs, and those of about fifty neuter verbs.

IMPERFECT. That I might not be humane and generous.
                  humain   ==.
That thou might'st be more careful. That she might not be so
                 soigneux.
arrogant. That we might be victorious. That you might not be
 —   ==
so stern. That they might not be so cruel.
sévère   —

FIRST CONJUGATION.

IN ER.

1 { In verbs ending in -*ger*, the *e* is preserved in those tenses where *g* is followed by the vowels *a* or *o*, in order to preserve to this letter its soft sound; as *mangeant, jugeons, je négligeai.*

2 { In verbs ending in -*cer*, for the same reason, a cedilla is put under *c*, when followed by *a* or *o*; as *suçant, plaçons, j'effaçai.*

3 { In verbs ending in -*oyer* and -*uyer*, the *y* is changed into *i* before a mute *e*; as *j'emploie, il essuie, j'appuierai, il nettoieroit.*

4 { This practice is extended by some to verbs in -*ayer*, and -*eyer*, as *il paie, j'essaierai, elle grasseye*, or *grasseie.*

5 { In some few verbs ending in -*eler* and -*eter*, the *l* and *t* are doubled in those inflections, which receive an *e* mute after these consonants, as from *appeler, il appelle*, from *jeter, je jetterai*, etc.

6 { The first person singular of the present of the indicative changes *e* mute into acute *é* in interrogative sentences. This remark is also applied to some verbs of the second conjugation ending in -*vrir*, -*frir* and -*lir*; as *néglige-je? aimé-je? offré-je? cueillé-je?*

EXERCISE.

PLUPERFECT. That I might have been more studious. That thou might'st have been more circumspect. That she might
circonspect.
have been more attentive to her duty. That we might have
devoir m. pl.
been less addicted to pleasure. That you might have been
livré   *à* art. m. pl.
more assiduous and more grateful. That they might have
assidu   *plus reconnoissant.*
been less daring.
hardi.

PARADIGM, OR MODEL.

INFINITIVE.

SIMPLE TENSES.		COMPOUND TENSES.	
PRESENT.		PAST.	
parl-*er*	*to speak*	avoir parl*é*	*to have spoken*

PARTICIPLES.

PRESENT.
parl-*ant* | *speaking*
PAST.
parl-*é* m. -*ée* f. | *spoken*

ayant parl-*é* | *having spoken* — PAST.

REMARKS.

1 { All the regular verbs of the First Conjugation adopt the terminations of the verb *parler;* EXAM.

	parl-*er*	aim-*er*	expliqu-*er*	avou-*er*
	parl-*ant*	annonç-*ant*	engag-*eant*	défray-*ant*
	parl-*é*	agré-*é*	décri-*é*	dédommag-*é*
je	parl-*e*	dans-*e*	iguor-*e*	renvoi-*e*
tu	parl-*es*	din-*es*	rejet-*tes*	renouvel-*les*
il	parl-*e*	chant-*e*	bégai-*e*	grassey-*e*
nous	parl-*ons*	berç-*ons*	choy-*ons*	chang-*eons*
vous	parl-*ez*	règn-*ez*	essuy-*ez*	épel-*ez*
ils	parl-*ent*	caress-*ent*	ennu-*ient*	appel-*lent*

And so on through the whole verb.

2 { Adverbs, with few exceptions, must be placed after the verb, in simple tenses, and between the auxiliary and the participle, in compound tenses, when this adverb is only a single word.

3 { The remarks prefixed to the exercises on the verb *avoir,* when *de* is to be placed between the verb and the substantive, ought to be attended to.

4 { The article *the,* after the verb, must always be expressed in French, though often understood in English.

EXERCISE.

INDICATIVE PRESENT. I willingly give that plaything to
volontiers donner joujou m.

INDICATIVE.

SIMPLE TENSES.		COMPOUND TENSES.		
PRESENT.		**PRETERIT INDEFINITE.**		
je parl-*e*	*I speak*	j'ai		*I have*
tu parl-*es*	*thou speakest*	tu as		*thou hast*
il parl-*e*	*he speaks*	il a		*he has*
nous parl-*ons*	*we speak*	nous avons	parl-*é*	*we have*
vous parl-*ez*	*you speak*	vous avez		*you have*
ils parl-*ent*	*they speak*	ils out		*they have*

(spoken.)

---

your sister. Do I prefer   pleasure to my duty?   Dost
   f.   *   *préférer* art.   m.   *devoir* m.
thou not incense thy euemies?   He does not propose salutary
    irriter   *ennemi*   *proposer un* =2
advîce to his friends.   We sincerely   love   peace and
avis m. 1.   *sincèrement*   art. *paix* f.   art.
tranquillity. We do not neglect (any thing) to   please you.
  = f.   *   *négliger rien*   *pour plaire*
Do you not admire the beauty of that landscape? Do not
   admirer   = f.   *paysage* m.   *
your parents comfort the afflicted?   They (make use of) all
  —   *consoler affligé* m. pl.   *employer*
 means   to   succeed.
art. *moyen* m. *pour réussir.*

PRETERIT INDEFINITE.   I have (given up) my favourite
              céder   *favori* 2
horse   to my cousin. Hast thou not exchanged watches
cheval m. 1.   — m.   *changer de montres*
with my sister? Has the tutor   given   fine engravings to
       précepteur   *de*   *gravure* f. pl.
his pupil?   We have spoken (a long-while) of your adventure.
pupille m.   *long-temps*   *aventure* f.
Have you not insisted too much upon that point? Have your
    insister   *   *sur*   — m.
aunts prepared their   ball dresses?
tantes préparer   *de bal* 2 *hàbit* m. pl. 1.

IMPERFECT.   I unceasingly thought of my misfortunes.
       sans cesse   penser à   *malheur* m. pl.
Didst thou dread   his presence and   firmness? He ex-
  *   *redouter*   — f.   pron. *fermeté* f.   *re-*
hibited in his person all the virtues of his ancestors. Did not
tracer en   f.   f.   *ancêtre*

SIMPLE TENSES.		COMPOUND TENSES.	
IMPERFECT.		PLUPERFECT.	
je parl-*ois*	*I did speak*, or *was speaking*	j'avois	*I had*
tu parl-*ois*	*thou didst speak*	tu avois	*thou hadst*
il parl-*oit*	*he did speak*	il avoit	*he had*
nous parl-*ions*	*we did speak*	nous avions parl-*é*	*we had* spoken
vous parl-*iez*	*you did speak*	vous aviez	*you had*
ils parl-*oient*	*they did speak*	ils avoient	*they had*

that woman accuse her friend of levity?   We did not protect
      accuser   ami f.   *légèreté* f.   *   *protéger*
that bad   man.   You despised a vain erudition.   Did the
    méchant   *mépriser* —   — f. 1   *
Romans disdain   so weak an enemy? The bees were there
Romain dédaigner   *foible* 2 m. 1.   *abeille* *   *y*
sucking the cups of the flowers.
sucer   *calice* m. *fleur*.

PLUPERFECT.   I had drained   an unwholesome marsh.
              dessécher   *malsain* 2   *marais* m. 1.
Hads't thou not married a man rich, but unluckily   without
         épouser   *malheureusement sans*
education?   Had his father rejected these advantageous
 — f.   *rejeter*   *avantageux* 2
offers?   We had not long   listened to the singing of
offre f. 1   *long-temps écouter*   *   *chant* m.
the birds.   Had you already studied   geography and
oiseau m.   *déjà*   *étudier* art. = f.   art.
history?   Had not his friends procured   him   a company of
=   *procurer* 2 *lui* 1   *compagnie* f.
cavalry?
cavalerie.

    There is a fourth preterit, called *preterit anterior indefinite,* which is used instead of the preterit anterior, when speaking of a time not entirely elapsed; as, *j'ai eu achevé mon ouvrage ce matin, cette semaine,* etc. and not *j'eus achevé:* as it is found in every conjugation, I shall insert it here; *j'ai eu parlé, tu as eu parlé, il a eu parlé, nous avons eu parlé, vous aves eu parlé, ils ont eu parlé.*

SIMPLE TENSES.		COMPOUND TENSES.	
PRETERIT. DEFINITE.		**PRETERIT ANTERIOR.**	
je parl-*ai*	*I spoke*	j'eus	
tu parl-*as*	*thou spokest*	tu eus	*I had*
il parl-*a*	*he spoke*	il eut	*thou hadst*
nous parl-*âmes*	*we spoke*	nous eûmes	*he had*
		parl-*é*	*we had*
vous parl-*âtes*	*you spoke*	vous eûtes	*you had*
ils parl-*èrent*	*they spoke*	ils eurent	*they had*

(spoken)

PRETERIT DEFINITE. Did I not gladly give
            *   *avec plaisir*   *de* art.
peaches and   flowers   to my neighbours? Thou for-
pêche f. pl.   pr. art. *fleurs* f. pl.   *voisin* m. pl.   *ou-*
gottest an essential circumstance. Did not your cousin
blier   *essentiel* 2 *circonstance* f. 1 *
relate that charming history with (a great deal) of grace?
raconter   —*mant* = f. *avec*   *beaucoup*
He lightly judged of my intentions. Did we not shew
  légèrement juger *   —   *   *montrer de*
courage,   constancy, and   firmness? Did
art. —m. pr—art. = f.   pr—art.   f.   *
you visit the grotto and the grove? They did not gene-
  visiter *grotte* f.   *bois* m.   *   *géné-*
rously   forgive their enemies.
reusement pardonner à

PRETERIT ANTERIOR. I had soon wasted my money,
             bientôt manger *argent* m.
and exhausted my resources. Had'st thou very soon reinforced
épuiser   *ressource* f.   * *vîte renforcer*
thy party? Had not Alexander soon surmounted all
  parti m.   *Alexandre* *surmonter tous* art.
obstacles? We had not soon enough shut the shutters, and
= m. pl.   *tôt* 2 *assez* 1 *fermer* *volet*
(let down) the curtains. Had you not quickly   dined?
baisser *rideaux*   *promptement dîner.*
In the twinkling of an eye, they had dispersed the mob.
Dans * *un clin* * *œil*   *disperser* *populace* f.

FUTURE ABSOLUTE. I shall relieve the poor.   Wilt
            soulager pauvre m. pl.
thou faithfully keep that secret? Will he consult
 fidèlement garder —m.   *consulter de* art.

SIMPLE TENSES.		COMPOUND TENSES.		
FUTURE ABSOLUTE.		FUTURE ANTERIOR.		
je parl-*erai*	*I shall, or will speak*	j'aurai		*I shall, or will*
tu parl-*eras*	*thou shalt speak*	tu auras		*thou shalt*
il parl-*era*	*he shall speak*	il aura		*he shall*
nous parl-*erons*	*we shall speak*	nous aurons	parl-*é*	*we shall*
vous parl-*erez*	*you shall speak*	vous aurez		*you shall*
ils parl-*eront*	*they shall speak*	ils auront		*they shall*

have spoken

enlightened judges? He will support you with all his credit.
éclairé 2   *juge* 1   *appuyer de*   — m.
We shall not prefer . pleasure to glory, and riches to
                préférer art. m.   art. f.   art. pl.   art.
honour. By such a conduct,   will you not afflict your father
              tel 2 1 *conduite* f. 3   *affliger*
and   mother? Will they astonish their hearers?
  pron.   *étonner*   *auditeur* m. pl.

FUTURE ANTERIOR. I shall soon have finished this book. By
                             achever   m.
thy submission, wilt thou not have appeased his anger? Will
soumission f.   *appaiser*   *colère* f.
the king have triumphed over his enemies? We, perhaps, shall
        triompher de   2   1
not have rewarded enough the merit of this good man.
  récompenser   *mérite* m.   *de bien* 2 1
Will you not have flown to his assistance? Will our servants
         voler   *secours* m.   *domestique* m.
have brought   money?
  apporter de art. *argent*

CONDITIONAL PRESENT. Should I form   conjectures
                         former de art.   f. pl.
without number? Thou would'st not avoid so great a danger?
  nombre m.   *éviter* 2 3   1 4
Would not his attorney (clear up) that business? We would
    procureur débrouiller   *affaire* f.
(drive away) the importunate. Would you not discover
chasser   *importun* m. pl.   *dévoiler*

M

CONDITIONAL.

SIMPLE TENSES.		COMPOUND TENSES.	
PRESENT.		**PAST.**	
je parl-*erois*	*I should, would, or could speak*	j'aurois	*I should, would, or could*
tu parl-*erois*	*thou should'st speak*	tu aurois	*thou should'st*
il parl-*eroit*	*he should speak*	il auroit	*he should*
nous parl-*erions*	*we should speak*	nous aurions	*we should*
vous parl-*eriez*	*you should speak*	vous auriez	*you should*
ils parl-*eroient*	*they should speak*	ils auroient	*they should*

(parl-é) ... (have spoken)

J'eusse parlé, tu eusses parlé, il eût parlé, nous eussions parlé, vous eussiez parlé, ils eussent parlé, is also used for the conditional past. This remark holds good for every verb.

---

that atrocious plot?   They would not unravel the clue of
    atroce 2   complot m. 1.   démêler   fil m.
that intrigue.
   —f.

PAST.   I should have liked   hunting,   fishing, and the
            aimer art. chasse f. art.   pêche f.
country.   Would'st thou not have played? Would he not have
campagne f.   jouer
bowed to the company? Would we gladly   have praised his
saluer *   compagnie f.   avec plaisir 2 louer 1
pride   and   incivility?   You would have awakened
argueil m.   pron. malhonnêteté f.   éveiller
every body.   Would those merchants have paid their debts?
tout le monde   marchand   payer   dette f. pl.

IMPERATIVE.   In all thy actions, consult the light of
         Dans   —f. pl. consulter   lumière art.
reason.   Never yield   to the violence of thy passions.
   f.   te abandonner   —f.   —
Let us love   justice,   peace, and   virtue.   Let us not
     art. —f.   art. f.   art. f.
cease   to work.   Sacrifice your own interest   to the
cesser de travailler   Sacrifier   * intérêt m. pl.

IMPERATIVE.

parl-*e**	*speak (thou)*
qu'il parl-*e*	*let him speak*
parl-*ons*	*let us speak*
parl-*ez*	*speak (ye)*
qu'ils parl-*ent*	*let them speak*

SUBJUNCTIVE.

SIMPLE TENSES.		**COMPOUND TENSES.**		
PRESENT.		**PRETERIT.**		
que	*that*	que	*that*	
je parl-*e*	*I may*, or *can speak*	j'aie	*I may*, or *can*	
tu parl-*es*	*thou may'st speak*	tu aies	*thou may'st*	
il parl-*e*	*he may speak*	il ait	*he may*	
nous parl-*ions*	*we may speak*	nous ayons	parl-é *we may*	*have spoken.*
vous parl-*iez*	*you may speak*	vous ayez	*you may*	
ils parl-*ent*	*they may speak*	ils aient	*they may*	

---

public good. **Do** not omit such useful and interest-
2 *bien* 1   ❋   *négliger de* art. *si utile* 2   *intéres-*
ing details.
sant 3 — m. pl. 1.

SUBJUNCTIVE PRESENT. That I may not always listen to
                                        écouter ❋
a severe censor of my defects.   That thou may'st find
   — 2 = m. 1   *défaut* m. pl.   *trouver*
real friends.   That he may adorn his speeches with the graces
de vrai   *parer*   *discours de*
of a pure diction.   That she may remain in her *boudoir.*
  — 2 — f. 1   *rester*   — m.
That we should so hastily   condemn   the world.   That you
      légèrement condamner   *monde* m.
may pout incessantly.   That they may work   more willingly.
  bouder sans cesse   *travailler plus volontiers*

❋ REM. The second person singular of the imperative of this
conjugation, and likewise of some verbs of the second ending in
-*rir, frir, -lir,* take *s* after *e,* before the word *y* and *en,* as *portes-*
en à ton frère, carry some to thy brother ; *offres-en à ta sœur,*
offer some to thy sister ; *cueilles-en aussi pour toi,* gather some
alike for thyself ; *apportes-y tes livres,* bring there thy books.

SIMPLE TENSES.		COMPOUND TENSES.	
IMPERFECT.		**PLUPERFECT.**	
que	that	que	that
je parl-*asse*	I might, could, or would speak	j'eusse	I might could, or would
tu parl-*asses*	thou might'st speak	tu eusses	thou might'st
il parl-*ât*	he might speak	il eût	parl-*é* he might
nous parl-assions	we might speak	nous eus—sions	we might
vous parl-*as*-siez	you might speak	vous eussiez	you might
ils parl-*as*-sent	they might speak	ils eussent	they might

have spoken.

PRETERIT. That I may have caressed insolence, and *caresser* art. — f.
flattered pride. That thou may'st have added nothing to
flatter art. *ajouter*
that work. That he may have carried despair into
ouvrage m. *porter* art. *désespoir* m. *dans*
the soul of his friend. That we may have blamed a conduct
âme *blâmer* *conduite* f.
so prudent and so wise. That you may have exasperated so
— *sage* *exaspérer*
petulant a character. That they may not have (taken advan—
— 2 *caractère* m. 1 *profiter*
tage) of the circumstances.
circonstance f. pl.

IMPERFECT. That I might not copy his example. That thou
imiter *exemple* m.
might'st (give up) perfidious friends. That he might inhabit
abandonner de art. —*de* 2 1 *habiter*
a hut instead of a palace. That we might fall at the
chaumière f. *au lieu* *palais* m. *tomber à*
feet of an illegitimate king. That you might respect the laws
pied m. *illégitime* 2 1 *respecter* *loi* f. pl.
of your country. That they might not speak at random.
pays m. *à tort et à travers*

PLUPERFECT. That I might not have burnt that work. That
brûler m.

SECOND CONJUGATION.

IN IR.

REMARK. This conjugation is divided into four branches.

The first, which contains a great many verbs, includes all the regular verbs terminated in *ir*, which do not fall under the three other branches.

The second contains only the seventeen following verbs in *mir, tir, vir:* all the others belong to the first branch.

Consentir	to consent	se rendormir	to fall asleep again
démentir	to give the lie	repartir*	to set out again, to reply
desservir	to clear the table	se repentir	to repent
dormir	to sleep	ressentir	to resent
endormir	to lull asleep	ressortir*	to go out again
mentir	to lie	sentir	to feel
partir	to set out	servir	to serve
pressentir	to foresee	sortir	to go out
redormir	to sleep again		

* *Repartir*, to set out again, to reply, and *ressortir*, to go out again, must not be confounded with *repartir*, to distribute, and *ressortir*, to belong to, which two last belong to the first branch, as well as *asservir*, to enslave, and *assortir*, to match; which were erroneously given as derivatives of *servir* and *sortir*.

The third branch contains the verbs *couvrir*, to cover; *offrir*, to offer; *ouvrir*, to open; *souffrir*, to suffer, and their derivatives.

The fourth branch contains the verbs *tenir* and *venir*, and their derivatives: respecting which the learner must observe, that *tenir* and all its derivatives are conjugated with *avoir* in their compound tenses; whereas *venir*, and its derivatives, are conjugated with *être*; except: 1st, *prévenir* and *subvenir*, which take *avoir*; 2dly, *convenir*, which takes *avoir* when it signifies to suit; and *être*, when it signifies to agree; 3dly, *contrevenir*, which takes indifferently *avoir* or *être*.

---

thou might'st not have contemplated the beauties of the country.
              contempler   =   campagne
That he might have perfected   his natural qualities.   That
          perfectionner   —rel 2   = f. pl. 1
we might not have gained   the victory. That you might have
          remporter   =f.
enchanted the public.   That they might have struck   their
—ter   — m.   frapper
enemies with fear.
     de crainte

PARADIGMS.
INFINITIVE.

PRESENT.

	BRANCH 1.	BRANCH 2.	BRANCH 3.	BRANCH 4.
Simple +	*to punish* pun-*ir*	*to feel* sen-*tir*	*to open* ouv-*rir*	*to hold* t-enir

PARTICIPLE PRESENT.

Simple +	*punishing* pun-*issant*	*feeling* sen-*tant*	*opening* ouv-*rant*	*holding* t-enant

PARTICIPLE PAST.

Simple	*punished* pun-*i*	*felt* sen-*ti*	*opened* ouv-*ert*	*held* t-enu
Comp. pres.	*to have punished* avoir pun-*i*	*felt* sen-*ti*	*opened* ouv-*ert*	*held* t-enu
Comp. partic.	*having punished* ayant pun-*i*			

INDICATIVE.

PRESENT.

Sim.				
I punish je pun-*is*	*feel* sen-*s*	*open* ouv-*re*	*hold* t-*iens*
tu pun-*is*	sen-*s*	ouv-*res*	t-*iens*
il pun-*it*	sen-*t*	ouv-*re*	t-*ient*
nous pun-*issons*	sen-*tons*	ouv-*rons*	t-*enons*
vous pun-*issez*	sen-*tez*	ouv-*rez*	t-*enez*
ils pun-*issent*	sen-*tent*	ouv-*rent*	t-*iennent*

INDICATIVE. PRESENT. I choose this picture. I feel all
          choisir   *tableau* m.
the unpleasantness of your situation. Whence comest thou?
  désagrément m.   —   *d'où* *venir*
Does he thus define that word? Does his mother (go out) so
  ainsi définir   *mot* m.   *sortir*
soon? Do we not (set off) for the country? Do you not
tôt   *partir*   *campagne* f.
pity   his sorrows? Do you not (tell a lie)? They (are
compatir à *mal* m. pl.   *mentir*
finishing) at this moment. They (act contrary) to your
finir *dans* * art. — m.   *contrevenir*
orders.
ordre.

IMPERFECT. I fortified his soul against the dangers of
       prémunir   *contre*   —

PRETERIT INDEFINITE.

Comp.	{ I have punished { j'ai pun-*i*	*felt* sen-*ti*	*opened* ouv-*ert*	*held* t-*enu*

IMPERFECT.

Simple	{ I did punish { je pun-*issois*	*feel* sen-*tois*	*open* ouv-*rois*	*hold* t-*enois*

PLUPERFECT.

Comp.	{ I had punished { j'avois pun-*i*	*felt* sen-*ti*	*opened* ouv-*ert*	*held* t-*enu*

PRETERIT DEFINITE.

Simple	I punished je pun-*is* tu pun-*is* il pun-*it* nous pun-*îmes* vous pun-*îtes* ils pun-*irent*	*felt* sen-*tis* sen-*tis* sen-*tit* sen-*tîmes* sen-*îtes* sen-*tirent*	*opened* ouv-*ris* ouv-*ris* ouv-*rit* ouv-*rîmes* ouv-*rîtes* ouv-*rirent*	*held* t-*ins* t-*ins* t-*int* t-*înmes* t-*întes* t-*inrent*

seduction. I served my friends warmly. Did'st not
art. —f. *servir* *avec chaleur*
thou amuse him with fair promises? He complied (at last)
entretenir de beau promesse f. pl. *consentir enfin*
with the wishes of his family. Did we not frequently
à *désir* m. pl. *famille* f. *fréquemment*
warn our friends of the bad state of their affairs? Did we
avertir *état*
sleep then? Did you not belie your character? Did
dormir alors *démentir* *caractère* m.
not the enemies invade an immense country? Did the
envahir — 2 *pays* m. 1.
wild beasts often (come out) from the bottom of
sauvage 2 *bête* f. 1 *souvent* *sortir* *fond* m.
their mountains?
montagne

PRETERIT. I softened my father by my submission. I
fléchir *soumission* f.
foresaw that terrible catastrophe. Thou did'st not (come again)
pressentir —2 —f. 1 *revenir*
as thou hadst promised. He did not succeed through
comme *le* ind-2 *promis* *réussir par*

N.B. Only the first person of those tenses, which are invariably conjugated alike, will now be given; the scholar will
easily supply the rest.

PRETERIT ANTERIOR.

Comp. { I had punished | felt | opened | held
j'eus pun-*i* | sen-*ti* | ouv-*ert* | t-*enu* }

FUTURE ABSOLUTE.

Simple { I shall punish. | feel | open | hold
je pun-*trai* | sen-*tirai* | ouv-*rirai* | t-*iendrai* }

FUTURE ANTERIOR.

Comp. { I shall have punished | felt | opened | held
j'aurai pun-*i* | sen-*ti* | ouv-*ert* | t-*enu* }

CONDITIONAL.

PRESENT.

Simple { I should punish | feel | open | hold
je pun-*irois* | sen-*tirois* | ouv-*rirois* | t-*iendrois* }

---

thoughtlessness.   Did his daughter not (set out again)
étourderie f.   *repartir*
immediately?   Did not Alexander sully his glory by his pride?
sur-le-champ   *ternir*
Did we (go-out) of the city   before him?   We never betrayed
               ville f. *avant lui*   *trahir*
that important secret. Did you not agree   to   trust
       — 2   — m. 1   *consentir de vous en rapporter*
to me?   They served their country with courage.   Did the
moi   *pays*   —
ancient philosophers   enjoy   great consideration?
      philosophe m. pl. *jouir de un*   — f.

FUTURE.   Shall I not obtain this of you? What will be-
                  obtenir cela de   *que*   *de-*
come of thee, if I forsake   thee?   Will he not embellish
venir * *tu*   *abandonner*   *embellir*
his country seat?   He will not sleep quietly.
   maison de compagne f.   *tranquillement* .
Shall we consent to that ridiculous bargain?   With
                    2   *marché* m. 1   *avec de* art.
time and   patience, you will compass   -your end. We
m.   pr. art. f.   *venir à bout de*   *dessein* m..
shall not sully the splendour of our life by an unworthy action,
          éclat m.   *indigne* 2 — 1
Will those men enrich their country by their industry? Will
         enrichir   *pays*   *industrie*
not our friends offer us their assistance?
         offrir   *secours*

PAST.

Comp. { *I should have punished* | *felt* | *opened* | *held*
{ j'aurois pun-*i* | seu-*ti* | ouv-*ert* | t-*enu*

IMPERATIVE.

Simple { *punish (thou)* | *feel* | *open* | *hold*
{ pun-*is* | sen-*s* | ouv-*re* | t-*iens*
{ qu'il pun-*isse* | sen-*te* | ouv-*re* | t-*ienne*
{ pun-*issons* | sen-*tons* | ouv-*rons* | t-*enons*
{ pun-*issez* | sen-*tez* | ouv-*rez* | t-*enez*
{ qu'ils pun-*issent* | sen-*tent* | ouv-*rent* | t-*iennent*

CONDITIONAL. I would open the door   and the window.
      porte f.   *fenêtre* f.
I should still cherish life. Would'st not thou interpose in
    chérir art.   *intervenir*
that affair? Would my brother (set off again) without taking
  f.   *repartir* *sans prendre*
leave of us? You would not succeed in injuring him in the
congé   *parvenir à* *nuire* *lui*
public opinion. Could'st thou soften that flinty heart?
— *s* — f. 1   *attendrir* *de rocher* 2 1
Could they foresee their misfortune? Would men always
  pressentir *malheur*   art.
(grow old) without growing wiser, if they reflected   on
vieillir *sans* *devenir* inf.-1   *réfléchir* ind.-2 *sur*
the shortness of life?
 brièveté f. art.

IMPERATIVE. Shudder with horror and terror. Support
    frémir de = *de effroi* m. *soutenir*
thy character in good and bad fortune. Do not
    art. *dans* art. *mauvais* — f.
obtain thy point but by means consistent with
parvenir à *fin* f. pl. *que* *des moyens que* *avoue* 2 * art.
delicacy. Let us feed the poor. Let us gain
délicatesse 1 *nourrir* m. pl. *obtenir* art.
glory by our perseverance. Let us not divulge our secrets
= f. —   *découvrir*   —
to every body. Never submit to · so unjust a yoke. Do not
 tout le monde *fléchir sous* *à* *joug* m. 1
maintain so absurd an opinion. Do not (come upon us) again
soutenir —de 2 — f. 1   *survenir* *plus*
(in that unexpected manner.)
 ainsi à l'improviste.

SUBJUNCTIVE.

PRESENT.

	that I may punish	feel	open	hold
	que je pun-*isse*	sen-*te*	ouv-*re*	t-*ienne*
	que tu pun-*isses*	sen-*tes*	ouv-*res*	t-*iennes*
Sim.	qu'il pun-*isse*	sen-*te*	ouv-*re*	t-*ienne*
	que nous pun-*issions*	sen-*tions*	ouv-*rions*	t-*enions*
	que vous pun-*issiez*	sen-*tiez*	ouv-*riez*	t-*eniez*
	qu'ils pun-*issent*	sen-*tent*	ouv-*rent*	t-*iennent*

PRETERIT.

	that I may have punished	felt	opened	held
Comp.	que j'aie.pun-*i*	sen-*ti*	ouv-*ert*	t-*enu*

IMPERFECT.

	that I might punish	feel	open	hold
	que je pun-*isse*	sen-*tisse*	ouv-*risse*	t-*insse*
	que tu pun-*isses*	sen-*tisses*	ouv-*risses*	t-*insses*
Sim.	qu'il pun-*ît*	sen-*tît*	ouv-*rît*	t-*int*
	que nous pun-*issions*	sen-*tissions*	ouv-*rissions*	t-*inssions*
	que vous pun-*issiez*	sen-*tissiez*	ouv-*rissiez*	t-*inssiez*
	qu'ils pun-*issent*	sen-*tissent*	ouv-*rissent*	t-*inssent*

PLUPERFECT.

	I might have punished	felt	opened	held
Comp.	que j'aie puni	senti	ouvert	tenu

SUBJUNCTIVE PRESENT. That 1 may never blemish my re-
flétrir
putation. That I may (be before-hand) with such dangerous
f.   *prévenir*   de art. *si*   =2
enemies. I will not have thee (go out) this morning. That he
    1   *veux*   que *tu*   sub-1   *matin* m.
may not enjoy   his glory.   That he may not obtain   his
            de   = f.   *parvenir* à
ends.   That we may become just, honest, and virtuous.
fin f. pl.   *devenir*   *honnête*   *vertueux*
That you may punish the guilty.   That you may return
            coupable pl.   *revenir*
covered with laurels.   That they may establish
couvert de   laurier m. pl.   *établir* de art.
wise and just laws.   That they may agree   about the
2   3   1   *convenir de*
conditions.

THIRD CONJUGATION.

IN -OIR.

PARADIGM.

This conjugation contains only seven regular verbs, which are:

perc-*evoir*	*to receive*	déc-*evoir*	*to deceive*
aperc-*evoir*	*to perceive*	d-*evoir*	*to owe*
conc-*evoir*	*to conceive*	red-*evoir*	*to owe again*

And *recevoir,* which serves as paradigm. *Percevoir* is a law term, and *apercevoir* is often *reflected.*

OBSERVE. In verbs ending in -*cevoir* the *c,* to preserve the *soft sound* of that letter, takes a *cedilla,* when followed by *o,* or *u.* See page 3.

INFINITIVE.

SIMPLE TENSES.		COMPOUND TENSES.	
PRESENT.		PAST.	
rec-*evoir*	to receive	avoir reç-*u*	to have received

PARTICIPLES.

PRESENT.			
rec-*evant*	receiving	ayant reç-*u*	having received
PAST.			
reç-*u*	received		

IMPERFECT. That I might stun   the whole neighbourhood.
       étourdir a   *tout* 1 *voisinage* m.
That I might not (bring about) my designs.   That thou
      venir à bout de   *projet* m. pl.
might'st (tell a wilful lie.)   That he might not bear
    mentir de dessein prémédité.   *soutenir*
his disgrace with firmness. That we might disobey   the laws.
  — f.   *fermeté*   *désobéir à*
That we might belong   to that great king. That you might
     appartenir
renounce your errors and   prejudices. That they might
revenir de   =   pr. pron. *préjugé*
weaken the force of their reasons.   That they might hold
affoiblir   f.   *raisonnement*   *tenir à*
the most absurd ideas.
    2   1.

INDICATIVE.

SIMPLE TENSES.		COMPOUND TENSES.	
PRESENT.		**PRETERIT INDEFINITE.**	
I receive, etc.	we receive		
je reç-*ois*	nous rec-*evons*	j'ai reç-*u*	I have re-
tu reç-*ois*	vous reç-*evez*		ceived
il reç-*oit*	ils reç-*oivent*	tu as, etc.	thou, etc.
IMPERFECT.		**PLUPERFECT.**	
I did receive	we did receive	j'avois reç-*u*	I had received
je rec-*evois*	nous rec-*evions*		
PRETERIT DEFINITE.		**PRETERIT ANTERIOR.**	
I received	we received	j'eus reç-*u*	I had received
je reç-*us*	nous reç-*ûmes*	tu eus, etc,	thou, etc.
tu reç-*us*	vous reç-*ûtes*		
il reç-*ut*	ils reç-*urent*		

EXERCISE.

INDICATIVE PRESENT. I perceive the summit, of the
apercevoir sommet
Alps covered with perpetual snow. What grati-
Alpes f. pl. de éternel 2 neige f. pl. 1. recon-
tude dost thou not owe to her who (has discharged)
noissance f. devoir celle 1 remplir 3
(the duty of a mother) (to thee) (in thy infancy)? Does
5 près de 4 2
your scholar understand well that rule which is so simple?
écolier concevoir bien règle f. * *
We do not owe a large sum. Do you not perceive the
devoir gros somme f.
snare? Ought firm and courageous men to yield to
piége m. devoir 5 des 1 3 . = 4 2 * céder
circumstances?
art. circonstance.

IMPERFECT. Did I not receive him kindly? Did he
le avec amitié
see the castle from such a distance? We did not re-
apercevoir château si * loin per-
ceive our income. Did you not receive great civilities?
cevoir revenu m. pl. de honnêteté

SIMPLE TENSES.		COMPOUND TENSES.	

FUTURE ABSOLUTE.

I shall receive	we, etc.	j'aurai reç-*u*	I shall have re-ceived
je rec-*evrai*	nous rec-*evrons*		

CONDITIONAL.

PRESENT.		PAST.	
I should receive	we should, etc.	j'aurois reç-*u*	I should have received
je rec-*evrois*	nous rec-*evrions*	lu, etc.	

IMPERATIVE.

reç-*ois*	receive thou	rec-*evons*	let us receive
		rec-*evez*	receive ye
qu'il reç-*oive*	let him receive	qu'ils reç-*oivent*	let them re-ceive

---

Did those tyrants conceive all the blackness of their
f. pl.   *tyran concevoir*   *noirceur* f.
crimes?

—

PRETERIT. I perceived him   walking by moon-
      le qui se promenoit à art. *clair de*
light.   Did the queen conceive a great esteem for that
la lune m.   *estime* f.
honest man? Did we not immediately perceive the snare?
de bien 2 1
You did not receive his letters in time.   Did the ministers con-
      lettres à temps.   —*tre*
ceive the depth of his plan?
    profondeur f.   —m.

FUTURE. Shall I receive visits to-day?   He will
      de art. *visite aujourd'hui*
not discover the spire of his village. We shall conceive
apercevoir clocher m.   —m.
well founded hopes.   Will you never conceive
de art. *fondé* 2 *espérance* f. pl. 1.
so luminous a principle? Shall men always owe their mis-
=2   1   art.   *mal-*
fortunes to their faults?
heur   *faute*

CONDITIONAL. Should I receive the offers of my enemy?
           offre

N

SUBJUNCTIVE.

SIMPLE TENSES.		COMPOUND TENSES.	
PRESENT.		**PRETERIT.**	
that I may receive	*that we, etc.*	que j'aie reç-*u*	*that I may*
que je reç-*oive*	que nous rec-*evions*	que tu, etc.	*have re-*
que tu reç-*oives*	que vous rec-*eviez*	qu'il, etc.	*ceived*
qu'il reç-*oive*	qu'ils reç-*oivent*		
IMPERFECT.		**PLUPERFECT.**	
that I might, etc.	*that we might, etc.*	que j'eusse	*that I might*
que je reç-*usse*	que nous reç-*ussions*	reç-*u*	*have re-*
que tu reç-*usses*	que vous reç-*ussiez*	que tu, etc.	*ceived*
qu'il reç-*út*	qu'ils reç-*ussent*		

Should a wise man thus (give himself up) to despair?
devoir 2 1 *ainsi* 2 *s'abandonner* 1 art. *désespoir* m.
Should we conceive such abstract ideas? You would
  de art. *si* 2 *abstrait* 3 1
easily perceive so gross a trick. Would not my sisters receive
  grossier 2 *ruse* f. 1
their friend with tenderness?
  f. *tendresse* f.

IMPERATIVE. Conceive the horror of his situation. Do not

receive that mark of confidence with indifference. Let us
  marque f. *confiance* —
entertain a horror of vice. Let us never owe (any
concevoir * *de* art. *pour* art. m.
thing). Receive his advice with respect and gratitude. Re-
rien *avis* — —
ceive no more of his letters.
  lettre f. pl.

SUBJUNCTIVE PRESENT. That I may receive consola-
  de art.
tions. That he should not conceive a thought so well explained.
  pensée f. *développé.*
That we may always receive false news. That you
  de *nouvelle* f. pl.
may not perceive the danger of books which are contrary
  — art. * * *contre*
to good morals. That they may not collect unjust
* art. *mœurs* f. pl. *percevoir de injuste* 2
taxes.
—f. pl. 1

FOURTH CONJUGATION.

IN -RE.

REMARK.—This conjugation has five branches.

The **FIRST** ends	in	-andre	as, répandre	to spill
	in	-endre	as, vendre	to sell
	in	-ondre	as, répondre	to answer
	in	-erdre	as, perdre	to lose
	in	-ordre	as, mordre	to bite
the **SECOND** ends	in	-aire	as, plaire	to please
			as, taire	to keep secret
the **THIRD** ends	in	-aître	as, repaître	to feed
	in	-oître	as, connoître	to know
the **FOURTH** ends	in	-uire	as, instruire	to instruct
the **FIFTH** ends	in	-aindre	as, contraindre	to constrain
	in	-eindre	as, peindre	to paint
	in	-oindre	as, joindre	to join

PARADIGMS.

INFINITIVE.

PRESENT.

BRANCH 1.	BRANCH 2.	BRANCH 3.	BRANCH 4.	BRANCH 5.
to render	to please	to appear	to reduce	to join
rend-re	pl-aire	par-oître	rédui-re	join-dre

PAST. (To have)

rendered	pleased	appeared	reduced	joined
avoir rend-u	pl-u	par-u	rédui-t	oi-nt

IMPERFECT. That I might conceive such a project. That
projet m.
he might perceive the secret designs of the enemy's general.
caché 2 *dessein* 1   2 *   1
That we might not receive every body with civility. That you
honnêteté.
might not conceive the depth of this book. That they
profondeur f.
might not perceive the masts of the ship.
mât m. pl.   *vaisseau* m.

PARTICIPLE PRESENT.

BRANCH 1.	BRANCH 2.	BRANCH 3.	BRANCH 4.	BRANCH 5.
rendering rend-*ant*	*pleasing* pl-*aisant*	*appearing* par-*oissant*	*reducing* rédui-*sant*	*joining* joi-*gnant*

PARTICIPLE PAST.

rendered rend-*u*	*pleased* pl-*u*	*appeared* par-*u*	*reduced* rédui-*t*	*joined* joi-*nt*

INDICATIVE.

PRESENT.

I render	*please*	*appear*	*reduce*	*join*
je rend-*s*	pl-*ais*	par-*ois*	rédui-*s*	joi-*ns*
tu rend-*s*	pl-*ais*	par-*ois*	rédui-*s*	joi-*ns*
il rend-	pl-*aît*	par-*oît*	rédui-*t*	joi-*nt*
nous rend-*ons*	pl-*aisons*	par-*oïssons*	rédui-*sons*	joi-*gnons*
vous rend-*ez*	pl-*aisez*	par-*oissez*	rédui-*sez*	joi-*gnez*
ils rend-*ent*	pl-*aisent*	par-*oissent*	rédui-*sent*	joi-*gnent*

PRETERIT INDEFINITE. (*I have*)

rendered j'ai rend-*u*	*pleased* pl-*u*	*appeared* par-*u*	*reduced* rédui-*t*	*joined* joi-*nt*

INDICATIVE PRESENT. I know his fiery and impetuous
       connoître   bouillant 2   = 3
temper.   I wait   his return with impatience. Does he
caractère m. 1   attendre   retour
fear   death? Does not virtue please every body? We do
craindre art. f.   à
not force   you to adopt   this opinion. We suppress for
  contraindre   de adopter   — f.   taire
the present several interesting circumstances. Do you not
  — m.   intéressant 2   f 1
confound these notions   one with   another? You seduce
confondre   art.   art.   séduire
your hearers   by your modest exterior. Do your sons
  auditeur m. pl.   2   = m. 1
acknowledge their errors? Do not those workmen waste their
reconnoître   =   ouvrier perdre
time about   trifles?
   à de art. bagatelle pl.
   IMPERFECT. I did not displease by my conduct. I was
        déplaire
pitying those sad victims   of the revolution. Did not
plaindre   triste victime f. pl.   —f.

IMPERFECT.

BRANCH 1.	BRANCH 2.	BRANCH 3.	BRANCH 4.	BRANCH 5.
I did render	*please*	*appear*	*reduce*	*join*
je rend-*ois*	pl-*aisois*	par-*oissois*	rédui-*sois*	joi-*gnois*

PLUPERFECT.

I had rendered	*pleased*	*appeared*	*reduced*	*joined*
j'avois rend-*u*	pl-*u*	par-*u*	rédui-*t*	joi-*nt*

PRETERIT DEFINITE.

I rendered	*pleased*	*appeared*	*reduced*	*joined*
je rend-*is*	pl-*us*	par-*us*	rédui-*sis*	joi-*gnis*
tu rend-*is*	pl-*us*	par-*us*	rédui-*sis*	joi-*gnis*
il rend-*it*	pl-*ut*	par-*ut*	rédui-*sit*	joi-*gnit*
nous rend-*îmes*	pl-*ûmes*	par-*ûmes*	rédui-*sîmes*	joi-*gnîmes*
vous rend-*îtes*	pl-*ûtes*	par-*ûtes*	rédui-*sîtes*	joi-*gnîtes*
ils rend-*irent*	pl-*urent*	par-*urent*	rédui-*sirent*	joi-*gnirent*

PRETERIT ANTERIOR.

I had rendered	*pleased*	*appeared*	*reduced*	*joined*
j'eus rend-*u*	pl-*u*	par-*u*	rédui-*t*	joi-*nt*

this dog bite? Did that man (at last) acknowledge his
chien mordre enfin
injustice? We did not appear convinced. We joined our
— f. convaincu pl.
sighs and tears. Were you painting an his-
soupir m. pl. pron. larme f. pl. peindre d'his-
torical subject? Did those orators throw the graces of
toire 2' tableau m. 1 = répandre —
expression into their speeches? They led the people
art. · — discours. induire m.
into an error.
en *

PRETERIT. I aimed at an honest end. Did his prudence
tendre à 2 but m. 1 — f.
extinguish the fire of a disordered imagination? Did not your
éteindre déréglé 2 — f. 1
conduct (do away) his prejudices? We led our
—duite f. détruire prévention f. pl. reconduire
friend back to his country-house. Did we offer our in-
· * de campagne 2 f. 1 vendre en-
cense to the pride of a blockhead? Did you feign to think
cens sot feindre de
as a madman? Did you conduct your children from truth to
en * fou conduire en

FUTURE ABSOLUTE.

BRANCH 1.	BRANCH 2.	BRANCH 3.	BRANCH 4.	BRANCH 5.
I shall render	*please*	*appear*	*reduce*	*join*
je rend-*rai*	pl-*airai*	par-*oîtrai*	rédui-*rai*	joi--*ndrai*

FUTURE ANTERIOR. (*I shall have*)

rendered	*pleased*	*appeared*	*reduced*	*joined*
j'aurai rend-*u*	pl-*u*	par-*u*	rédui-*t*	joi-*nt*

CONDITIONAL.

PRESENT.

I should render	*please*	*appear*	*reduce*	*join*
je rend-*rois*	pl-*airois*	par-*oîtrois*	rédui-*rois*	joi-*ndrois*

---

truth? Did those frightful spectres 　　　 appear 　　 again?
　　　　　　　effrayant 2 — m. pl. 1. *apparoître de nouveau*
Did not the children (come down) at the first summons?
　　　　　　　descendre 　*à* 　　　 *ordre* m. sing.

FUTURE. Shall I hear 　 the music 　　 of the new opera?
　　　　　　entendre 　　*musique* f.
I shall not conceal from you my mind. 　　　 Will the gene-
　　　　　taire 　*　 ✻* 　　　　*façon de penser*
ral constrain 　 the officers to join 　　 their respective corps?
　　contraindre 　*officier* 　　*rejoindre* 　　　 =
Will not a thought, true, grand, and well expressed, please
　　　　　　 f. 　　　　　　　　　 *exprimé*
at 　 all 　 times? We shall (make our appearance) on this great
dans art. m. pl. 　　　　　　　 *paroître* 　　　 *sur*
theatre, 　　 next 　　　 month. 　　 Shall we describe all the
　 — m. art. *prochain* 2 *mois* m. 1 　　　　　 *dépeindre*
horror of this terrible night? 　 Will you not new-model a
　　　 — 2 *nuit* f. 1 　　　　　　　 *refondre*
work so full of charming ideas? Will you know 　　 your
　　plein 　　 2 　　 1 　　　　 *reconnoître*
things 　　 again? Will they always reduce our duties 　　 to
effet m. pl. 　✻ 　　　　 · 　　　　 *devoir* m. pl.
　　 beneficence? 　 They will assiduously correspond with
art. *bienfaisance* f. 　　 · 　　　 *assidûment correspondre*
their friends.

CONDITIONAL. Should I, by these means, 　 gain 　　 the
　　　　 · 　　　　　 *moyen* m. s. *atteindre à*
desired end? 　 I should (carry on) the undertaking with suc-
désiré 2 *but* m. 1 　　　　 *conduire* 　 *entreprise* f.

PAST. (*I should have*)

BRANCH 1.	BRANCH 2.	BRANCH 3.	BRANCH 4.	BRANCH 5.
rendered	*pleased*	*appeared*	*reduced*	*joined*
j'aurois rend-*u*	pl-*u*	par-*u*	rédui-*t*	joi-*nt*

IMPERATIVE.

render (*thou*)	*please*	*appear*	*reduce*	*join*
rend-*s*	pl-*ais*	par-*ois*	rédui-*s*	joi-*ns*
qu'il rend-*e*	pl-*aise*	par-*oisse*	rédui-*se*	joi-*gne*
rend-*ons*	pl-*aisons*	par-*oissons*	rédui-*sons*	joi-*gnons*
rend-*ez*	pl-*aisez*	par-*oissez*	rédui-*sez*	joi-*gnez*
qu'ils rend-*ent*	pl-*aisent*	par-*oissent*	rédui-*sent*	joi-*gnent*

---

cess. Would his mother wait with (so much) patience? Could
            tant de
sincerity displease the man (of sense)? Should we sell
art. = f.   *à* *sensé*   *vendre*
our liberty? Should we build our house upon that plan?
        construire   — m.
Would you oblige   young people to live as you
    astreindre de art. *gens* pl. *vivre comme*
do? Would you reduce your child to despair? They
*   art. *désespoir* m.
should dread the public   censure. Would my pro-
 craindre 4 5 *de* 3 art. 1 f. 2
tectors introduce an unknown person into the world?
= *introduire* *inconnu* m. *

IMPERATIVE. Depict in thy idyl all the charms of a
     peindre   *idylle*   *douceur* f.
rural life. Expect not happiness from exter-
champêtre 2 1 *attendre* art.   art. *exté-*
nal objects; it is in thyself. Know the powers of thy mind
rieur 2 m. pl. 1   *force* f.
before thou write. Let us unite prudence with
avant de * *écrire*   *joindre* art. f *à* art.
courage. Let us not descend to useless particulars.
 m.   *descendre dans des* 2 —*larité* 1
Let us not (give offence) by an air of haughtiness. Seem
   déplaire * *des* m. pl.   *paroître* 2
 neither too cheerful nor too grave. Ye sovereigns, make
ne 1 *ni* *gai* *ni* *sérieux* * *souverain* pl. *rendre*
the people happy. Do not despise his friendship. Sweet
     dédaigner   *doux*

SUBJUNCTIVE.

PRESENT. (*that I may*)

BRANCH 1.	BRANCH 2.	BRANCH 3.	BRANCH 4.	BRANCH 5.
render	*please*	*appear*	*reduce*	*join*
que je rend-*e*	pl-*aise*	par-*oisse*	rédui-*se*	joi-*gne*
tu rend-*es*	pl-*aises*	par-*oisses*	rédui-*ses*	joi-*gnes*
il rend-*e*	pl-*aise*	par-*oisse*	rédui-*se*	joi-*gne*
nous rend-*ions*	pl-*aisions*	par-*oissions*	rédui-*sions*	joi-*gnions*
vous rend-*iez*	pl-*aisiez*	par-*oissiez*	rédui-*siez*	joi-*gniez*
ils rend-*ent*	pl-*aisent*	par-*oissent*	rédui-*sent*	joi-*gnent*

PRETERIT. (*that I may have*)

rendered	*pleased*	*appeared*	*reduced*	*joined*
que j'aie rend-*u*	pl-*u*	par-*u*	rédui-*t*	joi-*nt*

---

illusions, vain phantoms, vanish.   (Keep to yourself) such
 — f.   — *fantôme* m. *disparoître*   *taire*   *certain*
truths as may   offend.
f. pl. *qui peuvent offenser.*

SUBJUNCTIVE PRESENT.   That I may fear that cloud of ene-
                                    nuée f.
mies.   That I should please   every body,   is impossible.
              à   *ce*
That he may not reply to   such absurd criticism.   That
             répondre un si   2   *critique* f. 1
he may lead   his pupil step by step to a perfect knowledge
     conduire   *élève pas à*   *connoissance* f.
of the art of speaking and writing.   That we may entice by an
         inf-1   pr. inf-1   *séduire*
enchanting style.   That we may confound the arts with the
 —*teur* 2   m. 1
sciences. That you may have the same end   in view.   That
                      but m. 2   *tendre d* 1
they may not depend   on any body.   That they may not in-
        dépendre de personne   *ac-*
crease our sufferings.
croître   *peines*

IMPERFECT.   That I might not melt   into tears.   That
              fondre en larme
I might acknowledge the truth.   That he might (draw a picture)
    connoître   *peindre*
of   distressed   virtue.   That she might please by her accom-
* art. *malheureux* 2   1   *grâce*

IMPERFECT. *(that I might)*

BRANCH 1.	BRANCH 2.	BRANCH 3.	BRANCH 4.	BRANCH 5.
render	*please*	*appear*	*reduce*	*join*
que je rend-*isse*	pl-*usse*	par-*usse*	rédui-*sisse*	joi-*gnisse*
tu rend-*isses*	pl-*usses*	par-*usses*	rédui-*sisses*	joi-*gnisses*
il rend-*ît*	pl-*ût*	par-*ût*	rédui-*sît*	joi-*gnît*
nous rend-*issions*	pl-*ussions*	par-*ussions*	rédui-*sissions*	joi *gnissions*
vous rend-*issiez*	pl-*ussiez*	par-*ussiez*	rédui-*sissiez*	joi-*gnissiez*
ils rend-*issent*	pl-*ussent*	par-*ussent*	rédui-*sissent*	joi-*gnissent*

PLUPERFECT. *(that I might have)*

rendered	*pleased*	*appeared*	*reduced*	*joined*
que j'eusse rend-*u*	pl-*u*	par-*u*	rédui-*t*	joi-*nt*

PARADIGM, OR MODEL FOR PRONOMINAL VERBS.

Se repentir | *to repent.*

Pronominal verbs, as was said page 97, are conjugated throughout, in each person, with a *double personal pronoun,* and as all their compound tenses are formed by means of the auxiliary verb *être,* their participle past must always agree in gender and number with the *objective pronoun* when it is *direct,* otherwise not. Their inflections all follow the conjugations to which they belong.

---

plishments more than by her beauty. That we might conduct
f, pl.   *conduire*
him to   court. That we might affect   such low
     art. *cour* f.   *feindre de* art.   *si bas* 2
sentiments. That you might hear   their justification. That
     1   *entendre*
you might know your real friends. That they might (wait for)
          vrai   *attendre*
the opinion of   sensible persons. That they might not ap-
     art. *sensé* 2 f. pl. 1   f.
pear so scornful   and   vain.
     dédaigneux f. pl. *ni   si* f. pl.

In all participles past, except *absous, dissous, résous,* which are to be seen in their places, the feminine is formed by adding *e* mute to the masculine, and the plural by adding *s* to the singular, both masculine and feminine, when it does not already end with this letter, the French language not admitting a final *double consonant.*

As there is some difficulty in conjugating pronominal verbs, some few are here selected, which it will prove advantageous to practise.

s' alarm*er*	s' absten*ir*	s' habitu*er*	s' enorgueill*ir*
s' assoup*ir*	se serv*ir*	se nant*ir*	se méconnoît*re*
s' apercev*oir*	se souven*ir*	se contraind*re*	s' immortalis*er*
se défend*re*	se préval*oir*	se rend*re*	se dorlot*er*
se hât*er*	se repaît*re*	s' évertu*er*	s' ingéni*er*
se dépêch*er*	se condu*ire*	s' impatient*er*	s' oblig*er*
se ressent*ir*	s' enrhum*er*	se fâch*er*	se recueill*ir*
se pourv*oir*	s' ennuy*er*	se repos*er*	se bless*er*
se tai*re*	s' orient*er*	s' enquér*ir*	s' enrou*er*
se promen*er*	s' endorm*ir*	se méfi*er*	se réjou*ir*
se couch*er*	se morfond*re*	se formalis*er*	s' embarrass*er*
se lev*er*	se perd*re*	se rapétiss*er*	s' habill*er*
s' asse*oir*	s' évanou*ir*	se réconcili*er*	s' émancip*er*
s' arrog*er*	s' applaud*ir*	se sav*oir* gré	se dire
se procur*er*	s' attribu*er*	se prescri*re*	se rend*re* compte
se visit*er*	s' entr'aïd*er*	s' entr'ouvr*ir*	s' entrev*oir*

INFINITIVE.

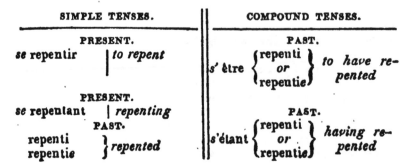

SIMPLE TENSES.	COMPOUND TENSES.
PRESENT.	**PAST.**
se repentir | *to repent*	s' être { repenti or repentie } *to have repented*
PRESENT.	
se repentant | *repenting*	**PAST.**
PAST.	
repenti repentie } *repented*	s'étant { repenti or repentie } *having repented*

INDICATIVE.

SIMPLE TENSES.	COMPOUND TENSES.

PRESENT.
I repent.

je	*me*	repens
tu	*te*	repens
il, *or* elle	*se*	repent
nous	*nous* repentons
vous	*vous* repentez
ils, *or* elles	*se*	repentent

PRETERIT INDEFINITE.
I have repented.

je	*me*	*suis*	repenti,
tu	*t'*	*es*	or
il, *or* elle	*s'*	*est*	repentie
nous	*nous sommes*	repentis,
vous	*vous êtes*	or
ils, *or* elles *se*	*sont*	repenties

IMPERFECT.
I did repent.

je	*me*	repentois
tu	*te*	repentois
il, *or* elle	*se*	repentoit
nous	*nous* repentions
vous	*vous* repentiez
ils, *or* elles *se*	repentoient

PLUPERFECT.
I had repented.

je	*m'*	*étois*	repenti,
tu	*t'*	*étois*	or
il, *or* elle	*s'*	*étoit*	repentie
uous	*nous étions*	repentis,
vous	*vous étiez*	or
ils, *or* elles *s'*	*étoient*	repenties

INDICATIVE. PRESENT. I commonly walk by
[*d'ordinaire se promener à* art.
moonlight. Dost thou not deceive thyself? He (is never
clair de la lune m. *se tromper* * ne se
happy) but (when he is doing) wrong. Do we not
plaire que à faire de art. *mal* m.
(nurse ourselves) too much? How do you do? They mean
s'écouter *se porter* *se proposer*
to travel in the spring.
de voyager à m.

PRETERIT INDEFINITE. I (have been) tolerably well for
se porter assez bien depuis
some time. Didst thou not lose thyself in the wood? (It
s'égarer *
is said) that he killed himself (out of) despair. Have we flat-
On dit se tuer * *de se flat-*
tered ourselves without foundation. Ladies, have you
ter * *fondement Mesdames, se*
walked this morning? Did those ladies recognise
p'omener matin m. *dame se reconnoître*
themselves in this portrait?
* *à* —m.

SIMPLE TENSES.	COMPOUND TENSES.

PRETERIT DEFINITE.	PRETERIT ANTERIOR.
I repented.	*I had repented.*

je	*me* repentis	je	*me*	*fus*	}	repenti,
tu	*te* . repentis	tu	*te*	*fus*		or
il, *or* elle	*se* repentit	il, *or* elle	*se*	*fut*		repentie
nous	*nous* repentîmes	nous	*nous fûmes*		}	repentis,
vous	*vous* repentîtes	vous	*vous fûtes*			or
ils, *or* elles *se*	repentirent	il, *or* elles *se*	*furent*			repenties

IMPERFECT. I tormented myself incessantly about the
 se tourmenter * *sans cesse pour*
affairs of others. Wast thou not (laying the foundation for)
 autrui *se préparer*
much sorrow by thy foolish conduct? He made himself
bien des regrets *se rendre* *
more and more unhappy every day. We despaired
 * * * *de* *en jour* *se désespérer*
without reason. Did you not laugh at us? They
 se moquer de
ruined themselves wantonly.
se perdre * *de gaieté de cœur.*

PLUPERFECT. I had trusted myself to (very uncertain) guides.
 se livrer des peu sûr 2 m. pl. 1
Didst thou not confide too inconsiderately in this man? Had
 se confier légèrement à
that officer rushed rashly into this danger? We
 —*cier se précipiter témérairement dans* —m.
had condemned ourselves. Had you not (been engaged) in
se condamner nous-mêmes *s'occuper de*
trifles? Had those travellers (gone out) of the right
bagatelle f. pl. *voyageurs se détourner droit*
way?
chemin m.

PRETERIT. I repented but too late of having taken such a
 tard imf.-2 *fait* 2 1
step. Wast thou not well entertained yesterday even-
démarche f. *s'amuser hier au*
ing? He suffered for his imprudence. We
 ne se trouver pas bien de
met in the street, but did not speak. Did you say
se rencontrer rue *se parler dites-vous*
nothing (to each other)? Did not those rash children ap-
 * *téméraire* 2 1 *s'ap-*

SIMPLE TENSES.	COMPOUND TENSES.

FUTURE ABSOLUTE.
I shall repent.

je	me	repentirai
tu	te	repentiras
il, *or* elle	se	repentira
nous	nous	repentirons
vous	vous	repentirez
ils, *or* elles	se	repentiront

FUTURE ANTERIOR.
I shall have repented.

je	me	serai ⎫ repenti,
tu	te	seras ⎬ or
il, *or* elle	se	sera ⎭ repentie
nous	nous	serons ⎫ repentis,
vous	vous	serez ⎬ or
ils, *or* elles	se	seront ⎭ repenties

plaud themselves for their folly?
*plaudir * de sottise* m.

PRETERIT ANTERIOR. (As soon as) I discovered that they
dès que s'apercevoir on
sought to deceive me, I was on my guard.
chercher ind-2 *tromper se tenir* ind-3 *garde* f. pl.
What did'st thou, when thou saw'st thyself thus forsaken?
*fis quand se trouver * ainsi abandonné*
When she recollected all the circumstances, she was quite
se souvenir de f. ind-3 *toute*
ashamed. When we had rejoiced sufficiently, (we parted).
honteux. se réjouir assez se séparer ind-3
When you had amused yourselves sufficiently at his expense, did
s'amuser à dépens m. pl.
you not leave him quiet? When they had walked enough,
laisser ind-3 *tranquille se promener*
they (sat down) at the foot of a tree.
s'assirent à

FUTURE ABSOLUTE. I will yield if they convince me.
se rendre on convainc
Wilt thou remember the engagement that thou makest?
se souvenir de prendre
What will not he reproach (himself for)? We shall not forget
se reprocher à lui-même s'oublier
ourselves (so far as) to (be wanting) in respect towards him.
* *jusque manquer de * lui*
Will you employ the means I (point out) to you? Will not
se servir de que indiquer
these flowers fade?
f. *se flétrir*

FUTURE ANTERIOR. Shall I have betrayed myself? Wilt
se trahir moi-même
thou not have degraded thyself in his eyes? He will have
*s'avilir * à*

o

CONDITIONAL.

SIMPLE TENSES.	COMPOUND TENSES.

PRESENT.			PAST.			
I should repent.			*I should have repented.*			
je	me	repentirois	je	me	serois	} repenti,
tu	te	repentirois	tu	te	serois	or
il, *or* elle	se	repentiroit	il, *or* elle	se	seroit	} repentie
nous	nous	repentirions	nous	nous	serions	} repentis,
vous	vous	repentiriez	vous	vous	seriez	or
ils, *or* elles	se	repentiroient	ils, or elles	} se	seroient	} repenties

---

(been proud)   of this trifling advantage.   We shall have
s'enorgueillir   *foible   avantage* m.
fatigued ourselves (to no purpose).   In the end, you will have
se fatiguer   *   *inutilement*   *à*
(been undeceived).   Will your children have (loved each other)
se désabuser   *s'entr'aimer*
too much?
*

CONDITIONAL.   PRESENT.   Should I suffer   myself to
                  se laisser   *   *
(be drawn) into the party   of the rebels?   Would'st thou be
entraîner   *parti* m.
(so easily)   frightened?   Would not the nation sub-
de si peu de chose 2 *s'effrayer* 1   —f. *se sou-*
mit   to so just a law?   We should not rejoice   to see the
mettre   5   4   1   2   *se plaire*   *voir*.
triumph of   guilt.   Would you dishonour   yourselves by
triomphe art. *crime* m.   *se déshonorer*   *
such an action?   Would those lords   (avail themselves) of
                seigneurs   *se prévaudroient de*
their birth   and   fortune, (in order to) hurt
    naissance   *de leurs richesses*   *pour*   *faire violence*
our feelings?
à   *sentiment.*
PAST.   Should I not have devoted myself entirely   to
             se dévouer   *   *entièrement*
the service of my country?   (Had it not been for) thy careless-
         pays m.   *sans*   *insouci-*
ness, thou would'st certainly have (grown rich).   Would this
ance f.   *s'enrichir*
pleasing hope have vanished so soon?   Should we have
doux espoir m.   *s'évanouir*

IMPERATIVE.

AFFIRMATIVE.	NEGATIVE.
Repent (*thou*).	*Do not repent.*

repens-*toi*	ne te repens
qu'il, or } qu'elle } se repente	qu'il, or } qu'elle } ne se repente
repentons-*nous*	ne nous repentons } pas
repentez-*vous*	ne vous repentez
qu'ils, or } qu'elles } se repentent	qu'ils, or } qu'elles } ne se repentent

SUBJUNCTIVE.

SIMPLE TENSES.	COMPOUND TENSES.
PRESENT.	PRETERIT.
That I may repent.	*That I may have repented.*

que			que			
je	*me*	repente	je	*me*	*sois*	repenti,
tu	*te*	repentes	tu	te	*sois*	or
il, *or* elle	*se*	repente	il, *or* elle se	*soit*		repentie
nous	*nous*	repentions	nous	*nous*	*soyons*	repentis
vous	*vous*	repentiez	vous	*vous*	*soyez*	or
ils, *or* elles *se*	repentent	ils, *or* elles } *se*	*soient*			repenties

---

degraded   ourselves to such a degree? You would have
se dégrader   *   2 1 point m.*
reduced   yourselves to every kind of want. They
se réduire   *   sorte f. privation f. pl.*
would have (been drowned), if (they had not had assistance).
    se noyer   on ne les avoit secourus.
IMPERATIVE. O man, remember that thou art mortal. Do
    se souvenir
not flatter   thyself (that thou wilt succeed easily). Let
   *te promets   *   un succès facile*
us take an exact account of our actions. Let us not deceive
se rendre —2 compte 1   se séduire
ourselves.   Rest   yourself under the shade of this tree.
*nous-mêmes. Se reposer   *   à   ombre*
Do not expose   yourself so rashly.
    s'exposer   témérairement.
SUBJUNCTIVE. PRESENT. I must   rise to-morrow at
    Il faut que se lever   de

SIMPLE TENSES.	COMPOUND TENSES.

IMPERFECT.	PLUPERFECT.
That I might repent.	*That I might have repented.*

que			que		
je	*me*	repentisse	je	*me*	*fusse*
tu	*te*	repentisses	tu	*te*	*fusses*
il, or elle *se*		repentit	il, or elle *se*		*fût*
nous	*nous*	repentissions	nous	*nous fussions*	
vous	*vous*	repentissiez	vous	*vous fussiez*	
ils, or elles } *se*		repentissent	ils, or elles } *se*		*fussent*

repenti, or repentie

repentis or repenties

an earlier hour. I wish that thou may'st be
* *meilleur heure* f. *souhaiter* *se porter*
better. I wish him to conduct himself better. Is it not es-
mieux *veux qu'il* * *se conduire* *
sential that we should contain ourselves? They wish that
—*tiel* *se contenir* * On *désirer*
you should habituate yourselves early to labour.
s'habituer * *de bonne heure* art. *travail* m.
It is time that they should (have relaxation) from the fatigue
se délasser —f.
of business.
art. f. pl.

PRETERIT. Can I have (been deceived) so grossly?
Se peut-il que *se tromper* *grossière-*
It is astonishing that thou hast determined to stay. It is
ment? *étonnant* *se décider* *rester On**
not said that he interfered in this business. It will never be
dit *se mêler de* On *
believed that we have conducted ourselves so ill. It is not
croira *se comporter* * *mal* On *
suspected that you have disguised yourselves so ingeniously.
soupçonner *se déguiser* * *adroitement*
It is not feared that they have behaved ill.
craindre *se conduire*

IMPERFECT. They required that I should (go to bed) at ten
On *exigeoit* *se coucher à*
o'clock. They wish that thou should'st walk oftener.
heure. On *voudroit* *se promener*
Did they not wish that he should practise fencing?
On *vouloit* *s'exercer à faire des armes*
Was it necessary that we should (make use) of this method?
= *se servir* *moyen* m.

CONJUGATION OF THE PASSIVE VERBS.

There is but one mode of conjugating passive verbs; it is by adding to the verb *être*, through all the moods and tenses, the participle past of the verb-active, which then must agree in gender and number with the subject; as,

Je suis aimé, *or* aimée	*I am loved*
tu étois estimé, *or* estimée	*thou wast esteemed*
il fut chéri de son peuple	*he was beloved by his people*
elle fut toujours chérie	*she was always beloved*
mon père fut respecté	*my father was respected*
ma mère fut révérée	*my mother was revered*
nous serons loués, *or* louées	*we will be praised*
vous en serez blâmés *or* blâmées	*you will be blamed for it*
ils seroient craints et redoutés	*they would be feared and dreaded*
elles seroient mieux instruites	*they would be better informed*
afin que mes fils soient connus	*that my sons may be known*
je voudrois que les portes fussent ouvertes.	*I should wish the doors were opened*

Did they wish that you should complain without reason?
    on   vouloit   *se plaindre*

Did they not wish   them (to make more haste)?
    on   désirer ind-2 *que ils   se hâter davantage?*

PLUPERFECT. Would they have wished that I had revenged
                    voulu   *se venger*
myself? I should have wished that thou hadst shewn
    *   désirer*   *se montrer*
thyself more accommodating. I should have wished that this
    *   moins difficile*   *voulu*
painter had (been less negligent). Would you have wished that
peintre · se négliger moins   *voulu*
we should have ruined ourselves in the public opinion, (in order
    se perdre +   2 f. 1   *pour*
to) satisfy your resentment? I could have wished perhaps
  satisfaire .ressentiment   *désirer peut-être*
that you had applied yourselves more to your studies.
    *s'appliquer * davantage*
We could have wished that they had extricated themselves
                .*se tirer*   *
more skilfully from the difficulties (in which) they (had
    adroitement   *embarras   où*
involved themselves).
s'étoient mis.

o 3

j'ai été dangereusemeut blessé, *or* blessée	*I have been dangerously wounded*
tu en avois été averti, *or* avertie	*thou hadst been apprised of it*
lòrsqu'il eut été mordu	*when he had been bitten*
après qu'elle eut été séduite.	*after she had been seduced*
le mur aura été détruit	*the wall will have been destroyed*
la ruse aura été découverte	*the artifice will have been disco- vered*
nous aurions été entendus, *or* entendues	*we should have been heard*
vous auriez été aperçus, *or* aperçues	*you should have been perceived*
supposez qu'ils aient été de- mentis	*suppose they were contradicted*
bien qu'elles aient été reconnues	*although they were recognised*
que les murs eussent été détruits	*that the walls might have been destroyed*
que les lumières eussent été éteintes	*that the lights might have been put out*

In the following exercises upon the verbs, the tenses will now be promiscuously intermixed.

EXERCISE.

That young lady is so mild, so polite, and so kind, that
   jeune demoiselle   *doux*   *honnête*   *bon*
she is beloved by every body. He performed with (so much)
   aimé de   *jouer* ind-4   *tant de*
ability, that he was universally applauded. He is known
intelligence   ind-4   *applaudi*
by nobody. How many countries, unknown to the ancients,
de   *que de pays*   *inconnu*
have been discovered by modern navigators?
     art.   2   *navigateur* m. pl. 1

CONJUGATION OF SOME NEUTER VERBS.

There are about six hundred neuter verbs in the French language, *fifty* of which taking the auxiliary *être* in their compouud tenses, their participles past must agree in gen- der and number with the subject; as,

Je suis tombé, *or* tombée	*I have fallen*
quand tu fus venu, *or* venue	*when thou hadst come*
il étoit arrivé avant moi	*he was arrived before me*
elle étoit déjà arrivée	*she was already arrived*

mon frère n'étoit pas encore parti	*my brother had not yet set off*
ma sœur étoit partie avant lui	*my sister had set off before him*
nous serons revenus, *or* revenues	*we shall have returned*
vous serez descendus, *or* descendues	*you shall have come down*
ils seroient repartis elles seroient reparties	} *they would have set off again*
que mes frères soient sortis	*that my brothers may have gone out*
que mes sœurs fussent sorties	*that my sisters might have gone out*

And so through all the compound tenses.

They came to see us with the greatest haste. When
    ind-4 * *voir*   *empressement* Quand
    did they arrive?   That estate   fell   to his
est-ce que   *arriver* ind-4   *terre* f. *lui est échu en* *
lot.   He fell   from his horse, but happily received
partage   *tomber* ind-4   *   *il* — ind-4
only a slight contusion on the knee.
ne que *léger*   — f.   *à*   *genou* m.

OF THE IMPERSONAL VERBS.

Observe that, in impersonal verbs, *il* has no relation to
a substantive, as may be seen by the impossibility of substituting a noun in its place.

IMPERSONAL VERBS.

il pleut	*it rains*	il bruïne	*it drizzles*
il neige	*it snows*	il importe	*it matters*
il grèle	*it hails*	il semble	*it seems*
il tonne	*it thunders*	il paroît	*it appears*
il éclaire	*it lightens*	il suffit que	*it suffices*
il gèle	*it freezes*	il importe	*it becomes*
il dégèle	*it thaws*	il s'ensuit que	*it follows that*
il arrive	*it happens*	il est à propos	*it is proper*
il sied	*it is becoming*	il faut	*it is necessary*
il messied	*it is unbecoming*	il y a, etc.	*there is, or are*

Does it rain   this morning?   Did it hail
   pleuvoir   *matin* m.   *grêler* ind-4 art.

last   night? It does not snow.   I thought   it had thun—
dernier 2 f. 1   neiger   croyois que   : ton—
dered.   Does it not lighten? Do you think   it freezes?
ner ind-6   .   éclairer   croyez que   geler
It is a remarkable thing. It was a terrible hurricane. It is ten
ce   ce ind-2   2   ouragan 1.
o'clock.   It (was not my friend's fault) that it   was   not
heure pl.   ne tenir ind-3 pas à mon ami   la chose subj-2 ne
so.   It will freeze long.   I do not think so ; it seems, on the
ainsi   long-temps.   crois   sembler à
contrary, that it thaws.   It (is fit)   to act so.   It (was of great
contraire   dégeler   convenir de   importer beau-
importance) to succeed. Would it be   proper to write to
coup ind-2 de réussir   être à propos de
your friends? It appears that he has not attended to that business.
    ¡   s'occuper de
Perhaps it (would be) better to (give up) · the undertaking. It
         vaudroit   * abandonner   entreprise
(was sufficient) to know his opinion.
     suffisoit   de

CONJUGATION OF THE IMPERSONAL VERB

Falloir, il faut, it must, it is necessary.

INFINITIVE.

SIMPLE TENSES.	COMPOUND TENSES.
PRESENT..... falloir	PAST .... avoir fallu
PARTIC. PRES. *wanted*	PAST .... fallu, ayant fallu

INDICATIVE.

PRESENT..... il faut	PRETERIT IND. il a fallu
IMPERFECT... il falloit	PLUPERFECT.. il avoit fallu
PRETERIT DEF. il fallut	PRETERIT ANT. il eut fallu
FUTURE ABSOL. il faudra	FUTURE ANT.. il aura fallu

CONDITIONAL.

PRESENT il faudroit	PAST........ il auroit fallu

SUBJUNCTIVE.

PRESENT...... qu'il faille	PRETERIT .... qu'il ait fallu
IMPERFECT... qu'il fallût	PLUPERFECT.. qu'il eût fallu

REMARK. The English verb *must*, not being impersonal,
may take any noun or pronoun for its subject; whereas the

French verb *falloir*, being always impersonal, a change of construction in the translation becomes necessary, and this may be done in two different ways:

The most common method is by putting the conjunction *que* after *il faut, il falloit,* etc. then transporting the subject of the English verb *must* to the second verb, which is to be put in the subjunctive in French: thus, I must sell my house, *il faut que je vende ma maison.*

The other way is by allowing the second verb to remain in the infinitive, as in English, and substituting in the place of the personal pronoun, which is the subject of the verb *must,* its corresponding objective *me, te, lui, nous, vous, leur,* which are to be placed between *il* and *faut, falloit,* etc. as I must begin that work to-day, *il* ME *faut commencer cet ouvrage aujourd'hui.*

OBSERVE. That all expressions implying necessity, obligation, or want, may be rendered by *falloir;* as I want a new grammar, *il* ME *faut une nouvelle grammaire.*

EXERCISE.

You *must* speak to him about that affair. It *was necessary*
    sub-1   de   f.   ind-2   que
for him to consent to that bargain. We *were obliged* to (set
* *il* * sub-2   *marché* m.   ind-3 *partir*
out) immediately.   Children *should* learn every day some-
▸ sub-2 *sur-le-champ* art.   cond-1 sub-2
thing by heart. *Shall* I suffer patiently such *an* insult? He
       ind-7   sub-4   1 2'
must have been a blockhead not to understand
cond-2 * sub-2   *sot*   2 *pour* 1 *comprendre* inf-1 *des*
such easy rules.   (How much) do you *want?* He does
si 2 3 *règle* f. 1   *combien*   *fait*
what is *requisite.* Do that as it (*should be*). What *must* he
           faites   ind-1   que 2 *lui* 1
have for his trouble? You are the man I *want.* Do not
*   *peine* f.   que
give me any more bread, I have already more than I
    *   de   en   déjà   ne
want. I *need* not ask you whether you will come. I do not
m'en *   inf-1   si

think that it is necessary to be a conjurer to guess his motives.
crois   il   sub-1   * sorcier pour deviner   motif
I could not   suspect   that I *ought*   to ask pardon for a
   pouvois   soupçonner   sub-2 * inf-1   —   de
fault   I have not committed.
faute f. que   commise

CONJUGATION OF THE IMPERSONAL VERB

Y avoir, there to be.

INFINITIVE.

PRESENT	y avoir	*there to be*
PAST	y avoir eu	*there to have been*
PARTIC. PRES...	y ayant	*there being*
PARTIC. PAST ..	y ayant eu	*there having been*

INDICATIVE.

PRESENT........	il y a	*there is, or there are**
PRET. INDEF...	il y a eu	*there has been, or there have been**
IMPERFECT	il y avoit	*there was, or there were**
PLUPERFECT ...	il y avoit eu	*there had been*
PRETERIT DEF..	il y eut	*there was, or there were**
PRETERIT ANT..	il y eut eu	*there had been*
FUTURE ABSOL.	il y aura	*there will be*
FUTURE ANTER.	il y aura eu	*there will have been*

CONDITIONAL.

PRESENT........	il y auroit	*there would be*
PAST	il y auroit eu	*there would have been*

SUBJUNCTIVE.

PRESENT	qu'il y ait	*that there may be*
PRETERIT......	qu'il y ait eu	*that there may have been*
IMPERFECT.....	qu'il y eût	*that there might be*
PLUPERFECT....	qu'il y eût eu	*that there might have been*

This verb in English is used in the plural, when followed by a substantive plural; in French it remains always in the singular.

EXERCISE.

There must *be* a great difference of age between those two
    il doit   —f.

persons. *There being* (so many) vicious people in this world,
          tant de   =2 *gens* m. pl. 1
is it astonishing that *there are* so many persons who become
  étonnant   sub-1   *devenir*
the victims of the corruption of the age? *It is* a thousand
        perversité f.   ·*siècle* m.   * *mille à*
   to one that he will not succeed. *There would be*
parier contre   *réussir*
more happiness if (every one) knew how to moderate his
  de bonheur   *chacun*   .*savoit* * * *modérer*
desires. I did not think that *there could be* (any thing) to
désir   *croyois*   ·subj-2   *rien*
blame   in his conduct. *There would* not be so many
reprendre   *conduite* f.
duels, did people reflect   , that one of the first obligations
 —   *si l'on*· *réfléchir* ind-2   'f.   —f.
of a Christian is to forgive   injuries. Could *there*
  chrétien   *de pardonner* art.   *pourroit-il*
be a king more happy than this, who has always been the
                    celui-ci
father of his subjects?
       .*sujet*

OF THE IRREGULAR VERBS.

For brevity's sake we shall give only the first person of
each tense, whenever all the others are formed regularly
from this first person.

IRREGULAR VERBS OF THE FIRST CONJUGATION.

Aller, to go.

Part. pres. allant. *Part. past*, allé.
Ind. pres. vais *or* vas, vas, va, allons, allez, vont.
Imperf. allois. *Pret.* allai.
Fut. irai. *Cond.* irois.
Imper. va, aille, allons, allez, aillent.
Subj. pres. aille, ailles, aille, allions, alliez, aillent.
Imperf. allasse.

REMARK. We say almost indifferently, *je fus* or *j'allai*,
j'ai été or *je suis allé*, *j'avois été* or *j'étois allé*, and *j'aurois
été* or *je serois allé*. This verb is, in its compound tenses,
conjugated with the verb *être*.

The imperative *va* takes an *s*, when followed by *y;* as *vas-y*, go thither : but it takes no *s*, when the *y* is followed by a verb; as *va y donner ordre*, go and order that matter.

Aller, when united to a personal pronoun and the word *en*, forms the verb *s'en aller*, to go away ; which is conjugated like *aller*.

S'en aller, s'en allant, allé. Je m'en vais, tu t'en vas, il s'en va, nous nous en allons, vous vous en allez, il s'en vont. Je m'en allois, je m'en allai, and in conversation, *je m'en fus. Je m'en suis allé, je m'en irai, je m'en irois.* IMPERATIVE. *Va-t'en, qu'il s'en aille, allons-nous-en, allez-vous-en, qu'ils s'en aillent. Que je m'en aille, que je m'en allasse.*

Puer, to stink, is by no means irregular, but simply defective in the preterit of the indicative, and in the imperfect of the subjunctive.

Tisser, to weave, is a verb defective, which, to form its compound tenses, borrows the participle past *tissu*, from the obsolete verb *tistre*.

Envoyer and *renvoyer* make in their future absolute and conditional present, *j'enverrai, j'enverrois*, and *je renverrai, je renverrois*.

EXERCISE.

Will you *go* this evening into the country ? I *am going* to
              soir   à   campagne f.   *

pay some visits, and if I be   early   (at liberty) I
faire   ind-1   *de bonne heure* 2   *libre* 1

shall certainly *go*   home.   Go there with thy brother.
        s'en aller   chez moi.

Go and *do* that errand.   *Go* there and put every thing in
   * *faire*   *commission* f.   * *mettre*   *en*

order. Let him *go* to   church on   holidays.   By
        art. *église* f. * art. *jour* pl. *de fête. à force*

being loaded with scents, and particularly amber,   he
de inf.-1 *chargé de odeur* f. pl.   *surtout* pr. *ambre* m.

offends the smell). They have *woven*　　silk and　　　cotton
　　　　puer　　　　　　　　 *de* art. f.　　 pr. art.　m.
together, and　.　made a very pretty stuff.　I shall *send*
　　　　　en ont fait　　　　　 *étoffe* f.　　　　　　 *de* art.
spring　　　flowers to those ladies.　I would *go* to Rome,　if I
printanier 2 f. pl. 1　　·　　*dame* f. pl.
could.　We would (*send back*) our horses.　Why　　do they *go*
pouvois　　　　　　　　　　　　　 *pourquoi*
away so soon?　My brother and　　　sister *went* yesterday to
　　　　　　　　　　　　　　　　　　 pron.
Windsor.　I shall not *go* (any more) a　　hunting.
　　　　　　　　　　　　 plus　à * art. *chasse* f.

IRREGULAR VERBS OF THE SECOND CONJUGATION.

Bénir, to bless, is regular through all its tenses, but has
two participles past; the one regular, as *bénie entre toutes
les femmes,* blessed among all women; and the other irregular, when speaking of things consecrated by the prayers
of the church.　In that case we say *bénit, bénite;* as *pain
bénit,* hallowed bread; *eau bénite,* holy water.

Fleurir, to blossom, used in its proper sense, is regular;
but used figuratively, that is, meaning *to flourish, to be
in repute, honour, esteem,* the participle present makes
always *florissant,* and the third persons of the imperfect of
the indicative make often *florissoit, florissoient.*

Haïr, to hate.　In the present of the indicative, the
three persons singular *je hais, tu hais, il hait,* and in the
imperative the second person singular *hais,* are pronounced
as a vowel, having the sound of *é* grave open, *je hès, tu
hès, il hèt, hès,* whilst in all other forms, the letters *aï*
form two syllables, and have each their proper sound; as,
*nous ha-ïssons, vous ha-ïssez, je ha-ïssois, je ha-ïs, je
ha-ïrai, ha-ï,* etc.

Gésir is a defective verb which signifies *être couché,* to
lie.　It is no longer used, except in the following expressions, *gisant, gît, nous gisons, ils gisent, il gisoit;* and is
only employed in light and familiar poetry.　When preceded by *ci,* however, it is very properly used in monu-
mental inscriptions: *ci-gît,* here lies.

P

EXERCISE.

May the name   of that good king be *blessed* from generation
　　　　　nom m.
to generation.   These trees *blossomed* twice   every   year.
en　　　　　　　　　 ind-2   *deux fois*   *   art.   *an*
The arts and　　　　sciences *flourished* at Athens in the time of Peri-
　　　　　—　　art.　—　　ind-2   *à Athènes*
cles. Horace and Virgil   *flourished* under the reign of Augus-
　　　　　　　　　 Virgile   ind-2   *sous*   *règne   Augus-*
tus.   We discovered from the top of the mountain a vast plain
te　　*découvrir*　　　　haut　　　　　　　　*plaine* f.
full   of *flowery*   meadows. The empire of the Babyloni-
rempli de fleurissant 2 *pré* m. pl. 1　—　　　—*nien*
ans was long   a *flourishing* one. We did not *hate* the
　ind-3 *long-temps*　*　　　*
man, but his vices.   Does she sincerely *hate* that vain pomp
　　　　　　　　　　　　　　　　　　　　pompe f.
and all the parade of   grandeur?
　　　appareil art.   —f.

BOUILLIR, *to boil.*

Part. pres. bouillant. *Part. past,* bouilli.
Ind. pres. bous, bous, bout, bouillons, bouillez, bouillent.
Imperf. bouillois. *Pret.* bouillis.
Fut. bouillirai. *Cond.* bouillirois.
Imper. bous. *Subj. pres.* bouille. *Imperf.* bouillisse.

N. B. Ebouillir, to boil away, and *rebouillir,* to boil
again, are conjugated in the same manner. The first is
commonly used only in compound tenses, and the infinitive
mood; as *cette sauce est trop ébouillie,* this sauce has
boiled away too much.

COURIR, *to run.*

Part. pres. courant. *Part. past,* couru.
Ind. pres. cours, cours, court, courons, courez, courent.
Imperf. courois. *Pret.* courus.
Fut. courrai. *Cond.* courrois.
Imp. cours. *Subj. pres.* coure. *Imperf.* courusse.

N. B. In the same manner are conjugated *accourir,* to
run to; *concourir,* to concur; *discourir,* to discourse;
encourir, to incur; *parcourir,* to run over; *recourir,* to have
recourse, and *secourir,* to assist.

EXERCISE.

Take that water off   the fire, it *boils* too fast.   Do not
Retirer   f. *de dessus*   m. f.   *fort*
let   the pot   (*boil away*) (so much).   That sauce has (*boiled*
laisser 1 m. 4   3   *tant* 2   f. *est* f.
away) (too much). *Boil*   that meat again ; it has not
                trop *faire rebouillir*   *viande* * f.
boiled long enough. He *runs* faster than I.   He *ran*   about
        * *assez*   *vite*   *moi*   ind-4   *
uselessly   all the morning. We *ran* at the voice of that honest
inutilement   *matinée* f.   ind-3   f.
man, and *assisted* him. (The moment) he saw us in danger, he
                    dès que   *vit* *en*
ran to us and delivered   us.   By so whimsical a conduct,
        * *délivrer* ind-3   *bizarre* 2   1
should we not *contribute* to our destruction? He *discoursed* so long
            concourir   *perte* f.
on the immortality of the soul,   and the certainty of another
sur   =   *certitude* f.
life, that he did not leave   (any thing) unsaid.   If we
            laisser ind-3   *rien* *en arrière*
(were to act) thus, we should certainly *incur* the displeasure of
agir ind-2 *ainsi*   *disgrâce* f.
our parents. I would not *have recourse* to so base a method.
                                bas 2 *moyen* m. 1
Will   men always *run* after   shadows?
    art.   *de* art. *chimère* f. pl.

Faillir, to fail. The authors of the Dictionary of the
French Academy give all the tenses of this verb, observing
only, that the greater part of them are obsolete. It is
now only used in the present of the infinitive *faillir*, and
participle past *failli*, in the preterit definite *je faillis, tu
faillis, il faillit, nous faillîmes, vous faillîtes, ils faillirent*,
and in the compound tenses, *j'ai failli, j'eus failli, j'avois
failli*, etc.

N. B. Its derivative *défaillir*, to faint, is conjugated in
the same manner, but it is now only used in the plural of
the present, *nous défaillons*, in the imperfect, *je défaillois*,
and the two preterits, *je défaillis, j'ai défailli*, and in the
present of the infinitive.

Fuir, *to fly, to run away.*
Part. pres. fuyant. *Part. past*, fui.
Ind. pres. fuis, fuis, fuit, fuyous, fuyez, fuient.

P 2

Imperf. fuyois. *Pret.* fuis.
Fut. fuirai. *Cond.* fuirois.
Imp. fuis, fuie, fuyons, fuyez, fuient.
Subj. pres. fuie, fuies, fuie, fuyions, fuviez. fuient.
Imperf. fuisse; *not commonly used.*

Conjugate in the same manner its compound *s'enfuir ,*
to run away.

MOURIR, *to die.*

Part. pres. mourant. *Part. past,* mort.
Ind. pres. meurs, meurs, meurt, mourons, mourez, meurent.
Imperf. mourois. *Pret.* mourus.
Fut. mourrai. *Cond.* mourrois.
Imper. meurs, meure, mourons, mourez, meurent.
Subj. pres. meure, meures, meure, mourions, mouriez, meurent.
Imperf. mourusse.

REMARK. *Mourir* in its compound tenses is conjugated
with the verb *être.* When *mourir* takes the form of the
reflected verb, it signifies *être sur le point de mourir,* to be
at the point of death; in this sense it is very seldom used,
except in the present and imperfect of the indicative, and it
has no compound tenses.

EXERCISE.

He (*was' near*) losing his   life in that rencounter. He
    *faillir   perdre * art.   *rencontre* f.
(*was near*) falling into the snare which was laid for him.
faillir ind-4 *donner   piège* m. *qu'on avoit tendu * *lui*
His strength *fails* him every day. Let us have
* art. f. pl. *défaillir lui*   art. m. pl. *Donnez-nous*
something to eat   directly; we *are fainting* with fatigue and
    *   *manger* a *vite* 1   *de —*
hunger. I cannot meet   him, he *flies* from me. When
pr. *faim   ne puis rencontrer*   *
we   have no employ, we endeavour to   *fly* from ourselves.
*on sait *   *s'occuper   chercher   se * soi-même*
Would he not *avoid*   flatterers,   if he knew all their false-
                fuir art. *flatteur* m. pl.   ind-a   *faus-*
hood. He *died* by a (very painful) disease.   She *died*   of
seté   de   cruel a   *maladie* f. 1   ind-4
grief   (for the loss of) her son. He *is dying.* She *was expiring*
chagrin m. *d'avoir perdu*   *se mourir.   se mourir*
with grief, when the fear   of   death at last wrested
    de   crainte f. art.   *enfin arracher* ind-3
her secret from her.
    —m. * *lui*

Quérir, to fetch, is used in this form only, and after the verbs *envoyer, venir, aller,* as *envoyer quérir,* send for; *aller quérir,* go and fetch. This verb is confined to familiar conversation only.

ACQUÉRIR, *to acquire.*

Part. pres. acquérant. *Part. past,* acquis.
Ind. pres. acqu-iers, —iers, —iert, acqué-rons, —ez, acquièrent.
Imperf. acquérois. *Pret.* acquis.
Fut. acquerrai. *Cond.* acquerrois.
Imper. acquiers, acquière, acquér-ons, —ez, acquièrent.
Subj. pres. acquièr-e, —es, —e, acquér-ions, —iez, acquièrent.
Imperf. acquisse.

S'enquérir, to enquire, and *requérir,* to request, to require, are conjugated as *acquérir.*

Conquérir, to conquer, is conjugated in the same manner, but it is almost obsolete in all simple tenses, except the preterit definitive of the indicative, *je conquis,* etc. and the imperfect of the subjunctive, *que je conquisse,* etc. It is very much used in the compound tenses.

Ouïr, to hear, is obsolete in several tenses. It is only used in the present of the infinitive *ouïr,* and participle past *ouï;* in the preterit definite of the indicative, *j'ouïs, tu ouïs, il ouït, nous ouïmes,* etc., and the imperfect of the subjunctive, *que j'ouïsse, que tu ouïsses, qu'il ouït, que nous ouïssions,* etc. Its principal use is in the compound tenses, but then it is generally accompanied by a verb; as *Je l'ai* or *je l'avois ouï dire,* I have or I had heard it said.

VÊTIR, *to clothe.*

Part. pres. vêtant.* *Part. past,* vêtu.
Ind. pres. vêts,* vêts,* vêt, vêtons, vêtez, vêtent.
Imperf. vêtois. *Pret.* vêtis.
Fut. vêtirai. *Cond.* vêtirois.
Imper. vêts,* vête,* vêtons, vêtez, vêtent.
Subj. pres. vête. *Imperf.* vêtisse.

This verb may be used through all its tenses, but seldom in the forms marked with an asterisk.
It is oftener used as a reflected verb, *se vêtir.*

N. B. Conjugate in the same manner *revêtir*, to invest; which is used through all its tenses, and *dévêtir*, to divest, which is principally used as a reflected verb, and in some forms only.

Send for the physician and follow exactly his advice.   *Go* and
.   *médecin*   *suivez*   *
fetch my cane.   Every   day   he *acquired*   celebrity by
   canne f.   · art. *jour* m. pl.   *de* art.   =f.
   works   calculated to   fix the attention of an enlight-
de art. *ouvrage* m. pl.   *fait   pour*   2
-ened public.   That I would *acquire*   riches at the
        1   subj-2 *de* art.   ,
expense   of my honesty!   He had *acquired* by his merit
dépens m. pl.   *probité*   *une*
great influence over the opinions of his contemporaries.   I have
        —f.   sing.   *contemporain*
inquired about that man   (every where) and have not (been able)
        de   -là *partout*   *pu*
(to hear any thing of him).   Who   has *requested* it   of |
   en avoir de nouvelles   *Qui est-ce qui*   5   4   *en* 2 *
you?   Sesostris, king of Egypt, *conquered* a great part of   Asia. |
·1   art.
The formidable empire which Alexander *conquered*   did not
        2   1   —*dre*   ind-6
last   longer   than his life. I have *heard*   that important
·*durer plus long-temps*   f.   *ouïr dire*   ·   2
news.   He *dressed* himself in   haste and (went out) imme-
sing. 1   *se vêtir*   *   *à* art. *hâte* f.   *sortir   sur-le-*
diately.   I wish   she would *dress*   the children with
·*champ*   *voudrois que*   *vêtir* sub-2
more 'care.   If his fortune permitted   him, he would *clothe* all
        de   *permettoit le lui*
the poor of the parish.   Two servants   *invested* him with his
        paroisse f.   *domestique revêtir*   *de*
ducal mantle.   He only passed   for a traveller, but
2   *manteau* m. 1   *ne*   ind-2 *que*
lately   he has *assumed* the character of an envoy.   It begins
depuis peu   *revêtir un*   * *envoyé*   *commencer*
to be   very warm; it is time to (*throw off some clothing*.)
   faire   *chaud*   *de*   *se dévêtir*

CUEILLIR, *to gather.*

Part. pres. cueillant.   *Part. past*, cueilli.
Ind. pres. cueille.   *Imperf.* cueillois.   *Pret.* cueillis.   -

Fut. cueillerai. *Cond.* cueillerois.
Imper. cueille. *Subj. pres.* cueille. *Imperf.* cueillisse.

N. B. Conjugate in the same manner *accueillir*, to welcome, and *recueillir*, to collect.

Saillir, to project, is commonly used in the two participles, *saillant* and *sailli*; however, it is sometimes used in the following forms of the third person, *il saille, il sailloit; il saillera, il sailleroit, qu'il saille, qu'il saillit.* But *saillir*, to gush out, does not belong to this branch. It is a regular verb, conjugated like *finir, je saillis, tu saillis, ils saillissent*, etc. Its principal use is in the third persons.

ASSAILLIR, *to assault.*

Part. pres. assaillant. *Part. past*, assailli.
Ind. pres. assaille. *Imperf.* assaillois. *Pret.* assaillis.
Fut. assaillirai. *Cond.* assaillirois.
Imper. assaille. *Subj. pres.* assaille. *Imperf.* assaillisse.

N. B. Tressaillir, to start, is conjugated like *assaillir.*

EXERCISE.

I will *gather* with pleasure some of these flowers and
pr.-prod.
fruits, since   you   wish   to have some.   Do not *gather*
   puisque   *être bien aise de*   *en*
these peaches before   they   are   ripe.   That is a country
  f. pl.   *avant que*   *ne* subj-1 *mûr*   *Ce*   *pays*
where they neither *reap*   corn, nor gather grapes.   We
 où \on   ne   recueillir. ni *blé   ni   *   *raisin*
shall *collect*   in ancient history   important and valuable
  recueillir   2   1   *de* art.   — 2   *précieux* 3
facts.   He *received* us in the most polite manner.   Po-
fait 1   *accueillir   de   2   manière* f. 1.   art.
verty,   misery,   sickness,   persecution, in a word, all
 f.   art.   f.   art. *maladie* f. art.   f.   *en*
the misfortunes   in the world (have *fallen   upon*) him.
 malheur m. pl. *de   accueillir*
You will   give six inches   to that cornice; it will
 voulez   pouce m. pl.   *corniche* f. f.
project too much.   That balcony *projected* too much;   it
   *   That balcony *balcon* m. ind-2   *
*darkened   the dining-room.   When Moses struck
obscurcir ind-2   *Quand Moïse frapper*
 the rock,   there *gushed out* (of it) a spring of (fresh
ind-5   *rocher* m.   *il*   ind-3   *en   source* f.

running) water.   The blood *gushed* from his vein   with
vif 2.   f. 1.   ind-2   *veine* f.
impetuosity.   We shall *assault* the enemy to-morrow in their
 =   ·   pl.   *demain*   ·
entrenchments.   Were we not *overtaken* by a horrible storm? ·
retranchement   ind-3   *assailli*   *tempête* f.
At every word   they said to him concerning his son, the good
à chaque   *que on disoit*   *de*
(old man) leaped   for joy.   Shall you not *shudder* with
vieillard tressaillir ind-2 *de joie*   *tressaillir*
fear?
peur f.

IRREGULAR VERBS OF THE THIRD CONJUGATION.

Avoir, to have, of which we have given the conjugation.
See p. 99.

Ravoir, to have again, is only employed in the present
of the infinitive, and even that in the familiar style.   To
make any other use of it, is to introduce a barbarous mode
of expression.

Choir, to fall, is defective, and hardly ever used but in
this form, and the participle past *chu*.

DÉCHOIR, *to decay*.

(*No Part. pres.*) *Part. past*, déchu.
Ind. pres. déchois, déchois, déchoit, déchoyons, déchoyez,
déchoient.
(*No Imperf.*) *Pret.* déchus.   *Fut.* décherrai.   *Cond.* dé-
cherrois.
Imper. déchois, déchoie, déchoyons, déchoyez, déchoient.
Subj. pres déchoie, déchoies, déchoie, déchoyi-ons, —ez, dé-
choient.
Imperf. déchusse.

Echoir, to fall to, to expire, has only the third person
of the present of the indicative now in use, *il échoit* or
échet; no imperfect; pret. *j'échus;* fut. *j'écherrai;* cond.
j'écherrois; no imperative; no present of the subjunctive;
imperf. *que j'échusse;* infinitive, *échoir;* part. pres. *échéant;*
part. past, *échu*.

These three verbs, *choir, déchoir* and *échoir*, are conjugated with *être*, in their compound tenses.

Falloir, to be necessary, is an impersonal verb, of which
we have given the conjugation.

EXERCISE.

I had   apartments that I liked ; I will endeavour to *have* them
  un logement   *aimer* *veux essayer de*   s.
again. Beware of   *falling.* How   has he *fallen* into po-
  Prenez garde inf-1.   *Comment*   *en pau-*
verty? Since the publication of his last   work, he has much
vreté. Depuis   *dernier*
fallen in the esteem of the public. If he do not alter
déchoir   *changer de*
his conduct, he will *decline* every day   in his reputation
  *   *déchoir de jour en jour* *de* —f.
and   credit. He has put in the lottery, and he hopes
   pr-pron. —m.   *mis à*   *loterie* f.
that a   capital prize will *fall* (to his share). That bill of
  * art. *gros lot* m. *échoir lui*   *lettre*
exchange has *expired.* The first term *expires* at Midsummer.
change échoir   *terme* m.   *à la Saint Jean*
You have drawn on me a bill of exchange; when *is* it *payable?*
   tirer sur moi   *échoir*
I did not believe that I *must* so soon (have taken) that journey.
   croyois * sub-2   *faire* *voyage* m.
He *must* have   sunk under the efforts of (so many)
  ind-4 *que succomber* sub-2   *tant de*
enemies.

Mouvoir, *to move.*

Part. pres. mouvant. *Part. past*, mu.
Ind. pres. meus, meus, meut, mouv-ons, —ez, meuvent.
Imperf. mouvois. *Pret.* mus.
Fut. mouvrai. *Cond.* mouvrois.
Imperf. meus, meuve, mouvons, mouvez, meuvent.
Subj. pres. meuv-e, —es, —e, mouv-ions, —iez, meuvent.
Imperf. musse.

N. B. Conjugate in the same manner *émouvoir,* to stir
up, to move, and *promouvoir,* to promote, and *démouvoir,*
to make one desist.

The first, whether employed in an actual or figurative
sense, is much used. The second is the proper expression
in speaking of a dignity. The third, which is a law-term,
is now only used in the present of the infinitive.

Pleuvoir, *to rain (impersonal).*

Part. pres. pleuvant. *Part. past*, plu.
Ind. pres. il pleut. *Imperf.* il pleuvoit. *Pret.* il plut.

Fut. il pleuvra. *Cond.* il pleuvroit:
Sub. pres. qu'il pleuve. *Imperf.* qu'il plût.

EXERCISE.

The spring   which *moves* the whole machine is very inge-
    ressert m.   2 *tout* 1   —f.
nious, though very simple.   It was   passion which *moved*
=   *quoique*   —   *Ce* ind-1 art.   f.   ind-4
him to that action.   Can   you doubt that the soul, though it
= f.   *Pouvez*
is spiritual, *moves* the body at pleasure?   That is a man whom
     ne sub-1   *à sa volonté*   *Ce*
nothing *moves*.   We had scarcely lost   sight   of   land
      émouvoir   *à peine perdu*   *vue* f. 3   2 art. *terre* f. 1
when there *arose*   a violent tempest.   We were *moved*
que   *il s'émouvoir* ind-2   *grande tempête* f.
with fear and pity.   When the famous d'Aguesseau was
de crainte f.   pr. *pitié* f.   *Quand*   *célèbre*
promoted to the dignity of chancellor, all   France shewed
       -= f.   *chancelier*   art.   f.   *en témoigner*
the greatest joy.   That bishop well deserved,   by his
ind-3   f.   *évêque*   *mériter* ind-2
talents and by his virtues, that the king should *promote* him to
                                     sub-2
the dignity of primate.   The people think that it *rains*
         primat   sing. *croît*   *de* art.
frogs   and   insects   at certain seasons. It will
grenouille f. pl.   pr. art. *insecte* m. pl. *en*   —   *temps* pl.
not *rain* to-day,   but I (am fearful) of its *raining* to-
     aujourd'hui   *craindre que* *   *ne* sub-1
morrow.

POUVOIR, *to be able.*

Part. pres. pouvant. *Part. past,* pu.
Ind. pres. puis *or* peux, peux, peut, pouv-ons,—ez, peuvent.
Imperf. pouvois. *Pret.* pus
Fut. pourrai. *Cond.* pourrois. (*No Imperative*).
Subj. pres. puisse. *Imperf.* pusse.

REMARK. Conversation and poetry admit the expression
je peux; but in interrogations, *je puis* alone is used. Say
puis-je and not *peux-je.*

SAVOIR, *to know.*

Part. pres. sachant. *Part. past,* su.
Ind. pres. sais, sais, sait, savons, savez, savent.
Imperf. savois. *Pret.* sus. *Fut.* saurai. *Cond.* saurois.

Imper. sache, sache, sachons, sachez, sachent.
Subj. pres. sache. *Imperf.* susse.

Seoir, to become, to befit, is not used in the infinitive, except sometimes in the participle present, *seyant.* In other moods, it is only used in the third person of the simple tenses, *il sied, ils siéent, il seyoit, il siéra, il siéroit, qu'il siée.* It is without preterit in the indicative, without imperfect in the subjunctive, and without compound tenses. But *seoir,* to sit, is used only in these two forms, *séant* and *sis* of the infinitive.

ASSEOIR, *to sit.*

Part. pres. asseyant. *Part. past,* assis.
Ind. pres. assieds, assieds, assied, assey-ons,—ez,—ent.
Imperf. asseyois. *Pret.* assis.
Fut. assiérai, *or* asseyerai. *Cond.* assiérois, *or* asseyerois.
Imper. assieds, asseye, assey-ous,—ez,—ent.
Subj. pres. asseye. *Imperf.* assisse.

N. B. This verb is oftener used as a reflected verb, *s'asseoir,* to sit down. The compound verb *rasseoir,* meaning either to sit again, to calm, or to sit down again, is conjugated in the same manner.

EXERCISE.

When he arrived   at home, he (was quite exhausted).
      ind-4 with *être chez lui*   *n'en pouvoir* ind-2 *plus*
The minister had (so many) people at his *levée* that I
   ministre ind-2 *tant* *de monde à*   *audience*
could not speak to him. Are you afraid   that he will
ind-3   -   * 2 craigniez* 1   *pouvoir*
  not   accomplish that affair? I *know* that he is not your
sub-1   *venir à bout de*   *de*
friend, but I *know* likewise that he is a man of probity. Let
pl.   *aussi* ·   *   bien*
them *know* that their pardon depends on their submission.
           grâce *dépendre de*   *soumission*
I could wish   that he *knew* a little better his lessons. Let
   désirer cond-1 ·   *sub-2*
us see   if this new-fashioned   gown   *becomes* you, or
  voyons   *d'un goût nouveau* s *robe* f. 1
not. Be assured that   colours too gaudy will not *become* you.
non.   art. f.   · *voyant*
The head-dress which that lady wore   *became* her very ill.
  coiffure f. *que* ‹   ·   *porter* ind-2 ind-2 *lui*

These colours *become* you. so well, you (would do wrong)
     part. pres.   *avoir tort* cond–1
to wear any others. *Set* that child in this arm-chair, and
de en porter de   *asseoir* in.   *fauteuil* m.
take care lest he fall. I will *sit down* on the top of that
prenez garde que ne subj–1 *s'asseoir* *sommet* m.
hill,   whence I shall discover a prospect no less magnifi-
côteau m.   *découvrir scène* f. —
cent than diversified. We (were seated) on the banks
que   *varié* • *s'asseoir* ind–6 *bord* m. pl.
of the Thames, whence we (were contemplating) myriads
  Tamise f.   ind–2   *de* art. *millier*
of vessels, which bring, every year, the riches of the two
 vaisseau *apporter* art.   •
hemispheres.
—

Voir, *to see.*

Part. pres. voyant. *Part. past,* vu.
Ind. pres. vois, vois, voit, voyons, voyez, voient.
Imperf. voyois. *Pret.* vis. *Fut.* verrai. *Cond.* verrois.
Imper. vois, voie, voyons, voyez, voient.
Subj. pres. voie, voies, voie, voyions, voyiez, voient.
Imperf. visse.

 Revoir, to see again, and *entrevoir,* to have a glimpse
of, are conjugated in the same manner; but *prévoir,* to
foresee, has a difference in the future and the conditional,
where it makes *je prévoirai,* etc. *je prevoirois,* etc.

 Pourvoir, to provide, differs likewise in some things ; it
makes in the preterit definite, *je pourvus, tu pourvus,* etc.,
in the future, *je pourvoirai,* etc., in the conditional, *je
pourvoirois,* etc., and in the imperfect of the. subjunctive,
que je pourvusse, etc.

 Surseoir, to supersede, though a compound of *seoir,* is
conjugated like *voir,* except in the future and conditional,
where it makes *je surseoirai,* etc., *je surseoirais,* etc. ; its
participle past is *sursis.*

Valoir, *to be worth.*

Part. pres. valant. *Part. past,* valu.
Ind. pres. vaux, vaux, vaut, valons, valez, valent.
Imperf. valois. *Pret.* valus. *Fut.* vaudrai. *Cond.* vaudrois
Imper. vaux, vaille, valons, valez, vaillent.
Subj. pres. vaille, vailles, vaille, val-ions,—iez, vaillent.
Imperf. valusse.

N. B. Revaloir, to return like for like, and *équivaloir*, to be equivalent, are conjugated in the same manner ; but *prévaloir*, to prevail, makes in the present of the subjunctive *que je prévale, que tu prévales, qu'il prévale, que nous prévalions*, etc.

VOULOIR, *to be willing.*

Part. pres. voulant. *Part. past,* voulu.
Ind. pres. veux, veux, veut, voulons, voulez, veulent.
Imperf voulois. *Pret.* voulus.
Fut. voudrai. *Cond.* voudrois.
Subj. pres. veuill-e, —es, —e, voulions, vouliez, veuillent.
Imperf. voulusse.

N. B. This verb is sometimes employed in the imperative, *veuille, veuillons, veuillez,* but then its signification is different, particularly in the second person plural. It means, *have the intention, the goodness, the resolution.*

EXERCISE.

See the admirable order of the universe : does it not announce
— 2   m. 1.
a supreme architect ?   Has he *again seen* with pleasure his
— 2   artisan m. 1.
country and his friends ?   (Had he *had a glimpse of*) the dawn
pays   aurore
of this fine day ? To finish their affairs, it would be necessary
                     Pour   falloir
     for them to (*see one another*). I clearly *foresaw*, (from that
que * ils * s'entrevoir subj-2 bien   dès-lors
time), all the obstacles he would have to surmount. *Would* you
              —m.   surmonter ind-2
have   the judge (*put off*)   the execution of the sentence that
* que   surseoir subj.2   arrêt
he had pronounced ? I shall not *put off* the pursuit   of that
     rendu   poursuite f. pl.
affair. If men do not *provide* (for it), God will *provide* for
          art.   y
it. Would this book *be good* for nothing ? You have not paid
          valoir *
for this ground more than it *is worth ;* (are you afraid) that it *is*
*   terre f.   f.   craindre   que
not *worth* six hundred pounds ?   Let us take
   subj-1   livre f. pl. *sterling*   prenons de art.
arbitrators. One ounce of gold *is equivalent* to fifteen ounces of
arbitre   once f.

Q

silver. Doubt not that reason and truth will *prevail*
              art.   art.   * *ne* subj-1
at last.   I can and   *will* tell the truth. If you *are*
à la longue   pron.   *dire*   *le*
willing, he will *be willing* too. Let us *resolve* to resist our
     le   *aussi*   *vouloir* * *combattre*
passions, and we shall be sure to conquer them. (*Be so good as*)
                   de vaincre   *vouloir*
to lend me your grammar.
* *prêter*

IRREGULAR VERBS OF THE FOURTH CONJUGATION.

BRANCH 1. *Rendre.*

RÉSOUDRE, *to resolve.*

Part. pres. résolvant. *Part. past*, résolu *or* résous.
Ind. pres. résous, résous, résout, résolv-ons, —ez, —ent.
Imperf. résolvois. *Pret.* résolus.
Fut. résoudrai. *Cond.* résoudrois.
Imper. résous, résolve, résolv-ons, —ez, —ent.
Subj. pres. résolve. *Imperf.* résolusse.

N. B. This verb has two participles past, viz. *résolu*, when it means decided, and *résous*, when it means reduced *into*; in this last sense, it has no feminine.

Absoudre, to absolve, defective, is conjugated like *résoudre*; it has neither preterit definite in the indicative, nor imperfect in the subjunctive; its participle past is *absous*, for the masculine, and *absoute*, for the feminine.

Dissoudre, to dissolve, is conjugated like *absoudre*, has the same irregularities, and wants the same tenses.

COUDRE, *to sew.*

Part. pres. cousant. *Part. past*, cousu.
Ind. pres. couds, couds, coud, cousons, cousez, cousent.
Imperf. cousois. *Pret.* cousis. *Fut.* coudrai. *Cond.* coudrois.
Imper. couds. *Subj. pres.* couse. *Imperf.* cousisse.

N. B. *Découdre*, to unsew, and *recoudre*, to sew again, are conjugated in the same manner.

METTRE, *to put.*

Part. pres. mettant. *Part. past*, mis.
Ind. pres. mets, mets, met, mettons, mettez, mettent.
Imperf. mettois. *Pret.* mis. *Fut.* mettrai. *Cond.* mettrois.
Imper. mets. *Subj. pres.* mette. *Imperf.* misse.

N. B. Conjugate in the same manner *admettre*, to admit; *commettre*, to commit; *compromettre*, to compromise; *démettre*, to turn out, to put out of joint; *omet re*, to omit; *permettre*, to permit; *promettre*, to promise; *remettre*, to put again, to restore; *soumettre*, to subject; *transmettre*, to transmit; and *s'entremettre*, to intermeddle.

EXERCISE.

Wood which is burned *resolves* itself into
art. *bois* m. on * *brûler* ind-1 *se résoudre* * *en*
ashes and smoke. Have they *resolved* on peace or
cendre f. pr. *fumée* f. on * art. f. art.
war? The fog has *resolved* itself into rain. Could
f. *brouillard* m. se *résoudre* ind-4 * *pluie* f. *
that judge thus lightly absolve the guilty?
si légèrement cond. 1 *coupable* m. pl. art.
Strong waters *dissolve* metals. Those drugs (were
fart 2 f. pl. 1 art. on 1 *drogue* 3
dissolved) (before they were put) into that medicine. My
ind-4 2 *avant que de les mettre* *remède* m.
daughter *was sewing* all day yesterday. That piece is not well
ind-3 * *hier* m.
sewed; it must (*be sewed over again*). Unpick that lace,
la inf-1 *découdre* *dentelle* f.
and *sew* it *again* very carefully. Does he *set* a great
2 1 *avec beaucoup de soin* *mettre*
value upon riches? I never *admitted* those principles. Has
prix m. *à* art.
he *committed* that fault? If he would take my advice, he would
faute f. *me croyoit*
resign his charge in favour of his son. He
se démettre cond-1 *de* f. *en* =
put his arm (out of joint) yesterday. I will
se démettre ind-3 * art. *bras* m. *
omit nothing that depends on me to serve you. God
de ce *dépendre* ind-7 *de* *pour*
frequently *permits* the wicked to prosper. *Put*
souvent *que* *méchant* m. pl. * *prospérer* subj-1 *remettre*
this book in its place again. Under whatever form of govern-
à —f. * *quelque* *gouverne-*
ment you (may live), remember that your first duty
ment m. *que* *viviez* *devoir* m.
is to be obedient to the laws. It frequently happens that
de *soumis* *à* *arriver*
fathers *transmit* to their children both their vices and their
art. *

virtues.　He has long　　　*meddled*　　with　　public affairs;
　　　　　　　　long-temps s'entremettre de art.　2　　1
but his endeavours have not been crowned　with　　success.
　　　　effort　　　　　　　*couronner de* art. m.

MOUDRE, *to grind.*

Part. pres. moulant.　*Part. past,* moulu.
Ind. pres. mouds, mouds, moud, mou-lons, —ez, —ent.
Imperf. moulois.　*Pret.* moulus.　*Fut.* moudrai.
Cond. moudrois.
Imper. mouds, moule, moulons, moulez, moulent.
Subj. pres. moule.　*Imperf.* moulusse.

N. B. In the same manner are conjugated *émoudre,*
to grind (knives, razors, etc.), and *remoudre,* to grind
again.

PRENDRE, *to take.*

Part. pres. prenant.　*Part. past,* pris.
Ind. pres. prends, prends, prend, pren-ons, —ez, prennent.
Imperf. prenois.　*Pret.* pris.　*Fut.* prendrai.　*Cond.* prendrois.
Imper. prends, prenne, prenons, prenez, prennent.
Subj. pres. prenn-e, —es, —e, pren-ions, —iez, —nent.
Imperf. prisse.

N. B. Conjugate in the same manner *apprendre,* to
learn; *comprendre,* to comprehend, to understand; *déprendre,* to separate; *désapprendre,* to unlearn; *entre-
prendre,* to undertake; *se méprendre,* to mistake, to be
deceived; *reprendre,* to take again, to reply; and *sur-
prendre,* to surprise.

ROMPRE, *to break.*

Part. pres. rompant.　*Part. past,* rompu.
Ind. pres. romps, romps, rompt, romp-ons, —ez, —ent.
Imperf. rompois.　*Pret.* rompis.
Fut. romprai.　*Cond.* romprois.
Imper. romps, rompe, rompons, rompez, rompent.
Subj. pres. rompe.　*Imperf.* rompisse.

N. B. In the same manner are conjugated *corrompre,*
corrupt, and *interrompre,* to interrupt.

EXERCISE.

I *took*　great　　　pains; but, at last, I *ground* all the coffee.
　ind-3 *beaucoup de* sing.　　*enfin*　　　　　*café* m.
Grind those razors　with care.　Those knives　(are just)
　　　rasoir m.　　　　　　*couteau* m. *venir d'être*

ground. This grain is not sufficiently *ground*, it should be
       assez   *falloir* ind-1 *le*
ground again. I wish that you may *take* courage. What news
inf-1   *vouloir.*   *
have you *learnt?* Philosophy *comprehends* logic,
    f. pl. art.   art. *logique* f. art.
ethics, physics, and metaphysics. It is (with difficulty)
morale f. art. *physique* f. art. *métaphysique* f. *ce difficilement*
that he *divests himself* of his opinions. He has *forgotten* all
que *se déprendre*   *désapprendre*
that, he knew. I fear you will *undertake* a task above
ce que ind-2   *que*   *ne* subj-1 *tâche* f. *au dessus de*
your strength. Could he have been *mistaken* so grossly?   I
   f. pl.   *   cond-2 *grossièrement*
reproved him continually for his faults, but (to no purpose.)
reprendre ind-2 *sans cesse de* *défaut* *inutilement*
We *surprised* the enemy, and cut them in pieces. In the
 ind-3   pl.   *tailler* *en*   *d*
middle of the road the axletree of our carriage *broke.*
  chemin *essieu* m. *carrosse se rompre* art.
Bad company *corrupts* the minds of young people. Why do
  f. pl.   sing   *gens. Pourquoi*
you *interrupt* your brother, when you see him busy?
      quand   *occupé*

Suivre, *to follow.*

Part. pres. suivant. *Part. past,* suivi.
Ind. pres. suis, suis, suit, suivons, suivez, suivent.
Imperf. suivois. *Pret.* suivis. *Fut.* suivrai. *Cond.* suivrois.
Imper. suis, suive, suivons, suivez, suivent.
Subj. pres. suive. *Imperf.* suivisse.

N. B. S'ensuivre, to ensue, only used in the third person singular and plural of every tense; and *poursuivre,* to pursue; are conjugated in the same manner.

Vaincre, *to conquer, to vanquish.*

Part. pres. vainquant. *Part. past,* vaincu.
Ind. pres. vaincs,* vaincs,* vainc,* vainqu-ons,* —ez, —ent.
Imperf. vainquois. *Pret.* vainquis.
Fut. vaincrai. *Cond.* vaincrois.
Imper. vaincs,* vainque, vainqu-ons,* vainqu-ez, —ent.
Subj. pres. vainque. *Imperf.* vainquisse.

N. B. All the persons of this verb, marked with an asterisk, are very little used. Conjugate in the same manner *convaincre,* to convince; which is used in all its tenses and persons.

BATTRE, *to beat.*

Part. pres. battant. *Part. past,* battu.
Ind. pres. bats, bats, bat, battons, battez, battent.
Imperf. battois. *Pret.* battis. *Fut.* battrai. *Cond.* battrois.
Imper. bats. *Subj. pres.* batte. *Imperf.* battisse.

Conjugate in the same manner, *abattre,* to pull down;
combattre, to fight; *s'ébattre,* to rejoice (an old word,
almost out of use); and *rebattre,* to beat again, to repeat
tediously.

Être, to be, which has already been conjugated at
length.

VIVRE, *to live.*

Part. pres. vivant. *Part. past,* vécu.
Ind. pres. vis, vis, vit, vivons, vivez, vivent.
Imperf. vivois. *Pret.* vécus. *Fut.* vivrai. *Cond.* vivrois.
Imper. vis. *Subj. pres.* vive. *Imperf.* vécusse.

N. B. Conjugate in the same manner *revivre,* to revive;
and *survivre,* to survive.

EXERCISE.

(For a long while) we *followed* that method, which was
 long-temps 2   ind-3 1   f.   ind-2
only calculated to mislead us. What (*is the consequence?*) See
ne que propre   égarer   Que   s'ensuivre
the errors which have *sprung*   from that proposition,
        s'ensuivre ind-4 f. pl.   —f.
which appeared so true. We *pursued* our course, when some
        ind-2   suivre ind-2 chemin lorsque de   art.
cries   which came from the midst of the forest excited
cri m. pl. * sortis   fond m.   forêt f. porter ind-3
 terror into our souls. The Greeks *vanquished* the Persians
art. effroi m.   Grec   Perse
at Marathon, Salamis,   Platea, and Mycale. I have, at
à   pr. Salamine, pr. Platée   pr.
last, *convinced* him, by   such powerful reasons, of the
          de art. si fort 2 f. pl. 1
enormity of his fault, that I (have no doubt)   but he will
  =   faute f.   ne douter nullement que ne
repair   it. It is during   winter that they *thrash* the
réparer subj-1 C'est pendant art.   on battre
corn in cold   countries. The enemy was so completely
    froid 2 art. pays m. pl. 1   pl.   —ment
beaten in that engagement, that he was forced to abandon thirty
    rencontre f.   pl.   de

leagues of the country. The cannon *(beat down)* the tower.
lieue f.   pays   canon   abattre ind-3   tour f.
They were *fighting* with unexampled   fury,   when a
    *   ind-2   *un sans example* 2 *acharnement* m. 1
panic   terror made them take   flight, and dispersed them
panique 2 =f. 1 ind-3 *leur*   art. *fuite* f.
in an instant, *Beat* these mattrasses   again.   Happy those who
  —m.   *rebattre*   *matelas* m. pl. *
live in   solitude!   Long   *live*   that good king!
   art. *retraite* f. que 1 *long-temps* 4 subj-1 5   2
He did not long *survive* a person who was so dear to him.
   ind-3 d   f.   art.
Fathers *live again* in their children.   He was in a strange dejec-
                                                              accable-
tion of mind; the news which he has received has
ment   f. pl.   f. pl.   ont *fait*
revived him.
inf-1

BRANCH II. *Plaire.*

Braire, to bray, a verb defective, is only used in the
present of the infinitive; in the third persons of the present,
and the future of the indicative, *il brait, ils braient, il
braira, ils brairont;* and the present of the conditional,
il brairoit, ils brairoient. However it may be used with
propriety in the other persons, when a comparison with an
ass requires it.

FAIRE, *to do, to make.*

Part. pres. faisant. *Part. past,* fait.
Ind. pres. fais, fait, faisons, faites, font.
Imperf. faisois. *Pret.* fis. *Fut.* ferai. *Cond.* ferois.
Imper. fais, fasse, faisons, faites, fassent.
Subj. pres. fasse. *Imperf.* fisse.

N. B. In the same manner are conjugated *contrefaire,*
to counterfeit, to mimic; *défaire,* to undo; *refaire,* to do
again; *satisfaire,* to satisfy; *surfaire,* to exact, to ask too
much; and *redéfaire,* to undo again. These four verbs,
forfaire, to trespass; *malfaire,* to do ill; *méfaire,* to misdo;
and *parfaire,* to perfect; are only used in this form, and
the participle past, *forfait, malfait, méfait* and *parfait.*

TRAIRE, *to milk* (defective).

Part. pres. trayant. *Part. past,* trait.

Ind. pres. trais, trais, trait, trayons, trayez, traient.
Imperf. trayois. (*No pret.*) *Fut.* trairai. *Cond.* trairois.
Imper. trais, traye, trayons, trayez, traient.
Subj. pres. traye. (*No Imperf.*)

N.B. Conjugate in the same manner *attraire*, to allure;
abstraire, to abstract, used only in this form; the participle
past, the present and the future of the indicative, and the
present of the conditional; *distraire*, to divert from; *ex-
traire*, to extract; *rentraire*, to fine-draw; *retraire*, to
redeem; *soustraire*, to substract, to take from. All these
verbs are principally used in the compound tenses; though
some of them may be used in the simple tenses which
they have.

EXERCISE.

What will ' you have him *do?* Do not *make* (so much)
Que vouloir * que il subj-1 tant
noise. Do they never *exact?* That woman *mimicked*
de bruit ind-2
all the persons whom she had seen; that levity rendered
f. pl. que li ' Pl. légéreté f. ind-3.
her odious. It was with difficulty he (divested himself) of the
f. ind-3 peine que se défaire
false opinions which had been given him in his infancy. Could
—f. où * f. pl. lui f.
it be possible that we should not again make a journey to Paris,
subj-2 art. * voyage de
Rome, and Naples? He says that you have offended him,
pr. pr. dit offensé
and that, if you do not *satisfy* him quickly, he will find
promptement art.
means to satisfy himself. Every night she *milked*
moyen sing. de se lui-même tout art. soir m. pl. ind-2
her sheep, which gave her a great quantity of wholesome milk.
brebis pl. ind-2 lui sain 2 lait m. 1
Have you *milked* your goats? Are the cows *milked?*
chèvre f. pl. vache f. pl. art.
Salt is good to *entice* pigeons. You will never know
sel m pour attraire art. m. pl. connoître
the nature of bodies, if you *abstract* not their accessory
art. =2
qualities from those which are inherent (in them). The least
= f. 1 — leur moindre
thing (diverts his attention). Will you not *extract* that charming
le distraire

passage? Have you *darned* your gown? Should he not *redeem*
                rentraire
that land? What! would you have   me *screen*   those
        Quoi ind-1   * que je soustraire* sub-1
guilty   persons from the rigour   of the laws?
coupable m. pl.   * à*   *rigueur* f.

BRANCH III. *Paroître.*

NAÎTRE, *to be born.*

Part. pres. naissant. *Part. past,* né.
Ind. pres. nais, nais, naît, naissons, naissez, naissent.
Imperf. naissois. *Pret.* naquis. *Fut.* naîtrai. *Cond.* naîtrois.
Imper. nais. *Subj. pres.* naisse. *Imperf.* naquisse.

This verb is conjugated in its compound tenses with *être.*

Renaître, to be born again, is conjugated in the same
manner: but it has no participle past, and, consequently,
no compound tenses.

PAÎTRE, *to graze* (defective).

Part. pres. paissant. *Part. past,* pu.
Ind. pres. pais, pais, paît, paissons, paissez, paissent.
Imperf. paissois. (*No pret.*) *Fut.* paîtrai. *Cond.* paîtrois.
Imper. pais. *Subj. pres.* paisse. (*No Imperf.*)

N.B. Repaître, to feed, to bait, is conjugated in the
same manner, but it has all its tenses. It makes, in the
preterit definite of the indicative, *je repus,* etc.; and in
the imperfect of the subjunctive, *que je repusse,* etc.

EXERCISE.

Was not Virgil *born* at Mantua? It is from that poisoned
       ind-3 *Mantoue Ça*   *empoisonné* 2
source that have *arisen*   all the cruel wars that have desolated
f. 1 *que*   *naître* f. pl.   f. pl.   *désoler*
the universe. The fable says, that as soon as Hercules had
      f. *dit*   *aussitôt que Hercule* h m.
(cut off) one of the heads   of the hydra,   others
couper   *tête* f. pl.   *hydre* f. *d'autres* 2 il
sprang up.   While their united flocks
en renaître ind-2 1 *tandis que* *réuni* 2 *troupeau* m. pl. 1
fed   on the tender and flowery grass, they sung
paître ind-2 * 2 fleuri* 3 *herbe* f. 1 *chanter* ind-2
under the shade of a tree the sweets of a rural   life.
à *ombre*   *douceur* f. pl. *champêtre* 2 f. 1

Your horses have not *fed*   to-day;   you must have
          repaître d'aujourd'hui * il   * faire
them *fed*. That is a man who   *thirsts*   (after nothing)
   -inf-1 *ce*   *ne se repaître de* 2   *
but blood and   slaughter.
que 1   pr. *carnage* m.

BRANCH IV. *Réduire.*

Bruire, to roar, is defective, being only used in this
form; in the present, *bruyant*, which is oftener used as a
mere adjective, *des flots bruyans;* and in the third person
of the imperfect of the indicative, *il bruyoit, ils bruyoient.*
Luire, reluire, to shine, to glitter; are only irregular in the
participle past; *lui, relui,* these two verbs have neither the
preterit definite, nor the imperfect of the subjunctive, at
least in use.

Nuire, to hurt, has the same irregularity; its participle
past is *nui,* but it has all the tenses.

CONFIRE, *to pickle.*

Part. pres. confisant. *Part. past,* confit.
Ind. pres. conf-is,—is,—it,—isons,—isez,—isent.
Imperf. confisois. *Pret.* confis.
Fut. confirai. *Cond.* confirois.
Imper. confis. *Subj. pres.* confise. *Imperf.* confisse.

Its derivative *déconfire,* to discomfit, to rout, is now
almost obsolete.

Circoncire, to circumcise; and *suffire,* to suffice; are conjugated like *confire,* except in the participle past, where
they make *circoncis* and *suffi.*

EXERCISE.

The thunder   which *roared*   from afar,   an-
   tonnerre m.   *bruire* ind-2 *dans* art. *lointain* m.
nounced a dreadful storm.   They heard *roar* the waves
ind-2   *terrible* 2 *orage* m. 1 *on* ind-2 inf-1 *flot* m. pl.
of an agitated sea.   That street is too *noisy* for those who
   agité 2 *mer* f. 1   *rue*   *bruyant*
love retirement and study. I (have a glimpse of) some-
  art. *retraite* f. art.   *entrevoir* . *quelque*
thing that *shines* through those trees. A ray   of hope
chose   *au travers de*   *rayon* m.
shone upon us in the midst of the misfortunes which over-
ind-4 *   *à* *milieu*   *malheur* m. pl.   ac-
whelmed us. Every thing is well rubbed in that house: every
cabler ind-2   *frotté*

thing *shines,* even the floor. . Would he not have *hurt*
y reluire jusqu'à · plancher m. * cond-2
you in that affair? Jesus-Christ was *circumcised* eight days after

his birth. Will you *preserve* these peaches with sugar,
naissance f. * *confire* *à* art.*sucre* m.
with honey, or with brandy? Have you *pickled*
art. *miel* m. art.*eau-de-vie* f. *de* art.
cucumbers, · purslane, and sea-fennel? If
concombre m. pl. pr. art. *pourpier* m. pr. art. *perce-pierre* f.
he loses his lawsuit, all his property will not *suffice.*
procès m. *bien*

Dire, *to say.*

Part. pres. disant. *Part. past,* dit.
Ind. prés. dis, dis, dit, disons, dîtes, disent.
Imperf. disois. *Pret.* dis *Fut.* dirai. *Cond.* dirois.
Imper. dis, dise, disons, dites, disent.
Subj. pres. dise. *Imperf.* disse.

N.B. Conjugate *redire,* to say again, in the same
manner; also the other compounds of *dire,* viz. *dédire,* to
unsay; *contredire,* to contradict; *interdire,* to forbid;
médire, to slander; and *prédire,* to foretel; except that
the second person plural of the present of the indicative
and of the imperative is regular: *vous dédisez, contredisez,
interdisez, médisez, prédisez.* *Maudire,* to curse, varies
by taking two *s* in the following forms; *nous maudissons,
vous maudissez, ils maudissent; je maudissois; qu'il maudisse; maudissons, maudissez, qu'ils maudissent; que je
maudisse, que tu maudisses,* etc. *maudissant.*

Écrire, *to write.*

Part. pres. écrivant. *Part. past,* écrit.
Ind. pres. écris, écris, écrit, écriv-ons,— ez, —ent.
Imperf. écrivois. *Pret.* écrivis.
Fut. écrirai. *Cond.* écrirois.
Imper. écris. *Subj. pres.* écrive. *Imperf.* écrivisse.

N.B. Conjugate in the same manner *circonscrire,* to
circumscribe; *décrire,* to describe; *inscrire,* to inscribe; *pre-
scrire,* to prescribe; *proscrire,* to proscribe; *récrire,* to write
again; *souscrire,* to subscribe; *transcrire,* to transcribe.

Lire, *to read.*

Part. pres. lisant. *Part. past,* lu.

Ind. pres. lis, lit, lisons, lisez, lisent.
Imperf. lisois.   *Pret.* lus.   *Fut.* lirai.   *Cond.* lirois.
Imper. lis.   *Subj. pres.* lise.   *Imperf.* lusse.

N. B. Conjugate in the same manner *relire,* to read over again, and *élire,* to elect.

RIRE, *to laugh.*

Part. pres. riant.   *Part. past,* ri.
Ind. pres. ris, ris, rit, rions, riez, rient.
Imperf. riois.   *Pret.* ris.   *Fut.* rirai.   *Cond.* rirois.
Imp. ris.   *Subj. pres.* rie.   *Imperf.* risse.

N. B. Sourire, to smile, is conjugated in the same manner.

Frire, to fry, is defective, having only the present of the infinitive, and the participle past, *frit;* in the indicative, the three persons singular of the present tense, *je fris, tu fris, il frit;* all the persons of the future and the conditional, *je frirai, nous frirons, tu frirois, vous fririez,* etc.; and in the imperative, the second person singular, *fris:* to supply the place of the other forms, we make use of the verb *faire,* and the infinitive *frire;* as, *faisant frire, je faisois frire,* etc. this verb is used through all its compound tenses.

EXERCISE.

Always *speak*   truth, but with discretion. Never *contradict*
.   dire art. f.
(any one) in public. You thought   you were serving me in
personne en   *penser* ind-4   *   *   inf-1   *en*
speaking thus: well,   (let it be so);   you shall not be con-
parler ainsi eh bien   *'soit en*   *dé-*
tradicted. What! would you *forbid* him a communication
dire   *quoi!*   *   *interdire*   — f.
with his friends? That woman who *slandered*   every one,
                         ind-2 *de*
soon lost   all kind of respect.   You had *foretold* that
     ind-3   *espèce* f. *considération*
event. Let us *curse* no one;   let us remember that our law
           ne personne   *se rappeler*
forbids us to *curse* even those who persecute us. *Write* every
défendre * *de*   *persécuter*   *tout* art.
day the reflections which you make on the books which you
pl.
read. Did he not *read* that interesting history with (a great
                2   1

deal) of pleasure? God is an infinite being who is *circum-*

      2 '*être* m. 1 *ne*

scribed neither by time nor   place. Shall you not *de-*

 ni .   art. *ni* pr. art. *lieu* m. pl.

scribe in that episode the dreadful tempest which assailed your

    —m.   *horrible* 2 f. 1

hero? Have those soles and   whitings *fried.* If you wish

   faire 1 .   — pron. *merlan* 3 inf-1 2 *vouloir*

to form your taste, *read* over and over, unceasingly, the

*   relire*   * sans cesse*

ancients. He was *elected* by a great majority of voices. We

   ind-4   à   *majorité* f.

have *laughed* heartily and have resolved to (go on). He

   de bon cœur *nous* *résolu de continuer*

did not answer   him (any thing): but he *smiled* at him,

  répondre ind-3 *lui* *rien*   iud-3 * *lui*

as a sign of approbation, in the kindest manner.

en *   —   de   *gracieux* 2 *air* m. 1.

BOIRE, *to drink.*

Part. pres. buvant, *Part. past*, bu.

Ind. pres. bois, bois, boit, buvons, buvez, boivent.

Imperf. buvois. *Pret.* bus. *Fut.* boirai. *Cond.* boirois.

Imper. bois, boive, buvons, buvez, boivent.

Subj pres. boive, —es, —e, buv-ions, buviez, boivent.

Imperf. busse.

N. B. Conjugate in the same manner *reboire,* to drink again ; and *emboire,* to imbibe, to soak in. This last is a technical term, principally employed in painting.

Clorre, to close, becomes obsolete, except in the three persons singular of the present of the indicative, *je clos, tu clos, il clot ;* in the future, *je clorrai, tu clorras,* etc. and the conditional, *je clorrois, tu clorrois,* etc. and in the second person singular of the imperative, *clos.*

Déclorre, to unclose; *enclorre,* to enclose; and *for- clorre,* to debar, are defective in the same tenses as *clorre.* The two former have the same tenses as *clorre ;* but the third, which is a term of law, is seldom employed, except in the present of the infinitive and in the participle past.

R

Éclore, to be hatched, to blow like a flower, is defective; it has in the infinitive only the present, and the participle past, *éclos;* in the indicative the two third persons of the present, *il éclot, ils éclosent;* of the future, *il éclora, ils écloront;* and of the conditional, *il écloroit, ils écloroient;* and in the subjunctive the two third persons, *qu'il éclose, qu'ils éclosent:* the compound tenses which are much used are formed with *être.*

CONCLURE, *to conclude.*

Part. pres. concluant. *Part. past,* conclu.
Ind. pres. conclus, conclus, couclut, conclu-ons, —ez, —ent.
Imperf. concluois. *Pret.* conclus.
Fut. conclurai. *Cond.* conclurois.
Imper. conclus. *Subj. pres.* conclue. *Imperf.* conclusse.

N. B. *Exclure,* to exclude, is conjugated like *conclure,* except that the participle past is *exclu,* or *exclus.*

CROIRE, *to believe.*

Part. pres. croyant. *Part. past,* cru.
Ind. pres. crois, crois, croit, croyons, croyez, croient.
Imperf. croyois. *Pret.* crus. *Fut.* croirai. *Cond.* croirois.
Imper. crois, croie, croyons, croyez, croient.
Subj. pres. croie, croïes, croie, croyions, croyiez, croient.
Imperf. crusse.

Its derivative *accroire* is only used in the present of the infinitive with the verb *faire,* when it signifies *faire croire ce qui n'est pas,* to induce a belief of what is not.

EXERCISE.

Seated under the shade of   . palm-trees, they were *milking*
    Assis à   art. *palmier* pl.   *   ind-2
their goats   and   ewes,   and merrily   *drinking*
    chèvre f. pl.   prou. *brebis* f. pl.   *avec joie* 2   ind-2 1
that nectar, which (was renewed)   every day. Should they
    m.   *se renouveler* ind-2 *tout* art. pl.
not have *drunk* with   ice? This window does not *shut* well;
    cond-2 à art. f.   f.
when you have made some alterations (in it) it will *shut* better.
    ind-8.   *réparation* f. pl. *y* f.   *mieux.*

He had scarcely *closed* his   eyes, when the noise which they
    à peine ind-6 * art.,   *que*   *que   on*
made at his door awoke   him.   Have they not *enclosed*
ind-3 *à*   *réveiller* ind-3   *an*
the suburbs   within the city? Will you *enclose* your park
   faubourg m. pl.   *ville* f.   *parc*
with a wall,   or   a hedge? Put the eggs   of those silk-
de   mur m. pr. *haie* f.   *mettez   œuf* m! pl   *ver-*
worms   in the sun,   that they may *hatch*. Those flowers
à-soie m. pl. *à   soleil* m.   sub-1
just   *blown*, spread the sweetest fragrance. When did
nouvellement   répandre   doux   parfum m.
they *conclude* this treaty? His enemies managed so well, that
   ind-4   *traité* m.   *faire* ind-3
he was unanimously *excluded* from the company.   Did you
   ind-3 *unanimement*   *compagnie* f.
think   me capable of so black an act?   He possesses
croire ind-4   *noir* a   *trait* m. 1   *avoir*
some kind of knowledge, but (not so much as he thinks).
   savoir   *il s'en faire trop accroire.*

OBSERVATIONS

UPON THE FOLLOWING TABLES.

The following tables, which exhibit at one view all
the primitive tenses, both of the regular and irregular
verbs, and most of the defective, with references to the
pages, where the other tenses are to be found, will, it is
presumed, prove useful to those who will consult them.

34

TABLE OF THE PRIMITIVE TENSES OF THE FOUR REGULAR CONJUGATIONS.

INFIN.	PARTICIPLES.		INDICATIVE.		
PRESENT.	PRESENT.	PAST.	PRESENT.	PRET. DEF.	

FIRST CONJUGATION.

					Page
arler.	Parlant.	Parlé.	Je parle.	Je parlai.	117

SECOND CONJUGATION.

unir.	Punissant.	Puni.	Je punis.	Je punis.	126
entir.	Sentant.	Senti.	Je sens.	Je sentis.	126
lentir.	Mentant.	Menti.	Je mens.	Je mentis.	
e repentir.	Se repentant.	Repenti.	Je me repens.	Je me repentis.	142
artir.	Partant.	Parti.	Je pars.	Je partis.	
ortir.	Sortant.	Sorti.	Je sors.	Je sortis.	
lormir.	Dormant.	Dormi.	Je dors.	Je dormis.	
ervir.	Servant.	Servi.	Je sers.	Je servis.	
uvrir.	Ouvrant.	Ouvert.	J' ouvre.	J' ouvris.	126
ffrir.	Offrant.	Offert.	J' offre.	J' offris.	
ouffrir.	Souffrant.	Souffert.	Je souffre.	Je souffris.	
enir.	Tenant.	Tenu.	Je tiens.	Je tins.	126
enir.	Venant.	Venu.	Je viens.	Je vins.	

THIRD CONJUGATION.

lecevoir.	Recevant.	Reçu.	Je reçois.	Je reçus.	131
)evoir.	Devant.	Dû.	Je dois.	Je dus.	

FOURTH CONJUGATION.

lépandre.	Répandant.	Répandu	Je répands.	Je répandis.	
lendre.	Rendant.	Rendu.	Je rends.	Je rendis.	135
oudre.	Fondant.	Fondu.	Je fonds.	Je fondis.	
lépondre.	Répondant.	Répondu	Je réponds.	Je répondis.	
ondre.	Tondant.	Tondu.	Je tonds.	Je tondis.	
erdre.	Perdant.	Perdu.	Je perds.	Je perdis.	
lordre.	Mordant.	Mordu.	Je mords.	Je mordis.	
ordre.	Tordant.	Tordu.	Je tords.	Je tordis.	
laire.	Plaisant.	Plu.	Je plais.	Je plus.	135
aire.	Taisant.	Tu.	Je tais.	Je tus.	
aroître.	Paroissant.	Paru.	Je parois.	Je parus.	135
roître.	Croissant.	Cru.	Je crois.	Je crus.	
onnoître.	Connoissant.	Connu.	Je connois.	Je connus.	
lepaître.	Repaissant.	Repu.	Je repais.	Je repus.	
léduire.	Réduisant.	Réduit.	Je réduis.	Je réduisis.	135
nstruire.	Instruisant.	Instruit.	J' instruis.	J' instruisis.	
raindre.	Craignant.	Craint.	Je crains.	Je craignis.	
eindre.	Peignant.	Peint.	Je peins.	Je peignis.	
oindre.	Joignant.	Joint.	Je joins.	Je joignis.	135

PRIMITIVE TENSES OF THE IRREGULAR WITH SOME DEFECTIVE VERBS.

INFIN.	PARTICIPLES.		INDICATIVE.		
PRESENT.	PRESENT.	PAST.	PRESENT.	PRETER. DEF.	

FIRST CONJUGATION.

					Page
Aller.	Allant.	Allé.	Je vais.	J' allai.	155

SECOND CONJUGATION.

Fleurir.	Fleurissant. / Florissant.	Fleuri.	Je fleuris.	Je fleuris.	1
Haïr.	Haïssaut.	Haï.	Je hais.	Je haïs.	15
Gésir.*	Gisant.		Il gît.		15
Bouillir.	Bouillant.	Bouilli.	Je bous.	Je bouillis.	15
Ebouillir.		Ebouilli.			15
Courir.	Courant.	Couru.	Je cours.	Je courus.	15
Faillir.	Faillant.*	Failli.	Je faux.*	Je faillis.	15
Défaillir.		Défailli.	Nous défaillons.	Je défaillis.	15
Fuir.	Fuyant.	Fui.	Je fuis.	Je fuis.	15
Mourir.	Mourant.	Mort.	Je meurs.	Je mourus.	15
Acquérir.	Acquérant.	Acquis.	J' acquiers.	J' acquis.	16
Conquérir.	Conquérant.	Conquis.	Je conquiers.	Je conquis.	161
Ouïr.	Oyant.*	Ouï.		J' ouïs.	161
Vêtir.	Vêtant.	Vêtu.	Je vêts.	Je vêtis.	161
Revêtir.	Revêtant.	Revêtu.	Je revêts.	Je revêtis.	162
Cueillir.	Cueillant.	Cueilli	Je cueille.	Je cueillis.	162
Saillir.	Saillant.	Sailli.	Il saille.	Il saillit.	163
Tressaillir.	Tressaillant.	Tressailli.	Je tressaille.	Je tressaillis.	163

THIRD CONJUGATION.

Avoir.	Ayant.	Eu.	J' ai.	J' eus.	199
Ravoir.					164
Choir.		Chu.			164
Déchoir.		Déchu.	Je déchois.	Je déchus.	164
Échoir.	Échéant.	Échu.	Il échoit.	J' échus.	164
Falloir.		Fallu.	Il faut.	Il fallut.	15a
Mouvoir.	Mouvant.	Mu.	Je meus.	Je mus.	165
Promouvoir.		Promu.		Je promus.*	165
Pleuvoir.	Pleuvant.	Plu.	Il pleut.	Il plut.	165
Pouvoir.	Pouvant.	Pu.	Je puis.	Je pus.	166
Savoir.	Sachant.	Su.	Je sais.	Je sus.	166
Seoir.*	Seyant.		Il sied.		167
Seoir.*	Séant.	Sis.			167
Asseoir.	Asseyant.	Assis.	J' assieds.	J' assis.	16
Surseoir.		Sursis.	Je sursois.	Je sursis.	16
Voir.	Voyant.	Vu.	Je vois.	Je vis.	168
Prévoir.	Prévoyant.	Prévu.	Je prévois.	Je prévis.	168
Pourvoir.	Pourvoyant.	Pourvu.	Je pourvois.	Je pourvus.	168
Valoir.	Valant.	Valu.	Je vaux.	Je valus.	168
Vouloir.	Voulant.	Voulu.	Je veux.	Je voulus.	169

N. B. The forms marked with an asterisk are obsolete.

INFIN.	PARTICIPLES.		INDICATIVE.	
PRESENT.	PRESENT.	PAST.	PRESENT.	PRETERIT.

FOURTH CONJUGATION.

INFIN. PRESENT.	PART. PRESENT.	PART. PAST.	IND. PRESENT.	IND. PRETERIT.	
Résoudre.	Resolvant.	Résous, résolu.	Je résous.	Je résolus.	170
Absoudre.	Absolvant.	Absous.	J' absous.		170
Dissoudre.	Dissolvant.	Dissous.	Je dissous.		170
Coudre.	Cousant.	Cousu.	Je couds.	Je cousis.	170
Mettre.	Mettant.	Mis.	Je mets.	Je mis.	170
Moudre.	Moulant.	Moulu.	Je mouds.	Je moulus.	172
Prendre.	Prenant.	Pris.	Je prends.	Je pris.	172
Rompre.	Rompant.	Rompu.	Je romps.	Je rompis.	172
Suivre.	Suivant.	Suivi.	Je suis.	Je suivis.	173
S'ensuivre.	S'ensuivant.	Ensuivi.	Il s'ensuit.	Il s'ensuivit	173
Vaincre.	Vainquant.	Vaincu.	Je vaincs.*	Je vainquis.	173
Battre.	Battant.	Battu.	Je bats.	Je battis.	174
Etre.	Étant.	Eté.	Je suis.	Je fus.	134
Vivre.	Vivant.	Vécu.	Je vis.	Je vécus.	174
Braire.			Il brait.		175
Faire.	Faisant.	Fait.	Je fais.	Je fis.	175
Traire.	Trayant.	Trait.	Je trais.		175
Naître.	Naissant.	Né.	Je nais.	Je naquis.	177
Renaître.	Renaissant.		Je renais.	Je renaquis*	177
Paître.	Paissant.	Pu.	Je pais.		177
Bruire.	Bruyant.				178
Luire.	Luisant.	Lui.	Je luis.		178
Nuire.	Nuisant.	Nui.	Je nuis.	Je nuisis.	178
Confire.	Confisant.	Confit.	Je confis.	Je confis.	178
Suffire.	Suffisant.	Suffi.	Je suffis.	Je suffis.	178
Circoncire.	Circoncisant	Circoncis.	Je circoncis	Je circoncis	178
Dire.	Disant.	Dit.	Je dis.	Je dis.	178
Médire.	Médisant.	Médit.	Je médis.	Je médis.	178
Maudire.	Maudissant.	Maudit.	Je maudis.	Je maudis.	178
Ecrire.	Écrivant.	Ecrit.	J' écris.	J' écrivis.	178
Lire.	Lisant.	Lu.	Je lis.	Je lus.	178
Rire.	Riant.	Ri.	Je ris.	Je ris.	180
Frire.		Frit.	Je fris.		180
Boire.	Buvant.	Bu.	Je bois.	Je bus.	181
Clore, clorre		Clos.	Je clos.		181
Conclure.	Concluant.	Conclu.	Je conclus.	Je conclus.	182
Exclure.	Excluant.	Exclu, or exclus	J' exclus.	J' exclus.	182
Croire.	Croyant.	Cru.	Je crois.	Je crus.	182

N. B. The derivatives, which are not in this Table, will be found with the primitives, to which we have given references.

CHAP. VI.

OF THE PREPOSITIONS.

Prepositions, which are so called, from being *prefixed* to the nouns, which they govern, serve to connect words with one another, and to shew the relation between them. Thus, in this phrase, *le fruit de l'arbre*, the fruit of the tree, *de* expresses the relation between *fruit* and *arbre*. Likewise in this, *utile à l'homme*, useful to man ; *à* forms the relation between the noun *homme* and the adjective *utile*. *De* and *à* are *prepositions*, and the word, to which they are *prefixed*, is called their *regimen*.

There are different kinds of prepositions.

Some are used—to denote *place*, as ,

CHEZ. *Il est* chez *lui*, he is *at* home.

DANS. *Il se promène* dans *le jardin*, he is walking *in* the garden.

DEVANT. *Il est toujours* devant *mes yeux*, he is always *before* my eyes.

DERRIÈRE. *Il ne regarde jamais* derrière *lui*, he never looks *behind* him.

PARMI. *Que de fous* parmi *les hommes !* how many fools *among* men !

SOUS. *La taupe vit* sous *terre*, the mole lives *under* ground.

SUR. *Il a le chapeau* sur *la tête*, he has his hat *on* (his head).

VERS. *L'aimant se tourne* vers *le nord*, the loadstone points *towards* the north.

EXERCISE.

We find less   real happiness *in* an elevated condition than *in*
On   de 2 bonheur 1   2   f. 1
a middling state.   One is never truly   peaceful   but *at*
moyen 2   1   véritablement   tranquille que
home.   He walked *before* me to   serve me as a guide.
soi   marcher .   pour   de *
There was   a delightful grove   *behind* his house.   Among
ind-2   2   bosquet m. 1

(so many)   different nations, there is not one that has   not
  tant   *de*   2   1   *y en avoir*   subj-1
a religious worship.   Nature displays her riches with
  2   *culte* m. 1 art.   *déployer*
magnificence *under* the torrid   zone.   Eternal snows
               torride 3 f. 1 *de* art. 3 5   f. pl. 4
:   (are to be seen) *on* the summit of the Alps.   *Towards*
on 1 *voir* iud-1 2   *sommet*
the north,   nature presents a gloomy and wild   as-
      art.   *triste* 2   *sauvage* 3 as-
pect.
pect m. 1.

Some—to mark *order,*

AVANT. *La nouvelle est arrivée* avant *le courrier,* the news
is come *before* the courier.

APRÈS. *Il est trop vain pour marcher* après *les autres,* he
is too proud to walk *after* other people.

ENTRE. *Elle a son enfant* entre *les bras,* she holds her
child *in* (for *between*) her arms.

DEPUIS. Depuis *la création jusqu'à nous, from* the creation to the present time.

DÈS. Dès *son enfance, from* his infancy; dès *sa source,
from* its source.

Some—to denote *union,* as,

AVEC. *Il faut savoir* avec *qui on se lie,* we ought to know
with whom we associate.

EXERCISE.

We (were up)   *before*   day-light, (in order to) enjoy
  se lever iud-6   art.   *   *pour*
the magnificent spectacle of the rising sun. *After* such
de   *magnifique* 2 — m. 1   *levant* 2 1   *de si*
great faults,   it only remained   for us   to repair
    faute f. pl.   *ne rester* ind-2 * *que* *réparer*
them (as well as we could). *Between* those two mountains is
    de notre mieux
a deep   hollow road.   Many   very asto-
 profond 3 *et creux* 2 *chemin* m. 1 * *de* art. 2   4
nishing events (have taken place) within these ten years.
    3   *il se passer* ind-4 1 *depuis* *

From my earliest infancy I have had an abhorrence of
  art. *tendre*   * *horreur* art.
lying.
mensonge m.

DURANT. Durant *la guerre, during* the war; durant *l'été, during* the summer.

PENDANT. Pendant *l'hiver, in* winter; pendant *la paix, in* time of peace. This preposition denotes a duration more limited than *durant.*

OUTRE. Outre *des qualités aimables, il faut encore,* etc., *besides* amiable qualities, there ought still, etc.

SUIVANT. *Je me déciderai* suivant *les circonstances,* I shall determine *according* to circumstances.

SELON. *Le sage se conduit* selon *les maximes de la raison,* a wise man acts *according* to the dictates of reason.

EXERCISE.

With wit, politeness, and a little (readiness to
    de art. pr. art. *peu de prévenance*
oblige), one generally succeeds in the world. We are fit
    réussir   *on propre*
for meditation *during* winter. (*In the course of*) that siege
à art. f. *pendant siège* m.
the commandant of the city made some very successful
    ind-3 *de* art. *heureux* 2
sallies. *Besides* the exterior advantages of figure and
sortie f. pl. 1   2   1   art.
the graces of deportment, she possesses an excellent heart, a
    art. *maintien* m. *avoir* 2   1
correct judgment, and a sensible soul. Always act
sain 2 *jugement* 1   2   1   *se conduire*
according to the maxims which I have given you.
    *   f. pl. *inculquer* f. pl.

Some—to express *opposition,* as,

CONTRE. *Je plaide* contre *lui,* I plead *against* him.

MALGRÉ. *Il l'a fait* malgré *moi,* he has done it *in spite of* me.

NONOBSTANT. Nonobstant *ce qu'on lui a dit, notwithstanding* what has been said to him.

EXERCISE.

We cannot long act (*contrary to*) our own character;
    savoir cond-1 *agir* contre *
notwithstanding all the pains we take to disguise it, it
    que pour
shews itself, and betrays us on many occasions. In
se montrer *trahir* *en bien de* art. *

vain we dissemble;   *in spite of* ourselves, we a̓re known at
   *   *avoir beau faire*   *on nous connoît à*
last.
la longue

Some—to express *privation*, or *separation*, as,

SANS. *Des troupes* sans *chefs,* troops *without* commanders.
EXCEPTÉ. Excepté *quelques malheureux, except* some
  wretches.
HORS. *Tous est perdu* hors *l'honneur,* all is lost *save*
  honour.
HORMIS. *Tous sont entrés* hormis *mon frère,* they are all
  come in *except* my brother.

EXERCISES.

(*Had it not been for*) your care, I should have been   ig-
      sans   pl.   *un*
norant all my life.   All the philosophers of   antiquity,
                                       art.
except a few,   have held the world to be eternal.   All
    très-petit nombre   *croire*   * *
laid   down their   arms, *except* two regiments, who pre-
mettre bas   *   *art.
ferred (making their way) through   the enemy. Every thing
    se faire jour   *au travers de*   pl.
is absurd and ridiculous in that work, *except* a chapter or two.

Some—to denote the *end,* as,

ENVERS. *Il est charitable* envers *les pauvres,* he is charitable to the poor.
TOUCHANT. *Il a écrit* touchant *cette affaire,* he has written
  respecting that business.
POUR. *Il travaille* pour *le bien public,* he labours *for* the
  public good.

EXERCISE.

I have written to you *concerning* that business, in which I
                               à laquelle
take the most lively interest; and as I know   your benevo-
                 vif   *connoître*   *bienveil-*
lence *towards* the unfortunate; I (make not the least doubt)
lance f.   *malheureux*   *ne douter nullement*

that you (will carefully attend) (to it), (not so much) *for* the
   ne donner tous vos soins sub-1 *y* moins
satisfaction of obliging me, as *for* the pleasure of justifying
    inf-1   justifier inf-1
innocence, and confounding calumny.
art.   pr. *confondre* art. f.

Others—to mark the *cause* and means, as,

PAR. *Il l'a fléchi* par *ses prières,* he has softened him
by his prayers.

MOYENNANT. *Il réussira* moyennant *vos avis,* he will
succeed *by* means of your counsels.

ATTENDU. *Il ne peut partir* attendu *les vents contraires,*
he cannot sail *on account of* contrary winds.

EXERCISE.

Is there any man that has never been softened *by* tears
   aucun . sub-1   fléchir art.
or disarmed *by* submission? *Through* the precautions
ni désarmer art.
which we took, we avoided the rocks of that dangerous
que ind-3 ind-3 *écueil* m. pl. 2
coast. *Owing to* the bad state of my father's health, I shall
côte f. 1   2 1
not travel this year.
 voyager *année* f.

The use of the prepositions, —*à,* —*de,* —*en,* is very
extensive.

A is generally used to express several relations, as *destina-
tion, tendency, place, time, situation,* etc. being often
a substitute for various other prepositions; EX. desti-
nation -*to: aller* à *Londres,* to go *to* London.—Tendency -*to, toward: courir* à *sa perte,* to hasten *to* one's
ruin.—Aim -*to, for: aspirer* à *la gloire,* to aspire *to*
glory.—Residence -*at,* in: *être* à *Rome,* to be *at* Rome.
—Time -*at:* à *midi,* at twelve o'clock.—Concern -*on:*
à *ce sujet,* on this subject.—Manner -*with: supplier* à
mains jointes, to intreat earnestly.—Means -*with:
peindre* à *l'huile,* to paint *in,* or *with* oil; -*with: bas* à
trois fils, three thread-stockings, that is, *with* three

threads.—Situation -*at, with: être à 'son aise,* to be *at*
ease.—Purpose -*for: une table à manger,* a dining table.
—Suitableness -*for,* to : *homme à réussir,* a man likely
to succeed : —desert: *crime à ne pas pardonner,* a crime
not *to* be forgiven, etc.

Fathers! give   good counsels, and still   better
        de   encore 5 pr. *meilleur* 1
examples *to* your children. A good minister only aims
        2   *ne aspirer*
at the glory of serving his country well. When we were
que à   inf-1 2   pays 3   1   ind-2
in the country,   -   we devoted   the morning *to*
à   *campagne* f.   *consacrer* ind-2   *matinée* f.   art.
study, we walked   *at* noon, and *at* three or four
        se promener ind-2   *midi*
o'clock   we went *a*   hunting, or   fishing.   Michael
heure pl.   ind-2 art. *chasse* f.   pr. art. *pêche* f.   *Michel*
Angelo has painted (a great deal) *in* fresco.   It is a bed *with*
Ange   *beaucoup*   art. *fresque* f. *ce*   *lit* m.
ivory posts and   mahogany feet. That man, *with* his
colonne d'ivoire pr. *pied d'acajou*   * art.
gloomy looks   and   surly   behaviour,   seems
sombre 2 *regard* m. 1   pr. art. *brusque* 2 *maintien* m. 1 *ne semble*
fit   only   *to* serve as a scare-crow.
propre   que   de * *épouvantail.*

DE is generally used to express *separation, extraction,
possession, appurtenance, cause, shift, result,* etc. and
supplies the place of several prepositions, as—*from :*
je viens de *France,* I come *from* France; *d'un bout à
l'autre, from* one end to the other.—*Of: le palais* du
roi, the palace *of* the king; *les facultés* de *l'âme,* the
faculties *of* the soul; *un homme* d'*esprit,* a man *of* wit.
In a partitive sense—*of: moitié* de, *quart* de, etc. the
half of, the fourth of, etc.: it is used for PAR—*by : il
est aimé* de *tout le monde,* he is beloved *by* every body;
for *through,* or *by,* etc.: *mourir* de *faim,* de *soif,* to
die *of* hunger, *of* thirst:—*on, upon, with: vivre* de
fruits, to live *upon* fruit.—*On account of,* or *for; sauter*
de *joie,* to leap *for* joy.

EXERCISE.

I come *from* London, where I have speut a   week very
         où   *passé huit jours*
agreeably. *From* one end   of the horizon to the other, the
        bout m.   m.
sky   was covered *with* thick   black clouds.
ciel m.   *épais* 2 *et noir* 3 *nuage* m. pl. 1.
The marble *of* Paros is not fiuer than that which we get
                           qui nous vient
from Carrara. Montaigne, Mad. de Sévigné, and la Fontaine,
  Carrare
were   writers *of*   truly original genius. One half
ind-2 *de* art. *écrivain*   *un* 2   3   1   *moitié* f.
of the terrestrial globe   is covered *with* water, and above a
    terrestre 2 *globe* m. 1   *plus de*
(third part) *of* the rest is uninhabited, either through extreme
tiers m.   *inhabité*   *ou*   *par*   *un* 2
heat,   or through excessive cold.   In that happy
chaleur f. 1   *un* =2   *froid* m. 1
retreat, we lived *on* the milk *of* our flocks, and the delicious
asile m.   ind-2   *brebis*   pr.   2
fruits *of* our orchards.
  1   *verger* m. pl.

EN serves to mark the relations of time, place, situation, etc. and is variously expressed, as *c'étoit* en *hiver,* it was *during* winter; *être* en Angleterre, to be *in* England; *aller* en *Italie,* to go *into* Italy; *elle est* en *bonne santé,* she is *in* good health; *il vaut mieux être* en *paix qu'en guerre,* it is better to be *at* peace than *at* war; *il l'a fait* en *haine de lui,* he did it out of hatred to him, etc.

EXERCISE.

He had for   a (long while) lived   *in* France; the
  3   *   *depuis* 1 * *long-temps* 2 *vivre* ind-2
troubles which agitated that fine kingdom   obliged him to
            ind-4   *royaume* m. ind-4   *de*
retire   *to* Switzerland, whence he soon after (set off)
se retirer   *Suisse*   *d'où* 3 1   2 *se rendre* ind-4
for Italy. We were *at* peace, and   enjoyed   all
         ind-2   pron. *en goûter* ind-2   art.
its blessings, when   ambition rekindled   the flames of
* *charme* m.   art.   *rallumer* ind-3   *feu* s.
  war, and forced us *to* put   our frontier   *in* a state
art.   ind-3.   *de mettre*   *frontière* f. pl.   *

of defence. The savage is almost continually *at* war; he can-
presque toujours
not remain *at* rest. He has acted on this occasion, *like*
en repos   *dans*
a great man.
*

CHAPTER VII.

OF THE ADVERB.

The *Adverb* is a word which is united to verbs, adjectives, or even adverbs themselves, to express their manner
and circumstances.

REMARK. There are adjectives which are sometimes
used as adverbs. We say, *il chante juste*, he sings right;
elle chante faux, she sings out of tune; *ils ne voient pas
clair*, they do not see clear; *cette fleur sent bon*, this
flower has a good smell, etc. These adjectives, *juste*,
faux, *clair* and *bon*, are employed as adverbs.

Adverbs are of different kinds: the most numerous are
those which express manner.

These adverbs are formed from adjectives in the following manner.

RULE I. When the adjective ends, in the masculine,
with a vowel, the adverb is formed by adding *ment:* as
modeste-ment, modestly; *poli-ment*, politely; *ingenu-
ment*, ingenuously, etc.

EXCEPTIONS. 1st. *Impuni* makes *impunément*.

2dly. These six adverbs, *aveuglément*, blindly; *com-
modément*, commodiously; *conformément*, conformably;
énormément, enormously; *incommodément*, incommo-
diously; and *opiniâtrément*, obstinately; take before *ment*
an *é* close, instead of the *e* mute in the adjective.

3dly. *Follement*, foolishly; *mollement*, effeminately;
nouvellement, newly; and *bellement*, softly; are formed
from the adjectives *fol, mol, nouvel* and *bel;* and, consequently, according to the following rule.

RULE II. When the adjective ends with a consonant, in the masculine, the adverb is formed from the feminine termination, by adding *ment;* as *grand, grandement;* greatly; *franc, franchement,* frankly; *naïf, naïvement,* artlessly, etc.

EXCEPTION. 1st. *Gentil* makes *gentiment,* prettily.

2d. These eight adverbs, *communément,* commonly; *confusément,* confusedly; *diffusément,* diffusedly; *expressément,* expressly; *importunément,* importunately; *obscurément,* obscurely; *précisément,* precisely; and *profondément,* deeply; take the *é* close instead of the mute *e* in the feminine of the adjectives from which they are formed.

REMARK. The adverbs *incessamment,* presently; *notamment,* especially; *profusément,* lavishly; *sciemment,* knowingly; and *nuitamment,* by night; are not derived from adjectives.

3d. The adjectives ending in *ant* and *ent,* form their adverbs by changing *ant* into *amment,* and *ent* into *emment;* as *constant, const-amment,* constantly; *éloquent, éloqu-emment,* eloquently. *Lent* and *présent* are the only two of this class that follow the general rule.

REMARK. In general, adverbs denoting a manner, and a few of the other classes, have the three degrees of comparison. We say *profondément, aussi, plus* or *moins profondément, fort, bien,* or *très-profondément,* and *le plus profondément.*

Mal, bad; *bien,* well; *peu,* little; make in the comparative, *pis,* worse; *mieux,* better; *moins,* less; and in the superlative, *le pis,* or *le plus mal,* the worst; *le mieux,* the best; and *le moins,* the least.

EXERCISE.

Bourdaloue and Massillon have both   spoken very
       l'un et l'autre

eloquently on   evangelical   truths; but the former has *prin-*
    art. *évangélique* 2 1

cipally (proposed to himself) to convince the mind; the latter
    se proposer   *de convaincre*

has *generally* had in view to touch the heart. Several of la
      en vue de   art.

Bruyere's characters are as *finely*   drawn as they are *delicately*
   2   1   *finement tracé*   *   *
expressed. Buffon is one of the best writers of the last age :
                                  2 *siècle* m. 1
he thinks *deeply*, describes *forcibly*, and expresses himself (with
                  peindre fortement   *no-*
dignity). Corneille and Racine are the two best French tragic
blement   3   *tragi-*
     poets; the pieces of the former are *strongly*, but *incorrectly*
que 2 1   f.   2   3
written; those of the latter are more *regularly* beautiful, more
  1   *beau*
purely expressed, and more *delicately* conceived.
                                      pensé

There are likewise various other sorts of adverbs.

1st. Those denoting affirmation; as *certes*, certainly; *oui*, yes; *soit*, be it so; *volontiers*, willingly.

Doubt. *Peut-être*, perhaps.

Denial. *Non, ne, ne pas, ne point*, no, not.

EXERCISE.

Certainly, either I mistake, or the business passed
            ou   *se tromper*   *se passer* ind-4
(in that manner). Do you think that he listens *willingly* to
   ainsi   *écouter*
this proposition? Have you ever read in Racine the famous

scene of Phædra's   delirium? *Yes*, I have, and I own
      Phèdre 2 art. *délire* m. 1   *la*   *lue*   *avouer que*
it is one of the finest of the French theatre. *Perhaps* you will
ce   2   m. 1
discover, on a second perusal of la Fontaine's   fables,
        dans   *lecture* f.   2   art. 1   *de* art.
beauties which you have not perceived at   first. Will you
f. pl. *que*   *aperçues* à art.   f.
have some? *No*. Will you not have some?   The man who
   *   *en*
(is willing) to do   good is *not* stopped by any   obstacle. I will
vouloir * * art.   *arrêté*   *aucun*
pay him what I owe, but *not* all at   once.
   lui ce que lui   *non pas* à art. *fois* f.

2dly. Some denote order or rank: as *premièrement*, first; *secondement*, secondly, etc. *d'abord*, at first; *après, ensuite*, after, afterwards; *avant, auparavant*, before, etc.

3dly. Others denote place or distance: the former are *où*, where; *ici*, here; *là*, there; *deçà*, on this side: *delà*, on that side; *partout*, every where: the latter, *près*, near; *loin*, far ; *proche*, nigh, etc.

We ought   *first* to avoid   doing   evil; *afterwards* we
   * *falloir* ind-1   *   *de* inf-1 art.   *
ought to do   good.   Read   books of instruction *first*, and
     *   art.   1   art.   3   4   2
afterwards you may proceed to those of entertainment. If you
          *   *passer* ind-7   .   *agrément*
will   go,   settle *first*   what is   to be done. The
vouloir s'en aller régler auparavant   *falloir* * * inf-1
painter had (brought together) in the same picture several dif-
          rassembler   *un*   *tableau*
ferent objects: *here*, a troop of Bacchants; *there*, a troop of
   2   1   *Bacchante*
young people; *here*, a sacrifice; *there*, a disputation of philoso-
      gens   -   *dispute* f.
phers.   Sesostris carried his conquests *farther* than Alexander
           pousser   *conquête*   *ne*
did   *afterwards.*   Call   upon your cousin ; he lives *near here.*
ind-4   *depuis*   *Passer chez*   *loger* 2' *ici* 1
I cannot see that, if I be   not *near*   it.   When he knew
         ind-1   *auprès* *   *Quand savoir* ind-3
where he was,   he began   to fear the consequences of his
       iud-2   *commencer* ind-3   *suite*
imprudence.   Contemplate (*at a distance*)   lofty mountains,
           de loin   art. *haut*
if you wish   to behold   prospects ever varied and ever
   vouloir * *découvrir de* art. *site* m.
new.

4thly. There are some that denote time, either in a determinate or in an indeterminate manner. Those de-noting a determinate time are, for the present ; *maintenant*, now; *à présent*, at present; *actuellement*, this moment, etc. for the past: *hier*, yesterday; *avant hier*, the day before yesterday; *autrefois*, formerly, etc. and, for the future: *demain*, to-morrow; *après demain*, the day after to-morrow, etc. Those denoting an indeterminate time are, *souvent*, often; *d'ordinaire*, generally; *quelquefois*, sometimes ; *matin*, early ; *tôt*, soon; *tard*, late, etc.

s 3

EXERCISE.

I have finished the work you prescribed me ; what do
  achever   *que* *ordonner* ind-6 . *que*
you wish me to do *now? Formerly,* education was
 vouloir 1 *que je* ＊ subj-1 3 2
neglected ; it is *now* (very much) attended to ; it is (to be hoped)
    on ＊ 3 *beaucoup* 2 *s'occuper en* 1 *falloir* *espérer*
that new views will *soon* (be adopted). They grieved
 on 4 2 *adopter* ind-7 1 *de* 3 *on s'affliger* ind-2
(at it) *yesterday ; now,* they laugh (at it) ; *to-morrow,* it will no
en   *rire en*   *on*
longer (be thought) of. It is one of those accidents which
 plus   *penser* ind-7 *y*
it is *sometimes* impossible to avoid. The dew incommoded
        de   *serein* m. ind-4
me (very much); I shall not (*in future*) walk so *late.*
      désormais *se promener*
Rude and coarse criticism *generally* (does greater injury)
malhonnête 2 *grossier* 3 *un* f. 1   *nuire plus*
to the person who indulges himself in it, than to him who is
   se permettre ＊   *celle*
the object (of it).
  en

5thly. Some express quantity; as *peu*, little; *assez*,
enough; *trop*, too much; *beaucoup*, much, very much;
tant, so much, etc.

And, lastly, some express comparison; as *plus*, more;
moins, less; *aussi*, so; *autant*, as much, etc.

EXERCISE.

There are many people who have pretensions ; but very
 beaucoup de ＊ *à* ＊
few who have such as are well founded. To embellish a
 en subj-1 ＊ ＊ ＊ ＊ *de fondé* ＊ 2
subject *too much*, frequently betrays a want of judgment and
 5 1 *souvent* *être* *faute*
taste. One *very often* experiences disgust in the midst of
     trouver art. *à*
the most riotous pleasures. She is a giddy and thought-
 bruyant 2 1 *ce* *léger* 2 *inconsé-*
less woman, who speaks *much* and reflects *little.* She has
quent 3 1   *réfléchir*
so much goodness, that it is impossible not to love her.
 de   *de*

These stuffs are beautiful; *consequently*   are   dear. This
    étoffe f.   *aussi*   *elles coûter cher*
book has   merit; but there are others   *as* good.   If he has done
    du   * *de*
that, I can   do (*as much*).   What I say to you (about it) is
    en   *autant*   .   *en*
meant *less* to   give you   pain than to apprize you of the
         pour faire   *de* art.   *avertir*
language that is used.   She is   six years *younger* than her
   propos   *on tenir*   *avoir*   *de moins*
brother. Nobody   is *more* interested than you are   (in the
       ne   * *à ce que réussir*
success) of the affair.   You do not offer   *enough* for this garden;
subj-1 2 *   1   *offrir*   *de*
give something   *more.*   *The more* ignorant we   are, *the less* we
       de   *   1   4   *on* 2   3   *
(believe ourselves so).
  croire   *l'être*

CHAPTER VIII.

OF CONJUNCTIONS.

The conjunction is a word which serves to connect sentences. When we say, *Il pleure et rit en même temps,* he
cries and laughs at the same time, the word *et* unites the
first sentence *il pleure* with the second *il rit.* Likewise
when we say, *Pierre et Paul rient,* Peter and Paul laugh,
the word *et* unites these two sentences into one, *Pierre rit*
and *Paul rit.*

There are different kinds of conjunctions.

1st. To unite two words, under the same affirmat on, or
under the same negation, we use *et* for the affirmation, and
ni, neither, nor, for the negation.

2dly. To denote an alternative, or distinction between
objects, we use *ou*, either, or ; *soit que*, whether, or;
tantôt, sometimes, etc.

3dly. To restrict an idea; *sinon*, but, except; *quoique,*
ncore que, though, although; *à moins que*, unless, till.

EXERCISE.

Gold *and*   silver are   metals *less* useful than   iron. To
art.   art.   *de* art.   art.
listen with joy to a slanderer, *and* to applaud him, is to warm
         *   *médisant*   *   *lui ce* * *réchauffer*

the serpent who stings, that　　he may sting more effectually.　I
　　　　　　　　piquer afin que　　　　　　　*plus sûrement*
like *neither* flatterers *nor* the wicked.　Those who have never
　　　　flatteur　　　　　　pl.
suffered, know nothing; they know *neither*　good　nor
　　　　　savoir　　　　　*connoître*　art. *bien* pl.　art.
evil.　You may　　choose *either*　　a happy mediocrity, *or* a
mal pl.　　*avoir à choisir*　　*de*　　　　　　　f.　　　*de*
sphere more elevated, but exposed to many　　dangers.　He is
　f.　　　　　　　　　　　　*bien de* art.　　　　　*ce*
an　　　inconsistent　man; he is *sometimes* of one opinion and
　sans consistance 2　1　　　　　*tantôt*　　　　*avis*
sometimes of another.　I have (nothing more) to say to you,
　　　　　　　　　　　ne　　　*autre chose*
only that I will　have　it so.　I shall not yet　pass to the pe-
sinon que　*vouloir* *　　*　　　　　　　*encore*　　　　*lec-*
rusal of the authors of the second class,　*unless* you　advise
ture f.　　　　　　　　*ordre* m.　　　　　*ne conseiller*
　　　me to it.
subj-1　　*

4thly. To express the opposition of an object to another; *mais*, but ; *cependant*, yet, nevertheless; *néan-*
moins, for all that, however ; *pourtant*, howsoever, though;
toutefois, *bien que*, although.

5thly. To express a condition; *si*, if ; *sinon que*, except
that; *pourvu que*, save that; *à condition que*, upon the
condition that.

6thly. To express consent ; *à la vérité*, indeed ; *à la*
bonne heure, very well.

7thly. To explain something; *savoir*, *c'est-à-dire*, viz.
that is to say; *comme*, as.

EXERCISE.

The serpent bites; it is only　　a bite; *but* from this bite
　　　　　　　　　　　ce　ne que　morsure
the venom communicates itself to the whole body : the slanderer
　venin
speaks; it is but　a word, *but* this word resounds every where.
　　　ne que parole f.　　　　　　*retentir*
(That is) certainly a superb picture; *nevertheless*, there is some
　voilà　　　　　　　　*tableau*
incorrectness of design.　Although Homer, according to Ho-
incorrection pl.　*dessin.*
race, slumbers　　　　　(at times , he is, *nevertheless*, the first
　sommeiller sub-1　*quelquefois en　ne pas moins*

of all poets. You will succeed, *provided* you act
art.   *réussir pourvu que agir* subj-1
with vigour. We have within us two faculties seldom united,
          en
viz. imagination and judgment.
          art.

8thly. To express relation or party between two propositions; *comme,* as ; *ainsi,* thus, so ; *de même,* as, just as ;
ainsi que, as: *autant que,* as much as ; *si que,* so as, etc.

9thly. To express augmentation or diminution ; for
augmentation, *d'ailleurs,* besides, moreover; *outre que,*
besides that; *de plus, au surplus,* besides, furthermore ;
and for diminution, *au moins, du moins, pour le moins,*
at least.

10thly. To express the cause or the wherefore of a
thing ; *car,* for ; *comme,* as ; *parce que,* because ; *puisque,*
since; *pour,* that, in order that, etc.

EXERCISE.

The most beautiful flowers last but a moment : *thus* hu-
         durer ne que   art. 2
man life passes away. The (greatest part) of mankind have,
4   5   1   *   *plupart* f.   art. *homme* pl.   pl.
like plants, hidden qualities that chance discovers.
  art.   de art. *caché* 2 *propriété* f. 1 art. *hasard faire découvrir*
Mad. de Sévigné's letters are models of elegance, sim-
        2   art.   f. 1   *de* art.   pr.
plicity, and taste ; *besides,* they are replete with interesting
       pr.   *plein de*   2
anecdotes. Nothing is more entertaining than history; *besides*
f. 1   * *de amusant*   art.
nothing is more instructive. Circumstances show
    * *de*   art. *occasion* pl.   *faire*
us to others, and still *more* to ourselves. I shall
connoître   *encore*
always advise you to take the ancients as your guides; *at least,*
    conseiller de   *pour* *
quit but seldom the way which they have traced for
pr. *s'écarter de ne que*   *route* f. *que*   *tracer* *
you. We must, *at least,* know the general principles of a lan-
   * *falloir*   2   1   *lan-*
guage, before (we take upon ourselves) to teach it. Certain
gue f.   *de se mêler de*   * *enseigner*   f.

people hâte   grandeur, *because* it   lowers   and   *humiliates*
gens   art.   —f.   pron. *rabaisser*   pron.
them, and   makes them feel the privation of the advantages
    *   *que elle*   *leur*   *bien* pl.
which they love.

11thly. To draw a conclusion; *or*, now; *donc*, then;
par conséquent, consequently; *c'est pourquoi*, therefore.

12thly. To express some circumstance of order or
time; *quand, lorsque*, when; *pendant que, tandis que*, etc.
whilst, while; *tant que*, as long as; *depuis que*, ever since;
avant que, before; *dès que, aussitôt que, d'abord que*, as
soon as; *à peine*, hardly, scarcely; *après que*, after that;
enfin, in fine, finally, to conclude, etc.

13thly. To express the transition from one circumstance
to another; *car*, for; *en effet*, indeed, in effect; *au reste*,
besides, otherwise; *à propos*, now I think of it; *après
tout*, after all.

We ought   to love what is amiable; *now*   virtue is
    * *falloir* ind-1 *   art.
amiable; *therefore* we ought to love virtue.   We ought to
                       *   *   * *falloir* *
practise what the Gospel   commands us ; *now* it commands
                    évangile m.
us- not only to forgive   our enemies, but also   to love
    non   *de pardonner à*   *encore* *de*
them. Despréaux was extremely   particular   in not
                         de la plus grande exactitude   *à*
coming   late, *when* he was invited to dinner ; he said, that
inf-1 *trop*   ind-2   ind-2
all the faults of those who (are waited for) present themselves
    défaut   *se faire attendre*
to those who await   for them. The pride which possesses us,
        attendre *   posséder*
    visible as   it is, escapes our eyes, *while* it manifests itself
tout   *que*   *à*
to the eyes of the public, and displeases every   one.   *After*
                          choquer tout art. *esprit* pl.
we had examined that singular effect, we (enquired into) its
        ind-5   2   1   *rechercher* ind-3 *en* art.
causes. We had *hardly* done, when (he came in). Pride coun-
        ind-2   *finir   que   entrer*   *con-*

terbalances all our imperfections ; *for,* whether it hides them,
tre-peser   *misère*·pl.   *ou*   *cacher*
or whether it discovers them, it glories in knowing them.　None
　si   *se glorifier de* inf-1   *il 'n'y a*
but   an Englishman   can   (be a judge of) Shakespeare:
　que   *qui* subj-1   *juger*
for, what foreigner is sufficiently versed in the English language
　 langue f.
to   discover the sublime beauties of that author?
pour   2   1

The conjunction *que* serves to conduct the sense to its
completion. It is always placed between two ideas, both
necessary in order to complete the sense; *Il est très-im-
portant que tout le monde soit instruit,* it is of great importance that every body should be well instructed.
It differs from the relative pronoun *que,* inasmuch as it
can never be turned into *lequel, laquelle.* The conjunction *que* is generally repeated before every number of a
period.

EXERCISE.

(As long as I live), this image will be   before my eyes ;
    toute ma vie   —f   *peint*
and, if ever the gods permit me to reign, I shall not forget, after
               faire   *
so terrible an example, *that* a king is not worthy to govern
                                 (*pas* not expressed)
nor   happy in his power,   (*but* in proportion as) he
et n'est   *puissance* f.   *qu'autant que*
subjects it to   reason. I am very glad   to see that you do
soumettre   art.   *de*
not love flattery, and *that* one (runs no risk)   in speaking to
                    ne hasarder rien   *à*   inf-1
you with sincerity.

CHAPTER IX.

OF INTERJECTIONS.

Interjections are words, which serve to express the
sudden emotions of the soul. They have no fixed
place in speech, but show themselves accordingly as the
sentiment that produces them comes to manifest itself
externally. The only thing to be attended to, is not

to place them between words which custom has made
inseparable.   There are interjections for every feeling, viz.

Of		
	pain	ahi, aïe! ouf! ah!
	grief	hélas! mon Dieu, etc.
	fear	ha! hé!
	joy	ah! bon, bon! o!
	aversion	fi! fi donc! oh, oh!
	disgust	pouah, pouah!
	indignation	foin de
	imprecation	peste de, la peste de
	disbelief	chansons, tarare
	surprise	ouais;
	astonishment	oh! bon Dieu! miséricorde! peste!
	warning	gare! hem! holà! ho!
	checking	tout beau! holà.
	encouraging	alerte! allons! ça, courage!
	applauding	bravo, vivat!
	encoring	bis, bis.
	calling	hola! ho! hem, hem!
	derision	oh! eh! zest! oh! oh! oh!
	silence	chut! paix! st.

PART II.

THE SYNTAX,

OR

WORDS CONSIDERED IN THEIR CONSTRUCTION.

CHAP. I.

OF THE SUBSTANTIVE.

THERE are some substantives which are never used in the plural; such are—1. The names of metals, considered in their original state; as *l'or*, gold; *le platine*, platina. 2. The names of virtues and vices; as *la chasteté*, chastity; *l'ivrognerie*, drunkenness. 3. Some words of a physical or moral nature; as *l'ouie*, hearing; *l'odorat*, smelling; *le sang*, blood; *le sommeil*, sleep; *la pauvreté*, poverty. 4. The infinitive of verbs, and adjectives used substantively, together with some other words, which cannot be reduced to any particular class.

Others, on the contrary, which likewise cannot be reduced to any particular class, are never used in the singular; as *annales*, annals; *ancêtres*, ancestors; *mouchettes*, snuffers, etc.

II.

OF COMPOUND NOUNS.

Of the formation of their plural.

1. When a noun is compounded of a substantive and an adjective, they both take the sign of the plural; as *un gentilhomme*, a nobleman; *des gentilshommes*, noblemen.

2. When a noun is compounded of two substantives, united by a preposition, the first only takes the sign of the plural; as *un arc-en-ciel*, a rainbow; *des arcs-en-ciel*, rainbows.

T

3. When a noun is compounded of a preposition, or verb, and a substantive, the substantive alone is put in the plural; as *un entresol* (a low room between two floors), *des entresols; un garde-fou* (rails on bridges), *des garde-fous.*

REMARK. There is a small number of substantives composed of a verb and an adverb, as *un passe-partout*, a master or general key; or of a verb repeated, as *passe-passe*, slight of hand: they never take the sign of the plural.

EXERCISE.

Gold is the most pure, the most precious, the most ductile,
art.   *parfait*
and, after platina, the heaviest of all   metals. *Chastity* is an obli-
                    pesant   art.   *.
gation of all   times,   all   ages, and   all   conditions.
        art.   pr. art.   pr. art. *état* m. pl. art.
Intoxication, which proceeds from   beer, is of longer duration
ivresse   *venir*   art.   *   *
than that which proceeds from   wine.   It is the sense of
                            art.   *ce*   art.
feeling, which teaches   to guard   against the errors of
toucher   *apprendre* *se garantir de*   art.
sight.   *Sleep* is the image of   death.   Early
    art.   art.   *de bonne heure* a
learn   to distinguish *truth* from   *falsehood.*   That is
apprendre 1   —*guer* art. *vrai*   art. *faux*
more bitter than   *wormwood.*   Dignity of
    amer   .. *de* art. *absinthe* art. *élévation* art.
mind   was formerly   the (distinguishing mark of)
sentiment m. pl. ind-2   *ce qui* *   *distinguer* ind-2
noblemen.   One of the *buttresses*   of the vault has fallen.
art.   *arc-boutant* m. pl.   *tomber*
He is always making   (cock and bull stories). The Tartars
    *   *fait*   *de* art. *coq-à-l'âne* m.pl.   *Tartare*
always form the *scouts*   of an army. The *fish-*
        être   *avant-coureur* m. pl.   *chasse-*
carriers   did not arrive in time. This door is only
marée m. pl.   ind-3 *à*   *ne que*
fastened with a   latch, and all (the persons) in the house
fermer   *à* * art. *loquet* m. *   *ceux*   *de*
have each their *key.*
            passse-partout m.

CHAP II.

OF THE ARTICLE.

1. The difficulty attendant on rendering into French the *a*, or *an*, which precedes a substantive, when it follows the verb *to be*, will easily be removed by examining whether that substantive be restricted by a particular idea; if it be not restricted, the *a* or *an* is not expressed in French; thus, *I am a Frenchman, I am a Prince*, must be translated by *je suis François, je suis prince*. But if it be restricted, then the *a* or *an* must be expressed by the word *un* placed before the substantive, as *I am a Frenchman of an illustrious family, I am a very unfortunate prince*, must be translated by *je suis un François d'une illustre maison, je suis un prince très-malheureux*.

2. When the verb *être* is preceded by the demonstrative *ce*, in phrases of this kind, *un* is always required before the substantive, as *c'est un trésor*, etc.

3. The French do not use the article before substantives expressing the quality of a preceding noun; though, in cases of this kind, the English usually employ the article *the*, and still more frequently *a* or *an;* as *Télémaque, fils d'Ulysse, roi d'Itaque*, Telemachus, *the* son of Ulysses, king of Ithaca; *le Duc d'York, prince du sang*, the Duke of York, *a* prince of the blood.

EXERCISE.

I am *a* Frenchman and *a* merchant; after having (been, at)
         négociant   inf-1, *parcouru*.
the most famous (trading towns) in the Levant, my commercial
   =   *échelle* f. pl. *de*   — m. *les affaires*
concerns   have brought me here. I am *an* unhappy
de mon commerce   *conduire*
Frenchman who, a striking   example of the vicissitudes of
    * *mémorable* 2 1   —
    fortune, seek   an asylum' where I may end my
art.   *chercher*   *asile* m.   *puisse finir*

days in peace. He was *a* man of   uncommon probity and of
          Ce   *un rare* 2   f. 1
tried   virtue; (as a) reward   for the services   he
un éprouvé 2 1   *pour le récompenser de*   *que*
had rendered to the church and   state, the king has made
   m. pl.   *église*   pr. art.
him *a* bishop.   Neoptolemus had hardly told me, that *he* was
      évêque   *Néoptolème eut à peine dit*
a Greek, when I (cried out)   O! enchanting words,   after
      que   *s'écrier* ind-3   *doux*   *parole* f. pl.
so many   years of silence and unceasing   pain, O my
     de   *sans consolation* 2 pr. 1
son, what misfortune, what storm,   or rather what propi-
     malheur m.   *tempête* f.   *plutôt*   *favo-*
tious wind has brought you hither to   end my woes?   He
rable 2 1   *conduire*   *pour*   *mal* m. pl.
replied,   I am of the island of Scyros, I am returning
répondre ind-3   *île*   *retourner*
thither; (I am said)   (to be) *the* son of Achilles.
  y   *on dit*   *que* ind-1

Without entering more minutely into this subject, the following comparative table, in which the same words are exhibited according to circumstances, both with and without the article, in conjunction with the phrases which have been inserted at the end of this grammar, will, it is presumed, be considered as a sufficient illustration of custom.

COMPARATIVE TABLE.

WITH THE ARTICLE.	WITHOUT THE ARTICLE.
The writings of Cicero are full *of the soundest* 2 ideas. 1	The writings of Cicero are full of *sound* 2 ideas. 1
Divest yourself *of the preju-* *se défaire* *préjugé* *dices* of childhood.	Have no *prejudice* (with regard to) this question. *sur*
The different kinds *of animals* that are upon the earth.	There are different kinds *of animals* upon the earth.
He enters into a detail *of the rules* of a good grammar.	He enters into a long detail of *frivolous* 2 rules. 1
He affects *circumlocutions.* *chercher de détour*	He affects long 1 *circumlocutions* 2 in order to explain the simplest 2 things. 1

WITH THE ARTICLE.	WITHOUT THE ARTICLE.
He loads his memory with *the verses of* Virgil and the *phrases* of Cicero.	He loads his memory *with insipid* 3 *verses* 1 and *phrases.* 2
Essays supported by *strong* 2 *discours soutenu* *expressions.* 1	Essays supported *by lively* 1 *vive* *expressions.* 2
He has collected *precepts* of *recueillir sur* morality. *mœurs* pl.	A * collection *of precepts* in *recueil sur* morals.
Make use *of the tokens* we *se servir signe (dont)* agreed upon.* *être convenu.*	We are obliged to use *some ex terior* 2 *signs* 1, in order to make ourselves understood. *nous entendre*
The choice *of studies,* proper, etc.	He has made a choice of *books,* which are, etc.
Knowledge has always been *connoissance* pl. the object of *the esteem, the praise,* and *the admiration of éloge* pl. men.	It is an object of esteem, of ce praise, and admiration.
The riches of the mind can only (be acquired) by study. *ne que s'acquérir*	There is in Peru a prodi *le Pérou* gious abundance *of useless* 2 *riches* 1
The gifts *of fortune* are uncertain. *fragiles.*	Gifts *of fortune.* *bien*
The connexion *of proofs* *enchaînement preuve* makes them please and per- *qu'elles* suade.	There is in this book an admirable connexion of solid 2 proofs. 1
It is by meditation upon what we read, that we acquire *fresh* 2 *knowledge.* 1 *connoissance* pl.	It is by meditation that we acquire fresh 1 knowledge 2. *nouveau*
The advantages *of memory.*	There are different *kinds of memory.*
The memory *of facts* is the most showy. *brillant.*	He has only a memory of facts.
The aim *of good masters* should be to cultivate *the devoir* ind-1 *de*	He has an air of pedantry *ton* m. *maître*

WITH THE ARTICLE	WITHOUT THE ARTICLE.
mind and reason of their pupils.	that shocks you at first sight. *abord*
The taste of mankind is liable *homme* pl. to great changes.	Society of chosen a men 1.
He has no need of the lessons you wish to give him.	He has no need of lessons. *avoir besoin*
France, Spain, England, etc.	Kingdom of France, of Spain, of England, etc.
The Island of Japan.	Island of Candia.
He comes from China.	He comes from Poland.
He arrives from America.	He arrives from Italy.
The extent of Persia.	He is gone to Persia. *en*
He is returned from the East Indies, from Asia, etc.	He is returned from Spain, from Persia, etc.
He lives in Peru, in Japan, in *à* the Indies, in Jamaica, etc.	He lives in Italy, in France, in London, in Avignon, etc. *à* *à*
The politeness of France.	The fashions of France.
The circumference of England.	The horses of England.
The interest of Spain.	The wines of Spain.
The invention of printing is attributed to Germany.	The empire of Germany is divided into a great number of states.
He comes from French Flanders.	He comes from Flanders.

III.

1. The English make use of *a,* or *an,* before nouns of measure, weight and purchase; as *wheat is sold for a crown a bushel; butter sells for sixpence a pound; wine sold yesterday for forty crowns a hogshead, 'tis more than a groat a bottle.* But the French make use of the article *le, la;* as *le blé se vend un écu le boisseau; la beurre se vend six sous la livre; le vin se vendit hier quarante écus le muid, c'est plus de quatre sous la bouteille.*

2. When speaking of *time, a* or *an* is expressed in French by the preposition *par,* as *so much a week, tant par semaine.*

3. In English, *a* is sometimes put between the pronoun which expresses admiration and the substantive that accompanies it, as *what a beauty!* but, in French, the *un* is never expressed in similar cases, as *quelle beauté!*

4. In English, when the adverbs *more* and *less* are repeated to express a comparison, they must be preceded by the article, as the more *difficult a thing is,* the more *honourable it is.* But, in French, the article is omitted, as plus *une chose est difficile,* plus *elle est honorable.*

EXERCISE.

Corn   sells   for eight shillings *a* bushel.   Veal and
art. *blé* m. *se vendre* *   *schelling   boisseau* art. *veau*
    mutton cost   ten pence *a* pound.   This lace is sold   at
art.   *coûter   sou   livre* f.   f. *se vendre* *
half   a guinea *an* ell.   The best French   wines are sold at
demi 2 1   f.   *aune   de France* 2 1   ind-1
from twelve to fifteen shillings *a* bottle.   My father goes to
                    bouteille f.   *va en*
Ireland   four or five times *a* year.   He gives his son seven
Irlande   *fois   an*
shillings *a* day.   It (is necessary), if you desire to   (im-
            falloir   * *faire des*
prove fast),   that you take   a lesson three times *a* week.
progrès rapides   *preniez* *
The more I contemplate those precious remains   of   anti-
                    = *reste* m. pl.   art.
quity, *the* more I am struck with wonder.   What *a* beautiful
=   *frappé de   étonnement*
morning! come, let us go and walk   into the fields.
matinée f.   *se promener   champ* m. pl.

CHAP. III.

OF THE ADJECTIVE.

1. It has been said (p. 71), that an adjective *agrees* in gender and number with the substantive which it qualifies; from this rule, however, must be excepted *nu,* bare, and *demi,* half, when placed *before* a substantive, and *feu,* late, when *before* the article or a pronominal

adjective ; as *il va nu-pieds*, he goes barefoot; *je suis à vous dans une demi-heure*, I will be with you in half an hour; *feu la reine*, the late queen; *feu ma mère*, my late mother. But the agreement takes place, if *nu* and *demi* be placed *after* the substantive, and *feu* between the article or pronominal adjective and the substantive; as *il a les pieds nus*, his feet are bare ; *je suis à vous dans une heure et demie*, I will be with you in an hour and a half; *la feue reine, ma feue mère*.

2. An adjective frequently serves to qualify two or more substantives expressing either persons or things of different genders.

If it be used to qualify more than two substantives, it must agree with them ; for, either these substantives perform the office of subject, as *la grammaire, la logique, et la rhétorique, méthodiquement enseignées, ne s'oublient guère*, grammar, logic and rhetoric, when taught with method, are seldom forgotten; or they constitute the regimen, as *c'est un homme d'une valeur, d'une vertu et d'une fidélité éprouvées*, he is a man of tried courage, virtue and fidelity.

If it be used to qualify only two substantives, the substantives of persons must be distinguished from the substantives of things; with the first, the rules of agreement are to be observed in all cases: with the second, custom allows, when the substantives form the regimen, to make the adjective agree with the last only ; as *elle avoit les yeux et la bouche ouverte*. Nevertheless, modern grammarians prefer the agreement even in this case.

3. With respect to phrases like the following, *les langues Angloise et Françoise sont fort cultivées*, though they are in opposition to the rules of grammar, yet it is allowable to use them. However, in strict propriety it seems better to say, *la langue Françoise et l'Angloise sont très-cultivées*.

EXERCISE.

He ran   through the streets   like a madman, *bare*-foot and
ind-2   *   *rue* f. pl.

bare-headed. His   legs   were   *bare*. Give me
  tête   *il* * art. *jambe* f. 2   *avoir* 1
half a guinea, and then you (will only owe)   me a guinea
                    *   *ne devoir plus que*
and a *half*. I shall be at   home in   *half* an hour. Come
                    chez moi dans
before *half* past one.   The *late* queen was   idolized.   The
        2 *une heure et* 1   2   1   ind-2 *adoré* .
late queen was   universally regretted.   His impetuosity and
        ind-5
        courage, long *restrained*, soon surmounted all   obsta-
pron.   *enchaîné*   ind-3   art.
cles.   The imagination and   genius of Ariosto, although *ir-*
                    art.   *l'Arioste quoique*
regular in their course,   yet   interest, (hurry along,) and
                    marche néanmoins attacher entraîner
captivate the reader, who can never be tired of admiring them.
        lecteur   *se lasser*   inf-1
There are in Gessner's   idylls   sentiments and a
            2   art. *idylle* 1 *de* art.
grace altogether *affecting.*   The good taste of the Egyptians
        tout-à-fait touchant
(from that   time) made them   love   solidity and unadorned
        dès lors ind-3 *l. ur*   art.   =   *tout nu* 2
regularity.   In those climates, the *dry* and the *rainy*   mon-
    = 1   sec   *pluvieux mous-*
soons   divide   the year.
son f. pl. *se diviser*   *année.*

II.

DIFFERENCE OF CONSTRUCTION BETWEEN THE ENGLISH AND
FRENCH LANGUAGES.

1. In English, the substantive of *measure* is placed before the substantive or adjective expressing the dimensions, as *a tower two hundred feet high*, or *in height*.
In French, the word which expresses dimension is .
placed first, if it be an adjective, and the preposition
de is added to it as a regimen; as *une tour haute de
deux cents pieds*. But if it be a substantive, or an
adjective used substantively, it is placed after, with the
preposition *de* either before the noun of measure or
of dimension; as *une tour de deux cents pieds de haut*,
or *de hauteur*. This last mode is the most elegant.

2. The English manner of expressing *dimensions*, is

to use the verb *to be*; as *the walls of Algiers are twelve feet thick, and thirty feet high*. The French in general make use of the verb *avoir*, then there are two constructions; as *les murs d'Alger ont douze pieds d'épaisseur, et trente de hauteur*; or *les murs d'Alger ont douze pieds d'épaisseur sur trente de hauteur*. This second mode of expression is most generally adopted.

3. In comparative sentences, to express difference, the English sentence often runs thus; *she is taller than her sister by the whole head*. The French in this manner; *elle est plus grand que sa sœur de toute la tête*.

EXERCISE.

This box, which is six feet *long*, is very convenient. You
　coffre m. 　　　　　　　　　　　　　　　commode
will be stopped in your march by a river three hundred feet *broad*.
　arrêté　　　　　　　　　　　　　　　f.
This observatory, (which is twelve hundred) feet *high*, is very pro-
　＝　　　　　　　　　　　　　deux cents　 toises
per for knowing the true position of the stars. It is a terrace
　inf-1　　　　　　　　　　　　　　　astre m. pl. *ce*　terrace f.
(a hundred and eighty) feet　　　　*broad*, and (twelve hundred)
　trente　　　　　　　toise f. pl. *large*　　deux cents
feet *long*. The walls　of our garden are twenty feet *high*
　*　　　　　　mur m. pl.
and three *broad*. It is one of the finest stones that　　was
　　　　　　　　　　　　　　　　　　　　　　　on ait
ever　seen: it is twenty feet *long*　and six *thick*. This
jamais vues　　　　　　　longueur　　　　épaisseur
ditch　is nine feet six inches　　*deep*,　　and six feet
fossé m.　　　　　　　pouce m. pl. profondeur f.
broad. My son is taller than yours *by two inches*.

REGIMEN OF THE ADJECTIVE.

Several adjectives have a regimen; some require the preposition *de*, and others the preposition *à* before a noun, or a verb, which then is called the regimen or government of the adjective.

EXAMPLES.

Digne de *récompense*,	Worthy *of* reward.
Utile à *l'homme*,	Useful *to* man.
Digne de *régner*,	Worthy *of* reigning.
Content de *son sort*, de *vivre*, etc	Satisfied *with* his lot, *with* living.
Beau à *voir*, *bon* à *manger*,	Fine *to* the sight, good *for* eating.
Apre au *gain*, *avide* d'*honneur*,	Eager *after* gain, greedy *of* honour.
Propre à *la guerre*,	Fit *for* war.

Récompense is the government of the adjective *digne*, as it is joined to that adjective by the word *de: l'homme* is the government of the adjective *utile*, because it is joined to that adjective by the word *à*, and so of the rest.

EXERCISE.

Virtuous men are always worthy *of esteem.* A weak
art. *Vertueux* 2 1 *toujours estime* f. *foible* 2
mind is liable *to many* contradictions. A heart free from
1 m. *sujet bien des —*f. pl. *cœur* m. *libre de*
cares enjoys the greatest possible felicity. Voltaire was
soin m. pl. *jouit de* 1 → 3 = f. 2 — *fut*
always greedy *of praise,* and insatiable *of glory.* Rous-
avide louange f. pl. — = =
seau, endowed *with* a strong and fiery imagination, was
doué de fort 2 *bouillant* 3 —f. 1
all his (life-time) subject *to frequent* fits of misan-
vie f. *enclin à de — accès* m. pl. . =
thropy, and liable *to all the variations* attendant upon it.
*sujet — *f. pl. *qui en sont la suite.*

PROMISCUOUS EXERCISES ON THE ARTICLE AND THE ADJECTIVE.

THE FAULTS OF INFANCY.
défaut m. pl. art. *enfance.*

The amiable Louisa and her young brother Charles were
Louise — ind-2
gentle, humane, and sensible. To the most interesting
doux sensible spirituel intéressant 2 art.
person, Louisa joined all the modesty, the pleasing ingenu-
figure f. 1 ind-2 = f. *heureux ingé-*
ousness and artless graces of her sex ; and Charles, the
nuité f. *naïf* 2 art. —f. *sexe* m.

vivacity,   the fire,   · and the manly gracefulness   of
= f.   *feu* m.   *mâle agrément* m. pl.
his.   But these advantages,   the precious gifts
          avantage m. pl.   *   = 2   *don* m. pl.
of   nature, were   obscured by   great defects.
   art.   —f. ind-2 *un peu obscurci de*   *défaut* m. pl.
They were both   inclined to   idleness, and liable
     ind-2 *l'un et l'autre enclin*   art. *paresse* f.   *sujets*
to fits of sullenness and   ill humour when   they were con-
des accès bouderie f.   *de* *   *h* m. *lorsque*   contradicted.   Faults are   diseases   of the soul, the cure
tredit   art. *défaut des maladies*   *guéri-*
   (of which) is the work   of time.
son f. 2 *dont* 1   *ouvrage*   art. m.

   In good dispositions, it is generally   the fruit of the
     les âmes bien nées elle   *d'ordinaire*   —m.
development ·of   reason, and   the desire of pleasing.
développement m.   art.   *de*   m.   inf-1
Though their parents   were   persuaded (of this), they em-
Quoique   —   sub-2 2 —*dé* 3   *en* 1   employed,   to   hasten it, an expedient which   succeeded.
ployer ind-3 *pour hâter* 2 *la* 1   *moyen* m.   *leur réussir* ind-3
If they were satisfied with them,   contentment and
* 2 ind-2 1 *content de*   art. *satisfaction* f   art.
joy were painted in their countenances ; if   dissatis-
f.   *peint sur figure* f. pl.   * *en étoient-ils* mécon-
fied, they did not   scold,   but they received them
teñt   *   *les gronder* ind-2   ind-2
with a sorrowful air,   a dejected countenance, and every
      triste 2   *regard* 1   *abattu* 2 *maintien* 1   *tous*
sign   of   chagrin and   trouble. Louisa and
art. *signe* m. pl.   art. — m.   *de* art. *douleur*
Charles were naturally   kind and feeling ; they could not
        naturellement bon   *sensible*   *ne pouvoient*
long   support the idea of having afflicted such ten-
long-temps résister à   *idée* inf-1 *affligé des si*   *ten-*
der parents. They felt their error, burst into tears,
dre 2 — 1   ind-2   ·*faute* f. *fondre en larme* 1 pl.
and asked pardon. All was immediately forgotten, and
       — m.   2   3 *aussitôt* 1   *oublié*   art.
satisfaction   again   smiled around.   It was by this
contentement m. *renaître* ind-2 *autour d'eux*   *Ce fut*
means   that these amiable children soon   became
moyen sing. *que*   *bientôt* 2 *devenir* 1 *des*
models   of docility,   complaisance, and   application.
modèle m. pl.   =   *de*   —   *de*   —

CHAP. IV.

OF THE PRONOUNS.

§. I.

OF PERSONAL PRONOUNS.

Of the Place of Personal Pronouns.

There is no difficulty in placing personal pronouns, when they act as subjects : the person who speaks always names himself last, and the person addressed is generally named first.

EXAMPLES.

Vous et moi, nous irons à la campagne,	You and I will go into the country.
Nous irons ce soir à la promenade, vous, votre frère, et moi,	We will take a walk this evening, you, your brother, and I.

EXERCISE.

My sister and I   were walking by the last rays   of
    nous   *   ind-2   *à*   *rayons* m. pl.
the setting sun, and we were saying: what a sweet splendour
   couchant   *   *disions*   *éclat* m.
does it   still spread   over all   nature! In the long
*   2   *pas* 3   4   *ne répand* 1   art.
   winter evenings,   my father, my brothers and I   (used to
de 2   *soirée* f. pl. 1   *nous passer*
spend) two hours in the library   and   to read there,
ind-2   *bibliothèque* f.   *nous* * *lisions y*
(in order to unbend our minds) from the serious studies of the
   pour   *se délasser*   = 2   1
day, those amiable poets who interest most   the heart, by the
   2   1   *le plus*
charms of a lively imagination, and make us love   truth, by
     riant 2   1   art.   *en*
disguising   it under the mask   of an ingenious fiction. You
déguiser inf-3   *trait* m. pl.   = 2   f. 1

and your friend shall accompany me to the museum, and there
      —pagner   *musée* m.   *   *où*
we shall study nature in her three kingdoms.
                          règne m. pl.

RULE. The pronouns *il* and *ils* always represent a
substantive masculine, the former, if it be singular, the
latter, if it be plural; and *elle* and *elles*, on the contrary,
represent a substantive feminine, *elle*, if it be singular, *elles*,
if plural.

Thus, in speaking of the *rose;* say, *elle a un parfum exquis, aussi est-elle la fleur la plus recherchée,* it has an
exquisite fragrance, and is indeed the choicest of flowers;
because *rose* is feminine and singular; and in speaking
of several ladies, *elles ont autant de modestie que de beauté,
d'esprit et de grâce,* they have as much modesty as they have
beauty, wit, and accomplishments; because *dames* is feminine and plural.

EXERCISE.

(Look at) that magnificent building; it unites gracefulness
Regardez   *—fique bâtiment* m. *réunir* art. *grâce* f.
to   beauty, and   elegance to   simplicity. Ignorance
art. = f.   art. — f.   art. = f.   — f.
is jealous, presumptuous, and vain: *it* sees difficulties
    présomptueux   —   *ne de*   = f. pl.
in nothing, (is surprised) at nothing, and stops at nothing.
à rien ne s'étonner de   *ne s'arrêter à*
Let us gather these roses; Heavens! what a sweet fragrance
    cueillir   *Ciel quel* *   *parfum*
they exhale! Never judge from appearances; *they* are often
    —ler   *sur* art.
deceitful: the wise man examines them, and does not decide
    *   *   *se décider*
upon *them,* till he has had time to fix his judgment.
d'après f. *que lorsque*   art. m. *de fixer*

With respect to pronouns, when used as a regimen,
custom has established the following rules.

RULE I. The pronouns *me, te, se, leur, le, la, les, y,* and
en, are generally placed before verbs, as are *nous, vous,* and
lui, when without a preposition.

EXAMPLES.

Il me dit,	He tells me.
Je le vois,	I see him.
Je les écoute,	I listen to them.
Je lui parle,	I speak to him.
J'y songerai,	I will think of it.
J'en suis ravi,	I am delighted at it.

EXERCISE.

(As soon as) he had explained   to us the maxims of So-
   Dès que   *expliquer* ind-5 *   * *So-*
crates, he said : you see that it is not without reason   he
crate   ind-3   *ce*   *que on le*
(is looked upon) as   truly wise.   He was continually saying
   regarde   . *un vrai*   '   ind-2
to *me,* yet a little   patience, and you will disarm   even   envy
*   *de*   *désarmer* * art.
itself.   You have, no doubt, (some foundation) for reproaching
        être sans doute   *fondé à*   inf-1
him with his   faults ; but is there (any man) on   earth that
lui de * art. m. pl.   *quelqu'un*   art.   *qui*
is   exempt (*from them*)?   To please *her,* you must never
subj-1   *en*   *lui* *
flatter *her.*   To abandon *one self* to   metaphysical abstrac-
      *   . art. *métaphysique* 2
tions,   is to plunge into an unfathomable abyss.
   1   *ce*   * *se jeter*   *sans fond* 2   *abîme* m. 1.

RULE II. The pronouns *moi, toi, soi, nous, vous, lui, eux, elle* and *elles,* are placed after verbs, when they are preceded by a preposition.

EXAMPLES.

Cela dépend de moi,	That depends on me.
Je pense à toi,	I think of thee.
On s'occupe trop de soi,	We are too attentive to ourselves.
Que dites vous d'eux,	What do you say of them.

EXERCISE.

My father loved me so tenderly that he thought   of
     ind-2   *penser* ind-2
none but *me,* (was wholly taken up) with *me,* and saw none but *me*
ne que   *ne s'occuper* ind-2 *que de*   ind-2

in the universe. If you wish to obtain that favour, you must
                                                        *
                            de
speak to *him himself.* It depended on *you* to excel   your
                            ind-2   *de*   *de l'emporter sur*
rivals, but you   would   not. Philip, father of Alexander,
            le vouloir ind-4   *Philippe 2*
being advised.   to expel from his dominions a man, who
comme on conseilloit à 1 de chasser   *état* m. pl.
(had been speaking) ill of *him;* I shall take care not to do that,
   parler ind-6   .   *se garder bien*   *   *   * *en*
said he, he would go and slander *me* every where.
ind-3   *   *médire de*   .

RULE III. In imperative phrases, with affirmation, *moi,*
toi, nous, vous, lui, leur, eux, elle, elles, le, la, les, y and *en*
are placed after verbs; but, if with negation, *me, te, se,*
nous, vous, lui, leur, le, la, les, y and *en,* are placed before
verbs.

EXAMPLES.

Dites-moi ce qui en est,	Tell me how things stand.
Donnez-en,	Give some.
Songez-y,	Think of it.

But we say :

Ne me *dites pas ce qui en est,*	Do not tell me how things stand.
Ne m'en *donnez point,*	Do not give me any.
N'y *songez pas,*	Do not think of it.

REMARK. 1st. When the pronouns *me, te, moi, toi,* are
placed betwixt an imperative and an infinitive, we make
use of *me, te,* when the imperative is without a regimen
direct.

EXAMPLES.

Venez me parler,	Come and speak to me.
Va te faire coiffer,	Go and get thy hair dressed.

But we make use of *moi, toi,* if the imperative have a
regimen direct.

EXAMPLES.

Laissez-moi faire,	Let me do it.
Fais-toi coiffer,	Get thy hair dressed.

2dly. If *moi, toi,* be placed after the imperative, and

followed by the pronoun *en*, they are changed into *me, te.*

Donnez-m'en,	Give me some.
Retourne-t'en,	Go back.

3dly. When there are two imperatives joined together by the conjunctions *et, ou,* it is more elegant to place the second pronoun before the verb.

*Polissez-*le *sans cesse et* le *re- polissez,*	Polish and repolish it continually.
*Gardez-*les *ou* les *renvoyez.*	Keep them or send them back.

Listen to *me,* do not condemn *me,* without a hearing. ·· *Com-*
écouter *   * m'écouter se plain-*
plain, thou hast   just cause of complaint; however, do not
dre   un   sujet ·   plainte
complain too bitterly   of the justice of   mankind.   Give
*   amèrement   art. homme* pl.
some. Do not give *any.* Think (*of it*).· Do not think *of it.*
                                                          y
Repeat *to them* continually that, without honesty, one can never
succeed in the world. Do not repeat *to them* continually the
same things. Acknowledge *him* as   your master, and obey *him.*
                reconnoître ^   pour   *lui*
Tread upon that spider   and kill   it.
marcher   ·   araignée f.   *écraser*

RULE IV. When several pronouns accompany a verb, *me, te, se, nous, vous,* must be placed first; *le, la, les,* before *lui, leur;* and *y* before *en,* which is always the last.

Prêtez-moi ce livre; je vous le *rendrai demain; si vous* me le *refusez, je saurai* m'en *passer.*	Lend me that book; I will return it you to-morrow; if you refuse me, I can make shift without it
Aurez-vous la force de le leur *dire?*	Will you have resolution enough to tell them it?
Il n'a pas voulu vous y *mener,*	He would not take you there.
Je vous y en *porterai,*	I will bring you some there,

EXCEPTION. In an imperative sentence, with affirmation, *le, la, les,* are always placed first, as *donnez–le–moi,* give it me; *offrez–la–lui,* offer it to him; *conduisez–les–y,* conduct them thither: and *moi* is placed after *y,* as *menez–y–moi,* carry me thither; but we say *menez–nous–y,* carry us thither.

EXERCISE.

You wish   to make a present to your sister. (There is) a
   vouloir *   *Voilà*
beautiful fan,   you should   present *her* with *it.* How
   éventail m.   *devoir* cond–1 *offrir* *lui* *   *Que*
many people are there without merit and without occupation,
   de gens * *
(who would be mere nothings) in   society,   did not   gaining
   ne tenir à rien cond–1   art.   *si* *   art. *jeu* m.
introduce   *them* (*into it*). I shall speak *to them* (*about it*)
introduire ind–2   *y*   *en*
and give   *you* a faithful account   *of it.* It is certain that
   je rendre ind–7   *exact* a *compte* m. 1
    old Géronte has refused his daughter to Valère; but because
art.
he does not give *her to him,* it does not follow   that he will
                      s'ensuivre
give *her to you.*

REMARK. The expression *même* is sometimes placed after the personal pronouns, *moi, toi, soi, nous, vous, eux, lui, elle, elles,* to mark more particularly the person or thing spoken of.

EXAMPLES.

Ils se sont perdus eux–mêmes,	They have ruined themselves.
Le monde estime bien des choses qui, en elles–mêmes, sont fort méprisables;	The world prizes many things which, in themselves, are worthless.

§ II.

OF THE RELATIVE PRONOUNS.

We have seen that the relative pronouns are *qui, que, dont, lequel, quoi.*

RULE I. *Qui,* when a relative, is always of the number, gender and person of its antecedents.

Moi qui suis son fils,	I who am his son.
Toi qui es si jeune,	Thou who art so young.
L'enfant qui joue,	The child who plays.
Nous qui étudions,	We who study.
Vous qui riez,	You who laugh.
Les livres qui instruisent,	The books which instruct.

In the first example, *qui* is singular, and of the first person, because the pronoun *moi* is in the singular, and of the first person. In the second it is singular, and of the second person, for the same reason; and it is farther masculine or feminine, according to the sex of the person addressed.

I who did not suspect   (so much) falsehood, cunning,
    *   *soupçonner* ind-2 *tant de fausseté* f. pr. *ruse* f.
and   perfidy, in a man whom I loved, blindly   followed
    pr. = f.   ind-2 *aveuglément* 3 *je suiv re* ind-2
his counsels. Thou *who* art   candour and   innocence itself,
    conseil m.   art.   =   art. — f.   *même*
trust not too lightly.   The great empire of the Egyptians,
te confie   légèrement   —m.   —tien
which was (as it were) detached from all   others, was not of
            comme   détaché   art.
long duration. We *who* know   the value of   time,
    durée f.   *connoître*   *pris* m. art.   *nous,*
ought   to make a good use   (of it), instead of wasting it in
devoir ind-1 *   *emploi* m. *au lieu   perdre   dans*
    idleness and   frivolity. What! is it you, my daughter, *who*
art. *oisiveté* f. art. *inutilité* f. *Quoi   ce*
(would wish) that I (should love) you less? The greatest men,
vouloir con-1 *que*   subj-2
who were the ornament and   glory of   Greece, Homer, Py-
    ind-4   *ornement* art. = f. art. *Grèce* f. *Homère,*
thagoras, Plato, even Lycurgus and Solon, went   to learn
— *gore, Platon, même* —*gue*   —   ind-3 * *apprendre*
    wisdom in Egypt.
art. *sagesse* f. *en Égypte.*

RULE II. *Que,* when a relative, is of the number and gender of its antecedent.

C'est moi que l'on demande,	It is I whom they ask for.
C'est toi qu'on appelle,	It is thou whom they call.
La femme que je vois si bien parée,	The woman whom I see so well dressed.
C'est nous que vous offensez,	It is we whom you offend.
C'est vous que je cherche,	It is you I am seeking.
Les dames que vous voyez,	The ladies whom you see.

I *whom* temptatiou surrounded on every side fell
    art. *séduction* f. *environner* ind-2 *de tout part* f. pl. *je tombai*
iuto the snare. It is thou *whom* the public voice calls to that
dans piége m. *Ce*   2 f. r *appeler*
employ. A power which terror aud force have
place f.   *puissance* f.   art. = f.   art. — f.
founded, cannot be of long duration. It is we *whom* they per-
fondé f.   *ne peut*   *durée* f.   *l'on pour-*
secute with unexampled rage. You *whom* every body
suivre avec une sans exemple 2 *fureur* f. 1   *tout le monde*
respects, hasten to (show yourself). (Every thing) in the
respecter se hater de   *paroître*   *Tout*   *dans*
universe alters and perishes; but the writings *which*
univers m. *s'altérer*   *périr*   *écrit* m. pl.   art.
genius has dictated, shall be immortal.
génie m. *dicté* pl.   —*tel*

Dont represents occasionally *de qui, duquel, de laquelle, desquels, desquelles,* and even *de quoi.*

L'homme dont vous parlez est parti,	The man of whom you are speaking is gone.
La tour dont nous apercevons les créneaux doit être très-élevée,	The tower whose battlements we perceive must be very high.
Ce dont je vous ai parlé l'autre jour n'a pas réussi,	What I was speaking to you of the other day did not succeed.

OBSERVE 1st, That *qui, que* and *dont* may equally apply to persons and things; but *qui* can never apply to things when it ought to be preceded by a preposition: in this case we must make use of *lequel, duquel, auquel,* etc.

2dly. *Lequel, laquelle,* apply both to persons and things.
3dly. *Quoi* applies only to things.
There is likewise an adverb which is employed as a relative pronoun; it is *où.* On this occasion, it is of both genders and both numbers, and signifies *dans lequel, auquel, dans laquelle,* etc.

EXAMPLES.

Voilà le but où il tend,	That is the object he has in view.
Ce sont des affaires où je suis embarrassé,	Those are affairs with which I am perplexed.

REMARK. *Où* is united with the preposition *de* and *par.*

EXAMPLES.

Voilà une chose d'où dépend le bonheur public,	That is an affair on which the public happiness depends.
Tels sont les lieux par où il a passé,	These are the places through which he passed.

EXERCISE.

Persons   of a middle   condition have not the   same
art. *personne* f. pl.   *commun* 2   — f. 1   *même*
need   of being cautioned   against the dangers *to which*
besoin m.   inf-1 *précautionné* f. pl. *contre*   *écueil* m. pl.
   elevation and   authority   expose those who are destined
art. — f.   art. *autorité* f. *exposer ceux*   *destiné* m. pl.
to govern   mankind. The protection on *which* he relied
 gouverner art. *homme* pl.   — f. *sur*   *compter*
   has been too weak. That after *which* a true philosopher
ind-2   *foible ce après*   *vrai* —*phe* m.
sighs   most ardently, is to spread   that sentiment of uni-
soupirer art.   *ardemment*   *de répandre*   — m.
versal benevolence   which should unite and (bring together)
— *sel* 2 *bienveillance* f. 1   *devroit unir*   *rapprocher*
all   men. These are   conditions without *which* the thing
    art.   *Ce sont des*   *sans*   f.
would not have been concluded.   Nature, of *whose*   secrets
       fait f.   art. — f.   *   1 art. —m.
   we (are ignorant), will be always a source of conjecture
pl. 4 2   *ignorer* 3   —f. 3   —f. pl. 4
to   mankind. That *of which* we complain   the most
pour 1 art. *homme* 2   *Ce*   *se plaindre*

bitterly is not always what affects us the most. The only
amèrement   *ce qui affecter*   *seul*
moments *in which* his soul still opens ✦ to pleasure
— m. pl.   *encore* 2 *s'ouvrir* 1 art.
are those which he devotes to study. The mountains *from*
ceux   *consacrer* art. *étude* f.   f. pl..
whence   gold (is extracted) are not in general fruitful.
  on 1 art. *or* 3 *tire* 2   * *en* — *infertile* pl.
The different countries through *which* he has passed have
   — *pays* m. pl. *par*   *passé*
furnished his pencil with , romantic and picturesque
fourni *à* *pinceau* m. *de* art. —*tique* 2 *pittoresque* 3
scenes.
 — 1.

---

§ III.

OF PRONOUNS ABSOLUTE.

We have seen that the pronouns absolute are, *qui, que, quoi, quel, lequel.*

Qui signifies *quel homme,* what man ; *quelle personne,* what person.

EXAMPLES.

Qui vous a dit cela?	Who told you that?
J'ignore qui a fait cela,	I don't know who did that.

Que signifies *quelle chose,* what thing.

EXAMPLES.

Que dit-on?	What do they say?
Je ne sais qu'en penser,	I don't know what to think of it.

Quoi has the signification of *que.*

EXAMPLES.

À quoi s'occupe-t-on?	What are they engaged in?
Dites-moi en quoi je puis vous servir,	Tell me how I can serve you.

REMARK. If *que* or *quoi* be followed by an adjective, the preposition *de* is placed before that adjective.

EXAMPLES.

Que dit-on de nouveau?	What news is there?
Quoi de plus instructif et de plus amusant?	What is more instructive and amusing?

EXERCISE.

Who will not agree that life has few real pleasures and
        convenir   art. f.   *peu de vrai*
many dreadful pains? (Some one) entered secretly;
beaucoup de affreux 2 peine f. pl. 1   *On*   *entra secrètement*
guess *who* it was. *What* have you read in that book
deviner   *   *   m.
that can have excited in your soul emotion and enthu-
qui puisse porté   art. — f.   art. *enthou-*
siasm? I know not *what* to think (of it). In *what* did you
siasme m. *savoir*   *   *A avez*
find them occupied? There is in that discourse I know not
trouvés occupé m. pl.   *discours* m. *savoir*
what which appears to me designing. *What* have you remarked
     sembler * *insidieux*   *remarqué*
good, beautiful and sublime in Homer? *What* more
pr.   pr.   pr.   pr.
brillant, and, at the same time, more false, than the expressions
brillant en * *même* pr.   —
of a man, who has (a great deal) of wit, but wants
         beaucoup esprit qui manque de
judgment?
jugement?

In interrogations, and after a verb, *quel* is used to ask
the name or qualities of a person or thing.

EXAMPLES.

Quel homme est-ce?	What man is it?
Quel temps fait-il?	What weather is it?
Je ne sais quel homme c'est,	I don't know what man it is.
Il sait quel parti prendre,	He knows what steps to pursue.

We have already seen, that the adverb *où* is employed
as a relative pronoun; it is likewise used as a kind of
absolute pronoun.

Où represents *en quel endroit*, in what place, or *à quoi*,
to what.

EXAMPLES.

Où allez vous?	Where are you going?
Où cela nous menera-t-il?	Where will that take us?
J'ignore où l'on me conduit,	I don't know where they are taking me.
Il n'a pas prévu où cette conduite le meneroit,	He did not foresee where such a conduct would lead him.

REMARK I. When *où* is joined to the preposition *de*, it marks the place or cause, according to circumstances of which you are speaking.

EXAMPLES.

D'où vient-il?	Where does he come from?
D'où sa haine procède-t-elle?	From whence proceeds his hatred.
Voilà d'où il vient,	It was there he came from.
Le mal me vient d'où j'attendois mon remède,	The evil proceeds from that quarter whence I had expected a remedy.

REMARK II. When *où* is preceded by the preposition *par*, it marks the place or means, according to the different circumstances of which you are speaking.

EXAMPLES.

Par où avez vous passé?	Which way did you come?
Par où me tirerai-je d'affaire?	Which way shall I extricate myself?
Voilà par où j'ai passé,	That is the way I came.
Je ne sais par où je me tirerai d'affaire,	I don't know which way I shall extricate myself.

EXERCISE.

What grace, *what* delicacy, *what* harmony, *what* colour-
    grâce f.   délicatesse f.   = f.   colo-
ing, *what* beautiful lines   in Racine! *What* then   must
ris m.   vers m.   —   1   donc 3 doit 2
have been that extraordinary man to whom seven cities
                    = 2   1   se sont
contested the glory of having given   birth?   He does not
.disputé   = f.   avoir donné art. jour m.   *
know *what* model   to follow. I have told you *what* man it is.
savoir   modèle m.* suivre   ce
Which of those ladies   do you think   the most amiable?
   f.   dames f. *   2 trouver 1   f.
Choose *which* of those two pictures   you like   best.
Choisir —m. 4   5   6 tableau m. 7   1 aimer 2 art. mieux 3
Where   am I?   He knows not *where* he   is. He is gone I don't
     en   savoir   en   allé   ne
know *where*. *Where* does he get   that pride?   (It is)   there
savoir   De   * lui vient   orgueil m. voilà de
he derives his origin.   (*Which way*) did you come? (That is)
   tirer   origine. Par   êtes-vous arrivé? Voilà
   (the road) I came.
par   venir ind-4

By the manner in which we have employed these pronouns, it will be seen they are only *interrogative* when
at the beginning of a sentence, and, consequently, the
most proper name for them is that of *pronouns absolute.*

§ IV.

OF DEMONSTRATIVE PRONOUNS.

Ce, cette,' ces, very often are joined to the adverbs of
place, *ci,* here, and *là,* there, in order to point out in a
more precise manner the thing spoken of; and then the
demonstrative pronoun is placed before the substantive,
and *ci* and *là* are placed after.

EXAMPLES.

Ce livre-ci,	This book.
Cette fleur-ci,	This flower.
Cet homme-là	That man.
Ces femmes-là,	Those women.

Celui, celle, ceux, celles, are followed by the preposition
de, when placed before a substantive, and by a pronoun
relative, when placed before a verb.

EXAMPLES.

Les maladies de l'âme sont plus dangereuses que celles du corps,	The disorders of the mind are more dangerous than those of the body.
L'homme dont je vous ai parlé est celui que vous voyez,	The man of whom I spoke to you is he whom you see.
De toutes les choses du monde, c'est celle que j'aime le moins,	Of all the things in the world, it is that which I like least.

REMARK. The pronouns *celui, celle, ceux,* and *celles,*
when followed by a pronoun relative, are expressed in
English by the personal pronouns, *he, she, they,* or by
that which, those which, such as, etc.

EXERCISE.

The pleasures of the wise resemble   in nothing *those* of a
           ressembler 2   3   1   4 *à*
dissipated man. *He that* suffers himself to (be ruled) by his
dissipé 2   1   *se laisse*   *   *dominer*
passions, must renounce   happiness. *This* stuff   will
     doit renoncer à art. *bonheur* m.   *étoffe-ci* f. *

x

become you wonderfully. *That* action is worthy of blame.
siéra *à merveille* f.-*là* *bláme.*
This scene is calculated to interest all men, but that
—f.-*ci* *faite* *pour intéresser* art. -*là*
cannot succeed.
ne sauroit *réussir.*

Celui-ci and *celui-là* adopt the gender and number
of the substantive whose place they supply. When they
are opposed to each other, *celui-ci* marks the object
which is the nearest; and *celui-là* that which is the most
distant.

EXAMPLE.

Celui-ci plaît, mais celui-là cap-tive;	This pleases, but that captivates.

Ci and *là* coalesce with *ce*, and form the two other
demonstrative pronouns *ceci* and *cela*, the first of which
signifies *cette chose-ci*, this object; the second, *cette chose-là*, that object.

They are used alone; but when they are opposed to
each other, *ceci* expresses the nearest object, and *cela* the
most distant.

EXAMPLE.

Je n'aime point ceci, donnez-moi cela;	I don't like this, give me that.

REMARK. When *cela* is alone and not opposed to the
pronoun *ceci*, it is, like *ceci*, used of an object which we
point to.

EXAMPLES.

Que dites-vous de cela?	What do you say of that?
Cela est fort beau,	That is very handsome.

EXERCISE.

(Here are) certainly two charming prospects; this
Voilà certainement *beau* *perspective* f. pl.
has something more cheerful, but many people
quelque chose de *riant* *bien de* art. *personne* f. pl.
think *that* more striking and more majestic. The body
trouver *imposant* *majestueux*

perishes, the soul is immortal; yet all our cares are for
périr   f.   —tel   cependant   soin
that, while   we neglect *this.* What means *this?* That
tandis que   négliger   veut dire
is true. It is not *that.* *This* is low and mean, but *that* is
            Ce   bas   rampant
grand and sublime.

— — —

§. V.

OF INDEFINITE PRONOUNS.

1st CLASS.

Those which are never joined to a Substantive.

Quelqu'un means *un, une,* one.

EXAMPLES.

Nous attendons des hommes, il	We expect men, some will
en viendra quelqu'un ;	come.
Plusieurs femmes m'ont promis	Several ladies have promised
de venir, il en viendra quel-	me to come, some will come.
qu'une ;	

Quelqu'un taken absolutely and substantively, is said
alike of both genders, and means *une personne,* a person.

EXAMPLE.

J'attends ici quelqu'un,	I wait here for somebody.

We no longer say, *un quelqu'un.*

Quelques-uns signifies *plusieurs dans un plus grand
nombre,* several out of a great number.

EXAMPLES.

Quelques-uns assurent,	Some people affirm.
Entre les nouvelles qu'il a dé-	Among the reports he has cir-
bitées, il y en a quelques-unes	culated, several are true.
de vraies,	

Quiconque, whoever; signifies *quelque personne que ce
soit, qui que ce soit,* any person whatever. It takes no
plural, and is never used but of persons.

Ce discours s'adresse à quicon-que est coupable,	This speech is addressed to whoever is guilty.

, *Chacun,* each, every one, is used either distributively or collectively. It has no plural.

When used distributively, it means *chaque personne, chaque chose,* each person, or thing. It is used in the feminine, and must be followed by the preposition *de.*

EXAMPLES.

Chacun de nous vit à sa mode,	Each of us lives as he pleases.
Voyez séparément chacune de ces médailles,	Look at each of these medals separately.

Used collectively, it signifies *toute personne,* every person.

EXAMPLE.

Chacun a ses défauts,	Every body has his faults.

We no longer say, *un chacun.*

EXERCISE.

Can *any one* (be still ignorant) that it is from the
Pourroit-il 2 1 *ignorer encore* *ce dès*
earliest infancy that we ought to form the mind, the heart
tendre enfance f. *on doit* * *former*
and the taste. Will not *some one* of these ladies be of the
*
party. *Some people* like to read (every thing new).
partie f. *aimer* *toutes les nouveautés.*
(These are) beautiful pictures; I could wish to buy
voilà de superbe tableau m. * *voudrois en acheter*
some. *Whoever* has studied the principles of an art, knows that
—*pes* — m. *savoir*
it (is only) (by length of time) and by deep reflexions
ce n'est que à la longue *de profond réflexion* f.
that he can succeed in making it his own. All the
réussir à 1 *se* 2 *rendre* 4 *le* 3 * *propre* 5.
ladies at the ball were very finely dressed, and *each*
bal m. ind-2 * *superbement paré avoit*
differently. *Every one* should, for (the sake of) his
une parure différente *devroit pour* *
own happiness, listen only to the voice of reason and of
propre *n'écouter que* * *voix* f. art. *raison* f.

.truth. What is the price. of *each* of these medals?
art. *vérité* f.   *prix* m.   f. ,   *médaille* f.

Autrui means *les autres personnes*, other people; it
only applies to persons, is never accompanied by an adjective, has no plural, and is never used in a sentence without
being preceded by a preposition.

EXAMPLE.

La charité se réjouit du bonheur d'autrui,	Charity rejoices in the happiness of others.

Personne, which is always masculine and singular,
means either *nul*, nobody, or *qui que ce soit*, whoever, any
body. In the first sense, it is preceded or followed
by the negative *ne*, which is placed after *personne*, when
this word stands before the verb; and before the verb
when *personne* stands after. The same observation applies
to *rien*.

EXAMPLES.

Il ne faut nuire à personne,	We must injure nobody.
Personne n'est assuré de vivre jusqu'au lendemain,	Nobody is certain of living till to-morrow.

REMARK I. The negative is sometimes understood; as
y a-t-il quelqu'un ici? is there any body here? *personne*,
nobody. *Personne* stands for *il n'y a personne*, there is
nobody here.

REMARK II. In interrogative phrases with an affirmation,
or in those expressing doubt, *personne* signifies *quelqu'un*,
any body.

EXAMPLES.

Personne oserait-il nier, etc.	Would any body dare deny?
Je doute que personne soit assez hardi,	I doubt whether any body be bold enough.

REMARK III. In comparative sentences, when *personne*
is placed in the second member of the comparison, it
means *any body*.

EXAMPLE.

Cette place lui convient mieux qu'à personne,	That place suits him better than any body.

x 3

Rien, nothing, which is masculine and singular, is used with or without a negation. When with a negation, it means *nulle chose*, nothing.

EXAMPLE.

Il ne s'attache à rien de solide,	He applies himself to nothing fixed.

When used without a negation, it means *quelque chose,* something.

EXAMPLE.

Je doute que rien soit plus pro- pre à faire impression que, etc.	I doubt whether any thing be more suited to make an impression than, etc.

The negation is sometimes understood; *que vous a coûté cela? rien;* how much did you pay for it? nothing.

It always requires the preposition *de* before the adjective or participle that follows it, and then if there be no verb in the sentence, the negation is not expressed; as *rien de beau que le vrai,* nothing is noble but truth.

EXERCISE.

To most men the misfortunes of *others* are
Pour la plupart de art. *mal* m. *ne*
but a dream. Do not to *others* what you would not wish
que songe m. * *vouloir*
to be done to you. *No one* knows whether he deserves
qu'on vous fît savoir si est digne de
love or hatred. An egotist loves *nobody*, not even his own
de égoïste pas même * *propre*
children; in the whole universe he sees no one but himself.
dans * *univers ne voit* * *que lui seul*
He is more than (*any body*) worthy of the confidence (with
digne confiance f.
which) the king honours him. I doubt whether *any one* ever
dont honorer que ait
painted nature, in its amiable simplicity, better than
jamais peint art. —f. =f.
the sentimental Gessner. Has *any body* called on me
sensible — * *à est-il venu* 1 *chez*
this morning? *Nobody.* There was *nothing* but great
matin m. *que de grand*

in the designs and works of the Egyptians. I
dans dessein m. pl. art. *ouvrage* m. pl. —*tiens*
doubt whether there is *any thing* better calculated to exalt
que * *soit* 2 1 *plus propre élever*
the soul than the contemplation of the wonders of nature.
f. *merveille* f. art. f.

2d CLASS.

Those which are always joined to a Substantive.

Quelque, some, signifies *un, une entre plusieurs*, one out
of several; it is of both genders, and adopts the number of
the substantive.

EXAMPLE.

Adressez-vous à quelque autre personne,	Apply to some body else.

Chaque, each, every, which is of both genders, has no
plural.

EXAMPLE.

Chaque pays a ses coutumes,	Each country has its customs.

Quelconque signifies *nul, aucun*, no, not any; *quel que
ce soit*, whatever it be; *quel qu'il soit*, whoever he be. It
is of both genders, is generally used with a negative, and
always placed after a substantive. When thus employed,
it is always singular.

EXAMPLE.

Il ne veut se soumettre à aucune autorité quelconque,	He will submit to no authority whatever.

Certain signifies *quelque*, certain, some. In this sense
it is used alike of persons and things; but it is always
placed before the substantive.

EXAMPLE.

J'ai ouï dire à certain homme, à un certain homme,	I have heard some man say.

Un, when it is not an adjective of number, and signifies

a or *an*, is used indefinitely, to express some person, or some thing indeterminately. In this acceptation it means *quelque, certain,* and takes the gender of the substantive with which it is joined. It makes in the feminine *une.* . .

J'ai vu un homme qui couroit.	I saw a man who was running.
Je me suis promené dans une grande et belle prairie,	I walked in a large fine meadow.

Some enlightened people   among the Egyptians
      éclairé 2 *esprit* m. pl. 1   *parmi*   —*tiens*
preserved   the idea of *a* first being, whose attributes they
conserver ind-2 *idée*   *être*   art.—*but* m. pl. 3 1
represented   under various symbols; this   (is proved)
représenter ind-2 2   *différent symbole* m. *c'est ce que prouve*
by the   following inscription upon a temple: "I am all that
  * * celle *   —f.   *de* —m.   *ce qui*
has been, is, and shall be; no mortal ever removed the veil
              5 *mortel* 2 1 *a levé*   *voile* m.
that covers me." *Every* nation has (in its turn) shone on the
            f.   *à son tour* 2 *brillé* 1
theatre of the world. There is no reason *whatever* that can
 m.   *raison* f.   *puisse*
bring   him to it. *Some* figures appear monstrous and
déterminer   —f.   —*trueux*
deformed, considered separately, or too near; but, if they
difforme   f. pl. *séparement* *de* *près*   *on*
are put in their proper light and   place, the true point of view
les met   * *jour* *à leur* —   —m. *vue* f.
    restores their   beauty and   grace. Yesterday I saw
leur *rend*   art. = f.   art. — f.   2   1
a lady   remarkably beautiful.
  d'une   *rare* 2   *beauté* 1

3d CLASS.

Those which are sometimes joined to Substantives, and sometimes not.

Nul, and *pas un,* no, not one, are employed either alone or in conjunction with the substantive. They are accompanied by the negation, assume the feminine, but have no plural, and may be followed by the preposition *de*.

EXAMPLES.

Nul de tous ceux qui y ont été n'en est revenu,	Not one of those who went there has returned.
Pas un ne croit cette nouvelle,	Not one believes that intelligence.
Je n'en ai nulle connaissance,	I have no knowledge of it.
Il n'y a pas une seule personne qui le croie,	There is not a single person that believes it.

Aucun signifies *nul*, no, none. It is generally accompanied by the negation, and may be followed by the preposition *de*.

EXAMPLE.

Vous n'avez aucun moyen de réussir dans cette affaire,	You have no means of succeeding in that affair.

This pronoun is seldom employed in the plural, except before substantives which have no singular, or are always employed in the plural in some particular sense.

EXAMPLE.

Il n'a fait aucunes dispositions, | He has made no dispositions.

REMARK. *Aucun* may be employed without a negation in interrogative sentences; or those which express doubt or exclusion.

EXAMPLES.

Aucun homme fut-il jamais plus heureux?	Was ever any man more successful?
On doute qu'aucune de ces affaires réussisse,	They doubt whether any of those affairs will succeed.
Le plus beau morceau d'éloquence qu'il y ait dans aucune langue, etc.	The finest piece of eloquence that exists in any language, etc.

EXERCISE.

No one likes (to see himself) as   he is.   *No* expression, *no*
            se voir.   *tel que.*   —f.

..truth of design and   colouring, *no* strokes of genius in that
  f.   *dessin   de coloris*   *trait*
great work.   He is as learned as *any* one.   *Not* one of these
  ouvrage m.   *savant*
engravings   announces any great skill.   *None* of his works will
gravure f. pl. *annoncer un   talent* m.
descend to   posterity.   He is so ignorant, and at the same
passer   art. = f.   —   en * même
time so obstinate, that he will not (be convinced) by *any* rea-
*temps   obstiné   *   - se rendre   à   rai-*
soning.   Did *any* man ever   attain   to such a pitch
sonnement m.   *jamais* 2 *parvenir* 1 ce * *comble* m.
of glory?   I doubt whether there be in *any* science a more evi-
  =   *que* subj-1   — f.   *plus lu-*
dent   principle.
mineux 2'   —*pe* m. 1

Autre, other, expresses distinction, the difference between two objects, or between one and several; as *quelle
autre chose souhaitez-vous de moi*, what else do you wish
for from me.

REMARK. *Autre* is sometimes used to express a person
indeterminately; as *j'aimé mieux que vous l'appreniez de
tout autre que de moi*, I had rather you learn it of any
other person than me.

Un is sometimes opposed to *autre;* in which case, these
two words are preceded by the article; supply the place of
the substantives to which they relate, adopt their gender
and number, and form the pronouns *l'un l'autre, l'un et
l'autre*, and *ni l'un ni l'autre*.

L'un l'autre, each other, one another, applies both to
persons and things: it takes both gender and number, and
requires the article before the two words of which it is
composed. If there be any preposition it must be placed
before the last. When these two words are used in conjunction, they express a reciprocal relation between several
persons or things.

EXAMPLE.

Il faut se secourir l'un l'autre, | We ought to assist each other.

When used separately, they denote a difference.

Les passions s'entendent les unes avec les autres; si l'on se laisse aller aux unes, on attire bientôt les autres;	Our passions have a relation with each other; if we indulge some, the others will soon follow.

REMARK. In the latter case *l'un* is used for the person or thing first mentioned, and *l'autre* for the person or thing last spoken of.

L'un et l'autre, both: these two words mark union. They require the verb to be in the plural.

L'une et l'autre sont bonnes,	Both are good.

Ni l'un ni l'autre, neither: these two words, on the contrary, mark separation. The verb must be in the plural.

Ni l'un ni l'autre n'ont fait leur devoir,	Neither has done his duty.

Ask   another.   Would *any other* have   been so
   Demander à   *   auroit-il eu   *   assez*
self-conceited   as to   think that his private   opinion could
*d'amourpropre * pour penser   particulier a — f. pût*
counterbalance the public sentiment?   Reason and   faith
   balancer   opinion f.   art. *raison* f.   art. *foi* f.
equally demonstrate that we were created   for *another* life.
   a   *démontrer* 1   -   *créer* ind-4   f.
They speak ill of *one another.*   The happiness of the people
      mal   m.
constitutes that of the prince; their true interests are connected
   faire   — m.   *intérêt* m.   *lié*
with each other.   Presumption and   pride easily insinuate
   à pl. pl. art. *présomption* f.   art. *orgueil* a   *se glis-*
themselves into the heart; if we allow   one (the) entrance,
ser 1   m.   *l'on y donne à* a f. 3   *entrée* 1
it is much to (be feared) that we shall soon   (abandon our-
   *bien   craindre   on * bientôt* a   ne. se .li-*
selves) to the *other. Both* relate   the same story, though
vre 1   .   *rapporter* . .   *fait* m. ·
neither believes   it to be true.
   *ne penser que * soit*

Même signifies *qui n'est pas autre,* which is not different.
It is of both genders, and takes the plural.

EXAMPLES.

C'est le même homme,	It is the same man.
La même personne,	The same person.
Ce sont les mêmes raisons,	They are the same reasons.
Ce poëme est le même que celui dont je vous ai parlé,	This poem is the same that I was mentioning to you.

Tel signifies *pareil, semblable, de même;* such, like,
similar, same. It assumes both genders and both numbers.

EXAMPLES.

Un tel projet ne sauroit réussir,	Such a scheme could not succeed.
Il n'y a pas de tels animaux, de telles coutumes;	There are no such animals, such customs.

When used alone, it either preserves its proper signification, or it expresses a person indeterminately.

EXAMPLES.

Vous ne sauriez me persuader rien de tel,	You cannot persuade me of any such thing.
Tel fait des libéralités, qui ne paye pas ses dettes,	The same man dispenses his bounty, who does not pay his debts.

Plusieurs, several, which is plural and of both genders,
is used indifferently of persons and things. When united
to a substantive, or relating to it, it generally signifies an
indeterminate number, without relation to another number.

EXAMPLES.

Plusieurs motifs l'ont déterminé,	Several reasons determined him.
Je crois cela pour plusieurs raisons,	I believe that for several reasons.

But it is used likewise of a greater or less number forming
part of a number still greater.

EXAMPLE.

Parmi un si grand nombre de | Out of so great a number of
gens, il y en eut plusieurs qui | persons, several objected to
s'y opposèrent; | it.

When *plusieurs* is employed absolutely, without either substantive or relative, it always means *plusieurs per-sonnes*, several persons, and supplies the place of a substantive.

EXAMPLE.

Plusieurs aiment mieux mourir | Many had rather die than for-
que de perdre leur réputation, | feit their character.

Tout is employed either alone or in conjunction with a substantive.

When employed alone, it signifies *toutes choses*, all things; *toute sorte de choses*, every kind of things.

EXAMPLE.

Tout nous abandonne au mo- | Every thing forsakes us at the
ment de la mort; il ne nous | moment of death; we retain
reste que nos bonnes œuvres; | nothing but our good works.

When united to a substantive, it is used either collectively or distributively.

Considered collectively, *tout* signifies the totality of a thing; in this acceptation, it is followed by the article.

EXAMPLES.

Tout l'univers, | The whole universe.
Tous les corps célestes, | All the celestial bodies

Considered distributively, *tout* signifies *chaque*, each, and in this case is not followed by the article.

EXAMPLE.

Tout bien est désirable, | Every good is desirable.

EXERCISE.

Does he always maintain the *same* principles? Yes, they are
        soutenir   *—pe*   *Oui . ce*

Y

absolutely the *same*. That general is the *same* that commanded
—*ment*   pl.   —   —*der*
. last   year.   *Such* a conduct   is inexplicable. There
art. *dernier* 2 *année* f. 1   2   1 *conduite* f.   —
are no   *such* customs   in this country.   I never heard
        de   *coutumes* f.   *pays* m.   ai   *entendu dire*
any thing   *similar*.   The *same man* sows who often reaps
        rien   de   *   *   *semer*   *recueillir*
nothing.   I this morning received *several* letters.   Of those
        1   3   *matin* 4   ind-4   2   *lettre* f. pl.   *Parmi*
manuscripts, there are *several*   much   esteemed. *Many* by
        —*crits   il y en a*   *qu'on beaucoup* 2 *estime* 1   *en*
endeavouring to injure   others   injure   themselves more
s'efforcer   de nuire à art.   *se nuisent à*
than they   think.   *All* is in God and God is in all.   The *whole*
        ne penser   *en*
course   of his life has been distinguished by   generous actions.
cours m.   f.   *marqué*   *des*   = 2   —f. 1
Every vice is odious.
        —m.   =

4th CLASS.

Those which are followed by QUE.

Qui que, whoever, is only used of persons, and signifies
quelque personne que, whatever person, in affirmative
sentences; it requires the following verb in the subjunctive.

Qui que ce soit qui ait fait cela, c'est un habile homme;	Whoever has done that, is a man of talents.
Qui que je sois,	Whoever I may be.
Qui que c'ait été,	Whoever it may have been.
Qui que c'eût été,	Whoever it might have been.
Qui que ce puisse être,	Whoever it may be.

REMARK. When *qui que*, followed by `ce soit`, is used
with a negative, it signifies *aucune personne*, nobody; as
je n'y trouve qui que ce soit, I find nobody there.

Quoi que, whatever it be, is only used of things, and
signifies *quelque chose que*, whatever thing, in affirmative
sentences; it requires also the following verb in the subjunctive.

Quoi que ce soit qu'il fasse ou qu'il dise, on se défie de lui;	Whatever he does or says, he is distrusted.
Quoi que vous disiez, je le ferai;	Whatever you may say, I will do it.

REMARK. When *quoi que*, followed by *ce soit*, is used with a negation, it signifies *aucune chose*, not any thing; as *sans application, on ne peut réussir en quoi que ce soit;* without application, it is impossible to succeed in any thing whatever.

Whoever   has told you so, he is mistaken.   Passenger,
    ce soit qui   *le*   *se tromper* ind-4 *Passant*
whoever thou be, contemplate with   religious veneration
      contempler   *un* $=2$ *respect* m. 1
this monument erected by   gratitude;   it is the tomb
   —m.   *élevé*   art. *reconnoissance* f. ce   *tombeau* m.
of a just and benevolent man.   How   , can he hope to
     2   *bienfaisant* 3 1   *Comment*   *espérer de*
be beloved   who   has regard for no one? *Whatever* he may
      lui   *ne*   *d'égards*
do or   say, he (will find it) very difficult to destroy
    qu'il   *aura*   *bien de la peine*   *détruire des*
prejudices so deeply   rooted. A mind vain, presumptuous,
préjugé m. *si profondément enraciné*   —   *présomptueux*
and inconsistent,   will never succeed in any thing whatever.
    sans consistance   *   *réussir*
Whatever a frivolous world   may   think of you, never swerve
      frivole 2 *monde* 1 *puisse*   *vous détournez*
from the path   of   virtue.
    chemin m.   art.   f.

Quel que signifies *de quelque sorte, de quelque espèce que ce soit*, of whatever sort, of whatever kind it may be, when relating to things; or *qui que ce soit*, whoever it may be, when relating to persons. It assumes both gender and number, according to the person or thing it relates to.

Quelles que soient vos affaires, venez;	Whatever business you may have, come.

| *Je n'en excepte personne, quel qu'il soit;* | I except nobody, whoever he may be. |

REMARK. We can likewise say, *lequel que,* whoever, whichever; as *lequel des trois que vous choisissiez, peu m'importe;* whichever of the three you choose, I care little.

Quelque que, of both genders, when united to a substantive, signifies *quel que soit le, quelle que soit la,* etc. whatever be the. It assumes both numbers.

EXAMPLE.

| *Quelque raison qu'on lui apporte, il n'en croit rien;* | Whatever reason is adduced, he believes nothing about it. |
| *Quelques efforts que vous fassiez, vous ne réussirez point;* | Whatever attempts you may make, you will never succeed. |

When united to an adjective, it operates as an adverb, and signifies *à quelque point que,* however great a degree; it neither takes gender nor number.

EXAMPLES.

| *Quelque belle qu'elle puisse être, elle ne doit pas être vaine;* | However beautiful she may be, she ought not to be vain. |
| *Quelque puissans qu'ils soient, je ne les crains point;* | However powerful they may be, I am not afraid of them. |

Tel que, such as, serves to mark the relation or resemblance of two objects which are compared.

EXAMPLE.

| *C'est un homme tel qu'il vous le faut;* | He is just such a man as you want. |

Tout que signifies *quoique, encore que,* though; *quelque,* however. On this occasion, *tout* is considered an adverb, and is employed with adjectives of every kind, and even with some substantives.

EXAMPLES.

| *Tout artificieux qu'ils sont, je doute que le public soit longtemps leur dupe;* | However artful they may be, I doubt whether the public will be long their dupe. |
| *Toute femme qu'elle est,* | Woman as she is. |

EXERCISE.

Let the laws be   (*what they may*), we must always
Que 2   *loi* f. 4 subj-1 3   *quel* 1
respect them. *Whatever* efforts you make, I doubt whether you
respecter   — f.   subj-1   *que*
will succeed.   All   men, *however* opposite they may be,
  * *réussir* subj-1   art.   *opposé*   * *soient*
agree   on that point. The man who   descends into himself
s'accorder   —m.   *ne rentrer en*
only to ·   discover his defects and   correct them, likes to
que pour y démêler   —m.   *se corriger en*
see himself as he is. *However* surprising that phenomenon
· ' '   *surprenant   phénomène* m. 2
may be, it is not against the order   of   nature. *Children as*
   1   *contre   ordre* m. art. — f.
they are, they   behaved remarkably well.
   se sont conduits   fort   bien.

A GENERAL EXERCISE ON THE PRONOUNS.

The   Evening Walk.
      du 2 soir 3   promenade *f.* 1.

On   a fine   summer evening, my brother, my sister, and
Dans   de 2   *soirée* f. 1
myself,   (were walking) (by the side) of a wood
moi   nous nous promenions   le long   bois m. *qui n'est*
not far   distant from the castle   which we inhabit. We
pas bien éloigné   château m.   *habiter*
(were. contemplating) with rapture   the majestic   scenery
contempler ind-2   *transport   —tueux* 2 *scène* f. 1
which   nature exhibits at the approach of   night, when we
art.   *déployer   approche* f. art. *nuit* f. *quand*
perceived, at the foot   of an ancient oak,   a boy   of a most
apercevoir à   pied m.   *vieux chêne* m. *enfant*   2
interesting   countenance. His beauty, his air   of ingenuous-
intéressant 3 art. *figure* f. 1   = f.   — m. *ingénuité*
ness and   candour, his gracefulness struck   us, and we
de =   grâce pl. *frappèrent   nous*
approached him. What! alone here, my boy?   said we,
approchâmes en   seul ici   enfant lui dîmes
Whence art thou? Whence comest thou? What art thou
d'où   *   2

Y 3

doing here alone? I am not alone, answered he, smiling,
fais 1 4 3   *répondre*   *d'un air riant*
I am not alone; but I was fatigued and I (have sat myself) under
                   fatigué · *me suis assis*   *à*
the shade of this tree, while my mother is busy in gather-
 ombre f.   *arbre* m. *tandis que*   *occupé à cueil-*
ing simples to give some relief   to the pains
lir des — *pour apporter*   *soulagement* m.   *douleur* f. pl.
which her aged father suffers. Ah! (how many) troubles
     ·2 *vieux* 3 4 *souffre* 1   *que*   *de peine* f. pl.
my good mamma has! How many troubles! Did you
2   3   *maman* 4 1   *si* *
know them, there is not one of you that would not be touched
connoissiez .   *qui* *   *fût touché*
with pity, and who could refuse the tribute of your tears.
de pitié   *. lui refusât un tribut*   * *larme* f. pl.
We said to him, lovely child, thy ingenuousness, candour,
    . aimable   =f.   pro. = f. pro.
innocence, (every thing) interests us in thy misfortunes and
— f.   *intéresser*   *à*   *malheur* m. pl.   *à*
those of thy mother. Relate them to us, whatever they be,
               raconter 2 * 1   *soient*
fear not to afflict us. (Woe be) to whoever cannot (be
crains de affliger   *malheur*   *ne sait pas s'at-*
affected) by the misfortunes of others. He immediately related
tendrir sur   *mal* m. pl.   2 *aussitôt* 1
the history of his mother, with an expression, an artlessness,
=   — f.   f.
a grace, altogether affecting. Our hearts felt· the live-
— f.   *tout-à-fait touchant* f. s.   *éprouver*   *vif*
liest emotions, tears (trickled down our cheeks), and we
— f.   *nos*   *coulèrent*
gave him what little money · we had about us.
       * art. *peu de argent que* ' ind-2 *sur*
(In the mean time) the mother returned. (As soon as) he
cependant   *revenir*   *dès que*
saw her, he exclaimed, run, mamma, run; see what these
apercevoir s'écrier accourir   *ce que*
good little folks have given me; I have related to them thy
     gens f. pl.
misfortunes; they have been affected (by them), and their sen-
          m.   *touché*   *en*
sibility (has not been satisfied) with shedding tears. See,
=   *ne s'est pas borné* f.   *à*   *   *des*
mamma, see what they have given me. The mother was
moved; . she thanked us, and said: Generous feeling
attendri   *remercier*   *nous dit*   =2   *et*   3

souls,   the good action which you (have just been doing)
âme f. pl. 1   — f.   *venez de faire*
will not be lost.   He who sees (every thing) and judges
       perdu   *juger*
(every thing) will not let   it go unrewarded.
      *   laisser * sans récompense.*

CHAPTER V.

OF THE VERB.

Agreement of the Verb with the Subject.

We have already seen, that the subject is that of which something is affirmed, and it may always easily be known by the answer to this question, *qui est-ce qui?* who or what is it? When we say, *Pierre vit*, Peter lives; *l'oiseau vole*, the bird flies; if we ask, *qui est-ce qui vit?* who is it that lives? *qui est-ce qui vole?* what is it that flies? The answers, *Pierre* and *l'oiseau*, shew that *Pierre* and *l'oiseau* are the subjects of the verbs *vit* and *vole*.

RULE. The verb must be of the same number and person as its subject.

EXAMPLES.

Je ris,	*I laugh.*	Nous parlons,	*We speak.*
Tu joues,	*Thou playest.*	Vous plaisantez,	*You jest.*
Il aime,	*He loves.*	Ils sont fous,	*They are mad.*

La vertu est aimable, *virtue is amiable.*

Ris is in the singular number and the first person, because *je*, its subject, is in the singular and the first person. *Joues* is in the singular and the second person, because *tu* is in the singular and the second person, etc.

EXERCISE.

The freest of all   men is he who can be free even in
   libre   *même*   art.
slavery.   Are we not often blind   to·our defects?
esclavage m.   *   s'aveugler* ind-1 *sur   défaut*
All   men (are inclined) to   laziness, but the savages of
   art.   *tendre* ind-1   art.   *sauvage*   art.

hot   countries are the laziest of all men. Do you think of
chaud a   pays 1
imposing long   on the credulity of the public? Thou canst
en imposer long-temps à   = f.   m.   pouvoir
not deny that he   is   a great man.
        nier   ne subj-1

REMARK I. When a verb has two subjects in the singular
number, it is put in the plural.

Mon père et ma mère m'aiment tendrement,	My father and mother love me tenderly.

His uprightness and   honesty make him courted by
    droiture f.   pron. honnêteté faire   rechercher de
every body.   Strength of   body and   of mind
        art.   f.   art.   celle   art.
    meet not always together.   A good heart and a noble
se rencontrer   ensemble.   m.   beau
soul are   precious gifts   of   nature.
f.   de art.   =   m. pl. 1   art. — f.

REMARK II. When a verb relates to subjects of different
persons, it agrees with the first in preference to the other
two, and with the second in preference to the third. We
name the person to whom we are speaking first, and always
name ourselves last. On this occasion, we place generally
before the verb the pronoun plural nous, if the first person
has been mentioned before, or the pronoun plural vous,
if no first person has been mentioned.

Vous, votre frère et moi, nous lisons ensemble la brochure nouvelle ;	You, your brother and I read together the new pamphlet.
Vous et votre ami, vous viendrez avec moi ;	You and your friend will come with me.

You, your friend, and I, have each   a different opinion.
        chacun   a   f. 1
In our childhood, you and I (were pleased) with playing to-
enfance f.   se plaire ind-2 à   inf-1

gether. Neither I, nor (any one else) has been able   to
       ni   *d'autres*   *ne*   *pouvoir* ind-4   *
understand (any thing) in that sentence.   (Take good care),
*comprendre*2 *rien* 1   *à* ~ *phrase* f.   *se garder bien*
you and your brother, not to (give way)   to the impetuosity
            * *de s'abandonner*
of your temper.
    caractère m.

REMARK III. When a verb has the relative pronoun *qui*
for its subject, it is put in the same number and person as
the noun or pronoun to which *qui* relates.

EXAMPLES.

Est-ce moi qui ai dit cette nouvelle?	Is it I who told this news?
Est-ce nous qui l'avons voulu?	Is it we who desired it?
Ceux qui aiment sincèrement la vertu sont heureux,	Those who sincerely love virtue are happy.

EXERCISE.

He that complains most of mankind, is not always he that
Celui   *se plaindre le plus* art. *homme* pl.
(has most reason) to complain (of them).   You that wish to
être le plus fondé   *en*   *vouloir* *
enrich your mind with thoughts vigorously conceived and no-
enrichir   *esprit de*   f. pl. *fortement conçu*   *no-*
bly   expressed, read the works of Homer and Plato.
blement exprimé   *ouvrage*

OF THE REGIMEN OF VERBS.

We have said that an active verb was that after which
we could put *quelqu'un* or *quelque chose;* and that the
word which is put after the verb is called the regimen
of that verb.   We then observed, that this regimen might
be known by asking the question, *qu'est-ce que?* This
regimen we call *direct*, and it may be either a noun or a
pronoun.

RULE. When the regimen of the active verb is a noun,
it is always placed after the verb; when it is a pronoun it
is generally placed before it.

EXAMPLE.

Ma mère aime tous ses enfans, | My mother loves all her children.

Je vous aime, and not, as in English, *j'aime vous*, I love you; *il m'aime*, and not *il aime moi.*

He has discovered to all   other nations   his ambitious
        montrer   art. *   *peuple* m. pl.   ═ 2
design   of   enslaving   them, and has left
dessein m. 1   *mettre dans l'esclavage* inf-1   *ne   laisser*
us no   means of defending our liberty, but by endeavouring
   aucun moyen   inf-1   *que en tâcher* inf-3
to overturn his new kingdom.   Homer represents Nestor as
de renverser   *royaume* m.
he that restrained the ungovernable wrath   of Achilles, the
celui   *modérer* ind-2   *bouillant courroux* m.
pride of Agamemnon, the haughtiness of Ajax, and the impetuous
               fierté f.   ═ 1
courage of Diomede. He dared   not (lift up) his   eyes,
—m. 1   *Diomède*   *oser* ind-2   *lever* * art.
lest   they should meet   those of his friend, whose
de peur de * * *rencontrer* inf-1
   very   silence condemned him.   He caresses them, because
art. *même* 2 m. 1   ind-2
he *loves* them.

Besides this regimen direct, some active verbs may have a second, which is called *indirect,* and is marked by the words *à* or *de.*

Il a fait un présent à sa sœur,	He has made a present to his sister.
Il accuse son ami d'imprudence,	He accuses his friend of imprudence.

This second regimen is known by the answer to these questions; *à qui?* to whom? *à quoi?* to what? *de qui?* of whom? *de quoi?* of what?

À qui a-t-il fait un présent?	To whom did he make a present?
À sa sœur,	To his sister.
De quoi accuse-t-il son ami?	Of what does he accuse his friend?
D'imprudence,	Of imprudence.

In submitting to the yoke of Asia, Greece would have
en subir inf-3 * joug m. art. art.
though't virtue subjected to voluptuousness, the mind
croire art. 2 assujettir inf-t 1 art. volupté f.
to the body, and courage to a senseless force, which con-
art. insensé 2 — f. r
sisted only in numbers. Three hundred Lacedemonians
ind-2 art. multitude f. —niens
hastened to Thermopilæ to certain death, content, in dying,
courir ind-3 art. — pl. un asssuré 2 f. 1 en
to have sacrificed to their country an infinite number of
de immoler pays m. 2 1
barbarians, and to have left to their countrymen the ex-
barbare de laisser compatriote
ample of an unheard bravery. You know the im-
inoui 2 hardiesse f. t savoir ind-2
portance which your parents attached to the success of that
— f. que — ind-2 réussite f.
affair: why have you not hastened to announce it
pourquoi s'empresser ind-4 de f.
(to them)?

The regimen of the passive verb is *de* or *par*, before
the noun or pronoun that follows them.

La souris est mangée par le chat,	The mouse is eaten by the cat.
Un enfant sage est aimé de tout le monde,	A good child is loved by every body.

REMARK. We ought never to use the word *par*, by,
before *Dieu*, God. We say, *les méchans seront punis de
Dieu*, which, in order to avoid making use of *by* may be
thus Englished; God will punish the wicked.

The city of Troy was taken, plundered, and destroyed by the
Troie prendre saccager détruire
confederate Greeks, 1184 before the Christian æra: this
confédéré 2 1 ans avant 2 ère f. 1
event has been celebrated by the two greatest poets of Greece
art.
and Italy. You will only be beloved, esteemed, and
pr. art. ne

courted   by men,   (in proportion as) you join   the
rechercher de   *que*   *autant que*   *joindre* ind-7
qualities   of the heart   to   those   of   the   mind.   God
=   f. pl.   pr.   3
punished   the Jews   every   time
punir (passive voice ind-3 2)   *peuple Juif* 1 *toutes les fois*
that,   deaf   to   the   voice   of   the   prophets,   they fell
      sourd   f.   *prophète*   sing. *tomber* ind-3
into   idolatry and   impiety.
dans art.   =   art. =

Some few neuter verbs have no regimen; as *dormir*, to
sleep; but many of them have.

RULE. We put *à* or *de* before the noun or pronoun that
follows the neuter verb.

Tout genre d'excès nuit à la santé.	Every kind of excess is hurtful to health.
Il médit de tout le monde.	He slanders every body.

This sentiment has pleased   the king and   all the nation.
                  à   *à*
In   his   retirement, he (has the full   enjoyment) of   the
dans   *retraite* f.   *jouir*   *tout*
faculties of the soul.   To slander (any one) is to assassinate
= f. pl.   *   *médire quelqu'un c'est* *
him in cold blood.   The honest man seldom   (permits himself)
    de 2 *sang* 1   *rarement se permettre de*
to   jest,   because   he knows   the most inno-
* art. *plaisanterie* f.   pl.   *parceque*   *savoir que*
cent jests may   sometimes hurt   reputation.   It is
f. pl.   *   *pouvoir quelquefois nuire à* art.   f.   *Ce*
only   in   retirement that one truly   enjoys one's self.
ne que   art.   *on véritablement jouir de   soi*
His work   has pleased   every   one,   because it unites to
    ouvrage m.   *à*   art. *monde*   *joindre un*
real utility the charms   of   style, and the beauties of
2   = f. 1   *agrément* m. pl.   art.   m.   sing.
    sentiment.
art.   pl.

The reflected verbs have for their regimen the personal pronouns, *me, te, se, nous* and *vous*, and this regimen is sometimes direct, and sometimes indirect.

OF THE NATURE AND USE OF MOODS AND TENSES.

Of the Indicative.

The indicative is that mood which expresses the different tenses, with a mere simple affirmation. It contains eight tenses, viz. the *present,* the *imperfect,* the *preterit definite,* the *preterit indefinite,* the *preterit anterior,* the *pluperfect,* the *future simple* and the *future anterior.*

The *present* marks a present time; that is to say, a time when a thing either exists or is doing.

EXAMPLES.

J'aime,	I love.
Ils jouent,	They play.

The *imperfect* expresses a present with respect to something past.

EXAMPLE.

J'entrois au moment où vous sortiez,	I came in at the moment you were going out.

Or it expresses a past but habitual thing, without fixing the time of its duration.

EXAMPLE.

César étoit un habile général,	Cæsar was an able general.

The *preterit definite* is that which marks a thing as done or as having happened at a time completely past.

EXAMPLE.

J'écrivis hier à Rome,	I wrote yesterday to Rome.

The *preterit indefinite* is that which expresses a thing as done, or as having happened at a time which is neither precise nor determinate.

z

EXAMPLE.

Il m'a fait un vrai plaisir en | He has given me real pleasure
venant me voir, | by coming to see me.

Or at a time which is not absolutely past.

EXAMPLE.

J'ai vu cette semaine beaucoup | I have seen many people this
de monde, | week.

EXERCISE.

My sister is in her chamber, where she (is occupied) in
           où   s'occuper   à
reading   ancient history, the study (of which) pleases her
inf-1 art.   2   1   2   dont 1   lui
extremely.   Benefits   bestowed   are (so many)
infiniment art. bienfait que on répandre ind-1   de   art.
trophies   erected   in the hearts of those whose   felicity
trophée que on s'ériger ind-1   1 art. =f. 4
(has been promoted) (by them). The great Corneille was
on 2   faire ind-1 3   *   —
busy   in his study   tracing the plan of one of his tragedies,
occupé   cabinet à inf-1   —m.   —
when a servant,   terrified,   came to tell him that his
     domestique m. tout effrayé ind-3 *   lui   * art.
house was   on   fire: go and find   my wife,
3   prendre à ind-6 2   * art. 1   * trouver
replied   he; I do not understand   household con-
répondre ind-3   entendre rien à art. affaire pl. du mé-
cerns.   Some   Hungarian noblemen revolted   from
nage m.   de art. Hongrois 2 seigneur 1 se révolter ind-3 contre
the emperor Sigismund; this prince heard   it, and
=   —mond   apprendre ind-3
marched boldly   against   them: Which, among you,
     fièrement au-devant de   d'entre
said   he (to them), will lay   hands   upon his king
ind-3   mettre 1 art. f. sing. 3.   4 art.
first? If there   be one bold enough, let him advance. This
2   en   un hardi
noble firmness struck.   the rebels   (with awe), who
     en imposer à   séditieux   *
returned immediately to   their duty. I have travelled through
rentrer aussitôt   dans le   devoir   voyager dans
almost all   Europe, and I have visited the most celebrated
    art. —f.   — bre 2

places in   Asia and   Africa;· if, on the one hand, I
lieu 1 *de* art. *Asie*   pr. art. *Afrique*   *de*   *côté* m.
admired the master-pieces of   art, of every kind, which the
ind-4   *chefs-d'œuvre* art.   *en tout genre*
protection of   enlightened governments has produced, on the
            art.   2   1   *faire naître*
other, I shed   tears, (on seeing) the ravages of   ignorance
      ind-4 *de* art.   *sur*   —   art. . f.
and   barbarism.   ·
      pr. art. *barbarie* f.

The *preterit anterior* expresses that a thing was done or
had happened immediately before a time which is passed,
and this tense is either definite or indefinite. There is
the same difference between its two forms as between the
two preterits, the definite and the indefinite.

EXAMPLES.

J'eus dîné hier à midi,	I had dined yesterday at twelve o'clock.
J'ai eu déjeûné ce matin à dix heures,	I had done breakfast this morning at ten o'clock.

The *pluperfect* is that past tense which expresses a thing
as done, or having happened, at any period antecedent
to the time when another thing was done; or it expresses
a thing done immediately before another, but indicating
a habit.

EXAMPLES.

J'avois soupé quand il entra,	I had supped when he came in.
Lorsque j'étois à la campagne, dès que j'avois déjeuné, j'allois à la chasse;	When I was in the country, as soon as I had breakfasted, I used to go a hunting.

The *future absolute* is that tense which expresses an
action to come; that is to say, that a thing will be done
or will happen at a time which does not yet exist.

EXAMPLE.

J'irai demain à la campagne,	I shall go to-morrow into the country.

The *future anterior* is the tense which expresses that
at a time when a thing will be done or will happen,

z 2

ánother thing will have been done, or will have happened.

Quand j'aurai fini, je sortirai, | When I have done, I shall go out.

I had done yesterday at noon. I (went out) (as soon as) I
   finir   *midi*   *sortir* ind-4 *dès que*
had dined. As soon as Cæsar had crossed the Rubicon, he had
                          passer   —
no longer to deliberate; he (was obliged) to conquer or to die,
  plus   *devoir* ind-2 * vaincre*   *
I had finished the task   that he had imposed upon me, when
        tâche f.   *imposer* f. *
he came in. Those who had contributed most to his eleva-
               —*buer le plus*
tion to the throne of his ancestors, were those who laboured
                         travailler
with the most eagerness   to precipitate him (from it). I
    de acharnement   *en*
shall shortly go into the country, where I intend · to
ne point tarder à *à*   *campagne*   *se proposer de*
(collect plants), (in order to) (make myself perfect) in the
herboriser inf-1   *pour*   *se perfectionner*
knowledge of   botany.   When I have done
         art. *botanique* f.   *achever* ind-8 *de*
reading the divine writings of Homer and Virgil, and   my
inf-1   2   *écrit* m. 1   *que*
mind has imbibed   their beauties, I shall read the other
    se pénétrer ind-8 *de*   ind-7
epic poets.
  2   1

The *conditional* is the mood which expresses affirmation in a dependance on a condition; it has two tenses, the *present* and the *past.*

The *present of the conditional* is that tense which expresses that a thing would be done or would happen on certain conditions.

Je ferois votre affaire avant qu'il | I would settle your business be-
soit peu, si elle dépendoit uni- | fore long, if it only depended
quement de moi; | upon me.

The *past of the conditional* is that tense which expresses that a thing would have been done or would have happened at a time which no longer exists, dependent on certain conditions.

EXAMPLE.

J'aurois ou *j'eusse fait votre affaire si vous m'en aviez* ou *eussiez parlé,*	I would have settled your business if you had mentioned it to me.

EXERCISE.

What would not be the felicity of man, if he always sought
  quel   — f.   *chercher* ind-2
his happiness in himself? I should be glad to see you harmonious,
                                  uni
happy, and comfortable. A dupe to my imagination, I should
      tranquille   *   *de*
have (been bewildered) (but for) you, in my   search   after
      s'égarer   *sans*   * art. *recherche* f.   *de*
   truth. Enquire   whether he would have consented to those
art.   *s'informer si*   *consentir*
conditions, in   case   he had thought himself able
        dans art.   *que*   *se croire* subj-4 *capable*
to fulfil   them.
de remplir

OF THE IMPERATIVE.

The *imperative* is that mood which, besides affirmation, expresses command, exhortation, entreaty. It has only one tense, which expresses a present with respect to the action of commanding, and a future with respect to the thing enjoined.

EXERCISE.

Be not fond   of   praise,   but seek   virtue, which
  sing. *passionné pour* art. *louange* f.   art.
procures to it. Let us remember that unless   virtue guide
attirer   *   *se souvenir*   *à moins que* art.   *ne*
us, our choice must   be wrong. Let us not be deceived
          devoir ind-1   *mauvais*   *se laisser prendre*
by the first appearances of   things; but let us take   time
à   art.   *se donner* art.
to fix our judgment. Arbiters of the destinies of   men, do
de   *arbitre*   =   art.   art.

good, if you wish   to be happy ; do good, if you wish that your
bien   vouloir *
memory should be honoured; do good, if you, wish that
            subj-1   art.
heaven should open to you its eternal gates.   Never forget
            subj-1   2   *porte* f. 1
that the truly   free. man is he, who, superior to all
    véritablement a 3   1   *dégagé   de*
fears and   all desires, is subject   only to the gods and to
. f-s.   pr. -   m-s.   *soumis ne que*
    reason.
art. . f.

N. B. In many verbs we may use a compound of the
imperative to express a command to do something pre-
viously to some other thing; as *ayez diné avant que je
revienne,* have dined before I return.

OF THE SUBJUNCTIVE.

The *subjunctive* is that mood which expresses the affirmation as subjoined to something that precedes.   This
dependance appears from its forming sense in conjunction
with the word which precedes, whilst it would form no
sense without it.   *Je voudrois qu'il lût,* forms sense, but
qu'il lût alone and unconnected does not.
    This mood contains four tenses, the *present* or *future,*
the *imperfect,* the *preterit,* and the *pluperfect.*
    The *present* and the *future* of the subjunctive can only be
distinguished by the sense: in this phrase, *il faut que je vous
ais bien attaché pour venir vous voir par le temps qu'il fait,*
I must have a great esteem for you to come and see you in
such weather as this ; *je sois* expresses a present time ; but
in this, *je ne crois pas que vous obteniez cela de lui,* I do not
think you will obtain that of him, *vous obteniez* expresses a
future and stands for *vous obtiendrez.*
    The. *imperfect,* the, *preterit,* and the *pluperfect* of the
subjunctive express also a past or future according to circumstances: in this phrase, *soupçonniez-vous qu'il ne le fît
pas,* did you suspect he would not do it, *fît* expresses a past;
but in this, *je désirerois qu'il vît du monde,* I wish him to
see company, *vît* marks a future.

EXERCISE.

Men must be (very much) blinded by their
art. 3. *il* 1 *que* 2 subj-1 *bien* *aveuglé*
passions, not to acknowledge that they ought to
pour *devoir* ind-1 *
(love one another) as parts of a whole; and as (the members
s'entr'aimer art. *tout* 2
of our body) (would do) if (every one) had a particular
1 *chacun* ind-2 *sa* 2
vitality. You asked him to come with us; but I doubt
vie f. 1 *prier* ind-4 *de*
whether he will have that complaisance. I could not persuade
que subj-1 ind-2
myself that he was so vain as to aspire to that place.
subj-2 *assez* * *pour* — f.
Though every body says so, I do not believe that he is
subj-1 *le* subj-1
gone to Rome. (Is it possible) that he should let slip so
se pouvoir *laisser* subj-3 *échapper*
good an opportunity of acquiring immortal glory? I could
beau *occasion* f. *un* 2 1
have wished that he had availed himself of his abode in the
profiter subj-4 *séjour à*
country, to perfect himself in the study of philosophy.
campagne *pour se perfectionner* art. = f.

OF THE INFINITIVE.

The *infinitive* is that mood which expresses the affirmation indeterminately without either number or person.

It denotes of itself neither *present*, *past*, nor *future*;
nevertheless it is considered as denoting those tenses, when
it follows other verbs. The *present* always expresses a present, relative to the preceding verb; as *je le vois, je le vis,
je le verrai venir.* I see, I saw, I shall see him come. The
past always expresses a past, relative to the verb that precedes it; *je crois, je croyois l'avoir vu venir,* I think, I
thought that I had seen him coming. To express a *future*
the infinitive must be preceded by the infinitive of the verb
devoir: as *je croyois devoir y aller,* I thought I was to go
there.

REMARK. The infinitive also expresses a future after the
verbs *promettre, espérer, compter, s'attendre,* and *menacer*:

as *il promet de venir* (*qu'il viendra*), he promises to come (that he will come); *il menace de s'y rendre* (*qu'il s'y rendra*); he threatens to go (that he will go) there.

EXERCISE.

We only shut our eyes to truth, because we fear to
ne * art. art. *que parce que de*
see ourselves as we are. We were yet far from the castle
2 *nous* 1 *tel que* ind-2 *encore*
when one of our friends came to join us. I did not think I
ind-3 * ind-2 *
was to set out so soon. He promises every day that he
devoir * art. pl. *de* *
will amend, but I do not rely upon his promises.
* *se corriger* *compter* *promesse* f. pl.
They talk of a secret expedition; he hopes to be (in it). He
on 2 —f. 1 * *en*
relies upon seeing you very soon to terminate
compter * inf-1 *au premier jour pour*
amicably his affair with you. You expected to take a
à l'amiable *s'attendre* ind-2 *de faire*
journey this year, but your father has changed his mind.
voyage m. *de* * *avis*
He threatens to punish us severely, if we (fall again) into the
de *sévèrement* *retomber*
same error.
faute.

OF THE PARTICIPLE.

The *participle* is a part of the verb which partakes of the nature both of a verb and adjective; of a verb, as it has its signification and regimen; of an adjective, as it generally performs its function, that is, expresses the quality of a person or thing.

There are two participles, viz. the *participle present* and the *participle past.*

OF THE PARTICIPLE PRESENT.

The *participle present* always terminates in *ant:* as *aimant, finissant, recevant, rendant.*

RULE. The participle present is invariable; that is, it takes neither gender nor number, when it expresses an action.

We say, *une montagne* or *des montagnes dominant sur*

des plaines immenses, a mountain or mountains commanding immense plains; *un homme, des hommes, une femme,
des femmes lisant, parlant, marchant*, a man, men, a woman, women reading, speaking, walking. But when it
expresses simply a quality, like an adjective, it takes both
the gender and number of its substantive. So we say, *un
homme obligeant*, an obliging man; *une femme obligeante*,
an obliging woman; *des tableaux parlans*, speaking portraits; *la religion dominante*, the established religion; *à
la nuit tombante*, at night-fall.

What grammarians call *gerund*, is nothing but the participle present, to which is prefixed the word *en; on se
forme l'esprit en lisant de bons livres*, we form our minds
by reading good books.

EXERCISE.

. That mountain being very high, and thus commanding a
  .   *élevé*   *ainsi   dominer sur*
vast   extent   of country, was   very well calculated for our
grande étendue   *pays* ind-2   *   *propre à*
observations.   This woman is of a good disposition, obliging
  .   *caractère* m.
every one,   whenever she (has it in her power).   They go
tout le monde   quand   *le pouvoir*
cringing before the great, that they may be   insolent to   their
ramper   devant   pl. *afin de* *   * inf-1 pl.   *avec*
equals.   The state of pure nature is the savage living in the desert,
égal
but living in his family,   knowing his children, loving them,
  famille f. *connoître*
(making use) of   speech, and (making himself understood).
user   art. *parole*   *se faire entendre*
An agreeable languour imperceptibly (laying hold) of my
  2   *langueur* f. *insensiblement   s'emparer*
senses, suspended   the activity of my soul, and I (fell asleep).
sens   suspendre ind-3   *s'endormir* ind-3
  Time is a real blunderer, placing, replacing, ordering, dis-
art.   *vrai brouillon   mettre   remettre   ranger dé-*
ordering, impressing, erasing, approaching, removing, and
ranger   imprimer   effacer   approcher   éloigner
making all things, good and bad; and almost always (impossi-
rendre   f. pl.   *presque*
ble to be known again).
méconnoissable.

OF THE PARTICIPLE PAST.

The participle past has various terminations; as *aimé, fini, reçu, ouvert, dissous,* etc.

This participle may either agree with its subject or its regimen.

AGREEMENT OF THE PARTICIPLE PAST WITH ITS SUBJECT.

RULE I. The participle past, when it is accompanied by the auxiliary verb *être,* agrees with its subject in gender and number ; that is, we add to it *e,* if the subject be feminine, and *s,* if it be in the plural.

EXAMPLES.

Mon frère est tombé,	My brother is fallen down.
Mes frères sont tombés,	My brothers are fallen down.
Ma sœur est tombée,	My sister is fallen down.
Mes sœurs sont tombées,	My sisters are fallen down.
La nuit sera bientôt passée,	The night will soon be over.
Les spectacles sont fréquentés,	The theatres are frequented.
Cette fleur est fort recherchée,	This flower is much sought after.
Ils sont fort estimés,	They are very much esteemed.

EXERCISE.

Fire-arms   were not known to the ancients.   Ishmael,
art. *arme à feu* f. pl. ind-4   *connu de*   *Ismaël,*
the son of Abraham, is known among the Arabs, as (the man)
*   —   parmi   Arabe   celui*
from whom they   sprung, and   circumcision has remained
          être sorti   art.   f.   être demeuré
(among them) as the mark of their origin. Heaven is that per-
    leur   f.   art.
manent city,   (into which) the just are   to be received after this
    — 2 *cité* f. 1   *où*   pl. *devoir*   *après*
life.   In Abraham's   time,   the threatenings of the true God
      de   2   art.   1   menace f. pl.
were   dreaded by Pharaoh,   king of Egypt; but, in the time of
ind-2 *redouté de Pharaon*
Moses,   all   nations were corrupted, and the world, which God
Moïse   art.   f.   *perverti*
has made   to   manifest his power,   was   become a temple of
    pour   puissance f.   *devenu*

idols. That dreadful crisis, which threatened the state with
         terrible 2 *crise* f. 1   ind-2   *de*
instant destruction, was happily   soon over.   She is
prochain 2   f. 1   ind-3 *heureusement*   *passé*
come to bring us all kinds   'of refreshments.   The sciences
        *   *sorte* f. pl.   *rafraîchissement*   f.
have always been protected by   enlightened governments.
            protégé   art. *éclairé* 2   1

RULE II. The participle past, when it follows the
verb *avoir*, never agrees with its subject.

EXAMPLES.

Mon frère a écrit,	My brother has written.
Mes frères ont écrit,	My brothers have written.
Ma sœur a écrit,	My sister has written.
Mes sœurs ont écrit,	My sisters have written.
Les Amazones ont acquis de la célébrité,	The Amazons have acquired celebrity.
J'ai contraint les soldats à marcher,	I have forced the soldiers to march.

REMARK. The participle of the verb *être*, and of all the
neuter verbs which are conjugated with the auxiliary verb
avoir, never vary. We say, *il* or *elle a été* he or she
has been ; *ils* or *elles ont été*, they have been ; *il* or *elle a
dormi*, he or she has slept; *ils* or *elles ont nui*, they have
annoyed.

EXERCISE.

The Romans successively   triumphed over the most
    Romain successivement 2   ind-4 1   *de*
warlike   nations. Lampridius relates that Adrian erected
belliqueux 2   1   *Adrien élever*
        to Jesus Christ some   temples, which (were still
ind-6   *de* art.   *on*   *encore* 2
to be seen) in his time.   Happy those   princes who have
voir ind-2 1 *de*   *   art.
never (made use) of their power but 'to do   good !   We
        user   *pouvoir que pour*   art.
have spent the whole day   in tormenting ourselves.   One
            journée f.   *à*   inf-1 2   *nous* 1
has seldom   seen a great stock   of good sense in a man of
    rarement   *fonds* m.   *sens*

imagination.　The errors of Descartes proved very　useful
　—　　　　　　=　　　　—　　*　*beaucoup servir*
　　to Newton.
ind-4

AGREEMENT OF THE PARTICIPLE PAST WITH ITS REGIMEN.

RULE I. The participle past always agrees with its regimen direct, when that regimen is placed before the participle, whether the auxiliary verb that accompanies it be *avoir* or *être.*

EXAMPLES.

Les écoliers que j'ai eus ont fait de grands progrès,	The pupils whom I have had have made rapid progress.
Lucrèce s'est tuée,	Lucretia has killed herself.
J'ai renvoyé les livres que vous m'aviez prêtés,	I have sent back the books which you had lent me.
Que de soins je me suis donnés,	What pains I have taken.
Quelle affaire avez-vous entreprise,	What business have you undertaken?
Quand la race de Caïn se fut multipliée,	When the race of Cain had multiplied.
Ces yeux que n'ont émus ni soupirs ni terreur,	Those eyes which neither sighs nor terror have moved.
Le dieu Mercure est un de ceux que les anciens ont le plus multipliés,	The god Mercury is one of those whom the ancients have multiplied the most.

REMARK. The regimen put before the participle is, in general, one of these pronouns, *que, me, te, se, le, la, les, nous* and *vous;* but it is sometimes a noun joined to the pronoun *quel,* or preceded by the word of quantity *que,* signifying *combien,* how much, as may be seen in the before mentioned examples.

EXERCISE.

All the letters which I have *received,* confirm　that impor-
　　　f. pl.　　　　　　　　　　　*confirmer*
tant news.　The agitated　life which I have *led*　till
　2　s. 1　　　*agité* 2 f. -1　　　　　　*mener jusqu'à*
now, makes me sigh　for　retirement.　The difficulties
présent　　*soupirer après* art. *retraite* f.　　　f. pl.
which the academies (have *proposed* to one another) do not
　　　　　　　se faire ind-4

seem   easy to (be resolved.)   The sciences which you have
paroître aisé   résoudre   f. pl.
studied, will prove infinitely useful (to you).   The death which
        être   f.
Lucretia (gave herself) has (made her immortal).   The
        se donner ind-4   immortaliser ind-4
cities   which those nations have (built for themselves) are
ville f. pl.   peuple   ⌐ se bâtir ind-4
but   a collection of huts. .   The persons whom you have
ne que   amas m.   chaumière   f. pl.
instructed appear to me possessed of reason and   taste. No-
          plein   pr.
thing can equal the   ardour of the troops which I have seen
         égaler   f. pl.
(setting off). The chimeras   which she has got   in her
inf-1   chimère f pl.   se mettre   * art.
head, (are beyond) all belief.   What measures   have I not
       passer   croyance f.   démarche f. pl.
taken! What fortunes has not this revolution ruined!   What
faire   f. pl.   renverser que
     tears has she not shed; what sighs has she not heaved!
de f. pl.   verser   m. pl.   pousser
The Amazons (made themselves) famous by their courage. The
       f. pl.   se rendre ind-4   célèbre
city of London has (made itself), by its commerce, the metro-
f   — m.
polis of the universe. I have thought her agitated by the furies.
—le f.   croire   —
This day is one of those which they have consecrated to.   tears.
       m. pl   consacrer   art.
The language in which Cicero and Virgil have written, will
    langue f. *   Cicéron
live in their works.   I could have wished to avoid entering
    par   ouvrage   *   vouloir * éviter d'entrer
into those details, but I thought   them necessary.   The
         — m.   croire ind-4   =
tribunes   demanded of Clodius the execution of the promise
tribun m. pl.   ind-3   à
which the consul Valerius had given them.
              faire leur

RULE II. The participle past never agrees with its
regimen, either when that participle is without regimen
direct, or when, having a regimen direct, that regimen
is placed after it.

2 A

EXAMPLES.

La lettre dont je vous ai parlé,	The letter which I have mentioned to you.
La perte et les profits auxquels il a participé,	The loss and profits which he has shared.
Les académies se sont fait des objections,	The academies have proposed objections to one another.
Vous avez appris à ces personnes à dessiner,	You have taught these persons to draw.
Lucrèce s'est donné la mort,	Lucretia has put a period to her existence.

EXERCISE.

The persons whose   visit you had *announced to* me, are not
    f. pl.   1   art. f. 5   2   4   3
come.   Men built   cities.   The Amazons
    art.   *se bâtir* ind-4 *de* art.
acquired great   celebrity.   I have *forced*   the soldiers to
ind-4   *beaucoup de*   =   *contraindre*
march.   That woman has *bestowed* on herself   fine gowns.   Let-
               se donner   *de*   art.
ters and   writing   were *invented* to present   speech.
4   art.   *écriture* 5 *on* 1 *a* 2   3   *pour peindre* art.
She has *cut*   two (of her) fingers.   Titus has *made* his wife
    se couper   *   *doigt* m. pl.   *rendre*
mistress of his riches.   I have *given* myself (a great deal of)
           bien   *bien*
    trouble.   Commerce has *made* this city flourishing.   They
art. *peine* f. art.   m.   f.   *florissant*
have *made*   an appointment.
    se donner * *rendez-vous*

RULE III. The participle past takes neither gender nor number, either when the participle and the auxiliary verb to which it is joined are used impersonally, or when that participle is formed by a verb, which governs the nouns or pronouns preceding it.

EXAMPLES.

Les chaleurs excessives qu'il a fait cet été, ont beaucoup nui à la récolte;	The excessive heats which we have had this summer, have done great injury to the harvest.
Quelle fâcheuse aventure vous est-il arrivé?	What unpleasant adventure have you met with?

La maison que j'ai fait bâtir,	The house which I have ordered to be built.
Imitez les vertus que vous avez entendu louer,	Imitate the virtues which you have heard praised.
Les mathématiques que vous n'avez pas voulu que j'étudiasse,	The mathematics which you would not permit me to study.
Elle s'est laissé séduire,	She has suffered herself to be seduced.

REMARK. To make a right application of the second part of this rule, we ought to examine whether we can put the regimen immediately after the participle. As we cannot say, *J'ai fait la maison, vous avez entendu les vertus, vous n'avez pas voulu les mathématiques,* it follows that the regimen belongs to the second verb. Sometimes, however, the regimen may relate either to the participle or to the verb, according to the meaning of the speaker. For instance, we must say, *Je l'ai vu peindre,* I saw her picture drawn; and *Je l'ai vue peindre,* meaning, I saw her painting.

Sometimes it happens too, that, in sentences which seem to resemble each other, the regimen in one belongs to the participle, and in the other to the verb which follows it. For instance, we ought to answer this question, *Avez-vous entendu chanter la nouvelle actrice?* Have you heard the new actress sing? *Oui, je l'ai entendue chanter;* yes, I have: but this question, *Avez-vous entendu chanter la nouvelle ariette?* Have you heard the new song? must be answered, *Oui, je l'ai entendu chanter;* yes, I have.

EXERCISE.

The great changes   which (have *taken* place) in   ad-
          changement   *y   avoir*   art.
ministration, have astonished many   people.   The heavy
                         bien des personnes   *grand*
rains   which we   have *had*   in the spring, have been
pluie f. pl.   * *il*   *faire* ind–4
the cause of many diseases.   The scarcity which there was
          maladie f. pl.   *disette* f.   ind–4
     last   winter, has afforded the opportunity of doing
art. *dernier* 2   1   *donner*   *occasion*   inf–1
much good.   What news   has *reached* you?   How many
     bien   *est-il venu*   .   *que   de*

2 A 2

imprudent steps   were *taken* on that occasion.   How
faux   démarche f. pl. *il s'est faire en*
many large ships   have been *built* in England within these fifty
    gros   il se construire ind-4   *depuis*   *
years.   The figures which you have *learned*   to draw   are of
                —   *apprendre   dessiner*
great beauty.   We ought   never to swerve   from the
*un   * falloir* ind-1   * s'éloigner*
good path   which we have *begun* to follow.   The measures
    route f.   *on*   *mesure* f.
which you *advised*   me to adopt   have not succeeded.
    conseiller ind-4   *de prendre*   *réussir*
The rule which I have *begun* to explain   seems   to me very
    règle f.   *expliquer sembler*
easy (to be understood).   You see that I have not (been mistaken)
        saisir   .   *se tromper* ind-4
on the affairs which I had *foreseen*   you would have in hand.
        prévoir que   *   *

CHAPTER VI.

OF THE ADVERB.

The Place of the Adverb.

RULE I. In the simple tenses, the adverb is generally
placed after the verb, and, in the compound tenses, between the auxiliary and the participle.

EXAMPLES.

L'homme le plus éclairé est ordinairement *celui qui pense* le plus modestement de lui-même,	The man who is most learned is generally he who thinks most modestly of himself.
Avez-vous jamais *vu un pédant plus absurde et plus vain?*	Have you ever seen a pedant more absurd and more vain?

The compound adverbs, and those which by custom have
preserved the regimen of the adjectives from which they
are derived, are placed always after the verb: as *c'est à
la mode*, that is fashionable; *il a agi conséquemment*, he
has acted consistently.

Those adverbs which denote time in an indeterminate
manner are likewise placed after the verb.

EXAMPLES.

Il eût fallu se lever plus matin,	It would have been necessary to rise earlier.
On a vu cela autrefois,	That has been seen formerly.

EXCEPTIONS. 1st. Adverbs of order and rank, and those which denote time in a determinate manner, are placed either before or after the verb.

EXAMPLES.

Nous devons premièrement *faire notre devoir,* secondement *chercher les plaisirs permis;*	We ought first to do our duty, secondly enjoy lawful pleasures.
Aujourd'hui *il fait beau, il pleuvra peut-être* demain;	To-day it is fine, it will rain perhaps to-morrow.

2dly. The five adverbs which serve for interrogation, are always placed before the verb.

EXAMPLES.

Comment vous portez-vous?	How do you do?
Où allez-vous?	Whither are you going?

RULE II. The adverb is always placed before the adjective which it modifies.

EXAMPLE.

C'est une femme fort *belle, très-sensible, et* infiniment *sage;*	She is a woman very beautiful, very sensible, and infinitely prudent.

RULE III. Adverbs of quantity and comparison, and the three adverbs of time, *souvent, toujours,* and *jamais,* are placed before the other adverbs.

Si poliment,	So politely.
Très-heureusement,	Very happily.
Le plus adroitement,	The most skilfully.
Ils ne seront jamais étroitement unis,	They never will be intimately united.
Ils sont toujours ensemble.	They are always together.
C'est souvent à l'improviste qu'il arrive,	He often comes unexpectedly.

2 A 3

The adverb *souvent* may, however, be preceded by an adverb of quantity or comparison; as *si souvent, assez, souvent.*

REMARK. When adverbs of quantity and comparison meet together in a sentence, the following is the order which custom has established; *si peu, trop peu, bien peu, très-peu; beaucoup* trop, bien plus, bien davantage, beaucoup moins, tant mieux, tant pis,* etc.

When *bien* is before another adverb, it means *very, much,* etc.: *bien assez,* quite enough; *bien moins,* much less, *frapper bien fort,* to strike very hard; but when it is placed after the adverb, it signifies *well:* as *assez bien,* pretty well; *moins bien,* not so well; *fort bien,* very well.

The above rules have been sufficiently exemplified in the exercises on the Verbs.

CHAP. VII.

OF THE CONJUNCTION.

The conjunction *que* serves, 1st, to complete a comparison; *l'Asie est plus grande que l'Europe,* Asia is larger than Europe: 2dly, to express a restriction in negative sentences; *on ne parle que de la nouvelle victoire,* they talk of nothing but the new victory.

The conjunction *que* also serves to give more force and grace, more spirit and precision to sentences.

1st. In elliptical turns: *Qu'il vive,* may he live; that is, *Je souhaite qu'il vive,* I wish he may live.

2dly. When it is put for *à moins que, avant que, sans que:* as *cela ne finira pas qu'il ne vienne,* there will be no end to it unless he come.

3dly. When it is used instead of *dès que, aussitôt que, si:* as *qu'il fasse le moindre excès, il est malade;* if he commits the least excess, he is ill.

4thly. When it is put for *jusqu'à ce que:* as *attendez qu'il vienne,* wait till he come.

5thly. When for *pourquoi:* as *que ne se corrige-t-il?* why does he not reform?

---

* *Beaucoup* is not, as the English *much,* susceptible of being modified by any adverb preceding; thus, *très-beaucoup, trop beaucoup* would be barbarisms.

We have every thing to fear from his wisdom,
even more than from his power. What men style
encore ce que art. appeler
greatness, power, profound policy, is in the eyes of
profond politique f. à
God only misery, weakness, and vanity. May
they understand, at last, that without internal
comprendre avec soi-même 2
peace there is no happiness. May she be as happy
art. 1 point de
as she deserves to be. Never write before you have
de le
thoroughly examined the subject which you propose
sous tous ses faces 2 1 se proposer
to treat. Let him but hear the least noise, his terrified imagi-
de traiter * effrayé
nation presents to him nothing but monsters. Do
f. * * ne que de art.
not sift this question, till I can (be your
approfondir ne subj-1 vous mettre
guide). Do not go out till your brother comes in. Why
sur la voie ne rentrer*
does he not (take advantage) of his youth, in order to acquire
profiter
the knowledge he wants?
connoissance pl. dont avoir besoin.

6thly. When it is used instead of comme, or parce que:
as, méchant qu'il est, wicked as he is.
7thly. When it is put for combien, and then it denotes
admiration and the sudden emotions of the soul: as que
Dieu est grand! how great is the Almighty! que je les
hais! how I hate them!
Another very frequent use of this conjunction is to put it
for comme, parce que, puisque, quand, quoique, si, etc.,
when, two phrases beginning with these words, others are
added under the same regimen, by means of the conjunction et: as si l'on aimoit son pays, et qu'on en désirât sincèrement la gloire, on se conduiroit de manière, etc.; if we
loved our country, and sincerely wished its glory, we
should act so as, etc.

Full *as* he was of his prejudices, he would not acknowledge
Rempli   ind-2   *préjugé*   ind-5   *convenir de*
(any thing).   Full of self-love (as he is), expect nothing
     rien   *pétri* 1   3   2   *de*
good (from him).   *How* beautiful is that cultivated nature!
          en   1   6   5 2   4   3
by the care of man *how* it is brilliantly and richly   adorned!
par   f.   *pompeusement*
    Had   profound philosophers presided at the formation of
si * *de*   ind-6 *à*   art.
languages, and *had* they carefully examined the elements of
langue   *avec soin* subj-4   — m.   art.
speech,   not only in their relations (to one another) but also
discours non   *entre eux*   *encore*
in themselves, it is not (to be doubted) that   languages
en   m.   *douteux*   art.   *ne*
would present ·   principles more simple, and at the
offrir subj-2 *de* art.
same time more luminous.

The conjunctions which unite sentences to one another,
are followed either by the infinitive, the indicative, or the
subjunctive.

Those that are followed by an infinitive, are: 1st. Such
as are distinguished from prepositions, only by being followed by a verb: as *il faut se reposer après avoir travaillé,*
one ought to rest after having laboured. 2dly. Those
which have the preposition *de* after them: as *je travaille
afin de vous surpasser,* I work that I may surpass you.

They   were going to spend a few   days in   town,
        ne * ind-2 * *passer * quelques*   *à* art.
only *that* they might return   with more pleasure to
que pour   *   *   *sè retrouver* inf-1   *dans*
their charming solitude.   Many persons work only (*in order to*)
                                        ne que   afin de
acquire   consideration and   riches, but the honest
      de art.   pr. art.   2   *et*
humane man spends   so much time in   study, only *to*
sensible 3 1 *ne employer*   *de*   *à* art.   *que pour*

be useful to his fellow-creatures. I unmask to you the plot
      semblables   *dévoiler*   *trame* f.
which your enemies have planned in   secret,   *in order*
     - *ourdir*   art. *ténèbres* f. pl.
to warn   you against their artifices.
prémunir

Those that govern the indicative are, *bien entendu que, à condition que, à la charge que, de même que, ainsi que, aussi bien que, autant que, non plus que, outre que, parce que, attendu que, vu que, puisque, lorsque, pendant que, tandis que, durant que, tant que, peut-être que;* to which may be added, *comme, comme si, quand, pourquoi,* etc. These conjunctions are followed by the indicative, because the principal sentence which they unite with the incidental one, expresses the affirmation in a direct, positive and independent manner.

REMARK. There are six conjunctions, the use of which varies according to the meaning expressed by the principal sentence, viz. *sinon que, si ce n'est que, de sorte que, en sorte que, tellement que, de manière que.* We say, *je ne lui ai répondu autre chose, sinon que j'avois exécuté ses ordres;* I made him no other answer, but that I had executed his orders; because the first verb expresses a positive affirmation. But we ought to say, *je ne veux autre chose, sinon que vous travailliez avec plus d'ardeur;* I desire nothing else, but that you should work with greater ardour.

EXERCISE.

When you have a more extensive knowledge of geometry
    ind-7   2   1   art.   f.
and   algebra, I shall give you a few   lessons in astronomy
  pr. art. *algèbre* f.   * *quelque*   *de*
and optics. Form your mind, heart, and taste,
  pr. *optique*   pron.   pron.
while you are still young. Do not keep truth a prisoner,
  encore   *retenir* art. * *captive*
though you should (draw upon you) a cloud of enemies.
quand *devoir* cond-1 *s'attirer* *nuée* f.
I will give you this fine picture *upon condition* that you
    tableau m. *à*
keep it as a testimony of my friendship.
conserver *témoignage* m.

The conjunctions which govern the subjunctive are,
soit que, sans que, pour que, quoique, jusqu'à ce que,
encore que, à moins que, pourvu que, supposé que, au
cas que, avant que, non pas que, afin que, de peur que,
de crainte que, and a few others. They are followed by
the subjunctive, because they always imply doubt, wish,
ignorance.

EXERCISE.

You know   too well the value of   time, *to*   make
   connoître   *prix* m. art.   *pour que être* 2
it   necessary to tell you to (make a good use of) it.   Study only
il 1   *de*   *de   bien employer*
    great models, *lest*   those which are but middling
art.   *de peur que*   * *médiocre ne*
should spoil   your taste, *before* it be entirely formed. I
   gâter subj-1
(make not the least   doubt) that your method   will succeed,
  ne douter nullement   f. ne   subj-1
provided it be well known. Several phenomena of   nature
  f.   art.
are easy (to be explained), *supposing* the principle of   universal
    (by the active)   art.   2
gravitation to be true.
  f. 1   *

PROMISCUOUS EXERCISE ON THE NINE PARTS OF SPEECH.

The Good Mother.

What a fine morning!   said   the amiable Charlotte to her
     matinée f. ind-3
brother George.   Come, let us go into the garden and enjoy
         sing.   *   inf-1
- the magnificent sight   ,   of   rich and abundant nature.
de   2   *spectacle* m. 1   *une* 2   *fertile* 3   1
We will gather there the freshest and   sweetest flowers.
     cueillir y   *frais* 2   art. adv. *odorant* 3 f. pl. 1
We will make a nosegay   which we will offer to mamma.   You
     bouquet m.   *maman.*   sing.
know   she loves   flowers. This attention will give her plea-
savoir que   art.   *faire lui*
sure. Ah!   brother, it will obtain us a smile, a caress, perhaps
     mon   f.   *valoir*   *sourire* m. f.

even a kiss.   Ah ! sister, replied   George, your proposal
   baiser m.   *ma*   *répondre* ind-3   sing. *projet*
delights me ; let us run, let us fly,   that we may offer her
enchanter   *courir*   *voler afin de* * *   *lui*
(when she rises) this tribute of our gratitude and our love.
à son lever   *hommage*   —   pr.
Full of this idea, Charlotte and George hastened
plein   *se hâter* ind-3 *de se rendre*
into the garden. Charlotte gathered   violets,   jes—
                 ind-3   *de* art.   pr. art.
samine, and young rose-buds   which (had but just begun)
            pr. *de* 2 *bouton* m. 1   *ne commencer que* ind-2
to open   their purple   cups,   while George prepared
entr'ouvrir   *de pourpre* 2 *calice* 1   ind-2
    green   sprigs of myrtle and   thyme, designed
de art. *verdoyant* 2 *jet* m. 1   *myrte*   pr. *thym destiné*
to support the flowers. Never had   these amiable children
soutenir   1   ind-2 3   2
worked with (so much) zeal and ardour. Satisfaction and
travailler   *tant de zèle* pr.   art. f.   art.
pleasure were painted in all their features, sparkled in their eyes,
    ind-2 *peint*   *trait* m. *pétiller*
and added still to their beauty.

While they (were employing themselves) (in this manner),
      s'occuper ind-2   *ainsi*
their mother, who had seen them in the garden, came to join
                         ind-3 * *joindre*
them. (As soon as) they perceived her, they flew to her, and
      dès que   ind-3   ind-3 *elle*
  said : Ah! mamma, how glad we are to see you ! how
lui   *que aise* 2 1 *de*
(impatient we were   ) for this pleasure. In the
il tardoit à notre impatience   *d'avoir*   *ce*
pleasing expectation (of it) we (were preparing) this nosegay for
doux attente f.   *   ind-2   *
you. What satisfaction should we have had in presenting
     -f.   *ne*   *pas*   *à offrir*
it to you ! Look at these rose-buds, these violets, this jessamine,
      voir *
this myrtle, and this thyme. Well,   we designed them for
                  Eh bien   *destiner*   *
you. These flowers, coming from us, would have been dear to
                                   cher
you. When you wore · them, you would have said : My
   En   * *porter* inf-2

children (were thinking) of me while I slept.   I am
    s'occuper ind-3   *dormir* ind-2
always as present to their minds as to their heart.   They love

me, and it is by giving me every   day   new proofs of their
    ce en'   art. pl. *de*   *preuve* f.
affection, that they acknowledge the care   ·I have taken
    reconnoître   *soin* m. pl. *que*
of them in their childhood, and all the marks of tenderness
                                             que
I am unceasingly giving them,
    ne cesser de inf-1.

My dear children, replied   the mother, embracing
    répondre ind-3   *en embrasser*
them, how charming you render   all my days! your
    quel charme   *répandre sur*   *
gratitude, your tenderness, your attention to me, make me
                                      pour
forget my former misfortunes, and open   my heart again to
  oublier   *ancien malheur* m.   *rouvrir*   *
the soft impressions of   pleasure. May   Heaven
   f.   art.   *Pouvoir* subj-1 art.
continue to bless my labours! May   it be your guide and your
continuer de   *soin*   *Pouvoir*   —
support in the career   which (will soon be opened) to   you!
soutien   *carrière* f.   *aller* ind-1 *s'ouvrir devant*
may it complete   its kindness   by preserving   you
  mettre le comble à   *bienfait* pl. *en garantir* inf-3
from the dangers to which you cannot fail   to be soon
                        *   *ne pas tarder* ind-7   *
exposed! Alas! I shudder (at them) beforehand, my dear chil-
    frémir   en   d'avance
dren; the moment is come when you must enter   the world.
         où   devoir   dans
Your persons,   your birth,   and your riches call   you there,
figure sing.   *naissance*   *appeler*   *y*
and insure you a distinguished rank (in it). I cannot always be
assurer   2   m. 1   *y*   ind-7
your guide. Young and inexperienced, you will   find
    sans expérience   *aller* ind-1 inf-1
yourselves surrounded by every kind   of temptation. (Every
  entouré   *sorte* f. *séduction*   *tout*
thing), even   vice, presents itself there under an
  jusque à art. m. *offrir*   *y* *sous* * *de* art.
agreeable form, and almost always in the shape of   pleasure,
  2   pl. 1   *sous*   *image* art.

which has (so many) attractions for youth. They will try
 tant de   *attrait* f.   art. *jeunesse*·f. *On*   *chercher*
to mislead you, to corrupt you; they (will make use of) artifice,
 égarer   *employer* art.
 railery, and even   ridicule, and, if   necessary,
art. =   *même* 2 art.   —1   *il est*
they will assume even   the mask   of virtue. If you
 prendre jusque à   *masque* m.   art.
abandon yourselves to first impressions, you are lost. The poison
 se laisser aller
of   example will insinuate itself into your hearts, will corrupt
art.   *se glisser*   *altérer*
the innocence and purity (of them), and will substitute
       en   *de* art.
violent   passions for the mild affections which have hitherto
déchirant 2   f. pl. 1   *à*   *doux*
formed your happiness.
faire.

Do not imagine, my dear children, that in placing before your
 croire   *en mettre sous*
eyes   a picture   of the dangers of the world, my intention
 art. *tableau* m.
is   to prohibit you every kind   of pleasure. God forbid,
subj-1   *interdire*   *espèce* f.   *à*   *ne plaire*
   pleasure is necessary to   man;   without it, our
subj-1 art.   *lui*
existence would be dreadful; (and therefore)   Providence,
    affreux   *aussi*   art.   f.
always attentive to our wants, has   multiplied the sources of
     besoin   *t-elle*
it both in   and out of ourselves. But, in tasting the pleasures
 *   *en nous*   *nous*   *en goûter*
of the world, never (abandon yourselves) (to them). Take care
       se livrer   *y*   *Avoir*
that they do not govern you ; know how to quit them,   the
     dominer   *savoir* *   *   *de*
moment   they have acquired (too much) empire over you. It
 que   *prendre* ind-7   *trop de*   *Ce*
is the only way   to enjoy with delight   that exquisite plea-
 moyen de   *volupté de*   *délicieux* 2
sure which we can only find in ourselves, and which has its
1   *en*
source in an upright and pure conscience. Ah ! why cannot I
 dans droit 2   3   f. 1.   *que*
give you all my experience ? why cannot you like me read   the
            dans

depths of the heart? with what astonishment would you often
abîme . . pl.

see . chagrin, agitation. and trouble, disguised under
art. . —m. art. art. —m. *déguisé sous*

the appearance of joy and tranquillity; hatred
apparence pl. art. pr. art. *calme* art. f.

and envy concealed under the air of confidence and
art. f. *caché* art. *confiance* f. pr. art.

friendship; indifference and selfishness, affecting the most
art. *égoïsme*

lively interest; the most dreadful and perfidious plots
vif 2 art. adv. 3 *trame* f. pl. 1

contrived deliberately in the dark; in a word, the
ourdi de sang froid et ténèbres f. pl. *en*

most odious vices endeavouring to show themselves under the
2 art. 1 *s'efforcer de*

features of (their opposite) virtues! In the world there
traits qui leur être opposé 2 art. 1

is but one moving principle; that is, self— interest.
ne que seul mobile m. *ce* art. *personnel* 2 1

To that every action refers; every thing tends to that
C'est à lui que art. pl. *se rapporter* . *lui*

as to its end. I know very well, my dear children, that your
fin f. *savoir*

hearts will not be infected by this vice. The sentiments of universal
de 2

benevolence with which I (have always) inspired you,
bienveillance 1 * *ne point cesser* ind-4 *de* inf-1

and of which I have seen you give (so many) proofs, (remove
tant de preuve rassurer

already every fear) (I might have) upon that subject: but will
d'avance. me sur point m.

you not yield to other vices not less dangerous? Cruel idea!
de· non f.

terrible uncertainty! If this misfortune were to happen,
affreux f. * * *arriver* ind-2

ah! my dear children, instead of being the joy and consola-
art. f.

tion of my life, you would be the torment, the shame, and the
honte f.

disgrace (of it). You would poison my days, and you
opprobre en empoisonner

would plunge a dagger into the very bosom which gave
; *porter* art. *mort* f. *même* 2 *sein* m. 1 ind-3

you life. But whither is my tenderness for you hurrying me?
, art *où* * . *emporter*

No, my children, no, I have nothing to fear, you love me (too
Non
much) to   wish   to afflict me so cruelly; and I shall have the
trop   pour vouloir *
pleasure, (as long as) I live, of seeing you walk in the ways
          tant que   ind-7   *sentier*
of   honesty and   virtue.
  art. *honneur*   pr. art.

~~~~~~~~

PART III.

OF WORDS CONSIDERED IN THEIR PARTICULAR RULES OR IDIOMS.

CHAP. I.

OF THE SUBSTANTIVE.

The substantive performs three functions in language, that of the subject, the regimen, or the apostrophe.

The substantive is the *subject* whenever it is that of which something is affirmed. When we say, *l'oiseau vole*, the bird flies; *le lion ne vole pas*, the lion does not fly; the substantives *oiseau* and *lion* are subjects, because it is affirmed of the first that it flies, and of the second that it does not fly.

It is to the substantive as the subject that every thing relates in a sentence. In the following, *un homme juste et ferme n'est ébranlé ni par les clameurs d'une populace injuste, ni par les menaces d'un fier tyran; quand même le monde brisé s'écrouleroit, il en seroit frappé, mais non pas ému:* the adjectives *juste* and *ferme* modify the subject *homme*, and all the rest modify *un homme juste et ferme*.

EXERCISE.

1. A king, who is inaccessible to men, is inaccessible to truth also, and passes his life in a ferocious 2 inhuman 3 grandeur 1 : as he is continually afraid of being deceived, he always 2 unavoidably 3 is 1 and deserves to be so; besides, he is at the mercy of slanderers and tale-bearers, a base 2 malicious 3 tribe 1, who feed upon venom, and invent mischief rather than cease to injure.

1. *Is inaccessible also*, l'est aussi; *ferocious*, sauvage; *inhuman*, et farouche; *as he is afraid*, craignant; *is*, l'est; *to be so*, de l'être; *besides*, de plus; *tale-bearers*, rapporteur; *tribe*, nation; *feed upon*, se nourrir de; *mischief*, mal; *to injure*, de nuire.

·2. The good which a man does is never lost; if men forget it,
God remembers and rewards it.

2. *Good*, bien; *a man*, on; *remember*, s'en souvenir.

The substantive forms the *regimen* when it is governed
by another word; now, a substantive may be governed
either by another substantive, by an adjective, by a verb,
or by a preposition: as *la loi de Dieu*, the law of God;
utile à l'homme, useful to man; *aimer son prochain*, to love
one's neighbour; *chez son père*, at his father's.

In French a substantive cannot be governed by another
substantive, but by the help of a preposition. This preposition is generally *de*: as *la difficulté de l'entreprise*, the difficulty of the undertaking; but sometimes, also, *à* and
pour are made use of: as *l'abandon à ses passions*, the
giving way to one's passions; *le goût pour le plaisir*, the
love of pleasure.

GENERAL RULE. When two substantives are found
together, the one *governing*, the other *governed*, the former
is generally placed first.

EXAMPLE.

La beauté *des sentimens*, la violence *des passions*, la grandeur *des événemens*, et les succès miraculeux *des grandes épées des héros, tout cela m'entraîne comme une petite fille.*—Sévigné.	The beauty of sentiments, the violence of passions, the grandeur of events, and the prodigious successes of the huge swords of heroes, all these transport me like a little girl.

REMARK. This order is not followed in English in these
two instances; 1st. when two substantives are joined by
an *s* and an apostrophe, placed after the first, thus, *'s*: as
the *king's palace*. 2d. When the two substantives form a
compound word; as *silk-stockings*.

EXERCISE.

1. The *silence* of the night, the *calmness* of the sea, the *trembling*2 *light*1 of the moon diffused over the surface of the water,

1. *Trembling*, tremblant; *diffused*, répandu; *dim*, sombre;

and *the dim azure of the* sky besprinkled with glittering 2 stars 1, served to heighten the beauty of the scene.

2. Nothing was heard but *the warbling* of birds, or the *soft breath* of the zephyrs sporting in *the branches* of the trees, or *the murmurs* of a lucid rill falling from the rocks, or *the songs* of the young swains who attended Apollo.

3. A smiling boy was, at the same time, caressing a lap-dog, which is his *mother's favourite*, because it pleases the child.

4. There are several *gold and silver mines* in this beautiful country; but the inhabitants, simple, and happy in their simplicity, do not even deign to * reckon gold and silver among their riches.

besprinkled, parsemé; *with,* de; *heighten,* rehausser; *scene,* spectacle.

2. *Nothing but,* on ne que; *breath,* haleine; *sporting,* qui se jouer,` ind-2; *branches,* rameaux; *lucid rill,* eau claire; *falling,* (which fell); *swains,* berger; *attended,* suivre, ind-2.

3. *Smiling boy,* enfant d'un air riant; *was caressing,* caresser, ind-2; *lap-dog,* bichon; *pleases,* amuser.

4. *Reckon,* compter.

The substantive is an *apostrophe,* whenever it is the person or thing addressed: as *rois, peuples, terre, mer, et vous, cieux, écoutez-moi!* In this sentence, the substantives *rois, peuples, terre, mer* and *cieux,* are an apostrophe.

REMARK. It is only when the language is highly oratorical that the speech is directed to inanimate objects.

EXAMPLE OF A BEAUTIFUL APOSTROPHE.

O Hippias! Hippias! I shall never see thee again * ! O my dear Hippias! it is I, cruel and * relentless, who taught thee to despise death. Cruel gods! ye prolonged my life, only that I might see the death of Hippias! O my dear child, whom I had brought up with so much care, I shall see thee no more. O dear shade, summon me to the banks of the Styx, the light grows hateful to me; it is thou only, my dear Hippias, whom I wish to see again. Hippias! Hippias! O my dear Hippias! I live but to pay the last duty to thy ashes.

Never, ne plus; *relentless,* moi impitoyable; *taught,* apprendre, ind-4; *prolonged,* prolonger, ind-1; *only that I might,* pour me faire; *brought up,* nourrir, ind-4; *with so much care,* et qui me coûter, ind-4, tant de soins; *shade,* ombre; *summon,* appeller; *to,* sur; *banks,* rive; *grows hateful,* être odieux; *I live but to,* ne vivre encore que pour; *pay,* rendre; *ashes,* cendre.

CHAP. II.

OF THE ARTICLE.

GENERAL PRINCIPLE. The article is to be used before all substantives common, taken in a determinate sense, *unless there be another word performing the same office;* but it is not to be used before those that are taken in an indeterminate sense.

CASES IN WHICH THE ARTICLE IS TO BE USED.

RULE I. The article necessarily accompanies all substantives common, which denote a whole species of things or determinate things.

EXAMPLES.

L'homme *se repaît trop souvent de chimères,*	Man too often feeds on chimeras.
Les hommes à imagination *sont toujours malheureux,*	Men of fanciful dispositions are always unhappy.
L'homme *dont vous parlez est très-instruit,*	The man you speak of is very learned.

In the first example, the word *homme* is taken in its fullest sense; it denotes a collective universality. In the second, *les hommes à imagination* denotes a particular class only. In the third, *l'homme* denotes but one individual, it being restricted by the incidental proposition *dont vous parlez.*

REMARK. In English, the article is not used before substantives taken in a general sense: as *men of genius, women of sound understanding.*

EXERCISE.

1. The moment elegance, the most visible image of fine taste, appears, it is universally admired. Men differ respecting the other constituent parts of * beauty, but they all unite without hesitation in acknowledging the power of elegance.

2. *Men of superior genius* 2, while 1 they * see 5 the rest of

---

1. *The moment,* du moment que; *fine,* délicat; *appears,* se montrer; *is,* elle est; *differ respecting,* différer sur; *constituent,* (which constitute); *hesitation,* hésiter; *in,* pour.

mankind painfully * struggling to comprehend obvious 2 truths 1,
glance themselves * through * the most remote consequences 1,
like lightning through a path that cannot be traced.

3. *The man who lives* under an habitual 2 sense 1 of the
divine 2 presence 1 keeps up a perpetual cheerfulness of temper,
and enjoys every moment the satisfaction of thinking himself *
in company with the dearest and best of friends.

2. *While*, tandis que ; *struggling*, se tourmenter ; *obvious*,
qui .'offreut d'elles-mèmes ; *glance*, ils pénètrent en un instant ;
lightning, foudre f. ; *through*, traverse ; *path*, espace ; *that*,
qu'on ; *be traced*, mesurer.

3. *Under*, dans ; *sense*, conviction ; *keep up*, conserver ; *perpetual*, constant ; *cheerfulness*, gaieté ; *temper*, caractère ; *enjoys*,
jouir de ; *of thinking*, se croire ; *in*, dans ; *with*, de.

RULE II. The article is put before substantives taken
in a sense of extract, or denoting only a part of a species ;
but it is omitted, if they be preceded by an adjective, or
a word of quantity.

EXAMPLES.

Du pain *et* de l'eau *me feroient plaisir*,	Some bread and water would please me.
Je vis hier des savans *qui ne pensent pas comme vous*,	I yesterday saw some learned men, who do not think as you do.
Voilà de beaux tableaux,	There are beautiful pictures.
J'achetai hier beaucoup de livres.	I bought yesterday many books.
Que de livres *j'achetai hier*,	How many books I bought yesterday.

REMARK. Among the words of quantity must be reckoned
plus, moins, pas, point and *jamais*.

EXAMPLES.

Il n'y eut jamais plus de lu-mières,	There never was more learning.
Il y a moins d'habitans à Paris qu'à Londres,	There are fewer inhabitants in Paris than in London.
Je ne manque pas d'amis,	I do not want for friends.

EXCEPTION. *Bien* is the only word of quantity which is
followed by the article.

EXAMPLES.

| *Il a bien de l'esprit,* | He has a great deal of wit. |
| *Elle a bien de la grâce,* | She is very graceful. |

REMARK. The sense of extract is marked in English by the word *some* or *any*, either expressed or understood, which answers to *quelque*, a partitive adjective, and consequently to *du, des*, which are elegantly used instead of *quelque*.

The expressions, *des petits-maîtres, des sages-femmes, des petits-pâtés*, etc. are not exceptions, because, in such cases, the substantives are so far united with the adjectives, as to form but one and the same word. We must likewise say, *le propre* des *belles actions, les sentimens* des *anciens philosophes*, etc. because, in expressions of this kind, the substantives are taken in a general sense.

EXERCISE.

1. We could not cast our eyes on either shore, without seeing *opulent* cities, *country houses* agreeably situated, *lands* yearly 2 covered 1 with a golden 2 harvest 1, *meadows* abounding in flocks and herds, *husbandmen* bending under the weight of the fruits, and *shepherds* who made 1 the echoes 5 around them 6 repeat 2 the sweet sounds 3 of their pipes and flutes 4.

2. Provence and Languedoc produce *oranges, lemons, figs, olives, almonds, chesnuts, peaches, apricots and grapes*, of an uncommon sweetness.

3. The man who has never seen this pure light, is as* blind as one who is born blind; he dies without having seen any thing; at most, he perceives but *glimmering and false lights, vain shadows*, and *phantoms* that have nothing of reality.

4. Among the Romans, those who were convicted of having

1. *Could*, pouvoir, ind-2; *our*, art; *seeing*, apercevoir; *yearly*, tous les ans; *covered with*, qui se couvrir de, ind-2; *abounding in*, remplis de; *flocks and herds*, troupeau; *husbandmen*, laboureur; *bending*, qui étoient accablés; *weight*, poids; *shepherds*, bergers; *pipes*, chalumeau; *the echoes*, aux échos; *around them*, d'alentour.

3. *Who is born blind*, aveugle-né; *without having*, n'avoir jamais, ind-3; *any thing*, rien : *at most*, tout au plus; *perceives*, apercevoir; *glimmering*, sombre; *lights*, lueur; *reality*, réel.

4. *Used*, employer; *illicit or unworthy means*, moyen illicite

used *illicit* or *unworthy means* to obtain an employ, were excluded from it for ever.

5. Those who govern are like the celestial 2 bodies 1, which have *great splendour* and *no rest*.

6. *What beauty, sweetness, modesty,* and, at the same time, *what mildness* and *greatness* of soul!

7. Themistocles, in order to ruin Aristides, made use of *many* artifices, which would have covered him with infamy in the eyes of posterity, had 1 not 4 the eminent services 2 which he rendered his country 3 blotted out 5 that stain.

8. The consequences *of great passions* are blindness of mind and depravity of heart.

9. *Noblemen* should never forget that their high birth imposes great duties* on them.

---

or voie indigne, pl.; *were,* ind-2; *from it,* en.

5. *Great,* beaucoup de; *splendour,* éclat; *no rest,* (that have no rest) repos.

6. *What,* que de.

7. *Ruin,* perdre; *made use of many,* employer bien; *artifices,* manœuvres; *covered,* cond-3; *with,* de; *infamy,* opprobre; *in,* à; *had,* si; *rendered,* ind-3, à; *blotted out,* effacer, cond-3; *stain,* tache.

8. *Of mind, of heart,* de art.

9. *Noblemen,* gentilhomme; *should,* devoir, ind-1.

RULE III. The article is put before proper names of countries, regions, rivers, winds and mountains.

EXAMPLES.

La France *a* les Pyrénées *et* la Méditerranée au sud, la Suisse *et* la Savoie à l'est, les Pays-bas au nord, *et* l'océan à l'ouest;	France is bounded on the south by the Pyrenees and the Mediterranean, on the east by Switzerland and Savoy, on the north by the Netherlands, and on the west by the ocean.
La Tamise, le Rhône, l'aquilon, les Alpes, le Cantal;	The Thames, the Rhone, the north wind, the Alps, the Cantal.

REMARK. We say, by apposition, *le mont Parnasse, le mont Valérien,* etc. *le fleuve Don,* etc. But we say, *la montagne de Tarare,* etc. *la rivière de Seine,* etc. We ought not to say *le fleuve du Rhône,* but simply *le Rhône.*

1. *Europe* is bounded' on the north by the Frozen Ocean; on the south, by the Mediterranean sea, which separates it from *Africa*; on the east, by the continent of *Asia*; on the west, by the Atlantic Ocean. It contains the following 2 states 1: on the north, *Norway, Sweden, Denmark*, and *Russia*; in the middle, *Poland, Prussia, Germany, United Provinces, the Netherlands, France, Switzerland, Bohemia, Hungary, the British Isles*; on the south, *Spain, Portugal, Italy, Turkey in Europe.*

2. The principal rivers in Europe are: the *Wolga*, the *Don* or *Tanaïs*, and the *Boristhenes* or *Nieper*, in Muscovy; the *Danube*, the *Rhine*, and the *Elbe*, in Germany; the *Vistula* or *Wezel*, in Poland; the *Loire*, the *Seine*, the *Rhone*, and the *Garonne*, in France; the *Ebro*, the *Tagus*, and the *Douro*, in Spain; the *Po*, in Italy; the *Thames* and the *Severn* in England; and the *Shannon* in Ireland.

3. The principal mountains in Europe are the *Daarne Fields* between Norway and Sweden; *Mount Krapel* between Poland and Hungary; the *Pyrenean Mountains* between France and Spain; the *Alps*, which divide France and Germany from Italy.

4. The bleak *north wind* never blows here, and the heat of summer is tempered by the cooling 2 *zephyrs* 1, which arrive to refresh the air towards the middle of the day.

1. *Bounded,* borné; *on,* à; *frozen ocean,* mer glaciale, f.; *south,* sud *or* midi; *Mediterranean sea,* Méditerranée, f.; *east,* est *or* orient; *west,* ouest *or* occident; *Norway,* Norwège; *Sweden,* Suède; *Denmark,* Danemark; *Russia,* Russie; *Poland,* Pologne; *Prussia,* Prusse; *Germany,* Allemagne; *Netherlands,* Pays-Bas; *Switzerland,* Suisse; *Bohemia,* Bohème; *Hungary,* la Hongrie; *British Isles,* îles Britanniques; *Spain,* Espagne; *Turkey in,* Turquie de.

2. *Muscovy,* Moscovie; *Vistula,* Vistule, f.; *Loire,* f.; *Seine,* f.; *Rhone,* m.; *Garonne,* f.; *Ebro,* Ebre; *Tagus,* Tage, m.; *Thames,* Tamise, f.; *Severn,* Saverne, f.

3. *Pyrenean Mountains,* Pyrénées.

4. *Bleak,* rigoureux; *north wind,* aquilon; *heat,* ardeur; *cooling,* rafraîchissant; *arrive,* venir; *to refresh,* adoucir.

EXCEPTIONS. The article is not used before the names of countries:

1st. When those countries have the names of their capitals: as *Naples est un pays délicieux*, Naples is a delightful country.

2dly. When those names are governed by the preposition *en:* as *il est en France,* he is in France; *il est en Espagne,* he is in Spain.

3dly. When those names are governed by some preceding noun, and have the sense of an adjective: as *vins de France,* French wines; *noblesse d'Angleterre,* the English nobility.

4thly. Lastly, when we speak of those countries as of places we come or are set off from: as *je viens de France,* I come from France; *j'arrive d'Italie,* I am just arrived from Italy. But, in this case, when we speak of the four parts of the world, the present practice favours the use of the article: as *je viens de l'Amérique, j'arrive de l'Asie.*

EXERCISE.

1. *Naples* may be called a paradise, from its beauty and fertility. From this country 2 some suppose 1 Virgil took the model of the Elysian 2 Fields 1.

2. I have been prisoner *in Egypt,* as a* Phœnician; under that name I have long suffered, and under that name I have been set at liberty.

3. *He* has received French and Spanish wines, Italian silks, Provence oil, and English wool.

4. We set sail *from Holland,* to go to the Cape of Good Hope.

5. I was but just arrived *from Russia,* when I had the misfortune to lose my father.

6. I had set off *from America,* when my brother arrived there.

1. *From,* à cause de; *from this country,* que c'est là où; *some suppose,* quelques personnes penser.

2. *Prisoner,* captif; *under that name,* c'est sous ce nom que (both alike).

4. *Set sail,* partir; *to go,* se rendre.

5. *I was but just,* ne faire que de.

6. *Set off,* partir; *there,* y.

The article is also used before the names of countries, either distant or little known; *la Chine,* China; *le Japon,* Japan; *le Mexique,* Mexico; and before those which have been formed from common nouns; *le Hâvre, le Perche, la Flèche,* etc.

REMARK. In English the article is generally omitted before names of countries.

CASES IN WHICH THE ARTICLE IS NOT USED.

RULE I. The article is omitted before nouns common, when, in using them, we do not say any thing on the extent of their signification.

·EXAMPLES.

Le sage n'a ni amour *ni* haine,	The wise man has neither love nor hatred.
Ils ont renversé religion, morale, gouvernement, sciences, beaux-arts, *en un mot, tout ce qui fait la gloire et la force d'un état ;*	They have overturned religion, morality, government, sciences, fine arts, in a word, every thing which constitutes the glory and strength of a state.

Hence the article is not employed before nouns.

1st. When they are in the form of a title or an address.

EXAMPLES.

Préface,	Preface.
Livre premier,	Book the first.
Chapitre dix,	Chapter the tenth.
Il demeure rue Piccadilly, quartier St. James;	He lives in Piccadilly, St. James's.

2dly. When they are governed by the preposition *en.*

EXAMPLES.

Regarder en pitié,	To look with pity.
Vivre en roi,	To live like, *or,* as a king.

3dly. When they are joined to the verbs *avoir* or *faire,* with which they form only one idea.

EXAMPLES.

Avoir peur,	To be afraid.
Faire pitié.	To excite pity.

2 C

4thly. When they are used as an apostrophe or interjection.

EXAMPLE.

Courage, soldats, tenez ferme ; | Courage, soldiers, stand firm.

5thly. When they serve to qualify a noun that precedes them.

EXAMPLES.

Il est quelquefois plus qu'homme,	He is sometimes more than man.
Son Altesse Royale le Duc d'York, Prince du sang royal d'Angleterre,	His Royal Highness the Duke of York, Prince of the blood royal of England.

6thly. The article is not put before the substantive beginning an incidental sentence, which is opposed to what has been said.

EXAMPLES.

Tous les peuples de la terre ont une idée plus ou moins développé d'un Etre suprême ; preuve évidente que le péché originel n'a pas tout-à-fait obscurci l'entendement :	All the nations of the earth have an idea more or less clear of a Supreme Being ; an evident proof that original sin has not totally obscured the understanding.

7thly. When they are governed by the words *genre, espèce, sorte,* and such like.

EXAMPLES.

Sorte de fruit,	A sort of fruit.
Genre d'ouvrage,	A kind of work.

EXERCISE.

1. The highways are bordered with *laurels, pomegranates, jessamines,* and the other trees which* are* always green and always in bloom. The mountains are covered with *flocks,* which yield a fine wool in great request with all the known 2 nations 1 of the world.

1. *Highways,* chemin : *with laurels,* de lauriers ; *pomegranates,* grenadiers ; *in bloom,* fleuri ; *yield,* fournir ; *wool,* laine, pl. *in great request,* recherché ; *with,* de ; *of the world*.

2. The fleets of Solomon, under the conduct of the Phœnicians, made frequent voyages to the land of Ophir and Tharsis (of the kingdom of Sophala, in Ethiopia), whence they returned at the end of three years, laden with *gold*, *silver*, *ivory*, *precious* 2 *stones* 1, and other kinds of merchandize.

3. *Costly furniture* 2 is not allowed there 1, nor *magnificent attire*, nor *sumptuous feasts*, nor *gilded palaces*.

4. We contemplated with pleasure the extensive fields covered with yellow ears of corn, the* *rich gifts* of bounteous Ceres.

5. He was *in a kind of ecstacy* when he perceived us.

6. In the most corrupt age, he lived and died *as a wise man**.

7. Are you surprised that the worthiest 2 men 1 are *but men*, and betray some remains of the weakness of humanity, amid the innumerable 2 snares 1 and difficulties which* are* inseparable from royalty ?

8. *He excited our pity*, when we saw him after his disgrace.

9. Hear then, *O nations* full of valour ! and you *O chiefs*, so wise and so united ! hear what I have *. to * offer you.

10. Out of this cavern issued, from time to time, a black 2 thick 3 smoke 1, which made a *sort of night* at mid-day.

2. *Made*, ind-2 ; *whence*, d'où ; *returned*, revenir ; *end*, bout ; *laden*, chargé.

3. *Is not allowed there*, on n'y souffre ni ; *furniture*, meuble ; *costly*, précieux ; *attire*, ornement ; *feast*, repas.

4. *Extensive*, vaste ; *fields*, campagne ; *yellow*, jaune ; *ears*, épi ; *bounteous*, fécond.

5. *In a kind of*, comme en.

6. *Age*, siècle.

7. *That*, de ce que ; *worthy*, estimable ; *but*, encore ; *betray*, montrer ; *remains*, reste ; *snares*, piége ; *difficulties*, embarras.

8. *He excited our pity*, il nous fit pitié.

9. *Hear*, écouter.

10. *Out of*, de ; *issued*, sortir ; *thick*, et épais ; *smoke*, fumée ; *mid-day*, milieu du jour.

RULE II. The article is not used, either before nouns preceded by the pronominal adjectives *mon, ton, son, notre, votre, leur, ce, nul, aucun, chaque, tout* (used for *chaque*), *certain, plusieurs, tel,* or before those which are preceded by a cardinal number without any relation whatever.

EXAMPLES.

Nos mœurs *mettent le prix à* nos richesses,	Our manners fix the value of our riches.
Toute nation *a ses lois,*	Each nation has its laws.
Cent ignorans *doivent-ils l'emporter sur un homme instruit?*	Are a hundred blockheads to be preferred to one learned man?

EXERCISE.

1. That *good father* was happy in his children, and his children were happy in him.

2. *These imitative 2 sounds* 1 are common to all languages, and form, as it were, their * real basis.

3. *Every man* has his foibles, his moments of humour, even his irregularities.

4. *Each plant* has virtues peculiar to it, the knowledge 2 of which 1 could not but be infinitely useful.

5. *In all his instructions,* he is careful to remember that grammar, logic, and rhetoric, are three sisters that ought never to be disjoined.

2. *Common,* fondu ; *to,* dans ; *and form, as it were,* et ils en font comme ; *real,* fondamentale.

4. *Peculiar,* qui sont propres ; *to it,* lui ; *could,* cond-1 ; *not but,* ne que.

5. *He is careful to remember,* ne point perdre de vue; *ought,* en devoir, ind-1 ; *to be disjoined,* séparer.

RULE III. Proper names of deities, men, animals, towns, and particular places, are without the article, but they take it when used in a limited sense.

EXAMPLES.

Dieu *a créé le ciel et la terre,*	God has made heaven and earth.
Jupiter *étoit le premier des dieux,*	Jupiter was the first of the gods.
Bucéphale *étoit le cheval d'Alexandre.*	Bucephalus was Alexander's horse.
Rome *est une ville d'une grande beauté,*	Rome is a city of great beauty.

But we ought to say, *le Dieu des Chrétiens,* the God of the Christians; *le Dieu de paix,* the God of peace; *le*

Jupiter d'Homère, Homer's. Jupiter; *le Bucéphale d'A-lexandre,* Alexander's Bucephalus ; *l'ancienne Rome,* ancient Rome ; *la Rome moderne,* modern Rome.

If, in imitation of the Italians, we use the article before the names of painters and poets of that nation, except *Michel-Ange* and *Raphael,* it is because the expression is elliptical, the words *peintre, poète,* or *seigneur,* being understood.

EXERCISE.

1. *Jupiter,* son of *Saturn* and *Cibele* or *Ops,* after having expelled his father from the throne, divided the paternal * inheritance with his two brothers, *Neptune* and *Pluto.*

2. On a dispute at a feast of the gods, between *Juno, Pallas,* and *Venus,* for the pre-eminence of beauty, *Jupiter* not being able to bring them to an agreement, referred the decision to *Paris,* a shepherd of mount Ida, with directions that a golden apple should be given to the fairest. *Paris* assigned to *Venus* 2 the golden * prize 1.

3. *God* said : let there* be 2 light 1, and there* was 2 light 1.

4. The *Apollo di Belvidere* and *the Venus di Medicis,* are valuable 2 remains 1 of antiquity.

5. *May* and *September* are the two finest months of the year in the south of France.

6. The *God of Abraham, Isaac,* and *Jacob,* was the only true God.

1. *Expelled,* chasser ; *divided,* en partager ; *inheritance,* héritage.

2. *On,* dans ; *at a feast,* qu'il y eut à un festin ; *being able,* pouvoir ; *to bring to an agreement,* accorder ; *referred,* renvoyer ; *directions,* ordre ; *that a golden apple,* etc. *to give a golden apple to ; assigned,* adjuger.

4. *Di Belvidere,* de Belveder ; *di,* de ; *valuable,* précieux.

6. *Only,* seul.

CHAP. III.
OF THE ADJECTIVE.
I.
OF THE ADJECTIVE WITH THE ARTICLE.

RULE I. Adjectives taken substantively are, like
2 c 3

substantives common, accompanied by the article, if the occasion require it.

EXAMPLE.

| Les fous *inventent les modes, et les sages s'y conforment;* | Fools invent fashions, and wise men conform to them. |

EXERCISE.

1. Were the learned of antiquity to come to life again, they would be much astonished at the extent of our knowledge.
2. The ignorant have, in a * large stock of presumption, what they want in real knowledge, and that is the reason they are admired by fools.

1. *Were the,* si les; *to come again,* revenir, ind-2; *life,* monde; *at,* de; *knowledge,* connoissance, pl.
2. *Large stock,* forte dose; *they want,* il leur manquer; *knowledge,* science; *the reason,* ce qui fait que; *they are admired,* the fools admire them.

RULE II. When a noun is accompanied by two adjectives, expressing opposite qualities, the article must be repeated before each adjective.

EXAMPLES.

| Les vieux *et* les nouveaux *soldats sont remplis d'ardeur,* | The old and the new soldiers are full of ardour. |
| Il faut fréquenter la bonne compagnie *et fuir* la mauvaise, | We ought to frequent good and shun bad company. |

REMARK. This rule must be strictly attended to, when the qualities expressed by the adjectives are opposite: but those qualities may be either nearly synonimous, or merely different, without being opposite. In the first instance, the article is not repeated: as *Le sage et pieux Fénélon;* in the second, it is perhaps better to repeat it: as *Le sensible et l'ingénieux Fénélon.*

N.B. In French the substantive must be joined to the first adjective, when it is governed by different words.

EXERCISE.

1. The ancient 1 and modern 3 writers 2 are not agreed upon that point.
1. *Writers,* auteur; *are agreed,* s'accorder.

2. The wise man preserves the same tranquillity of mind in good or bad fortune.

3. The man who is jealous of his reputation frequents good and shuns bad company.

4. Grand and vigorous thoughts were always the offspring of genius.

2. *The wise man,* le sage; *preserves,* conserver.
3. *Shuns,* éviter.
4. *Vigorous,* fort; *offspring,* fruit.

RULE III. The article is used before the adjective which is joined to a proper name, either to express its quality, or to distinguish the person spoken of from those who might bear the same name.

EXAMPLES.

Le sublime Bossuet,	*Le vertueux Fénélon,*	*Le tendre Racine,*
The sublime Bossuet.	The virtuous Fénélon.	The tender Racine.
Louis le Gros,	*Louis le Juste,*	*Louis le Grand,*
Louis the Fat.	Louis the Just.	Louis the Great.

REMARK. The adjective which is joined to a proper name, may either precede or follow that name. If it precede, it expresses a quality which may be common to many; if it follow, it expresses a distinguished quality. These two expressions, *Le savant Varron* and *Varron le savant,* do not convey the same meaning: in the first, we merely give *to Varron* the quality of *savant;* in the second, we mean to say, that there are several persons of the name of *Varron,* and that the one we are speaking of is distinguished for his learning.

EXERCISE.

1. The great Corneille astonishes by beauties of the first class, and by faults of the worst taste. If the tender Racine does not often rise so high, at least he is always equal, and possesses the art of always interesting the heart.

2. The more we read the fables of the good and artless La Fontaine, the more we are convinced they are a book for all ages, and the manual of the man of taste.

1. *By,* par des; *class,* ordre; *is always equal,* se soutenir; *possesses,* avoir.

2. *The more we,* plus on; *artless,* simple; *are convinced,* on se convaincre; *they are,* que c'est; *a,* le; *for,* de; *manual,* manuel.

3. It was only under the reign of Louis the Just (XIII) that good taste began to show itself in France; but it was under that of Louis the Great that it was carried to perfection.

3. *Only*, ne que; *show itself*, se montrer; *carried*, porter à.

RULE IV. When a superlative relative is placed before a substantive, the article serves for both; if after it, the article is to be repeated before each.

EXAMPLE.

Les plus habiles *gens font quelquefois* les plus grandes *fautes*,
or
Les *gens* les plus habiles *font quelquefois* les *fautes* les plus grandes,
The ablest men sometimes commit the grossest blunders.

EXERCISE.

1. It has been said of the Telemachus of the virtuous Fenelon, that it is the most useful 2 present 1 the Muses have made to man; for, could the happiness of mankind be produced by a poem, it would be by that.
2. The smoothest 2 waters 1 often conceal the most dangerous 2 gulfs 1.

1. *It has been said*, on a dit; *present*, don que; *have made*, subj-3; *could* (if the, etc. could, ind-2); *mankind*, genre humain; *be produced by*, naître de; *would be*, naître, cond-1.
2. *Smoothest*, tranquille.

II.

THE PLACE OF THE ADJECTIVES.

RULE I. Pronominal adjectives, and adjectives of number, are placed before the substantive, as are generally the following sixteen, viz. *beau, bon, brave, cher, chétif, grand, gros, jeune, mauvais, méchant, meilleur, moindre, petit, saint, vieux* and *vrai*, when taken in their literal sense.

EXAMPLES.

Mon père,	*quel homme,*	*plusieurs officiers,*	*grand homme,*
My father,	what man.	several officers.	great man.

| *Vieille femme,* | *dix guinées,* | *six arbres, etc.* |
| Old woman. | ten guineas. | six trees, etc. |

EXCEPTIONS. 1st. We must except the pronoun *quelconque.*

EXAMPLE.

| *Raison quelconque,* | Reason whatever. |

2d. The adjectives of number, joined to proper names, pronouns, and substantives, as quotations and without the article.

EXAMPLES.

George trois,	George the third.
Lui dixième,	He the tenth.
Chapitre dix,	Chapter the tenth.
Page trente,	Page thirty.

3d. The sixteen adjectives before mentioned, when they are joined by a conjunction to another adjective, which is to be placed after the substantive.

EXAMPLE.

| *C'est une femme grande et bien faite,* | She is a woman tall and well made. |

REMARK. In English, two or even several adjectives may qualify a substantive, without a conjunction : but in French, they are generally joined by a conjunction : as *c'est un homme aimable et poli,* he is an amiable, well-behaved man; except when custom allows the substantives to be placed between two adjectives; as *c'est un grand homme sec,* he is a tall thin man.

EXERCISE.

1. There have been ages, when a *great man* was a sort of prodigy produced by a mistake of nature.
2. In almost all nations, the *great geniusses* that have adorned them were contemporaries.

1. *Ages,* des siècles; *when,* où; *produced,* enfanter.
2. *In,* chez; *nations,* peuple; *adorned,* illustrer, ind-4.

3. *Young people*, says Horace, are supple to the impressions of vice, lavish, presumptuous, and equally impetuous and light in their passions ; *old people*, on the contrary, are covetous, dilatory, timid, ever alarmed under the future, always complaining, hard to please, panegyrists of times past, censors of the present, and great givers of advice.

4. *What man* was ever satisfied with his fortune, and dissatisfied with his wit?

5. *Thirty chambers* which have a communication one with another, and each of them an iron door, with six huge bolts, are the places where he shuts himself up.

3. *People,* gens; *supple,* souple; *lavish,* prodigue; *impetuous,* vif; *old,* f. pl. (the following adjectives m. pl.); *covetous,* avare; *dilatory,* temporiseur; *about,* sur; *complaining,* plaintif; *hard,* difficile; *please,* contenter; *times,* sing.; *givers,* donneur.

4. *Dissatisfied,* mécontent.

5. *Have a communication,* communiquer; *each of them,* dont chacun avoir; *huge,* gros; *bolts,* verrou; *places,* lieu, sing.; *shuts himself,* se renfermer.

RULE II. In general, adjectives formed from the partiple present of verbs are always placed after the substantive; *ouvrage divertissant,* entertaining work; and those formed from the participle past always; *figure arrondie,* round figure; those denoting form: *table ovale,* oval table; colour: *maison blanche,* white house; taste: *herbe amère,* bitter herb; sound : *orgue harmonieux,* harmonious organ; an idea of action: *procureur actif,* active attorney; or, an effect produced: *coutume abusive,* custom founded in abuse; a quality relative to the nature of a thing: *ordre grammatical,* grammatical order; or, to the species of a thing: *qualité occulte,* occult quality; adjectives expressing a nation: *générosité Angloise,* English generosity; those in esque, il, ule, ic, ique: *style burlesque,* burlesque style; *jargon puéril,* childish jargon; *femme crédule,* credulous woman; *bien public,* public welfare; *ris sardonique,* sardonic grin ; and perhaps a few others ; but in this, custom is to be consulted as the best guide.

1. An *affected* simplicity is a *refined* imposture.

2. The *smiling* images of Theocritus, Virgil, and Gessner, excite in the soul a soft sensibility.

3. In that *antique* palace are to · be seen neither *wreathed* columns, nor *gilded* wainscots, nor *valuable* basso-relievos, nor ceilings curiously *painted*, nor *grotesque* figures of animals which never had existence but in the imagination of a child or a madman.

4. If *human* life is exposed to many troubles, it is also susceptible of many pleasures.

5. A *ridiculous* man is seldom so by halves.

6. *Spanish* manners have, at first sight, something harsh and uncivilized.

7. *French* urbanity has become a proverb among *foreign* nations.

1. *Refined*, délicat.

2. *Smiling*, riant; *excite*, porter; *soft*, doux.

3. *Are to be seen*, on ne voit; *wreathed*, torse; *wainscots*, lambris; *basso-relievos*, bas relief; *ceilings*, plafond; *curiously*, artistement; *had existence*, exister.

4. *Many*, bien de; *troubles*, peine.

5. *So*, le; *by halves*, à demi.

6. *Spanish*, Espagnol; *manners*, mœurs; *at first sight*, au premier abord; *uncivilized*, sauvage.

7. *Become*, passer en; *among*, chez.

RULE III. Although it may seem that adjectives expressing moral qualities are placed indifferently before or after the substantive, yet it is taste alone, and a correct ear, that can assign their proper situation.

In conversation, or in a broken, loose style, it may be indifferent to say *femme aimable*, or *aimable femme*: *talens sublimes* or *sublimes talens*, etc. but in the dignified style the place of the adjective may, in a variety of instances, affect the beauty of a sentence.

1. An *amiable* woman gives to every thing she says an *inexpressible* grace; the more we hear the more we wish to hear her.

1. *Give to*, répandre sur; *inexpressible*, inexprimable; *we*, on.

2. The *majestic* eloquence of Bossuet is like a river which carries away every thing in the rapidity of its course.

3. The *sublime* compositions of Rubens have made 1 an English traveller 3 say 2, that this *famous* painter was born in Flanders through a mistake of nature.

2. *Majestic,* majestueux; *river,* fleuve; *carries away,* entraîner; *course,* cours, m.

3. *Say,* dire à; *famous,* célèbre; *through,* par; *mistake,* méprise.

III.

REGIMEN OF THE ADJECTIVE.

RULE. A noun may be governed by two adjectives, provided those adjectives do not require different regimens. Thus we say, *Cet homme est* utile et cher à sa famille, that man is useful and beloved by his family; because the adjective *utile* does not govern the preposition *de.*

EXERCISE.

1. A young man whose actions are all regulated by honour, and whose only aim is perfection in every thing, is *beloved and courted* by every body.

2. Cardinal Richelieu was all his life-time feared and hated by the great whom he had humbled.

3. A young lady, mild, polite, and delicate, who sees in the advantage of birth, riches, wit, and beauty, nothing but incitements to virtue, is very certain of being beloved and esteemed by every body.

1. *Actions are regulated by honour,* l'honneur dirige les actions: *whose only aim is,* qui ne se propose que; *courted,* recherché.

3. *Young lady,* demoiselle; *delicate,* décent; *nothing but,* ne que; *incitements,* encouragement; *certain,* assuré.

IV.

ADJECTIVES OF NUMBER.

Unième is used only after *vingt, trente, quarante, cin-*

cinquante, soixante, quatre-vingt, cent, and *mille. C'est la vingt-unième fois,* it is the twenty-first time.

Cent in the plural takes *s,* except when followed by another noun of number: as *ils étoient deux cents,* they were two hundred; but we say, *ils étoient deux cent dix,* they were two hundred and ten; *trois cents hommes,* three hundred men. *Vingt,* in *quatre-vingt* and *six-vingt,* also takes *s* when followed by a substantive; as *quatre-vingts hommes,* eighty men; *six-vingts abricots:* but it takes no *s* when followed by another number, *quatre-vingt-un arbres, quatre-vingt-dix hommes.* The ordinal numbers, collective and distributive, always take the mark of the plural: *les premières douzaines,* the first dozens; *les quatre cinquièmes,* the four fifths.

In dates we write *mil:* as *mil sept cent quatre-vingt-dix-neuf,* one thousand seven hundred and ninety-nine. On all other occasions we write *mille,* which never takes the sign of the plural: as *dix mille hommes,* ten thousand men; *quatre mille chevaux,* four thousand horses.

REMARK. *Cent* and *mille* are used indefinitely: as *il lui fit cent caresses,* he showed him a hundred marks of kindness; *faites-lui mille amitiés,* present him a thousand compliments.

EXERCISE.

1. It was the thirty-first year after so glorious a peace, when the war broke out again with a fury of which history offers few examples.
2. There were only three hundred, and, in spite of their inferiority, they attacked the enemy, beat and dispersed them.
3. He has sold his country house for* two thousand five hundred and fifty pounds.
4. Choose out of your nursery eighty fruit-trees and ninety dwarf-trees, divide them into dozens, and put in the two first dozens of each sort, those whose fruits are the most esteemed.

1. *Year,* année; *when,* que; *broke out again,* se rallumer.
2. *Only,* ne que; *in spite of,* malgré.
3. *Pounds,* livre sterling.
4. *Out of,* dans; *nursery,* pépinière; *fruit-trees,* pied d'arbre fruitier; *dwarf-trees,* arbre nain; *divide,* partager.

2 B

5. When Louis the Fourteenth made his entry into Strasbourg, the Swiss deputies being come to pay their respects to him, Le Tellier, archbishop of Rheims, who saw among them the bishop of Basle, said to one near him : That bishop is apparently some worthless character.—How, replied the other, he has a hundred thousand livres a year.—Oh! oh! said the archbishop, he is then an honest man ; and shewed him a thousand civilities.

5. *Swiss* (of the Swiss); *pay*, présenter ; *respect*, hommage, pl.; *one near him*, son voisin ; *that bishop*, etc. c'est un misérable apparemment que cet évêque ; *a year*, de rente ; *shewed*, faire ; *civilities*, caresse.

We say, *le onze, du onze, au onze, sur les onze heures, sur les une heure*, pronouncing the words *onze* and *une* as if they were written with an *h* aspirated.

The cardinal numbers are used instead of the ordinal.

1st. In speaking of the hours and in calculating time: as *il est trois heures*, it is three o'clock ; *l'an mil sept cent dix*, the year one thousand seven hundred and ten.

2dly. In speaking of all the days of the month except the first: *le premier de Mars*, the first of March.

3dly. In speaking of the order of sovereigns and princes: as *Louis seize, Georges trois ;* except the first two of the series: as *Henri premier, Georges second.* We also say, *Charles-Quint, Sixte-Quint,* instead of *Charles cinq, Empereur,* and *Sixte cinq, Pape ;* but this expression *quint*, derived from the Latin word *quintus,* is only used in these two instances.

EXERCISE.

1. They made in the parish and in the neighbouring places a collection which produced a hundred and twenty-one guineas.

2. William, surnamed the Conqueror, king of England and duke of Normandy, was one of the greatest generals of the eleventh century : he was born at Falaise, and was the natural son of Robert, duke of Normandy, and of Arlotte, a furrier's daughter.

1. *They*, on; *neighbouring places*, voisinage, sing.; *collection*, quête.

2. *William*, Guillaume ; *century*, siècle ; *furrier*, fourreur.

5. Make haste; it will soon be ten o'clock. We shall have a good deal of difficulty to arrive in time.

4. The winter was so severe in one thousand seven hundred and nine, that there was but one olive tree that resisted it* in a plain where there had been more than ten thousand.

5. It was the twenty-first of January one thousand seven hundred and ninety-three, that the unhappy Louis the sixteenth was led to the scaffold.

3. *Make haste,* se dépêcher; *will be,* ind-1; *a good deal of difficulty,* bien de la peine; *in,* à.

4. *Severe,* rude; *but,* ne que; *olive-tree,* olivier; *had been,* ind-2.

CHAPTER IV.

OF THE PRONOUN.

I.

PERSONAL PRONOUNS.

I.

Office of Personal Pronouns:

The personal pronouns have the three characteristics of the substantive; that is, subject, regimen, and apostrophe; but with this difference, that some always form the subject; two only are used as an apostrophe; some always form the regimen; and lastly others are sometimes the subject and sometimes the regimen.

Je, tu, il, and *ils* are always the subject; these four pronouns cannot be separated from the verb which they govern, but by personal pronouns acting as a regimen, or by the negative *ne.*

EXAMPLES.

Je ne lui en veux rien dire,	I will say nothing to him about it.
Tu en apprendras des nouvelles,	Thou wilt hear news of it.
Il nous raconta son histoire,	He told us his history.
Ils sont survenus à l'improviste,	They are come unexpectedly.

The two acting as an apostrophe are *toi* and *vous,*

2 D 2

whether they stand alone or are preceded by the interjection *ó:* as *toi, ó toi, vous, ó vous.*

1. The better to bear the irksomeness of captivity and solitude, I sought for books : for I was overwhelmed, with melancholy, for want of some instruction to cherish and support my mind.

2. Since thou art more obdurate and unjust than thy father, mayest thou suffer evils more lasting and cruel than his.

3. What ! say they, do not men die fast enough without destroying each other ? Life is so short, and yet it seems that it appears too long to them. Are they sent into the world to tear each other in pieces, and to make themselves mutually wretched ?

4. O thou, my son, my dear son, ease my heart; restore me what is dearer to me than my life. Restore to me my lost son, and restore thyself to thyself.

5. O ye, who hear me with so much attention, believe not that I despise men : no, no, I am sensible how glorious it is to toil to make them virtuous and happy ; but this toil is full of anxieties and dangers.

1. *To bear,* pour supporter ; *irksomeness,* ennui ; *overwhelmed with,* accablé de ; *for want,* faute ; *to cherish,* qui pût nourrir ; *support,* soutenir.

2. *Obdurate,* dur ; *mayest,* pouvoir, subj-1 ; *lasting,* long.

3. *Die fast enough,* être assez mortel ; *destroying each other,* se donner encore une mort précipitée ; *sent into,* sur ; *world,* terre ; *tear in pieces,* se déchirer ; *make themselves,* se rendre.

4. *Ease,* soulager ; *restore,* rendre ; *lost* (whom I have lost), perdre.

5. *I am sensible,* savoir ; *glorious,* grand ; *to toil,* travailler à ; *toil,* travail ; *anxiety,* inquiétude.

Me, te, se, leur, le, la, les, y, and *en,* are always used as a regimen ; direct, if they are the object of the action expressed by the verb, or indirect, if they bear a relation which may be expressed by the prepositions *à* or *de.* They always precede the verb, except sometimes in the imperative, and can never be separated from it by another word, not even by the negation.

Remark. However, some of these pronouns may be

separated from the verb in the infinitive by the words *tout, rien,* and *jamais.*

C'est leur tout refuser,	It is refusing them every thing.
C'est ne me rien permettre,	It is allowing me nothing.
Il a juré de ne lui jamais pardonner,	He has sworn he would never pardon him.

Me, te, se, are sometimes regimen direct, and sometimes regimen indirect; they are regimen direct, when they represent *moi, toi, soi ;* they are the regimen indirect, when they supply the place of *à moi, à toi, à soi.*

Vous me soupçonnez mal-à-propos,	You suspect me unjustly.
Je t'en remercie,	I thank thee for it.
Il se perd de gaieté de cœur,	He ruins himself out of wantonness.
Vous me donnez un sage conseil,	You give me prudent advice.
Je te donne cela,	I give thee that.
Il se donne du mouvement,	He is always in motion.

Leur is always indirect, because it stands for *à eux* or *à elles.*

Je leur représentai le tort qu'ils ou qu'elles se faisoient,	I represented to them the injury they did themselves.

1. He has been speaking to them with such energy as has astonished them.

2. Women ought to be very circumspect; for a mere appearance is sometimes more prejudicial to them than a real fault.

5. He comes up to me with a smiling air, and pressing my hands, says, My friend, I expect you to-morrow at my house.

1. *Such energy as,* une force qui.

2. *Mere,* simple; *is more prejudicial,* faire plus de tort.

3. *Comes up .. with,* aborder .. de ; *pressing,* serrer; *my hands,* la main ; *at my house,* chez moi.

4. He said to me: Wilt thou torment thyself incessantly for advantages, the enjoyment 2 of which 1 could not render thee more happy! Cast thy eyes round thee, see how every thing smileth at thee, and seemeth to invite thee to prefer a retired and tranquil life to the tumultuous pleasures of a vain 2 world 1.

5. The ambitious man* agitates, torments, and destroys himself to obtain the places or honours to which he aspires; and when he has obtained them, he is still not satisfied.

4. *Incessantly*, sans cesse; *advantages*, des biens; *could*, savoir, cond-1; *cast*, porter; *thy*, art.; *smileth*, sourire.

6. *Destroys*, consumer; *to*, pour.

Le, la, les, are always direct, and *y* indirect: as *je le vois, je la vois, je les vois*, that is, *je vois lui, je vois elle, je vois eux* or *'elles; je n'y entends rien*, I understand nothing of it; that is, *je n'entends rien à cela.*

En is *generally* indirect, because its principal use is to represent a substantive and the preposition *de.*

REMARK. We have said *generally*, because, in our opinion, *en* may be the regimen direct, or at least perform the function of it, whenever it is substituted for the member of an elliptical phrase: *avez-vous reçu de l'argent? oui, j'en ai reçu;* have you received any money? yes, I have received some: in phrases of this kind there is an ellipsis of these words, *un peu, beaucoup, une portion*, or some similar expressions.

EXERCISE.

1. I have known him since his childhood, and I always loved him on account of the goodness of his character.

2. This woman is always occupied in doing good works; you see her constantly consoling the unhappy, relieving the poor, reconciling enemies, and promoting the happiness of every one around her.

1. *Have known*, connoître, ind-1; *loved*, ind-4; *on account*, à cause; *the goodness of his* (his good).

2. *In*, à; *works*, œuvres, f. pl.; *constantly*, sans cesse; *consoling*, etc., inf-1; *promoting*, faire; *every one around her*, tout ce qui l'environne.

3. The more you live with men, the more you will be convinced that it is necessary to know them well before you* form a connection with them.

4. Enjoy the pleasures of the world, I consent to it; but never give yourself up to them.

5. I shall never consent to that foolish scheme; do not mention it any* more.

6. Have you received some copies of the new work? Yes, I have (received some.)

3. *Live,* ind-η; *be convinced,* se convaincre; *before,* avant de; *form a connection,* vous lier.

4. *Enjoy,* jouir de; *give yourself up,* se livrer.

5. *Scheme,* entreprise; *mention,* parler de.

6. *Copies,* exemplaire.

Those which are sometimes the subject and sometimes the regimen are *nous, vous, moi, toi, lui, elle, eux, elles.*

Nous and *vous* may be the subject; *nous aimons, vous aimez;* the regimen direct, *ils nous aiment, ils vous aiment;* and indirect, *ils nous parlent, ils vous parlent.*

In general, *moi, toi,* are only the subject by apposition or reduplication, whether they follow the verb, as *je prétends moi, tu dis donc toi;* or precede it, as *moi, dont il déchire la réputation, je ne lui ai jamais rendu que de bons offices;* I, whose reputation he is blackening, always did him acts of kindness; *toi, qui fais tant le brave, tu oserois,* etc. wouldst thou who pretendest to be so brave, dare, etc.

REMARK. Sometimes the personal pronouns *je* and *tu* are not expressed, but understood: as *moi, trahir le meilleur de mes amis!* I, betray my best friend! *faire une lâcheté, toi!* thou, be guilty of such baseness! where it is easy to supply the expression *je voudrois, tu pourrois.*

They are likewise the subject when they are placed in a kind of apposition expressed by *ce* and *il* in impersonal verbs: as *qui fut bien aise? ce fut moi; ce ne peut être que toi; que vous reste-t-il? moi.*

After a conjunction, they are either the subject or regimen, according to the nature of the phrase: as *nous y étions, mon père et moi; il ne craint ni toi ni moi.*

In phrases which are not imperative, *toi* and *moi* can only be the regimen by apposition before or after the verb: as *voudriez-vous me perdre, moi, votre allié*, etc. *toi, je te soupçonnerois de perfidie.*

After a preposition they alone can be employed: as *vous servirez-vous de moi; selon moi, vous avez raison; il est fâché contre toi.*

What I have just remarked of *toi* and *moi*, is applicable to *lui*, but with this difference, that in the imperative, *lui* can only be the regimen after *que*, signifying *only*, or in distributive phrases: as *n'aimer que lui, je ne le trouve pas mauvais, mais ne me haïssez pas;* that you should like only him, I do not disapprove, but do not hate me; *protégez-nous, lui à cause de,* etc. *et moi, parce que,* etc. it may likewise be said so by apposition, *aimez-le, lui qui,* etc.

Eux is employed in the same manner as *lui*, but differs from it in this, that it cannot be the regimen indirect, except after a preposition: as *parliez-vous d'eux? est-ce à eux que vous parlez?*

REMARK. *Lui* and *eux* may be the subject in distributive phrases without being in apposition: as *mes frères et mon cousin m'ont secouru; eux m'ont relevé, et lui m'a pansé;* my brothers and cousin have assisted me; they have taken me up, and he has bound up my wounds.

The natural office of *elle* and *elles*, is to form the subject; however, all the other uses of which we have now been speaking suit them, except that they cannot be the regimen indirect, unless preceded by a preposition: as *c'est à elles que je parle.*

EXERCISE.

1. In the education of youth, we should propose to ourselves to cultivate, to polish their understanding, and thus to enable them to fill with dignity the different stations assigned them; but above all, we ought to instruct them in that religious worship which God requires of them.

.1. *Youth*, jeunes gens; *should*, devoir, ind-1; *'to cultivate*, (to them); *to polish*, (to them), orner; *understanding*, l'esprit; *enable*, disposer; *stations*, place; (which are) *assigned* (to) *them; worship*, culte; *requires*, demander.

2. What! you would suffer yourself to be overwhelmed by adversity!

3. I! stoop to the man who has imbrued his hands in the blood of his king.

4. Thou! take that undertaking upon thyself! Canst* thou think of it?

5. Your two brothers and mine take charge of the enterprise; they find the money, and he will manage the work.

6. It is I who have engaged him to undertake this journey.

7. It is thou who hast brought this misfortune on thyself.

8. When you are at Rome, write to me as often as you can, and give me an account of every thing that can interest me.

9. He told it to thee thyself.

10. Fortune, like a traveller, shifts from inn to inn; if she lodges to-day with me, to-morrow, perhaps, she will lodge with thee.

11. Whom dost thou think we were talking of? it was of thee.

12. Descartes deserves immortal praise, because it is he who has made reason 1 triumph 2 over authority in philosophy.

13. He is displeasing to himself.

14. She is never satisfied with herself.

15. The indiscreet often betray themselves.

16. Saumaise, speaking of the English authors, said, that he had learned more from them than from any other.

17. To love a person, is to render him, on every occasion, all the services in our power, and to afford him, in society, every comfort that depends upon us.

2. *Suffer yourself,* se laisser, cond-1; *to be overwhelmed,* abattre.

3. *Stoop to,* m'abaisser devant; *imbrued,* souiller; *in,* de.

4. *Take upon thyself,* te charger; *of it,* y.

5. *Take charge,* se charger; *find,* fournir; *money,* fonds, pl.; *manage,* conduire.

6. *Undertake,* faire; *journey,* voyage.

7. *Hast brought on thyself,* s'attirer, ind-4.

8. *Are,* ind-7; *can,* ind-7; *give,* faire; *an account,* le détail.

9. *Told,* dire, ind-4.

10. *Shifts from inn to inn,* changer d'auberge; *with,* chez; *she will lodge,* ce être.

11. *Were talking,* parler, subj-2.

12. *Triumph over,* triompher de.

13. *Is displeasing,* se déplaire.

15. *Betray,* se trahir.

17. *In our power,* dont on est capable; *afford,* procurer à; *comfort,* agrément; *depends upon,* dépendre de.

II.

ON THE PRONOUN *soi*.

Soi is generally placed with a preposition and in phrases where there is an indeterminate pronoun either expressed or understood: *on doit rarement parler de soi, il est essentiel de prendre garde à soi.* In this case, it is the regimen indirect. .

But it may stand without a preposition. 1st. With the verb *être:* as *en cherchant à tromper les autres, c'est souvent soi qu'on trompe,* or *on est souvent trompé soi-même;* in attempting to deceive others, we frequently deceive ourselves. In this situation it is the subject.

2dly. After *ne que:* as *n'aimer que soi c'est n'être bon à rien,* to love only ourselves, is being good for very little; or by apposition: as *penser ainsi c'est s'aveugler soi-même,* to think in this manner is to blind one's self. It is in these examples the regimen.

When *de soi* and *en soi* are used in a definite sense speaking of things, they mean *de sa nature,* and *dans sa nature.*

EXERCISE.

1. To excuse in one's self the follies which one cannot excuse in others, is to prefer being a fool one's self to seeing others so.
2. To be too much dissatisfied with ourselves is a weakness; but to be too much satisfied (*with ourselves*) is (*a*) folly.
3. We ought to despise no one : how often have we needed the assistance of one more insignificant than ourselves?
4. If we did not attend so much to ourselves, there would be less egotism in the world.
5. Vice is odious in itself.
6. The loadstone attracts iron (to itself.)

1. *Follies,* sottises; *others,* autrui; *prefer,* aimer mieux; *fool, sot; to seeing,* que de voir; *so,* tel.
3. *We ought,* falloir, ind-1; *how often,* combien de fois; *we,* on; *needed the assistance,* n'avoir pas besoin; *insignificant,* petit.
4. *We,* on; *attended to,* s'occuper de; *egotism,* égoïsme.
6. *Loadstone,* aimant.

III.

CASES WHERE THE PRONOUNS *elle, elles, eux, lui, leur*, MAY APPLY TO THINGS.

The personal pronouns *elle* and *elles*, when the regimen, generally apply to persons only. We say, speaking of a woman: *Je m'approchai d'elle, je m'assis près d'elle;* but we say, speaking of a table: *Je m'en approchai, je m'assis auprès.*

But when these pronouns are governed by the prepositions *avec, après, à, de, pour, en,* etc. they may very well be applied to things. We say,

Speaking of a river: *Cette rivière est si rapide quand elle déborde, qu'elle entraîne avec elle tout ce qu'elle rencontre; elle ne laisse après elle que du sable et des cailloux:* that river is so rapid when it overflows, that it carries away every thing it meets with in its course; it leaves nothing behind but sand and pebbles.

And speaking of an enemy's army: *nous marchâmes à elle,* we marched up to it. We cannot even express ourselves in any other way.

In speaking of things, reasons, truth, etc. we say also: *ces choses sont bonnes d'elles-mêmes,* these things are good in themselves; *j'aime la vérité au point que je sacrifierois tout pour elle,* I love truth to that degree, that I would sacrifice every thing for it; *ces raisons sont solides en elles-mêmes,* those reasons are solid in themselves.

After the verb *être,* they are applied only to persons; and likewise when they are followed by the relatives *qui* and *que:* as *c'est à elle, c'est d'elles que je parle, c'est elle-même qui vient.*

The same may be said of the pronoun *eux,* which is also generally applied to persons only; yet custom allows us to say, *ce chien et ces oiseaux font tout mon plaisir, je n'aime qu'eux; eux seuls sont mon amusement, je ne songe qu'à eux:* this dog and these birds are all my pleasure, I love nothing but them; they alone are my diversion, I think of nothing else. *Lui* and *leur* are generally applied to persons, but are sometimes used in speaking of animals, plants, and even inanimate objects: *ces chevaux*

sont rendus, faites-leur donner un peu de vin; those horses
are exhausted, give them a little wine; *ces orangers vont
périr, si on ne leur donne de l'eau;* those orange-trees
will die unless they have a little water; *ces murs sont
mal faits, on ne leur a pas donné assez de talus;* those
walls are badly built, they have not sufficient inclination.

Thus much being premised, we shall give the following—

RULE. The pronouns *elle, elles, eux, lui,* and *leur,*
ought never to be applied to things, except when custom
does not allow them to be replaced by the pronouns *y*
and *en.*

EXERCISE.

1. Virtue is the first of blessings; it is from it alone we are to
expect happiness.
2. The labyrinth had been built upon the lake Meris, and they
had given it a prospect proportioned to its grandeur.
3. Mountains are frequented on account of the air one breathes
on them: how many people are indebted to them for the recovery
of their health?
4. War brings in its train numberless evils.
5. It is a delicate 2 affair 1 which must not be too deeply investigated; it must be lightly passed over.
6. I have had my house repaired, and have given it an appearance quite* new.
7. Those trees are too much loaded, strip them of part of their
fruit.
8. This book costs me a great deal, but I am indebted to it for
my knowledge.

1. *Blessings,* bien; *are,* devoir.
2. *Had been built,* on bâtir, ind-6; *prospect,* vue.
3. *On account,* à cause; *breathes,* respire; *on them,* y; *are
indebted for,* devoir; *recovery,* rétablissement.
4. *Brings,* entraîner; *in its train,* avec elle; *numberless,*
bien de.
5. *Affair,* matière; *must,* ind-1; *be deeply investigated,* approfondir, inf-1; *be passed,* glisser; *over,* dessus.
6. *Have had,* faire, ind-4; *appearance,* air.
7. *Strip,* ôter; *of part,* une partie.
8. *A great deal,* cher; *knowledge,* instruction.

9. Self-love is captious; we, however, take it for our * guide; to it are all our actions directed, and from it we take counsel.

10. These arguments, although very solid in themselves, yet made no impression upon him; so strong a chain is habit.

11. These reasons convinced me, and by them I formed my decision.

12. I leave you the care of that bird, do not forget to give it water.

9. *We* (it is it that we); *to it*, (it is to it that we direct all, etc.); *direct*, rapporter; *from it*, (and it is from it that, etc.)

10. *No*, ne aucun; *so strong*, etc. (so much habit is a, etc.); *habit*, habitude.

11. *And from*, (and it is from them that); *by*, d'après; *formed my decision*, se décider.

IV.

A DIFFICULTY RESPECTING THE PRONOUN *le* CLEARED UP.

Le, la, les, are sometimes used as pronouns, and sometimes as articles. The article is always followed by a noun, *le roi, la reine, les hommes,* whereas the pronoun is always joined to a verb, *je le connois, je le respecte, je les estime.*

The pronoun *le* may supply the place of a substantive, or an adjective, or even of a member of a sentence.

There is no difficulty, when it relates to a whole member of a sentence; it is always then in the masculine singular: as *on doit s'accommoder à l'humeur des autres autant qu'on le peut,* we ought to accommodate ourselves to the humour of others as much as we can.

EXERCISE.

1. The laws of nature and decency oblige us equally to defend the honour and interest of our parents, when we can do it without injustice.

2. We ought not to condemn, after their death, those that have not been condemned during their life-time.

1. *Decency*, bienséance.
2. *We ought*, falloir; *condemned*, le; *time*.

Neither is there any difficulty when *le* supplies the

2 x

place of a substantive; it being evident that it then takes the gender and number of that substantive: as *Madame, êtes-vous la mère de cet enfant? Oui, je la suis.*—Madam, are you the mother of that child? Yes, I am. *Mesdames, êtes-vous les parentes dont Monsieur m'a parlé? Oui, nous les sommes.*

REMARK. Though the word relating to the interrogative sentences, in the following exercises, is not expressed in English, yet it must always be in French: this word is *le,* which takes either gender or number, according to its relation.

EXERCISE.

1. Was that your idea? Can you doubt that it was?
2. Are you Mrs. Such-a-one? Yes, I am.
3. Are those your servants? Yes, they are.

1. *Idea,* pensée; *that it was,* ce être, subj-2.
2. *Mrs.* Madame; *such-a-one,* un tel.
3. *Those,* ce; *they,* ce.

It only remains, therefore, to lay down the following

RULE. The pronoun *le* takes neither gender nor number, when holding the place of an adjective.

EXAMPLES.

Madame, êtes-vous enrhumée?—Oui, je le suis.
Mesdames, êtes-vous contentes de ce discours?—Oui, nous le sommes.
Fut-il jamais une femme plus malheureuse que je le suis?

REMARK. This rule is observed, when the substantives are used adjectively: *Madame, êtes-vous mère?—Oui, je le suis. Mesdames, êtes-vous parentes?—Oui, nous le sommes. Elle est fille, et le sera toute la vie.* But not if the adjectives be used substantively: as *Madame, êtes-vous la malade?—Oui, je la suis.* Therefore, this question: *Etes-vous fille de M. le duc?* is to be answered: *Oui, je le suis;* and this: *Etes-vous la fille de M. le duc?—Oui, je la suis.*

EXERCISE.

1. Ladies, are you glad to have seen the new piece? Yes, we are.

2. I, a* slave! I, born to command! alas! it is but too true that I am so.

3. She was jealous of her authority, and she ought to be so.

4. Was there ever a girl more unhappy, and treated with more ridicule than I am.

5. You have found me amiable : why have I ceased to appear so to you?

6. Have we ever been so quiet as we are?

7. Madam, are you married? Yes, I am.

8. Madam, are you the bride? Yes, I am.

1. *Ladies,* Mesdames.

2. *Slave,* esclave ; *but,* ne que.

3. *Ought,* devoir, ind-2.

4. *With more ridicule,* plus ridiculement.

We likewise observe the same rule with the article placed before *plus* or *moins* and an adjective. It takes neither gender nor number, when there is no comparison : as *la lune ne nous éclaire pas autant que le soleil, même quand elle est le plus brillante ;* the moon does not give us so much light as the sun, even when it shines brightest: but it takes gender and number, when there is a comparison : as *de toutes les planètes, la lune est la plus brillante pour nous ;* of all the planets the moon is the most brilliant to us.

EXERCISE.

1. This father could not bring himself to condemn his children, even when they were most guilty.

2. This woman has the art of shedding tears, even 2 at the time 1 when she is least afflicted.

3. Out * of so many criminals only the most guilty should be punished.

1. *Could,* ind-2 ; *bring himself,* se résoudre.

2. *Shedding,* répandre de ; *at,* dans ; *when,* que.

3. *Only the most,* etc. (one must punish only the most guilty) *only,* ne que.

4. Although that woman displays more fortitude than the others, she is not, on that account, the least distressed.

4. *Displays*, montrer; *fortitude*, fermeté; *on that account*, pour cela; *distressed*, affligé.

V.

REPETITION OF THE PERSONAL PRONOUNS.

RULE I. The pronouns of the first and second persons, when the subject, must be repeated before all the verbs, if those verbs are in different tenses; and it is always better to repeat them, even when the verbs are in the same tense.

EXAMPLES.

Je soutiens, et je soutiendrai toujours;	I maintain, and (I) will always maintain.
Vous dites, et vous avez toujours dit;	You say, and (you) have always said.
Accablé de douleur, je m'écriai et je dis;	Overwhelmed with sorrow, I exclaimed and (I) said.
Nous nous promenions sur le haut du rocher, et nous voyions sous nos pieds;	We were walking upon the summit of the rock, and (we were) seeing under our feet, etc.

REMARK. In all cases the pronouns must be repeated, though the tenses of the verbs do not change, if the first of these is followed by a regimen: as *Vous aimerez le Seigneur votre Dieu, et vous observerez sa loi;* you shall love the Lord your God, and (you shall) observe his law.

EXERCISE.

1. My dear child, I love you, and I shall never cease to love you: but it is that very love that I have for you which obliges me to correct you for your faults, and to punish you when you deserve it.

2. I heard and admired these words, which comforted me a

1. *Correct for*, reprendre de.

2. *Heard*, écouter, ind-2; *words*, discours; *my mind*, etc.

little, but my mind was not sufficiently at liberty to make him a reply.

3. Thou wast young, and thou aimed'st without doubt at the glory of surpassing thy comrades.

4. God has said, you shall love your enemies, bless those that curse you, do good to those that persecute you, and pray for those who slander you. What a difference between this morality and that of philosophers!

(I had not the mind, etc.) *sufficiently at liberty*, assez libre; *to make a reply*, répondre à.

3. *Aimed'st at*, aspirer à; *surpassing*, l'emporter sur.

4. *Slander*, calomnier; *between*, de ; *and that*, à celle.

RULE II. The pronouns of the third person, when the subject, are hardly ever to be repeated before the verbs, when those verbs are in the same tense, and they may be repeated or not, when the verbs are in different tenses.

EXAMPLES.

La bonne grâce ne gâte rien; elle ajoute à la beauté, relève la modestie, et y donne du lustre;	A graceful manner spoils nothing; it adds to beauty, heightens modesty, and gives it lustre.
Il n'a jamais rien valu et ne vaudra jamais rien;	He never was good for any thing, and never will be.
Il est arrivé ce matin, et il repartira ce soir;	He is arrived this morning, and (he) will set off again this evening.

REMARK. We have said *hardly ever*, because perspicuity requires the repetition of the pronoun, when the second verb is preceded by a long incidental phrase: as *Il fond sur son ennemi, et après l'avoir saisi d'une main victorieuse, il le renverse, comme le cruel aquilon abat les tendres moissons qui dorent la campagne.*

EXERCISE.

1. He took the strongest cities, conquered the most considerable provinces, and overturned the most powerful empires.

2. He takes a hatchet, completely cuts down the mast which

1. *Overturned*, renverser.

2. *Hatchet*, hache f.; *completely cuts down*, achever de

was already broken, throws it into the sea, jumps upon it amidst the furious billows, calls me by my name, and encourages me to follow him.

5. He marshals the soldiers, marches at their head, advances in good order towards the enemy, attacks and breaks them, and, after having entirely routed them, (he) cuts them in pieces.

couper; *broken,* rompre; *throws,* jeter; *jumps upon it,* s'élancer dessus; *billows,* onde.

5. *Marshals,* ranger en bataille; *breaks,* renverser; *entirely routed,* achever de mettre en désordre; *cuts,* tailler.

RULE III. The personal pronouns, when the *subject,* of whatever person they may be, must always be repeated before verbs, either when we pass from an affirmation to a negation, or, on the contrary, from a negation to an affirmation, or when the verbs are joined by any conjunction, except *et* and *ni.*

EXAMPLES.

Il veut et il ne veut pas,	He will and he will not.
Il donne d'excellens principes, parce qu'il sait que les progrès ultérieurs en dépendent;	He lays down excellent principles, because he knows that upon them depends all further progress.

But we say: *il donne et reçoit,* he gives and receives; *il ne donne ni ne reçoit,* he neither gives nor receives.

EXERCISE.

1. It is inconceivable how whimsical she is; from one moment to another, she will and she will not.

2. The Jews are forbidden to work on the sabbath; they are as it * were * locked in slumber; they light no fire, and carry no water.

3. For nearly a week she has neither eaten nor drank.

1. (She is of a whimsical cast inconceivable) *whimsical cast,* bizarrerie f.

2. (It is forbidden to) *forbidden,* défendre; *sabbath,* jour du sabbat; *locked,* enchaîné; *slumber,* repos; *light,* allumer.

3. *For,* depuis; *nearly,* près de; *a week,* huit jours; *has eaten....drank,* ind-1.

4. The soldier was not repressed by authority, but stopped from satiety and shame.

4. *Repressed*, réprimer; *stopped*, s'arrêter, ind-3; *from*, par.

RULE IV. Pronouns, when the regimen, are repeated before all the verbs.

EXAMPLES.

L'idée de ses malheurs le pour- suit, le tourmente et l'accable;	The idea of his misfortunes pur- sues (him), torments (him), and overwhelms him.
Il nous ennuie et nous obsède sans cesse,	He wearies (us) and besets us unceasingly.

REMARK. The pronoun, when the regimen, is not re- peated before such compound verbs as express the repeti- tion of the same action: as *je vous le dis et redis, il le fait et refait sans cesse.* This, however, is the case only when the verbs are in the same tense.

EXERCISE.

1. It is taste that selects the expressions, that combines, arranges and varies them, so as to produce the greatest effect.

2. Horace answered his stupid critics not so much to instruct them, as to shew their ignorance, and let them see that they did not even know what poetry was.

3. Man embellishes nature itself; he cultivates, extends and polishes it.

1. *So as to*, de manière à ce qu'elles, subj-1.

2. *Stupid*, sot; *not so much*, moins; *as to*, pour; *show* (to them), *their*, etc.; *let see*, faire entendre; *was*, c'étoit que.

VI.

RELATION OF THE PRONOUN OF THE THIRD PERSON TO A NOUN EXPRESSED BEFORE.

RULE. The pronouns of the third person, *il, ils, elle, elles, le, la, les,* must always relate to a noun, whether subject or regimen, taken in a definite sense; but they must not be applied, either to a subject and regimen at the same time, or to a noun taken in an indefinite sense,

or to a noun that has not been before expressed in the
same-sense.

EXAMPLES.

La rose *est la reine des fleurs,* *aussi est*-elle *l'emblême de la beauté ;*	The rose is the queen of flowers; therefore it is the emblem of beauty.
J'*aime* l'ananas ; ,il *est exquis :*	I like the pine-apple; it is delicious.

But we cannot say: Racine *a imité* Euripides *en tout ce
qu'il a de plus beau dans sa Phèdre,* Racine has imitated
Euripides in all that he has most beautiful in his Phedra;
because, as the pronoun *il* may relate either to *Racine*
or to *Euripides,* the sentence is equivocal. Neither can
we say : *Le légat publia une sentence d'interdit;* il *dura
trois mois :* the legate published a sentence of interdiction;
it lasted three months: because *il* cannot, from the construction of the sentence, relate to *interdit.* Again, it is
not altogether correct to say, Nulle paix *pour l'impie ; il*
la *cherche,* elle *fuit ;* no peace for the wicked; he seeks it,
it flies: because, from the construction, the pronouns *la*
and *elle* seem to be used for *nulle paix;* whereas, according to the meaning, they supply the place of the substantive *paix,* which is the opposite state.

EXERCISE.

1. Poetry embraces all sorts of subjects; *it* takes in every thing
that is most brilliant in history; *it* enters the fields of philosophy ; *it* soars to the skies ; *it* plunges into the abyss ; *it* pene-
trates even to the dead ; *it* makes the universe its domain ; and
if this world be not sufficient, *it* creates new ones; which *it*
embellishes with enchanting abodes, which *it* peoples with a
thousand various inhabitants.

2. Egypt aimed at greatness, and wanted to * strike the eye
at a distance, but always pleasing *it* by the justness of proportion.

1. *Subjects,* matière ; *takes in,* se charger de: *that is,* y avoir
de; (in) *the fields; soars,* s'élancer dans; *plunges,* s'enfoncer;
to, chez (its domain of the universe); *be sufficient,* suffire ;
ones, monde; *enchanting,* enchanté ; *abodes,* demeure ; *various,*
divers.

2. *Greatness,* grand ; *wanted,* vouloir; *at a distance,* dans
l'éloignement; (in) *pleasing,* contenter.

5. Egypt, satisfied with its own territory, where every thing was in abundance, thought not of conquests ; *it* extended itself in another manner, by sending colonies to every part of the globe, and, with *them,* politeness and laws.

4. The Messiah is expected by the Hebrews; *he* comes and calls the Gentiles, as had been announced by the prophecies ; the people that acknowledge *him* as come, is incorporated with the people that expected *him,* without a single moment of interruption.

3. *Was in abundance,* abonder ; *thought,* songer ; *in,* de ; *by,* en ; *to,* par ; *part of the globe,* terre.

4. *Gentiles,* Gentil (the prophecies had announced it); *acknowledge,* reconnoître ; *with,* à; *without,* sans qu'il y ait; *single,* seul.

II.

POSSESSIVE PRONOUNS.

EXPLANATION OF SOME DIFFICULTIES ATTENDANT ON THE POSSESSIVE PRONOUNS.

FIRST DIFFICULTY. The possessive pronouns *son, sa, ses, leur, leurs,* relate either to persons or to things personified, or simply to things. If they relate to persons or personified things, we always use those possessive pronouns: but if they relate to things, they are used as follows.

The possessive pronouns are always employed,

1st. When the object to which they relate is either named or designated by a personal pronoun in the same member of a phrase.

EXAMPLES.

L'Angleterre *étend* son com- *merce par toute la terre,*	England extends her commerce over the whole globe.
Elle *envoie ses flottes dans toutes les mers,*	She sends her fleets into every part of the sea.

2dly. Before a noun, when qualified even by a single adjective, unless the noun form the regimen.

EXAMPLE.

Ses *ressources* immenses *sont inépuisables,*	Her immense resources are inexhaustible.

3dly. After every preposition.

EXAMPLE.

C'est par *sa position, jointe à la sagesse* de *son gouvernement, qu'elle réunit* dans *son sein de si grands avantages;*

It is by her situation, joined to the wisdom of her government, that she unites such vast advantages within herself.

4thly. Before all words which can govern the preposition *de.*

EXAMPLES.

Son *parlement est le* sanctuaire de *la plus sage politique,*
Son *roi n'a de pouvoir que pour faire le bien,*

Her parliament is the seat of the wisest policy.
Her king possesses power only to do good.

On all other occasions, the article must be employed with the pronoun *en,* which is placed immediately before the verb to which the word serves as a subject or regimen.

EXAMPLE.

Tout enfin contribue à m'en faire aimer le séjour; j'en admire surtout l'exacte police, en même temps que les lois m'en paroissent extrémement sages;

In short, every thing conspires to make me love that residence; I particularly admire the strictness of her police, at the same time that her laws appear to me extremely wise.

EXERCISE.

1. A new custom was a phenomenon in Egypt; for which reason, there never was a people that preserved so long *its* customs, *its* laws, and even *its* ceremonies.

2. Solomon abandoned himself to the love of women; *his* understanding declines, *his* heart weakens, and *his* piety degenerates into idolatry.

3. That superb temple was upon the summit of a hill; *its* columns were of Parian marble, and *its* gates of gold.

1. *Phenomenon,* prodige ; *for which reason,* aussi ; *à,* de ; *preserved,* subj-3.

2. *Understanding,* esprit; *declines,* baisser; *weakens,* s'affoiblir.

3. *Summit,* haut ; *hill,* colline; *Parian,* de Paros.

4. The Laocoon is one of the finest statues in France ; not only *the whole,* but all *its* features, even the least, are admirable.

5. The Thames is a magnificent river ; *its* channel is so wide and so deep below London-bridge, that several thousands of vessels lie at their ease in it.

6. This fine country is justly admired by foreigners; *its* climate is delightful, *its* soil fruitful, *its* laws wise, and *its* government just and moderate.

7. The trees of that orchard have sun enough, yet *its fruits* are but indifferent.

8. The Seine has its source in Burgundy and *its* mouth at Havre-de-Grace,

9. The pyramids of Egypt astonish, both by the enormity of *their* bulk and the justness of their proportions.

10. Egypt alone could erect monuments for posterity; *its* obelisks are to this day, as well for their beauty as for their height, the principal ornaments of Rome.

11. History and geography throw mutual light on each other ; a* perfect knowledge *of them* ought to enter into the plan of good education.

4. *In,* qu'il y ait en ; *the whole,* l'ensemble ; *even,* jusqu'à.

5. *Channel,* lit ; *below,* au-dessous de ; *lie at,* être à ; *in it,* y.

6. *Justly,* avec raison ; *soil,* sol.

7. *Have sun enough,* être bien exposé ; *but indifferent,* assez mauvais.

8. *Mouth,* embouchure ; *Havre,* le Hâvre.

9. *Both,* également et ; *bulk,* masse; *and,* et par.

10. *Egypt alone could,* il n'appartenoit qu'à l'Egypte de ; *erect,* élever ; *to this day,* encore aujourd'hui ; *as well for,* autant par ; *height,* hauteur.

11. *Throw mutual light,* etc. s'éclairer l'une par l'autre ; *of them* (their).

SECOND DIFFICULTY. The learner is sometimes at a loss to know whether the possessive pronoun ought to be used or not before a noun that is the regimen. The following is the

RULE. The article, not the possessive pronoun, must be put before a noun forming the regimen, when a pronoun which is either subject or regimen sufficiently supplies the place of that possessive, or when there is no sort of ambiguity.

EXAMPLES.

J'ai mal à la tête,	I have the head-ache.
Il faudroit lui couper la jambe,	It would be necessary to take off his leg.
Ce cheval a pris le mors aux dents,	That horse has run away.

EXERCISE.

1. For the whole winter he had sore eyes.
2. I had a fall yesterday, and hurt my back and head.
3. It would be better for a man to lose his life than forfeit* his honour by a criminal 2 action 1.
4. In this bloody battle, he received a wound by a shot in his right arm, and another in his left leg: by dint of care his arm was saved, but it was necessary to cut off his leg.

1. *For,* pendant; *he had sore,* avoir mal à.
2. *Had a fall,* se laisser tomber; *hurt,* se faire mal à.
3. *Would be better,* valoir mieux, cond-1.
4. *A wound by a shot,* un coup de feu; *in,* à; *by dint,* à force; *his arm,* etc. (they saved the arm to him); *was necessary,* falloir, ind-3; *to* cut off,* (to him).

But should either the personal pronoun or circumstances not remove all ambiguity, then the possessive pronoun must be joined to the noun. We say, je *vois que* ma *jambe s'enfle,* I see that my leg is swelling. For the same reason we say, il *lui donna* sa *main à baiser,* he gave him his hand to kiss; elle *a donné hardiment* son *bras au chirurgien,* she courageously presented her arm to the surgeon.

EXERCISE.

1. In this interview they made each other presents; she gave him her portrait, and he gave her his finest diamond.
2. A young surgeon preparing to bleed the great Condé, this prince said to him smiling, do not you tremble to bleed me? I, my Lord, no, certainly; it is not I, it is you who ought to tremble.

1. *Interview,* entrevue; *made each other,* se faire mutuellement.
2. *Preparing,* se disposer; *bleed,* saigner; *smiling,* d'un air

The prince, charmed with the reply, immediately gave him his arm.

riant; *it is not I*, (it is not to me); *it is you*, (it is to you); *who ought* to, de; *reply*, repartie.

REMARK. 1st. Although verbs which are conjugated with two pronouns of the same person remove every kind of amphibology, at least in general, yet custom authorises some proverbial expressions, in which the possessive pronoun seems to be useless: as, il se *tient ferme sur* ses *pieds*, he stands firm upon his feet.

2dly. Custom likewise authorises certain pleonasms, which seem to form exceptions to this rule: as, je *l'ai vu* de mes propres yeux, I have seen it with my own eyes.

3dly. When we speak of an habitual complaint, we use the possessive pronoun: as, sa *migraine l'a repris*, his headache is returned.

The possessive pronouns perform the office of the article, and are subject to the same rules; they must therefore be repeated before all substantives which are either subject or regimen, and before adjectives which express different qualities: as, son *père*, sa *mère*, et ses *frères sont de retour;* his father, mother, and brothers are come back; je *lui* ai montré mes *plus beaux et* mes *plus vilains habits*, I have shown him my finest and my ugliest dresses. This rule, which is not always observed in English, is common, in French, to all pronominal adjectives.

1. Whatever he may do, he always finds himself safe.
2. Can you yet doubt the truth of what I tell you? Would you ask a stronger proof than that I gave you, it is that I heard it, yes, heard it with my own ears.
3. My gout does not allow me a moment's repose.

1. *Finds himself*, se retrouver; *safe*, sur ses jambes.
2. *Can*, cond-1; *doubt*, douter de; *ask*, exiger.
3. *Allow*, laisser.

2 F

4. It is in vain that I exhort you to work and study; *your*
idleness, that cruel disease under* which you labour, renders
useless all the exhortations of friendship.

5. If you wish to be beloved, fail not to perform the promises
you have just made.

6. In the retreat that I have chosen for myself, my study and
garden are my greatest delight.

7. He brought me into his laboratory, and shewed me his
large and small vessels.

4. *It is in vain that I,* je avoir beau ; *you labour,* vous travailler.

5. *Fail not,* ne pas manquer ; *perform,* remplir ; *have just
made,* venir de faire.

6. *For myself,* (to me) ; *study,* cabinet ; *are,* faire ; *greatest,*
plus cher.

7. *Brought,* mener ; *laboratory,* laboratoire ; *vessels,* vaisseau.

III.

RELATIVE PRONOUNS.

Qui, when the subject may very properly relate both
to persons and things.

EXAMPLES.

L'homme qui *joue perd son temps,*	The man who games loses his time.
Le livre qui *plaît le plus n'est pas toujours le plus utile.*	The book which pleases most is not always the most useful.

But when it is the regimen, it can only be used of
persons or of things personified, whether the regimen be
direct or indirect.

EXAMPLES.

Quand on est délicat et sage dans ses goûts, on ne s'at-tache pas, sans savoir qui *l'on aime ;*	He who is wise and discriminate in his choice, does not form an attachment, without knowing the person he loves.
L'homme à qui *appartient ce beau jardin est très-riche,*	The man to whom this fine garden belongs is very rich.
La femme de qui *vous parlez,*	The woman of whom you are speaking.

REMARK. When the regimen indirect is expressed by the preposition *de*, we ought to prefer *dont* to *de qui*. It is better to say, *la femme* dont *vous parlez*; however, when the verb expresses a kind of transfer or conveyance, *de qui* must be used: as *celui de qui je tiens cette nouvelle*, the person from whom I had that intelligence.

RULE I. *Qui* must not be separated from its antecedent, when that antecedent is a noun.

EXAMPLES.

Un jeune homme qui *est docile aux conseils qu'on lui donne, et* qui *aime à en recevoir, aura infailliblement du mérite;*	A young man who is obedient to the advice that is given him, and who loves to receive this, will infallibly have merit.

REMARK. In some phrases, *qui* may be separated from the substantive by several words: that is, when the sense obliges us to refer it to that substantive: as *il a fallu, avant toute chose, vous faire lire dans l'écriture sainte* l'histoire du peuple de Dieu, qui *fait le fondement de la religion.* This sentence is very correct, because as *du peuple* determines the kind of history, and *de Dieu* the kind of people, the mind necessarily goes back to the substantive *histoire*, to which it refers the incidental phrase.

Qui, however, may be separated from its antecedent, when this antecedent is a pronoun used as the regimen direct: as *il la trouva* qui *pleuroit à chaudes larmes*, he found her crying bitterly; *je le vois* qui *joue*, I see him playing; because, in this case, the place of the pronoun is before the verb, and it is the same as saying, *il trouva elle* qui *pleuroit*, etc. *je vois lui qui joue*. Also in this kind of sentence, which are real gallicisms: ceux-là *ne sont pas les plus malheureux* qui *se plaignent le plus*, those are not the most unhappy who complain the most.

2 F 2

1. A young man *who* loves vanity of dress, like a woman, is unworthy of wisdom and glory ; glory is only due to a heart *that* knows how * to * suffer pain and trample upon pleasure.

2. Thyself, O my son, my dear son, thou * thyself *that* now enjoyest a youth so chearful and so full of pleasure, remember that this delightful age is but a flower *which* will be ɪ withered § almost as soon 2 as blown.

3. Men pass away like flowers, *which* open in * the morning, and at night are withered and trampled under foot.

4. You must have a man *that* loves nothing but truth and you, *that* will speak the truth in spite of you, *that* will force all your entrenchments ; and this necessary character is the very * man whom you have sent into exile.

5. We perceived him waiting for us, quietly seated under the shade of a tree.

1. *Vanity of dress*, à se parer vainement ; *trample upon*, fouler aux pieds.

2. *Chearful*, vif ; *full of*, fertile eu ; *remember*, se souvenir ; *delightful*, bel ; *withered*, sécher , *blown*, éclore.

3. *Open*, s'épanouir ; *and*, (which) ; *at night*, le soir ; *withered*, flétrir ; *under*, à ; *foot*, art. pl.

4. *You must have*, il vous falloir ; *nothing but*, ne que ; *will speak, will force*, subj-1 ; *entrenchments*, retranchement ; *character*, homme ; *man*, même ; *sent into exile*, exiler.

5. *Waiting for*, (who waited), attendre ; *under*, à.

RULE II. The relative *qui* must always have a reference to a noun taken in a determinate sense.

L'homme est un animal raisonnable, qui, etc. *Il me reçut avec* une politesse, qui, etc.

But we cannot say, l'*homme est* animal raisonnable, qui, etc. *Il me reçut avec* politesse, qui, etc.

REMARK. Though, in many phrases, the determinate nature of the nouns is not expressed, yet it is clearly understood. Thus, all these phrases are correct :

Il n'a point de livre qui *ne sait* de son choix,	He has not a book that is not of his own selecting.

Y a-t-il ville dans le royaume qui *soit plus favorisée ?*	Is there *a city* in the kingdom that is more favoured ?
Il se conduit en homme qui *connoît le monde,*	He behaves himself like *a man* who knows the world.
Il est accablé de maux qui *ne lui laissent pas un instant de repos,*	He is overwhelmed with *misfortunes* that do not allow him a moment's rest.
C'est une sorte de fruit qui *ne mûrit pas en Europe,*	It is a sort of *fruit* that does not ripen in Europe.

From the translation of all the above examples, it is evident that *livre, ville, maux,* are really determinate ; the meaning being, *il n'a pas* un livre qui, etc. *y a-t-il* une ille qui, etc.

EXERCISE.

1. He received us with such goodness, civility, and grace, as charmed us, and made us forget all we had suffered.

2. There is no *city* in the world where there are more riches and a greater population.

3. Is there a *man* can say ; I shall live till to-morrow?

4. He has no friend but would make for him every kind of sacrifice.

5. He is surrounded *by enemies*, who are continually observing him, and would be very glad to detect him in a fault.

6. In his retreat, he lives like a philosopher, *who* knows mankind and mistrusts them.

7. The pine-apple is *a sort of fruit*, that in Europe ripens only in hot-houses.

8. That man is *a sort of pedant*, who takes words for ideas and facts confusedly heaped up for knowledge.

1. *Such—as,* un—qui.
2. *There are,* subj.
3. *Man,* who) ; *can,* subj.
4. *But,* qui ne : *would make,* subj-2.
6. *Like a,* en ; *philosopher,* sage ; *mistrusts,* se défier de.
7. *Pine-apple,* ananas ; *hot-houses,* serre-chaude.
8. *Heaped up,* entasser ; *knowledge,* savoir.

Que relates both to persons and things, in all cases. It is always the regimen direct in a sentence, and cannot subsist without an antecedent expressed, which it generally follows. *L'homme que je vois,* la pêche que *je mange.* We say *generally,* because, in some instances, it may be separated from the antecedent by several words :

2 F 3

that is, when the mind necessarily goes back to that antecedent, as in the sentence of Flechier: *Qu'est-ce qu'une
armée? c'est un corps animé d'une infinité de passions différentes*, qu'un *homme habile fait mouvoir pour la défense
de la patrie.*

REMARK. There are instances where *que* appears to be
the regimen indirect, as it seems to be used instead of *à qui*
or *dont:* as *c'est à vous* que *je parle; c'est de lui* que *je
parle: de la façon* que *j'ai dit la chose.* In this case, *que*
is a conjunction.

EXERCISE.

1. The God *whom* the Hebrews and Christians have always
served, has nothing in common with the deities full of imperfec-
tion and even of vice worshipped by the rest of the world.

2. The Epic poem is not the panegyric of a hero *who* is proposed as a* pattern, but the recital of great and illustrious actions
which are exhibited for imitation.

3. The good *which* we hope for† presents itself to us, and disappears like an empty dream, *which* vanishes when we awake—to
teach us, that the very things *which* we think we hold fast in our
hands, may slip away in an instant. ..

4. Plato says, that, in writing, we ought to hide ourselves, to
disappear, to make the world forget us, that we may present
nothing but the truths we wish to impress.

1. (That the rest of the world worshipped.)

2. *Is proposed*, on propose; *as*, pour; *pattern*, modèle; *is exhibited*, on donner; *imitation*, exemple.

3. *Good*, bien; *disappears*, s'envoler; *empty*, vain; *vanishes*,
etc.; le réveil fait évanouir; *we* hold fast, tenir le mieux; *in our
hands*; *slip away*, nous échapper.

4. *We*, on; *to make the world forget*, se faire oublier; *that
we may present but*, pour ne produire que; *wish*, vouloir; *impress*, persuader.

Lequel and *dont* relate both to persons and things. It
is a general rule, that *lequel* ought never to be used either
as a subject or object, except to avoid ambiguity; for,
whenever the sense is evident, *qui* or *que* must be used:
that is conformable to the present practice.

Lequel with the preposition *de*, is either followed or
preceded by a noun, which it unites to the principal sen-

tence. If it be followed, *dont* is preferable to *duquel* both for persons and things. Thus we say, *la Tamise* dont *le lit;* and not, *de laquelle; le prince* dont *la protection*, and not *duquel*. If *lequel* be preceded by the noun, we can only make use of *duquel* when speaking of things: as *la Tamise, dans le lit* de laquelle; and it is always better to use it, when speaking of persons: as *le prince à la protection* duquel; *de qui* would not be so well.

·· With the preposition *à* we can only make use of *auquel*, when speaking of things: as *les places* auxquelles *il aspire;* but we ought to prefer *à qui*, when speaking of persons: as *les rois* à qui *on doit obéir; auxquelles* would not do so well.

It is easy to see that the relative *qui*, preceded by a preposition, never relates to things, but to persons only.

1. The grand principle on *which* the whole turns is, that all the world is but one republic, *of which* God is the common father, and in *which* every nation forms, as it were, one great family.

2. Homer, *whose* genius is grand and sublime like nature, is the greatest poet, and perhaps the most profound moralist of antiquity.

3. The celebrated Zenobia, *whose* noble firmness 2 you have admired 1, preferred dying with the title of queen, rather than accept the advantageous 2 offers 1 which Aurelian made her.

4. The Alps, on the summit *of which* the astonished eye discocovers perpetual snow and ice, present, at sun-set, the most striking and most magnificent spectacle.

5. A king, *to whose* care we owe a good law, has done more for his own glory than if he had conquered the universe.

6. The ambitious man sees nothing but pleasures in the possession of the employs *to which* he aspires with so much eagerness, instead of seeing the trouble that is inseparable from them.

1. *Turns*, rouler; *every,* chaque; *as it were*, comme.

3. *Preferred*, aimer mieux; *than*, que de.

4. *Snow, ice*, pl.; *sun-set*, soleil couchant; *striking*, imposant.

5. *Care*, sollicitude.

.7. Kings, *whom* religion makes it our duty to obey, are, upon earth, the true representation of the providence of God.

7. (To) *whom*; *makes it our duty to*, faire un devoit de.; *representation* image.

Quoi can only relate to things. It is placed after the word to which it relates, but is always preceded by a preposition, and is generally followed by the subject of the phrase with which it is connected. Formerly it was more used than at present: we used to say, *la chose à quoi on pense; voilà les conditions* sans quoi *la chose ne peut se faire.* This mode of expression is still to be met with in some writers; but *lequel, duquel, auquel* are much better; for *quoi* has a vague signification, for which reason it is never used with any degree of propriety, but when it relates to a vague and indefinite subject, such as *ce* or *rien:* as *c'est* de quoi *je m'occupe sans cesse; il n'y a* rien à quoi *je sois plus disposé.*

Où, d'où, par où, relate only to things. They are never used but when the nouns to which they refer express some kind of motion or rest, at least, metaphorically: as *voilà le but* où *il tend,* that is the end he aims at; *c'est une chose* d'où *dépend le bonheur public,* it is a thing upon which the public happiness depends: *les lieux* par où *il a passé,* the places through which he has passed.

EXERCISE.

1. *What* a young man, who begins the world, ought principally to attend *to*, is not to give it a high opinion of his understanding, but to gain numerous friends by the qualities of his heart.
2. A youth passed in idleness, effeminacy, and pleasure, lays up for* us nothing but sorrow and disgust in old age: this, however, is *what* we little think of when we are young.

1. *To what*, ce à quoi; *begins*, entrer dans; *to attend*, s'attacher; *opinion*, idée; *understanding*, esprit; *to gain*, se faire; *numerous*, beaucoup de.
2. *Idleness*, inutilité; *effeminacy*, mollesse; *pleasure*, volupté; *lays up*, préparer; *of*, à; *we*, on.

3. There is nothing *by which* we are more affected than the loss of fortune, although, being frail and perishable by its nature, it cannot contribute to our happiness.

4. A grove *in which* I brave the ardours of the dog-star, a retired valley *where* I can meditate in peace, a high hill whence my eye extends over immense plains, are the places *where* I spend the happiest moments of my life.

3. *By*, à; *we*, on; *affected*, sensible; *frail*, frêle; *by*, de; *cannot*, sub-1 ; *our*, (the).

4. *Grove*, bosquet; *dog-star*, canicule ; *spend*, passer.

IV.

ABSOLUTE PRONOUNS

Quoi relates to persons only; it presents to the mind nothing but a vague indeterminate idea: as, qui *sera assez hardi pour l'attaquer?* who will be bold enough to attack him? It is likewise used in the feminine, and in the plural : as, qui *est cette* personne? who is that person? qui *sont ces femmes?* who are those women?

Que and *quoi* relate to things only : as, que *pouvoit la valeur en ce combat funeste?* what could valour do in that fatal combat? *à* quoi *pensez-vous?* what are you thinking of? *Que* is sometimes used for *à quoi, de quoi:* as, que *sert la science sans la vertu?* what avails learning without virtue? *Que sert à l'avare d'avoir des trésors?* what use is it to the miser to possess treasures? that is, *à quoi sert,* etc. *de quoi sert,* etc.

Quoi sometimes relates to a whole sentence, and in this case it is the only expression authorized by custom : as *la vie passe comme un songe; c'est cependant* à quoi *on ne pense guères.*

REMARK. *Que* and *quoi* govern the preposition *de* before the adjective that follows them : as, que *dit-on de nouveau?* quoi *de plus agréable?* *Que* governs it likewise before substantives.

Quel relates both to persons and things: as quel *homme peut se promettre un bonheur constant? quelle grâce! quelle beauté! mais quelle modestie!*

Où, d'où, par où, never relate but to things.

EXERCISE.

1. *Who* could ever persuade himself, did not daily experience convince us of it, that, out of a hundred persons, there are ninety who sacrifice, to the enjoyment of the present, all the best founded hopes of the future?

2. *Who* would not love virtue for its own sake, could he see it in all its beauty?

3. He who does not know how* to apply himself in his youth, does not know *what* to do when arrived at maturity.

4. He was a wise legislator, who, having given to his countrymen laws calculated to make them good and happy, made them swear not to violate any of those laws during his absence; after *which*, he went away, exiled himself from his country, and died poor in a foreign land.

5. *What* people of antiquity ever had better laws than the Egyptians? *What* other nation ever undertook to erect monuments calculated to triumph over both time and barbarism?

6. *What more instructing* and *entertaining* than to read celebrated authors in their own language! *What beauty! what delicacy* and *grace*, which cannot be conveyed into a translation, are discovered in them!

7. When Menage had published his book on the Origin of the French Language, Christina, queen of Sweden, said, "Menage is the most troublesome 3 man i in the world 2: he cannot let one word 2 go 1 without its passport: he must know *whence* it comes, *where* it has passed *through*, and *whither* it is going."

1. *Out of*, sur; *future*, avenir.

2. *Its own sake*, elle-même; *could he*, si on pouvoir, ind-2.

3. (To) *what; to do*, s'occuper; *when arrived*, etc., dans l'âge mûr.

4. *He*, ce; *calculated*, propre; *not to*, (that they would not); *went away*, partir.

5. *Calculated to* fait pour; *both*, également; *over*, de.

6. *Language*, langue; *delicacy*, finesse; *which cannot*, qu'on ne peut: *be conveyed*, faire passer; *translation*, traduction; *are*, etc. n'y découvre-t-on pas.

7. *When*, après que; *Christina*, Christine; *troublesome*, incommode; *in the*, de, art.; *cannot*, ne sauroit; *go*, passer; *must*, vouloir.

V.

DEMONSTRATIVE PRONOUNS.

Ce, joined to the verb *être*, always governs this verb in the singular, except when it is followed by the third person plural. We say, *c'est moi, c'est toi, c'est lui, c'est nous, c'est vous;* but we must say, *ce sont eux, ce sont elles, ce furent vos ancêtres qui,* etc.

Ce is often used for a person or thing mentioned before, and, in this case, it supplies the place of *il* or *elle*. *Ce* must always be used when the verb *être* is followed by a substantive taken in a determinate sense; that is, accompanied by the article, or the adjective *un*.

EXAMPLES.

Lisez Homère et Virgile; ce sont les *plus grands* poètes *de l'antiquité:*	Read Homer and Virgil; they are the best poets of antiquity.
La douceur, l'affabilité et une certaine urbanité, distinguent l'homme qui vit dans le grand monde; ce sont là les marques *auxquelles on le reconnoît:*	Gentleness, affability and a certain urbanity, distinguish the man that frequents polite company; these are marks by which he may be known.
Avez-vous lu Platon? c'est un *des plus beaux génies de l'antiquité;*	Have you read Plato? he is one of the greatest geniusses of antiquity.

But when the verb *être* is followed by an adjective, or by a substantive taken adjectively, we make use of *il* or *elle*.

EXAMPLES.

Lisez Démosthène et Cicéron; ils sont très-éloquens:	Read Demosthenes and Cicero; they are very eloquent.
J'ai vu l'Hôpital de Greenwich; il est magnifique et digne *d'une grande nation:*	I have seen Greenwich Hospital; it is superb and worthy of a great nation.
Compteriez-vous sur Valère? ignorez-vous qu'il est homme à ne jamais revenir de ses premières idées?	Would you rely upon Valère? do you not know that he is a man who will never abandon his first opinions?

1. It *is we* who have drawn that misfortune upon * us, through our thoughtlessness and imprudence.

2. *It was* the Egyptians that first observed the course of the stars, regulated the year, and invented arithmetic.

3. Peruse attentively Plato and Cicero: *they are* the two *philosophers* of antiquity who have given us the most sound and luminous ideas upon morality.

4. If you be intended for the pulpit, read over and over again Bourdaloue and Massillon: *they are* both very *eloquent;* but the aim of the former is to convince, and that of the latter to persuade.

1. *Have drawn*, s'attirer; *thoughtlessness*, légèreté.

2. *First*, les premiers; *stars*, astre.

3. *Peruse*, lire; *sound*, sain; *morality*, morale.

4. *Be intended for*, se destiner à; *pulpit*, chaire; *read over and over again*, lire et relire sans cesse; *aim*, but.

Ce, joined to a relative pronoun, relates to things only. It is always masculine singular, because it only denotes a vague object, which is not sufficiently specified to know its gender and number.

EXAMPLE.

Ce qui flatte *est plus dangereux que* ce qui offense,	What flatters is more dangerous than what offends.

REMARK. *Ce,* joined to the relative pronouns, *qui*, *que, dont* and *quoi*, has, in some instances, a construction peculiar to itself. *Ce* and the relative pronoun that follows it, form, with the verb which they precede, the subject of another phrase, of which the verb is always *être.* Now, *être* may be followed by another verb, an adjective, or a noun.

When *être* is followed by another verb, the demonstrative *ce* is to be repeated: as, ce que *j'aime le plus* c'est *d'être seule*, what I like most is to be alone.

When followed by an adjective, the demonstrative is not repeated: as, ce dont *vous venez de me parler* est *horrible*, what you have been mentioning to me is horrid.

When it is followed by a substantive, the demonstrative may either be repeated or not, at pleasure, except in the case of a plural, or a personal pronoun. Thus we can say, ce *que je dis est*, or, c'est *la vérité*, what I say is truth; though the former is best. But we say, ce qui *m'indigne*, ce sont *les injustices qu'on ne cesse de faire*; what provokes me, are the injuries which are continually committed: ce qui *m'arrache au sentiment qui m'accable*, c'est vous; what alleviates the grief that oppresses me, is you. Most of these rules essentially contribute to the elegance of language.

EXERCISE.

1. *What* is astonishing *is* not always *what* is pleasing.
2. *What* the miser thinks least of, is to enjoy his riches.
3. *What* pleases us in the writings of the ancients, *is* to *see* that they have taken nature as a model, and that they have painted her with a noble simplicity.
4. *What* that good king has done for the happiness of his people deserves to be handed down to the latest posterity.
5. *What* constitutes poetry *is not* the exact number and regular cadence of syllables ; but *it is* the sentiment which animates every thing, the lively fictions, bold figures, and beauty and variety of the imagery : *it is* the enthusiasm, fire, impetuosity, force, a something in the words and thoughts which nature alone can impart.
6. *What* we justly admire in Shakspeare *are* those characters always natural and always well * sustained.
7. *What* keeps me attached to life *is you*, my son, whose tender age has still need of my care and advice.

1. *Is astonishing*, étonner; *is pleasing*, plaire.
2. *What* (that to which); *miser*, avare; *to*, de.
3. *As a*, pour.
4. *Deserves*, être digne; *to be handed down*, être transmis; *latest*, la plus reculée.
5. *Constitutes*, faire; *exact*, fixe; *lively*, vif; *imagery*, image, pl. ; *a something*, un je ne sais quoi; *words*, parole; *impart*, donner.
6. *We*, on; *justly*, avec justice; *natural*, dans la nature; *sustained*, soutenus.
7. *Keeps attached*, attacher; *care, advice*, pl.

There are two ways of employing *celui*. In the first

2 G

it is followed by a noun or pronoun preceded by the preposition *de*.

Celui de vous qui, etc.	Whichever of you that, etc.
Cette montre ressemble à celle de votre frère,	That watch is like that of your brother.

In the second instance, it is followed by *qui*, *que*, or
dont : as,

Celui qui ne pense qu'à lui seul dispense les autres d'y penser,	He who thinks of nobody but himself exempts others from thinking of him.
Votre nouvelle est plus sûre que celle qu'on débitoit hier,	Your intelligence is more authentic than that which was circulated yesterday.

In these two cases it is applied both to persons and
things.

REMARK. In this last instance we sometimes omit *celui*,
and this turn gives strength and elegance to the expression:
as *qui veut trop se faire craindre se fait rarement aimer*;
he who wishes to make himself too much feared, seldom
makes himself beloved.

Ceci and *cela* apply only to things.

REMARK. In the familiar style, custom authorises us to
say, in speaking of a child, or of country people amusing
themselves, *cela est heureux!*

1. *Whichever of you* shall be found to excel the others both
in mind and body, shall be acknowledged king of the island.

2. There are admirable pictures : *these* are after the manner of
Rubens, and *those* after the manner of Van-Huisum.

3. Why are the statues of the most celebrated modern sculp-
tors, notwithstanding the perfection to which the arts have been
carried, so much inferior *to those* of the ancients?

1. *Be found to excel the others*, on juger vainqueur; *both
in*, et pour (repeated).

2. *There are*, voilà de; *picture*, tableau ; *are after*, être dans;
manner, genre.

3. *Are*, (to be placed before *so much inferior*) ; *have been
carried*, (active voice with *on*) ; *inferior*, au-dessous.

4. *He* whose soul glowing, as it were, with divine fire, shall represent to himself the whole of nature, and shall breathe into objects that spirit of life which animates them, those affecting traits which delight and ravish us, will be a man of real genius.

5. *He that* judges of others by himself, is liable to many mistakes.

6. *He that* is easily offended, discovers his weak side, and affords his enemies an opportunity of taking advantage of it.

7. *He who* loves none but himself deserves not to be loved by others.

4. *Glowing with*, enflammé de ; *as it were*, pour ainsi dire ; *the whole of*, tout ; *shall breathe into*, répandre sur ; *affecting*, touchant ; *delight*, séduire ; *real*, vrai.

5. *By*, d'après ; *liable*, exposé ; *mistake*, méprise.

6. *Is offended*, s'offenser ; *weak side*, foible ; *affords*, fournir à ; *of taking advantage*, profiter.

VI.

PRONOUNS INDEFINITE.

Though the pronoun *on* is generally followed by the masculine, as in the phrase, *on n'est pas toujours maître de ses passions*, there are occasions which show so evidently that a female is spoken of, that *on* is, in these cases, followed by a feminine ; as *on n'est pas toujours jeune et jolie;* it may likewise be followed by a plural : as *on se battit en désespérés ; est-on des traîtres?*

The pronoun is repeated before all the verbs of a sentence, but care must be taken that it refer to one and the same subject. Thus this sentence, *on croit être aimé et l'on ne nous aime pas,* is incorrect ; we must say, *on croit être aimé et l'on ne l'est pas.*

Quiconque is masculine ; however, it is sometimes feminine, and in speaking to women we can say, *quiconque de vous*, etc. Though, perhaps, *celle de vous*, etc. is preferable.

EXERCISE.

1. Do you sincerely think, said Emily to Lucilla, that when

1. *Sincerely*, de bonne foi ; *Emily*, Emilie ; *women*, on ;

2 G 2

women are sensible and pretty, *they* are ignorant of* it ; no, *they* know it very well : but if *they* are watchful over their character, *they* are not proud of these advantages.

2. *We* are not slaves, to receive such treatment.

3. Do you know what *they* do here? *They* eat, *they* drink, *they* dance, *they* play, *they* walk ; in a word, *they* kill time in the gayest manner possible.

4. *Whoever* of you is bold enough to slander me, I will make him repent it.

5. *Whoever* of you is attentive and discreet, shall receive a reward that will flatter her.

they, on ; *know*, savoir ; *watchful over*, jaloux de ; *character*, réputation ; *are proud*, s'énorgueillir.

2. *We*, on ; *slaves*, (des) esclave ; *to receive*, pour essuyer de.

3. *They*, on ; *in the gayest manner*, le plus gaiment ; *possibly*, (that they can).

4. *Is*, ind-7 ; *to slander*, pour médire de ; *it*, (of it).

5. *Is*, ind-7 ; *that will*, fait pour.

Chacun, though always singular, may be followed, sometimes by *son*, *sa*, *ses*, and sometimes by *leur*, *leurs*, which, in many instances, is very perplexing.

There is no difficulty in those phrases where *chacun* does not belong to a plural number ; we then make use of *son*, *sa*, *ses* : as *donnez à chacun sa part*, give to each his share ; *que chacun songe à ses affaires*, let every one mind his own business.

But it is not so in phrases where *chacun* belongs to a plural number.

RULE. In phrases where *chacun* is contrasted with a plural to which it belongs, we make use of *son*, *sa*, *ses*, when *chacun* is placed after the regimen ; but we must use *leur*, *leurs*, when *chacun* is placed before the regimen.

EXAMPLES.

Remettez ces médailles chacune en sa place,	Return those medals each into its proper place.
Les hommes devroient s'aimer, chacun pour son propre intérêt ;	Men ought to love one another, each for his own interest.

But we must say :

Les hommes devroient avoir, chacun pour leur propre intérêt, de l'amour les uns pour les autres ;	Men ought, for their own interest, to have an affection for each other.

REMARK. In phrases where *chacun* is contrasted with a plural, there are two senses, the collective and the distributive. When *chacun* is placed after the regimen, the collective sense expressed by the plural is finished; and the distributive *chacun* must perform the office peculiar to it, by considering the whole kind separated into individuals : but when *chacun* is placed before the regimen, the collective sense is not completed, and consequently it must be carried on to the end.

The pronoun which follows *chacun* is put in the plural : as *la reine dit elle-même aux députés qu'il étoit temps qu'ils s'en retournassent chacun chez eux.*

EXERCISE.

1. Go into my library, and put the books which have been sent back to me, *each* into *its* place.
2. They have all brought offerings to the temple, *every one* according to *his means* and devotion.
3. Thierry charged Uncelanue to carry his orders to the mutineers and to make them retire *each* under *his* colours.
4. *Each* of them has brought *his* offering and fulfilled *his* religious duty.
5. Had Ronsard and Balzac, *each* in *his* manner of writing, a sufficient degree of merit to form *after them* any very great men in verse and in prose?
6. After a day so usefully spent, we went back, *each* to *our* own home.

2. *Offerings,* offrande.
5. *To carry,* aller porter ; *mutineers,* mutin ; *colours,* drapeau.
4. (They have brought each their, etc.); *fulfilled,* remplir.
5. *Manner of writing,* genre; *a sufficient degree,* assez; *any,* un.
6. *Day,* journée; *went back,* retourner ; *to,* chez ; *our own home,* (pron. personal).

2 G 3

7. Minds that possess any correctness, examine things with attention, in order to give a fair judgment of them ; and they place *each* 2 of* them 1 in the rank *it* ought to occupy.

7. *Possess any,* avoir de ; *correctness,* justesse ; *give a fair judgment,* juger avec connoissance ; *place,* mettre ; *to occupy,* avoir.

Personne, used as a pronoun, is always masculine ; of course the adjective relating to it must be of that gender : as *personne n'est aussi heureux qu'elle,* nobody is so happy as she.

It has been said that *l'un et l'autre* require the verb they govern to be in the plural. The most respectable grammarians are of opinion that *ni l'un ni l'autre* ought likewise to govern the verb in the plural ; and indeed this pronoun evidently expresses two objects. However, some think that if the action expressed by the verb applies only to a single object, this verb ought to be preserved in the singular, and that therefore we ought to say : *ni l'un ni l'autre n'est mon père ; ni l'un ni l'autre ne sera nommé à cette ambassade ;* but when *ni l'un ni l'autre* elegantly stand after the verb, there is no such distinction ; the verb is always in the plural : as *ils ne sont morts ni l'un ni l'autre.*

EXERCISE.

1. Nobody is so severe, so virtuous in public, as some women who have the least restraint in private.

2. Nobody could be happier than she ; but by the consequence of that levity which you know she has, she has lost all the advantages that she had received from nature and education.

3. Racine and Fenelon will always be the delight of sensible hearts : both 2 possessed 1 in the highest degree the art of exciting in us at their pleasure the most tender and the most lively emotions.

1. *So,* aussi ; *some,* certain ; *have the least restraint,* être le moins retenu.

2. *Could,* ind-2 ; *the,* un ; *levity,* légèreté ; *know she has,* lui connoître.

3. *Always,* dans tous les temps ; *both,* l'une et l'autre ; *in the,* au ; *pleasure,* gré.

4. Balzac and Voiture enjoyed in their time great celebrity: but neither a has been read 1 since good taste has made 1 the native and simple graces 3 to be preferred 2 to the bombast of the first, and the affectation of the second.

4. *Enjoyed*, ind-4; *neither*, ni l'un ni l'autre; *has been read*, (they read them no more); *native*, du naturel; *simple*, de la simplicité; *be preferred*, (active voice); *bombast*, bouffissure.

Tout, when the regimen direct, is placed after the verb, in simple tenses, and between the auxiliary and the participle, in compound tenses: as *il avoue tout; il a tout avoué.* But when it is the regimen indirect, it is always placed after the verb, either in simple or compound tenses: as *il rit de tout; il a pensé à tout.* *Rien* follows the same order of construction.

Tout is sometimes used as an adverb, and merely as an expletive: *il lui dit tout froidement,* he told him (quite) coolly. Sometimes also, instead of *quoique très, entièrement, quelque;* in which case the following rules must be observed.

RULE I. *Tout* does not alter its number before an adjective masculine: as *les enfans,* tout *aimables qu'ils sont,* children, all amiable as they are; *ils sont tout interdits,* they are quite disconcerted.

RULE II. *Tout* takes neither gender nor number before an adjective feminine, beginning with a vowel or *h* mute: but it takes both gender and number before an adjective feminine, beginning with a consonant. We say, *la vertu,* tout *austère qu'elle paroît; ces images,* tout *amusantes qu'elles sont:* but we say, *c'est une tête* toute *vide; ces dames,* toutes *spirituelles qu'elles sont.*

EXCEPTION. *Tout* takes neither gender nor number before an adjective feminine, beginning with a consonant, when it is immediately followed by an adverb. Thus we say, *ces fleurs sont* tout aussi *fraîches que celles que vous avez; ces dames sont,* tout ainsi que, tout comme *vous, belles, jeunes et spirituelles.* In this sense, *tout* is a mere expletive.

1. Children, *amiable* as they are, have, nevertheless, many faults which it is of importance to correct.

2. The philosophers of antiquity, *although* very* much* *enlightened,* have given us but very confused ideas of the deity, and very vague notions about the principal duties of the law of nature.

3. These flowers, *inodorous* as they are, are not the less esteemed.

4. Virtue, *austere* as it is, makes us enjoy real pleasures.

5. Fables, *although* very* entertaining, yet truly 5 interest only when they convey to us instruction, under the disguise of an ingenuous allegory.

6. Although that absurd pedant is an incessant 2 scribbler 1, yet his head is *altogether empty.*

7. Far be from us those maxims of flattery, that kings are born with talents, and that their favoured souls come out of God's hand *completely wise* and *learned.*

8. Those fountains glide *quite* gently through a mead enamelled with flowers.

9. The peaches are quite as good as those of the south of France.

1. *Have, nevertheless,* ne laisser pas d'avoir; *faults,* défaut; *of importance,* essentiel.

2. *Enlightened,* éclairés qu'ils étoient ; *of nature,* naturel.

3. *Inodorous,* inodore ; *not,* n'en.

4. *Enjoy,* goûter de.

5. *Entertaining,* amusantes qu'elles sont; *truly,* véritablement; *convey,* offrir; *disguise,* voile.

6. *Incessant,* infatigable ; *scribbler,* écrivailleur; *his head is,* (he has not less the head) ; *not,* n'en ; *altogether,* tout.

7. *Far be,* loin; *of,* de, art.; *are born,* naître; *with talents,* habile; *favoured,* privilégié; *come out,* sortir ; *learned,* savant.

8. *Glide,* couler ; *gently,* doucement; *through a mead,* sur un gazon.

9. *South,* midi.

Quelque que joined to a substantive, either single or accompanied by an adjective, takes the mark of the plural.

EXAMPLES.

Quelques *richesses que vous ayez,*	Whatever riches you may have.
Quelques *bonnes œuvres que vous fassiez,*	Whatever good actions you may do.
Quelques *peines affreuses que vous éprouviez,*	However dreadful pains you may suffer.

But when joined to an adjective separated from its substantive, it does not take the mark of the plural.

EXAMPLES.

Tous les hommes, quelque *opposés qu'ils soient;*	All men, however opposite they may be.
Ces actions, quelque *belles qu'on les trouve;*	Those actions, however brilliant they may be found.

We have seen that *quelque que* and *quel que,* joined to a substantive, have the same meaning, although they are not used indifferently for each other. If the pronoun stands before the substantive, we make use of *quelque que:* as *quelques richesses que vous ayez;* but if the substantive be after the *que* and the verb, then we make use of *quel que* in two separate words: as *quelles que soient les richesses que vous ayez.*

EXERCISE.

1. *Whatever talents* you may possess, *whatever advantages* you may have received from nature and education, with* *whatever perfections* you may be endowed, expect the suffrages but of a small number of men.

2. *Whatever great services* you may have rendered mankind, rather look for their ingratitude than their acknowledgments.

3. *However useful, however well written* the works which you have published, yet think not that you will immediately reap the fruits of your labours ; it is but by slow degrees that light introduces itself among men. The course of time is swift; but it seems to lag, when it brings reason and truth along with it.

1. *Possess,* avoir; *have received,* tenir ; *be endowed,* posséder; *expect,* ne s'attendre à ; *but,* que.

2. *Mankind,* homme, pl. ; *rather look for,* compter plutôt; *acknowledgment,* reconnoissance.

3. *Immediately,* de suïte ; *reap,* recueillir ; *by slow degrees,* avec lenteur; *among,* chez; *swift,* rapide; *to lag,* se traîner; *along with it,* à sa suite.

4. Whatever may be the obstacles which ignorance, prejudice, and envy oppose to the true principles of an art, yet we ought never to be deterred from propagating them : the sun does not cease to shine, because its light the hurts eyes of nightbirds.

5. *Whatever be your birth, whatever your riches* and dignities, remember that you are frustrating the views of providence, if you do not make use of them for the good of mankind.

4. We, on ; *to be deterred,* se rebuter ; *propagating,* répandre ; *shine,* éclairer ; *its,* the article ; *hurts,* blesser ; *nightbirds,* oiseau de nuit.

5. *Are frustrating,* frustrer.

CHAPTER V.

OF THE VERB.

AGREEMENT OF THE VERB WITH ITS SUBJECT.

It has been observed that the verb which has two subjects, both singular, is put in the plural : but to this rule there are the following

EXCEPTIONS.

1st. Though a verb may have two subjects in the singular, yet that verb is not put in the plural, when the two subjects are joined together by the conjunctions, *ou, comme, aussi bien que, autant que,* etc.

EXAMPLES.

La séduction ou *la terreur l'a entraîné dans le parti des rebelles,*	Either persuasion or terror *has* drawn him into the party of the rebels.
Le roi, aussi bien que *son ministère,* veut *le bien public ;*	The king, *as well* as his ministry, *wishes* for the public good.
Son honnêteté, autant que *son esprit, le* fait *rechercher ;*	His honesty, as much as his wit, makes him courted.
L'envie, comme *l'ambition,* est une *passion aveugle ;*	Envy, like ambition, *is* a blind passion.

2dly. The verb is likewise put in the singular, notwithstanding plurals may precede it, either when there is an expression which collects all the substantives into one, such as *tout, ce, rien,* etc. or when the conjunction *mais* is placed before the last substantive.

EXAMPLES.

Biens, dignités, honneurs, tout disparoît *à la mort;*	Riches, dignities, honours, every thing *vanishes* at death.
Jeux, conversations, spectacles, rien *ne la distrait;*	Games, conversations, shows, nothing *diverts* her.
Perfidies, noirceurs, incendies, massacres, ce n'est *là qu'une foible image,* etc.	Perfidies, enormities, conflagrations, massacres, all this *is* but a feeble representation, etc.
Non-seulement. toutes ses richesses et tous ses honneurs, mais toute sa vertu s'évanouit;	Not only all his riches and honours, but all his virtue *vanishes.*

EXERCISE.

1. Either fear *or* inability prevented them from moving.

2. The fear of death, *or* rather the love of life, began to revive in his bosom.

3. Alcibiades, *as well as* Plato, was among the disciples of Socrates.

4. Lycurgus, *like* Solon, was a wise legislator.

5. Euripides, *as much as* Sophocles, contributed to the glory of the Athenians.

6. Riches, dignities, honours, glory, pleasure, every thing loses its charms from the moment we possess it, because none of those things can fill the heart of man.

7. The gentle zephyrs which preserved, in that place, notwithstanding the scorching heat of the sun, a delightful coolness; springs gliding with a sweet murmur through meadows interspersed with amaranths and violets; a thousand springing flowers which enamelled carpets ever green; a wood of those tufted trees that bear golden apples, and the blossom of which

1. *Inability,* impuissance; *moving,* remuer.

2. *Began to revive,* se réveiller; *in,* au fond de; *bosom,* cœur.

3. *Among,* au nombre de.

6. *We,* on; *none,* rien; *those things,* tout cela.

7. *Preserved,* entretenir; *scorching heat,* ardeur; *interspersed with,* semer de; *springing,* naissant; *carpets,* tapis; *tufted,* touffu; *golden* (of gold); *renewed,* (which renews) se

348   PARTICULAR RULES OF THE VERB.

renewed every season, yields the sweetest of all perfumes; the
warbling of birds, the continual prospect of a fruitful country;
in a word, nothing of what till then had made him happy.
could deaden the feeling of his grief.

renouveler; (in) *every season*; *yields*, répandre; *prospect,*
spectacle; *made*, rendre; *deaden*, l'arracher à; *feeling*, sentiment.

OF THE COLLECTIVE PARTITIVE.

The collectives general have nothing to distinguish them
from substantives common, with regard to the laws of
agreement; but the collectives partitive apparently break
through those laws in some instances.

RULE. The verb, which relates to a collective partitive, is put in the plural when that partitive is followed
by the preposition *de* and a plural; but it is put in the
singular, either when the partitive is followed by a regimen singular, or when it expresses a determinate quantity,
or lastly, when it presents an idea independent of the
plural which follows it.

EXAMPLES.

La plupart des hommes sont *bien prompts dans leurs juge-mens*,	The greatest part of men are very hasty in their judg-ments.
Bien des philosophes *se* sont *trompés*,	Many philosophers have been mistaken.

But we ought to say:

Une infinité de peuple est *accourue* (regimen singular),	An immense number of people flocked together.
La moitié des soldats a *péri* (determinate quantity),	One half of the soldiers has perished.
Le plus grand nombre des troupes a *péri* (idea independent of the plural),	The greater number of the troops has perished.

We see, then, that the substantives partitive, *la plupart, une infinité, une foule, un nombre, la plus grande
partie, une sorte,* etc. and words signifying quantity, such
as *peu, beaucoup, assez, moins, plus, trop, tant, combien,*
and *que* used for *combien,* followed by a noun joined to

them by the preposition *de*, have not the least influence on the verb, and consequently, it is not with them that the verb agrees, but with the noun which follows them.

REMARK. The words *infinité* and *la plupart*, used by themselves, require the verb in the plural : as *une infinité pensent, la plupart sont d'avis.*

EXERCISE.

1. *Many persons* experience that human life is every where a state in which much is to be endured and little to be enjoyed.

2. *Many poets* think that poetry is the art of uniting pleasure with truth, by calling imagination to the help of reason.

3. *Few persons* reflect that time, like money, may be lost by unseasonable avarice.

4. *So many years* of familiarity were chains of iron which linked me to those men who beset me every hour.

5. *How many wise* men* have thought that to seclude one's self from the world, was to pull out the teeth of devouring animals, and to take away from the wicked the use of his poniard, from calumny its poisons, and from envy its serpents!

6. *A company of young Phœnicians* of uncommon beauty, clad in fine linen, whiter than snow, danced a * long while the dances of their own * country, then those of Egypt, and lastly those of Greece.

7. *A troop of nymphs,* crowned with flowers, whose lovely tresses flowed over their shoulders and waved with the wind, swam in shoals behind her car.

8. At the time of the invasion of Spain by the Moors, an *innumerable multitude of people* retired into the Asturias, and there proclaimed Pelagius king.

1. *Much is,* etc. (one has a great deal of pains, and little of real enjoyments).

3. *Unseasonable,* hors de propos.

4. *Familiarity,* habitude ; *linked,* lier ; *beset,* obséder.

5. *How many,* que de ; *to seclude one's self,* se retirer ; *pull out of,* arracher à ; *to take away from,* ôter à.

6. *Company,* troupe ; *clad in,* et vêtu de ; *linen,* lin.

7. *Lovely,* beau ; *tresses,* cheveu ; *flowed,* pendre : *waved,* flotter ; *with,* au gré de ; *swam,* nager ; *shoals,* foule ; *car,* char.

8. *Moors,* Maure ; *retired,* se retirer ; *Asturias,* Asturies ; *Pelagius,* Pélage.

2 H

9. *A third part of the enemy* were left dead on the field of battle; the rest surrendered at discretion.

10. *The innumerable crowd of carriages* which are to be seen in London during the winter, astonishes foreigners.

9. *A third part*, un tiers ; *enemy*, pl. ; *surrendered*, se rendre.

10. *Crowd*, quantité; *which are*, (active voice, on).

PLACE OF THE SUBJECT WITH REGARD TO THE VERB.

We have seen that the subject of a verb is either a noun or a pronoun, and that this subject must always be expressed in French. It now only remains to know its place with respect to the verb.

RULE. The subject, whether noun or pronoun, is generally placed before the verb.

EXAMPLES.

L'ambition effrénée *de quelques hommes* a, *dans tous les temps*, été *la vraie cause des révolutions des états;*	The unbridled ambition of a few men has, in all ages, been the real cause of the revolutions of empires.
Quand nous nageons *dans l'abondance, il est bien rare que* nous *nous* occupions *des maux d'autrui;*	When we roll in plenty, we seldom think of the miseries of others.

EXERCISE.

1. *Youth* is full of presumption ; *it* expects every thing from itself; although frail, it thinks itself all-sufficient, and that it has nothing to fear.

2. *Commerce* is like certain springs; if you attempt to * divert their course, *you* dry them up.

3. *It* is enough that falsehood is falsehood, to be unworthy of a man who speaks in the presence of God, and who is to sacrifice every thing to truth.

4. The *ambition* and *avarice* of man are the sources of his unhappiness.

1. *Full of presumption*, présomptueux; *expects*, se promettre; *itself all-sufficient*, pouvoir tout; *that it has*, avoir.

2. *Springs*, source ; *attempt*, vouloir ; *dry up*, faire tarir.

3. *It is enough*, suffire ; *falsehood*, mensonge; *is*, subj. ; *in*, en ; *is to sacrifice*, doit.

5. *They* punish, in Crete, three vices which have remained unpunished in all other nations: ingratitude, dissimulation and avarice.

6. Like the Numidian lion, goaded by cruel hunger, and rushing upon a flock of feeble sheep, *he* tears, *he* slays, *he* swims in blood.

5. *Punished*, ind-2; *have remained*, être; *in*, chez.

6. *Like*, semblable à; *goaded by*, etc. (that cruel hunger goads), dévorer; *rushing*, (which rushes upon), entrer dans; *tears*, déchirer; *slays*, égorger.

EXCEPTIONS.

1st. In interrogative phrases, the question is made either with a prónoun or a noun; if with a pronoun, this is always placed after the verb: as *que dit-on? irai-je à la campagne? de qui parle-t-on?* if with a noun, the noun is sometimes placed before, and sometimes after the verb; it stands before when the pronoun personal which answers to it, asks the question: as *cette nouvelle est-elle sûre? les hommes se rendent-ils toujours à la raison?* it stands after, when a pronoun absolute or an interrogative adverb, placed at the beginning of the phrase, allow the suppression of the personal prónoun: as *que dit votre ami? à quoi s'occupe votre frère? où demeure votre cousin?*

REMARK. In interrogative sentences, when the verb which precedes *il, elle, on,* ends with a vowel, the letter *t* is put between that verb and the pronoun: as *arrive-t-il? viendra-t-elle? aime-t-on les vauriens?* When *je* is after a verb, which ends with *e* mute, we change that *e* mute into *é* acute: as *aimé-je? puissé-je?* But, as custom does not always admit *je* after the verb, we must adopt another turn, and say, in interrogating: *est-ce que je cours? est-ce que je dors?*

1. *Have you* forgotten all that Providence has done for you? how *have you* escaped the shafts of your enemies? how *have you* been preserved from the dangers which surrounded you on all

1. *Escaped*, échapper à; *shafts*, trait; *preserved*, garantir;

2 H 2

sides? *could you be* so blind as not to acknowledge and adore the all-powerful hand that has miraculously saved you?

2. What *will posterity say* of you, if, instead of devoting to the happiness of mankind the great talents which you have received from nature, you make use of them only to deceive and corrupt them?

3. Do not *the misfortunes* which we experience often contribute to our prosperity?

4. Why are *the works of nature* so perfect? Because each work is a whole, and because she labours upon an eternal plan, from which she never deviates. Why, on the contrary, are *the productions* of man so imperfect? It is because the human mind being unable to create any thing, and incapable of embracing the universe at a single glance, can * produce, only after having been enriched by experience and meditation.

on all sides, de toutes parts; *so as*, assez pour; *saved*, conserver.

2. *Devoting*, consacrer; *mankind*, homme, pl.; *deceive*, égarer.

3. *Experience*, éprouver; *turn out*, tourner en.

4. *Because*, c'est que; *and because*, et que; *being unable*, ne pouvoir; *incapable*, (not being able); *at*, de; *glance*, vue; *enriched*, fécondé.

2dly. In the incidental sentences which express that we are quoting somebody's words: as *je meurs innocent, a dit Louis XVI.* I die innocent, said Louis XVI. *Je le veux bien, dit-il;* I am very willing, said he.

3dly. With an impersonal verb, and these words, *tel*, *ainsi. Il est arrivé un grand malheur*, a great misfortune has happened. *Tel étoit l'acharnement du soldat que*, etc. such was the fury of the soldier that, etc. *Ainsi finit cette sanglante tragédie*, thus ended that bloody tragedy.

1. True glory, *said he*, is founded in humanity: whoever prefers his own glory to the feelings of humanity, is a monster of pride, and not a man.

2. There have happened for these * ten years, *so many events*,

1. *Is founded*, ne se trouve pas hors de: *feelings*, sentiment.

2. *There have happened for*, il se passer depuis; *exceeding*,

exceeding all probability, that posterity will find it very difficult to credit them.

3. *Such* was *that incorruptible Phocion*, who answered the deputies of Alexander, who were telling him that this powerful monarch loved him as the only honest man; well, then*, let him allow me 1 to be and to appear so.

4. *Thus* ended, by the humiliation of Athens, *that dreadful war* of twenty-seven years, to * which ambition gave rise, which hatred made atrocious, and which was as fatal to the Greeks, as their ancient confederation had proved advantageous to them.

hors de; *probability*, vraisemblance; *will find very difficult*, avoir bien de la peine; *to credit*, ajouter foi à.

3. *Loved*, chérir; *honest man*, homme de bien; *well*, ho! *to be so*, d'être tel; *appear so*, le paroître.

4. *Ended*, se terminer; *gave rise*, faire naître; *made*, rendre; *had proved*, être.

4thly. When the subjunctive is used to express a wish, or for *quand même* and a conditional: as *puissent tous les peuples se convaincre de cette vérité*, may all nations be convinced of this truth; *dussé-je y périr, j'irai;* should I perish there, I will go.

5thly. When the subject is followed by several words which are dependent upon it. This exception is strictly to be attended to, when the words which depend on the subject form an incidental sentence which, by its length, might obscure the relation of the verb to the subject. Perspicuity here requires that the subject should be so displaced.

Sometimes, however, this displacing of the subject is only the effect of taste, and happens when we wish to avoid an inharmonious cadence: or when, in the middle of a speech, an orator wishes to rouse the attention of his hearers by a bold and unexpected turn.

EXERCISE.

1. The gods grant that you may never experience such misfortunes!

2. May you, O wise old man! in a repose diversified by pleasing occupations, enjoy the past, lay hold of the present, and charm your latter days with the hope of eternal felicity.

1. *Grant*, faire; *experience*, éprouver de.

2. *Old man*, vieillard; *lay hold of*, saisir; *with*, de.

2 H 3

3. What is not in the power of the gods! were you at the lowest depths, the power of Jupiter could draw you from thence: were you in Olympus, beholding the stars under your feet, Jupiter could plunge you to the bottom of the abyss, or precipitate you into the flames of gloomy Tartarus.

4. There, through meadows enamelled with flowers, glide a thousand various rivulets, distributing every where their pure (limpid) waters.

5. Already, for the honour of France, there* had come into administration a man more distinguished for his understanding and virtues, than for his dignities.

3. *Is not in the power*, ne peuvent; *were,* subj-2; *lowest depths*, fond de l'abîme; *power*, puissance; *could*, pouvoir, cond-1; *Olympus*, Olympe; *stars*, astre; *gloomy*, noir; *Tartarus*, Tartare.

4. *Through*, au milieu de; *with*, de; *glide*, serpenter; *rivulets*, ruisseau; *distributing*, (which distribute).

5. *Had come*, être entré; *administration* (of affairs); *understanding*, esprit.

GOVERNMENT OF THE VERBS.

We have already observed, that when the regimen of a verb is a noun, it is generally placed after the verb: but to this rule there is one exception, besides those which will hereafter be mentioned.

EXCEPTION. In an interrogative sentence, the regimen is placed before the verb, when this regimen is joined to an absolute pronoun.

EXAMPLES.

Quel objet voyez-vous?	What object do you see?
À quelle science vous appliquez-vous?	To what science do you apply yourself?
De quelle affaire vous occupez-vous?	About what business are you employed?

REMARK. In French, a verb can never have two regimens direct; therefore, when a verb has two regimens, one of them must necessarily be preceded by a preposition.

EXAMPLES.

Donnez ce livre à votre frère,	Give that book to your brother.
On a accusé Cicéron d'imprudence et de foiblesse,	Cicero has been accused of imprudence and weakness.

According to the natural order of the ideas, it should seem that the regimen direct ought to be placed before the indirect.: however, as the perspicuity of the sentence does not allow it in all cases, the following rule must be observed.

RULE. When a verb has two regimens, the shorter is generally placed first; but if they be of equal length, the regimen direct must be placed before the indirect.

EXAMPLES.

Les hypocrites s'étudient à parer le vice *des dehors de la vertu,*	Hypocrites make it their study to deck vice with the exterior of virtue.
Les hypocrites s'étudient à parer des dehors de la vertu *les vices les plus honteux et les plus décriés,*	Hypocrites make it their study to deck with the exterior. of virtue the most shameful and most odious vices.
L'ambition sacrifie le présent à *l'avenir, mais la volupté sacrifie* l'avenir *au présent;*	Ambition sacrifices the present to the future, but pleasure sacrifices the future to the present.

EXERCISE.

1. Illustrious examples teach us, that God has hurled *from their thrones princes who contemned his laws :* he reduced *to the condition of beasts the haughty Nebuchadnezzar, who wanted to usurp divine honours.*

2. Wretched is* the man who feeds *his mind with chimeras.*

3. Our interest should prompt us to prefer *virtue to vice, wisdom to pleasure, and modesty to vanity.*

1. *Teach,* apprendre; *hurled,* renverser; *haughty,* superbe; Nabuchodonosor; *wanted,* vouloir.

2. *Feeds,* repaître.

3. *Should,* devoir, ind-1; *prompt,* porter; *pleasure,* volupté.

RULE. A noun may be governed at once by two verbs, provided those verbs do not require different regimens.

EXAMPLES.

On doit aimer et respecter les rois,	We ought to love and respect kings.
Ce général attaqua et prit la ville,	That general attacked and took the city.

But we must not say, *cet officier attaqua et se rendit maître de la ville*, that officer attacked and made himself master of the city. A different turn should be given to the sentence, by placing the noun after the first verb, and *en* before the second: as *cet officier attaqua* la ville *et s'en rendit maître*, that officer attacked the city and made himself master of it.

EXERCISE.

1. Luxury is like a torrent, which *carries away* and *overturns* every thing it meets.

2. Nothing can* resist the operation of time: it, at length, *undermines, alters* or *destroys* every thing.

5. Among the Spartans, public education had two objects: the first, to harden their bodies by fatigue; the second, to *excite* and *nourish* in their minds the love of their country, and an enthusiasm for what is great.

1. *Carries away*, entraîner; *overturns*, renverser; *every thing*, tout ce que.

2. *Operation*, action; *at length*, à la longue; *undermines*, miner.

5. *Among the Spartans*, à Sparte; *to*, de; *harden*, endurcir; *by*, à; *their* must be rendered by the article; *for*, de.

OF THE USE PROPER OR ACCIDENTAL OF MOODS AND TENSES.

INDICATIVE.

The *present* is used to express an existing state: as *je suis ici*, I am here; an invariable state: as *Dieu est de toute éternité*, God is from all eternity; a future near at hand: as *c'est demain fête*, to-morrow is a holiday: or even a preterit, when we mean to give a sort of picture of what would have been a mere narration. Thus, we find in Racine: *j'ai vu votre malheureux fils traîné par ses chevaux*, I have seen your unhappy son dragged along by his horses: but suddenly passing from the preterit to the present, he adds: *il veut les rappeler, et sa voix les effraie ;* he calls out to stop them, but his voice frightens them.

In English, the verb *to be* is frequently used with the participle present: as *I am reading, I was translating*, *I shall be writing*; a construction not adopted in French, and whenever found, it is to be translated in French simply by the verb put in the tense expressed by the verb *to be*. Thus, *am* being in the present tense of the verb *to be*, *I am reading* must be expressed by *je lis*, the present tense of the verb *lire*, to read; and *shall be* being the future tense of the verb *to be*, *I shall be writing* must be rendered *j'écrirai*, being the future tense of the verb *écrire*, to write.

EXERCISE.

1. *He is* in his chamber, where he is unbending his mind from the fatigue of business, by some instructive and agreeable reading.

2. Truth, eternal by its nature, *is* immutable as God himself.

3. I never *let* a day *pass* without devoting an hour or two to reading the ancients.

4. It is this week that the new piece comes out.

5. The armies were in sight, nothing was heard on all sides but dreadful cries: the engagement began. Immediately a cloud of arrows *darkens* the air and *covers* the combatants; nothing *is* heard but the doleful cries of the dying, or the clattering of the arms of those who *fall* in the conflict; the earth *groans* beneath a heap of dead bodies, and rivers of blood *stream* every where; *there is nothing* in this confused mass of men enraged against one another, but slaughter, despair, revenge and brutal rage.

1. *Is unbending*, délasser; *reading*, lecture.

2. *By*, de; *immutable*, immuable.

3. *Let*, *; *devoting*, consacrer.

4. *Comes out*, on donner.

5. *Sight*, présence; *nothing was*, etc., on ne que, ind-2 *the. engagement began*, on en venir aux mains, ind-3; *cloud*, nuée; *arrows*, trait; *darkens*, obscurcir, *nothing is*, etc. on ne plus que; *doleful*, plaintif; *clattering*, bruit; *conflict*, mêlée; *groans*, gémir; *beneath*, sous; *heap*, monceau; *rivers*, ruisseau; *stream*, couler; *there is nothing in*, etc., ce ne être dans; *mass*, amas; *enraged*, acharné; *but*, que; *slaughter*, massacre; *rage*, fureur.

The *imperfect* is used to denote the repetition of an action at a time which is past: as *quand j'étois à Paris*, *j'allois souvent aux Champs Elysées ;* when I was at Paris, I often went to the *Champs Elysées :* 2dly. For a past which has some duration, especially in narrations : as *Rome étoit d'abord gouvernée par des rois,* Rome was at first governed by kings.

EXERCISE.

1. When *I was* at Paris, *I went* every morning to take a walk in the *Champs Elysées,* or the *Bois de Boulogne ;* afterwards I *came* home, where I employed myself till dinner, either in reading or writing ; and in the evening, I generally went for amusement to the French Theatre or the Opera.

2. When *I was* in the prime of life, like the light butterfly I *fluttered* from object to object, without being able to settle to any thing : eager for pleasure, I *seized* every thing that had its appearance : alas ! how far *was* I then from foreseeing that I should deplore with so much bitterness the loss of this precious time.

3. For a short time after Abraham, the knowledge of the true God still *appeared* in Palestine and Egypt. Melchisedec, king of Salem, *was* the priest of the Most High a God 1. Abimelech, king of Gerar, and his successor of the same name, *feared God,* *swore* by his name, and *reverenced* his power. But in Moses's time, the nations *adored* even beasts and reptiles. Every thing *was* God but God himself.

1. *Take a walk,* se promener ; *in,* à ; *came home,* rentrer chez soi ; *was busy,* s'occuper ; *reading,* (by the verb) ; *for amusement,* me délasser ; *French Theatre,* Comédie Françoise.

2. *Prime of life,* fleur de l'âge ; *butterfly,* papillon : *fluttered,* voler ; *being able,* pouvoir : *settle,* me fixer ; *eager for,* avide de : *had its appearance,* m'en présentoit l'image ; *how,* que ; *with so much bitterness,* (so bitterly).

3. *Swore,* jurer ; *reverenced,* admirer ; *the nations,* on ; *even,* jusqu'à ; *but,* excepté.

In French, the *preterit definite* and the *preterit indefinite* are not used indifferently.

We make use of the preterit definite, when speaking of a time which is entirely past, and of which nothing remains : as *je fis un voyage à Bath le mois dernier,* I took a journey to Bath last month ; *j'écrivis hier à Rome,* I wrote yesterday to Rome. To authorise the use of this tense, there must be the interval of at least one day. It is most used in the historic style.

EXERCISE.

1. Amenophis *conceived* the design of making his son a conqueror. He *set about* it, after the manner of the Egyptians, that is, with great ideas. All the children who *were born* on* the same day as Sesostris, *were brought* to court by order of the king; he *had* them educated as his own children, and with the same care as Sesostris. When he *was* grown up, he made him serve his apprenticeship in a war against the Arabs : this young prince *learned* there to bear hunger and thirst, and *subdued* that nation, till then invincible. He afterwards *attacked* Lybia, and *conquered* it. After these successes, he *formed* the project of subduing the whole world. In consequence of this *, he entered Ethiopia, which he *made* tributary. He *continued* his victories in Asia. Jerusalem *was* the first to feel the force of his arms: the rash Rehoboam *could* not resist him, and Sesostris *carried* away the riches of Solomon. He *penetrated* into the Indies, farther than Hercules and Bacchus, and farther than Alexander did afterward. The Scythians *obeyed* him as far as the Tanais ; Armenia and Cappadocia *were* subject to him. In a word, he *extended* his empire from the Ganges to the Danube.

1. *Making,* faire de ; *set about it,* s'y prendre ; *after,* à ; *ideas,* pensée ; *brought,* amener ; *had educated,* faire élever ; *grown up,* grand ; *made serve,* faire faire ; *apprenticeship,* apprentissage ; *in,* par ; *entered,* entrer dans; *made,* rendre ; *as far as,* jusqu'à ; *Cappadocia,* Cappadoce.

The preterit indefinite is used either for a past indeterminate, or for a past of which something still remains : as *j'ai voyagé en Italie,* I have travelled in Italy ; *j'ai déjeuné ce matin à Londres et dîné à Richmond,* I breakfasted this morning in London and dined at Richmond.

The preterit indefinite is sometimes used instead of a future just approaching : as *avez-vous bientôt fini?* have you soon done? *oui, j'ai fini dans le moment ;* yes, I shall have done in a moment.

EXERCISE.

1. Enflamed with the desire of knowing mankind, I have

1. *With,* de ; *mankind,* homme, pl. ; *to,* chez ; *polished na-*

travelled, not only to the most polished nations, but even to the most barbarous. I have observed them in the different degrees of civilization, from the state of simple nature to the most perfect state of society, and wherever I went, the result was the same : that is to say, I have every where seen beings occupied in drying up the different sources of happiness that nature had placed within their reach.

2. I have *travelled* this year in Italy, where I *had* an * opportunity of seeing several master-pieces of antiquity, and where I *made* a valuable collection of scarce medals. I there *admired* the perfection to which they *have brought* architecture, painting, and music : but what *pleased* me most there, was the beauty of the climate of Naples.

tions, peuple policé; *savage nations,* nation sauvage ; *from,* depuis ; *to,* jusqu'à; *wherever I went,* dans tous les pays ; *the result was the same,* (I had the same result); *in drying up,* à tarir; *within their reach,* à leur portée.

2. *Opportunity,* occasion; *master-pieces,* chef-d'œuvre ; *scarce,* rare ;' *pleased me most,* faire le plus de plaisir ; *was,* ind-1.

The two preterits anterior differ in the same manner as the two preceding preterits, but they are always accompanied by a conjunction or an adverb of time : as *je suis sorti dès que j'ai eu dîné,* I went out as soon as I had dined; *j'eus fini hier à midi,* I had done yesterday at noon.

The *pluperfect* denotes that a thing was done before another, which was itself done at a time which is past: as *j'avois soupé quand il entra,* I had supped when he came in.

EXERCISE.

1. As soon as I had examined this phenomenon, I tried to find out its causes.

2. As soon as we had crossed the river, we found ourselves in a wood where there was not a single path-way traced.

3. As soon as the great Sesostris had satisfied his ambition,

1. *As soon as,* dès que ; *tried to find out,* en rechercher.

2. *Crossed,* traverser ; *found ourselves,* se trouver engagé ; *path-way,* sentier de.

3. *The whole of the day,* jour entier ; *administering,* rendre,

by the conquest of so many empires, he returned into Egypt, where he devoted the whole of the day to administering strict justice to his people, and in the evening, he recreated himself by holding conferences with the learned, or by conversing with the most upright people of his kingdom.

4. I *had only received*, like most of the grandees, an education in which I had imbibed nothing but sentiments of pride and insensibility; that is, they had done every thing in their power, to stifle in me the happy and benevolent dispositions which I *had received* from nature.

inf-1; *strict*, exact; *recreated*, délasser; *by holding conferences*, à s'entretenir; *upright*, honnête; *people*, gens.

4. *Grandee*, grand; *imbibed*, puiser; *they*, on; *in their power*, ce qu'on pouvoir; *stifle*, étouffer; *benevolent*, bienfaisant.

As foreigners find the use of these different preterits attended with great difficulty, we shall give the following analysis, in order more clearly to explain the manner in which we use them.

We read in Marmontel:

Célicour, à l'âge de quinze ans, avoit été dans le monde ce qu'on appelle un petit prodige;	Celicour, at the age of fifteen, *had been* in the world what is called a little prodigy.

The author employs the pluperfect, because he speaks of a period of time anterior to all those which he is going to mention.

Il faisoit *des vers les plus galans du monde; il n'y* avoit *pas dans le voisinage une jolie femme qu'il n'eût célébrée; c'étoit dommage de laisser tant de talens enfouis dans une petite ville; Paris* devoit *en être le théâtre.*	He *composed* the most agreeable love-sonnets imaginable: there *was* not a pretty woman in the neighbourhood that he had not celebrated; it *was* pity to let so many talents be buried in a little town; Paris *was* the theatre on which they ought to be exhibited.

Here the author makes use of the imperfect, because he speaks of the habitual employ of Celicour.

2 I

Et l'on fit si bien, que son père se résolut de l'y envoyer;	And they *contrived* matters so, that his father *determined* to send him there.

Now the author passes to the preterit definite, because he is no longer speaking of what Celicour used to do, but of what he did at a time past, and of which nothing remains.

Ce père étoit un honnête homme, qui aimoit l'esprit sans en avoir, et qui admiroit, sans savoir pourquoi, tout ce qui venoit de la capitale. Il avoit même des relations littéraires, et du nombre de ses correspondans étoit un connoisseur nommé M. de Fintac.	This father *was* a good sort of man, who *was* fond of wit, without having any, and *admired*, without knowing why, every thing that *came* from the metropolis. Nay, he even *had* some literary connexions, and among his correspondents *was* a connoisseur of the name of Fintac.

Here, again, the author resumes the form of the imperfect, because he is now speaking of the habitual state of Celicour's father, in his little town, and because in this passage he merely relates what that father was doing at a time past, which has no kind of relation to the present.

Ce fut principalement à lui que Célicour fut recommandé,	It *was* particularly to him that Celicour was recommended.

The form of the preterit definite is now resumed, because this is an action passed, at a time of which nothing is left, etc.

EXERCISE.

1. God, who *had created* his angels in holiness, *would* have their happiness depend upon themselves: they *might* insure their felicity, by giving themselves willingly to their Creator; but they *delighted* in themselves, and not in God: immediately those spirits of light *became* spirits of darkness.

1. *Have their happiness to depend*, (that their happiness), dépendre, subj-a; *might*, pouvoir; *delighted in*, se plaire en; *of light*, lumineux; *darkness*, ténèbres.

2. There is a letter which Philocles *has written* to a friend of his, about his project of making himself king of Carpathus. I *perused* that letter, and it *seemed* to me to be the hand of Philocles. They had perfectly imitated his'writing. This letter *threw* me into a strange surprise. I *read* it again and again, and could not persuade myself that it *was* written * by Philocles, when I recalled to my mind the affecting marks which he *had given* me of his disinterestedness and integrity.

3. Those who *had shewn* the greatest zeal for the state and my person *did not think* themselves obliged to undeceive me, after so terrible an example. I myself *was afraid* lest truth should break through the cloud, and reach me in spite of all my flatterers. I *felt* within myself that it would have raised in me bitter remorse. My effeminacy, and the dominion which a treacherous minister had gained over me, *threw* me into a kind of despair of ever recovering my * liberty.

2. *There is*, voilà; *about*, sur; *Carpathus*, Carpathie; *to be*, de; *they*, on; *again and again*, sans cesse; *by*, de; *when I recalled to*, repasser dans, inf-3; *integrity*, bonne foi.

3. *Think not themselves obliged to*, se croire dispensé de; *was afraid lest*, craindre que; *break through*, percer, subj-2; *reach*, parvenir jusqu'à; *in spite of*, malgré; *raised in*, causer à; *effeminacy*, mollesse; *dominion*, ascendant; *treacherous*, perfide; *gained*, prendre; *threw*, plonger; *recovering*, rentrer en.

The difference between the two future tenses is, that the period of time expressed by the future absolute may or may not be determined: as *j'irai à la campagne*, or, *j'irai demain à la campagne;* while, in the future anterior, the time is necessarily determined: as *j'aurai fini quand vous arriverez.*

EXERCISE.

1. Remember that youth is but a flower, which *will wither up* almost as soon as open. Thou *wilt see thyself* gradually changed. Smiling graces, sweet pleasures, strength, health, and joy, *will vanish* like a pleasing dream; nothing but the sad remembrance will be left thee.

2. I *shall* next year *take* a journey into Greece, and I am preparing myself for it by reading that of the young Anarcharsis.

1. *Will wither*, (will be almost as soon withered) sécher; *open*, éclore; *gradually*, insensiblement; *lively*, riant; *nothing will be left*, il n'en rester.

2. *Take*, faire; *for it*, y; *reading*, lecture de.

3. When you have read the celebrated discourse of Bossuet on Universal History, and studied in it the causes of the grandeur and the fall of states, you will be less astonished at the revolutions, more or less sudden, that modern empires have experienced, which appeared to you in the most flourishing state.

5. *Have read*, ind-8; *and*, que vous, ind-8; *in it*, y; *fall*, chute; *sudden*, subite; (that have experienced the modern empires, which, etc.); *appeared*, ind-2.

CONDITIONAL.

We make use of the conditional:

1st. To express a wish: as *que je serois*, or *j'aurois été, content de réussir dans cette affaire*, how glad I should be, or should have been, to succeed in that affair.

2dly. With *si*, if, whether, expressing a doubt: as *Demandez-lui s'il seroit venu avec nous, supposé qu'il n'eût pas eu affaire;* ask him whether he would have come with us, had he not been busy.

3dly. Before or after the imperfect, or pluperfect of the indicative, preceded by *si:* as *nous nous épargnerions bien des peines, si nous savions modérer nos désirs;* we should spare ourselves much pain, did we know how to moderate our desires: *vous auriez été plus heureux, si vous aviez suivi mes conseils;* you would have been more happy, if you had followed my advice.

4thly. With *quand*, used instead of *si*, *quoique*, or *quand même*, the verb preceded by *quand* is generally in one of the conditionals: as *quand l'avare posséderoit tout l'or du monde, il ne seroit pas encore content;* were the miser to possess all the gold in the world, still he would not be satisfied.

5thly. Lastly, for various tenses of the indicative: as *croiriez-vous votre fils ingrat?* could you think your son ungrateful? which means *croyez-vous*, etc. *l'auriez-vous soupçonné d'un tel vice?* could you have suspected him of such a vice? which means *l'avez-vous*, etc. *quelle raison pourrait m'empêcher d'aller vous voir*, what cause could prevent me from coming to see you? which means *quelle cause pourra*, etc.

EXERCISE.

1. If it were even possible for men always to act conformably to equity, as it is the multitude that must judge their conduct, the wicked would always blame and contradict them from malignity, and the good sometimes from mistake.

2. What false steps I should have made but for you, at my entrance into the world!

3. But for your counsels, I should have failed in this undertaking.

4. How satisfied I should have been, if you had sooner informed me of your happiness!

5. If we gave to infancy none but just and clear notions, *there would be* a much less considerable number of false wits in the world.

6. Had Alexander *conquered* the whole world, his ambition *would not have been* satisfied; he *would* still *have found* himself *confined* in it.

7. *Could you believe* him vain enough to aspire to that high degree of honour?

8. *Could you* ever *have thought* him capable of deserting the good cause, to go and side with the rebels?

9. *Would you renounce* being useful to the present generation, because envy fastens on you?

1. *If even,* quand même; *were,* cond-1; *for men* (that men); *to act,* subj-2; *judge,* juger de; *would blame,* ind-7; *contradict,* croiser, ind-7.

2. *What,* que de; *steps,* démarche; *but for,* sans.

3. *But for,* sans; *failed,* échouer.

4. *How,* que.

5. *We,* on; *a much less considerable number,* bien moins.

6. (When Alexander would have conquered); *confined,* trop à l'étroit.

8. *Deserting,* abandonner; *to go and side with,* pour se ranger sous les drapeaux de.

9. *Renounce,* renoncer à; *fastens,* s'attacher; *on you,* à vos pas.

REMARK ON THE USE OF THE CONDITIONAL AND FUTURE.

Foreigners are very apt to use the future or the conditional after *si,* when meaning *supposé que.* They say *j'irai demain à la campagne, s'il fera beau;* I shall go

2 I 3

into the country to-morrow, if the weather be fine : *vous auriez vu le roi* si *vous* seriez *venu,* you would have seen the king if you had come. The impropriety of this construction will be obviated by attending to the following

RULE. When a verb is preceded by *si,* meaning *supposé que,* the present is used instead of the future absolute ; the preterit indefinite, instead of the future anterior ; the imperfect instead of the conditional present, and the pluperfect instead of the conditional past.

EXAMPLES.

J'irai demain à la campagne, s'il fait *beau ;*	I shall go to-morrow into the country, if it be fine weather.
Il aura eu l'avantage, s'il a suivi vos conseils ;	He will have had the advantage, if he has followed your advice.
Je serois content, si je vous voyois *appliqué ;*	I should be pleased, if I saw you apply to study.
J'aurois été content, si je vous avois vu *appliqué ;*	I should have been pleased, if I had seen you attentive to your studies.

REMARK. This rule does not hold good, either when *si* is placed between two verbs, the first of which implies doubt, uncertainty : as *je ne sais s'il viendra ;* or with the second conditional past : as *vous m'eussiez trouvé si vous fussiez venu ce matin.*

EXERCISE.

1. A young man who is just entering the career of letters, *will conciliate* the good will of the public, *if he consider* his first successes only as an encouragement to do better.

2. That absurd criticism *will have amused* only fools or malicious people *, if attention *has been paid* to the spirit that pervades the whole, and the manner in which it is written.

1. *Is just entering,* débuter dans ; *career,* carrière ; *will conciliate,* s'attirer ; *good will,* bienveillance ; *consider,* regarder.

2. *Fools,* sot ; *malicious,* méchant ; *paid,* faire ; *pervades the whole,* régner d'un bout à l'autre ; *in which,* dont.

3. Life *would possess* many more sweets and charms, *if men*, instead of tearing one another to pieces, *formed* but one society of brethren.

4. The Athenians *would have found* in the young Alcibiades the only man capable of insuring their superiority in Greece, *had not* that vain thoughtless people *forced* him by an unjust, or at least imprudent, sentence, to banish himself from his country.

5. I know not *whether* reason *will* soon *triumph* over prejudice and ignorance, but I am certain it will be the case, sooner or later.

6. Rome *had never attained* that high degree of splendour and glory which astonishes us, *had it* not *extended* its conquests as much by its policy as by its arms.

3. *Possess*, avoir; *tearing one another to pieces*, s'entredé-chirer.
4. *Superiority*, prépondérance; *thoughtless*, léger.
5. *Know*, savoir; *it will be so*, cela être.
6. *Attained*, parvenir à; *policy*, politique.

SUBJUNCTIVE.

We have said that there are conjunctions which govern the indicative, and others which govern the subjunctive. We call *principal proposition* the phrase which is followed by the conjunction, and *incidental*, or *subordinate proposition*, that which is placed after the conjunction. In this sentence, *je crois que vous aimez à jouer; je crois* is the principal proposition, and *vous aimez à jouer* is the subordinate proposition: *que* is the conjunction that unites the two phrases.

GENERAL RULE. The verb of the subordinate proposition must be put in the indicative, when the verb of the principal proposition expresses affirmation, in a direct, positive, and independent manner; but it is put in the subjunctive, when that of the principal proposition expresses doubt, wish or uncertainty.

We say, *je sais qu'il est surpris*, I know he is surprised; *je crois qu'il viendra*, I believe he will come. But we ought to say, *je doute qu'il soit surpris*, I doubt his being surprised; *je doute qu'il vienne*, I doubt his coming; *je souhaite qu'il réussisse,* I wish he may succeed; *je tremble qu'il ne succombe,* I tremble lest he should fail.

1. The glory which has been ascribed to the Egyptians of being the most grateful of all men, *shows* that *they were* likewise the most sociable.

2. In Egypt, when it *was proved* that the conduct of a dead man * *had been* bad, they condemned his memory, and he was denied burial.

3. *I am sure* that, by moderation, mildness and politeness, you *will disarm* even * envy itself.

4. The new philosophers *say* that colour *is* a sensation of the soul.

5. I *believe you are* as honest and disinterested as you seem to be.

6. I *doubt* whether the Romans *would* ever *have triumphed* over the Gauls, if the different chiefs of this warlike people had not been disunited.

7. I *could wish* that the love which we ought to have for one another *were* the priciple of all our actions, as it is the basis of all virtues.

8. *Fear* lest it *should be said* that you feed upon chimeras, and that you take the shadow for the reality.

9. The new philosophers *will have* colour *to be* a sensation of the soul.

10. I *will have* you to be as honest and disinterested as you seem to be.

1. *Which has,* etc. qu'on; *ascribed,* donner; *grateful,* reconnoissant.

2. *Was denied,* priver de; *burial,* sépulture.

3. *By,* avec; *politeness,* honnêteté.

4. *Sensation,* sentiment.

5. *Seem to be,* le paroître.

6. *Whether,* que.

8. *It,* on ne; *feed upon,* se repaître de.

9. *Will have,* vouloir; *colour to be,* (that colour be).

Do, did, will, would, should, can, could, may, and *might,* are sometimes, with respect to the French language, simply signs of tenses; at others they are real verbs.

There can be no difficulty about *do* and *did;* these are mere expletives, denoting interrogation, negation or merely emphasis, when they are joined to a verb. *I do love,* j'aime ; *I did love,* j'aimois or j'aimai ; *do I love,* aimé-je ; *did I love,* aimois-je or aimai-je ; *I do not love,* je n'aime pas ; *I did not love,* je n'aimois pas or je n'aimai pas. In all these cases they are not expressed in French. But when they are followed by a noun or pronoun, then they are real verbs, and mean *faire.* *Do me that favour,* faites-moi ce plaisir ; *he did it,* il le fit; or, in short, by any thing else except the verb with which they are necessarily connected: as *he did more than could have been expected,* il fit plus qu'on n'eût pu espérer.

Should is only a sign of the conditional, when it expresses a thing which may happen upon some condition : *I should like a country life, if my affairs would permit me to indulge my inclination :* j'aimerois la vie champêtre, si mes affaires me permettoient de suivre mon goût. But, when it implies duty or obligation, it is a verb, and must be expressed by the verb *devoir :* as *we should never swerve from the path of virtue,* nous ne devrions jamais nous écarter du sentier de la vertu.

Can, could, may and *might,* are not so difficult as they appear at first sight; because, in almost every instance, there is no impropriety in rendering them by the verb *pouvoir.* In general, the first two imply a power, a possibility, a capability, etc. and the others, permission, probability, etc.

Do, did, shall, will, etc. are sometimes used elliptically in the answers to interrogative sentences. This construction is not used in French. We must repeat the verb, accompanied with a pronoun expressive of the idea of the interrogative sentence : *shall you do your exercise to-day?* *yes, I shall ;* must be translated by, *ferez-vous votre thème aujourd'hui ? oui, je le ferai.*

RELATIONS BETWEEN THE TENSES OF THE INDICATIVE.

RULE. When the first verb is in the imperfect, the preterit or the pluperfect, and the second denotes a tem-

porary action, this second verb is put in the imperfect, if
we mean to express a present.

Je croyois, j'ai cru, j'avois cru, que vous étudiiez les mathématiques ;	I thought, I have thought, I had thought, that you were studying the mathematics.

In the pluperfect, if we mean to express a past.

EXAMPLE.

Il m'assura qu'il n'avoit jamais tant ri,	He assured me that he had never laughed so much.

And in the present of the conditional, if we mean to
express a future absolute.

EXAMPLE.

On m'a dit que votre frère viendroit à Londres l'hiver prochain,	I was told your brother would come to town next winter.

But, although the first verb may be in some of these
tenses, yet the second is put in the present, when this
second verb expresses a thing which is true at all times.

EXAMPLE.

Je vous disois, je vous ai dit, je vous avois dit, que la santé fait la félicité du corps, et le savoir celle de l'âme ;	I told you, I have told you, I had told you, that health constitutes the happiness of the body, and knowledge that of the soul.

REMARK. In phrases where the imperfect is preceded by
que, it denotes sometimes a past, sometimes a present,
with respect to the preceding verb. It denotes a past, when
the verb which is joined to it by the conjunction *que* is in
the present or future.

EXAMPLE.

Vous savez ou vous saurez que le peuple Romain étoit aussi avide qu'ambitieux,	You know *or* you must know that the Romans were a people as covetous as they were ambitious.

But it denotes a present, when the verb which precedes it is in the imperfect, one of the preterits or the pluperfect.

EXAMPLES.

On disoit, on a dit, on avoit dit , que Phocion étoit *le plus grand et le plus honnête homme de son temps;*	It was said, it has been said, it had been said, that Phocion was the greatest and most upright man of his age.
Dès qu'on eut appris à Athènes qu'Alcibiade étoit *à Lacédémone, on se repentit de la précipitation avec laquelle on l'avoit condamné;*	As soon as it was known at Athens that Alcibiades was at Lacedemon, the Athenians repented of the precipitation with which they had condemned him.

Nevertheless, the imperfect denotes the past, in this last instance, when it signifies an action which was past before that which is expressed by the first verb.

EXAMPLE.

En lisant l'histoire des temps héroïques, vous devez avoir remarqué que ces hommes, dont on a fait des demi-dieux, étoient *des chefs féroces et barbares, dignes à peine du nom d'homme ;*	In reading the history of heroic times, you must have remarked that those men who have been made demi-gods, were ferocious and barbarous chiefs, scarcely deserving the name of men.

EXERCISE.

1. I *thought* you *were not ignorant* that, to teach others the principles of an art or science, one needs to have experience and skill.

2. I *had been told*, that your sweetest occupation *was* to form your taste, your heart and your understanding.

3. Darius, in his flight, being* reduced to the necessity of drinking water muddy and infected by dead bodies, *affirmed* that he never *had drunk* with so much pleasure.

1. *Were ignorant*, ignorer; *teach*, instruire dans; *needs*, avoir besoin; *skill*, habileté.

2. *I had*, etc. (by the active voice), on.

3. *Flight*, déroute; *muddy*, bourbeux; *affirmed*, assurer.

4. Care *has been taken* to inculcate in me, from infancy, that I *should succeed* in the world, only in proportion as I should join to the desire of pleasing, a great deal of gentleness and civility.

5. Ovid *has said*, that *study softens* the manners and *corrects* every thing that is found in us rude and barbarous.

6. You *know* that those pretended heroes, of whom pagan antiquity has made gods, *were* only barbarous and ferocious kings, who overran the earth, not so much to conquer as to ravage it, and who left every where traces of their fury and of their vices.

7. It *has been said of* Pericles, that his eloquence was like a thunderbolt which nothing could resist.

8. As soon as Aristides *had said*, that the proposal of Themistocles *was* unjust, the whole people *exclaimed*, that they must not think of it any longer.

9. Had you read the history of the early ages, *you would know* that Egypt *was* the most enlightened country in the universe, and that whence knowledge *spread* into Greece and the neighbouring countries.

4. *Care has*, etc. (active voice), on avoir; *in me*, me; *in proportion*, autant ; *civility*, honnêteté.

5. *Corrects*, effacer ; *is found*, se trouver de.

6. *Overran*, parcourir; *not so much*, moins.

7. *It*, on ; *thunderbolt*, foudre, m. ; (to) *which*.

8. *Exclaimed*, s'écrier; *they must*, falloir, ind-2 ; *of it*, y ; *any longer*, plus.

9. *Ages*, temps ; *whence*, celui d'où ; *neighbouring*, circonvoisin ; *countries*, lieu.

RELATIONS BETWEEN THE TENSES OF THE SUBJUNCTIVE AND THOSE OF THE INDICATIVE.

RULE I. When the verb of the principal proposition is in the present or future, we put in the present of the subjunctive that of the subordinate proposition, if we mean to express a present or future ; but we put it in the preterit, if we mean to express a past: we say,

Il faut que celui qui parle se mette à la portée de celui qui l'écoute,	He that speaks should accommodate himself to the understanding of him that listens.

Il voudra que votre frère soit de | He will wish your brother to be
la partie; . | one of the party.

But we must say,

Pour s'être élevée à ce point de | To have risen to that pitch of
grandeur, il faut que Rome | grandeur, Rome must have
ait eu une suite non inter- | had an uninterrupted suc-
rompue de grands hommes; | cession of great men.

EXCEPTION. Though the first verb be in the present or future, yet we may put the second in the imperfect, or pluperfect of the subjunctive, when some conditional expression is introduced into the sentence.

EXAMPLES.

Il n'est point d'homme, quelque | There is no man, whatever
mérite qu'il ait, qui ne fût | merit he may have, that
très-mortifié, s'il savoit tout | would not feel very much
ce qu'on pense de lui; | mortified, were he to know
| all that is thought of him.

Où trouvera-t-on un homme | Where will you find the man
qui ne fît la même faute, s'il | who would not have com-
étoit exposé aux mêmes ten- | mitted the same error, had
tations? | he been exposed to the same
| temptations?

Je doute que votre frère eût | I doubt whether your brother
réussi sans votre assistance, | would have succeeded, had
| it not been for your assist-
| ance.

EXERCISE.

1. He who wishes to teach an art, must *know* it thoroughly; he must *give* none but clear, precise, and well-digested notions of it; he must *instil* them, one by one, into the minds of his pupils, and, above all, he must not overburthen their memory with useless or unimportant rules.

2. He *must yield* to the force of truth, when they *shall have suffered* it to appear in its real light.

1. (*It must* that he who, etc. know it); *he must* (not repeated), que; *instil*, faire entrer; *by*, à; *overburthen*, surcharger.

2. (It must ind-7, that he); *yield*, se rendre; *suffered*, permettre; *it to appear*, (that it appear); *real light*, vrai jour.

2 K

3. There is no work, however perfect people may suppose it, that would not be liable to criticism, if it were examined with severity and in every point of view.

4. I doubt whether his piece would have had the approbation of *connoisseurs*, if he had not determined to make in it the changes you judged necessary.

3. *Would be, liable*, prêter, subj-2; *with severity*, à la rigueur; *in*, sous; *point of view*, face.

4. *Had determined*, se décider; *in it*, y; *judged*, ind-4.

RULE II. When the first verb is in the imperfect, either of the preterits, the pluperfect, or either of the conditionals, we put the second in the imperfect of the subjunctive, if we mean to express a present or a future: but we put it in the pluperfect, if we mean to express a past.

We say *je voulois, j'ai voulu, j'eus voulu, je voudrois,* or *j'eusse voulu que* vous finissiez *cette affaire;* but we ought to say *je ne savois pas, je n'ai pas su,* etc. *que* vous *eussiez étudié les mathématiques.*

REMARK. With the preterit indefinite the second verb is put in the present, if it expresses an action which is, or may be done at all times: as *Dieu a entouré les yeux de tuniques fort minces, transparentes au dehors, afin qu'on puisse voir à travers;* God has surrounded the eyes with very thin tunics, transparent on the outside, that we may see through them: and in the preterit, if we mean to express a past: as *il a fallu qu'il* ait sollicité *ses juges,* he must have been obliged to solicit his judges.

EXERCISE.

1. M. de Turenne never *would* buy any thing on credit, of tradesmen, for fear, he used to say, they *should lose* a great part of it, if he happened to be killed. All the workmen who were employed about his house, had orders to bring in their bills before he set out for the campaign, and they were regularly paid.

1. *Would*, vouloir, ind-2; *buy on credit*, prendre à crédit; *of*, chez; *happened*, venir; *were employed*, travailler; *about*, pour; *bills*, mémoire; *he*, on; *set out for*, se mettre en.

2. It *would be better* for a man who truly loves himself, *to lose* his life, than to forfeit his honour by some base and shameful action.

3. Lycurgus, in one of his laws, *had forbidden* the lighting of those who came from a feast in the evening, that the fear of not being able to reach their houses might *prevent* them from getting drunk.

4. People *used* the bark of trees, or skins, to write upon*, before paper was known.

5. Go and * ask that old man, for whom you are planting? he will answer you, for the immortal gods, who *have ordered*, both that I *should profit* by the labour of those that have preceded me, and that those who should come after me *should profit* by mine.

2. *To lose*, (that he *would lose*); *forfeit*, ternir.

3. *In*, par; *the lighting of*, que on éclairer, subj-2; *that*, afin que; *reach their houses*, se rendre chez eux; *getting drunk*, s'enivrer.

4. *People*, on; *bark*, écorce; *skins*, peau; *known*, en usage.

5. *Have ordered*, vouloir; *both*, et; *by*, de.

In interrogative and negative sentences, the second verb is generally in the subjunctive: as *quel est l'insensé qui tienne pour sûr qu'il vivra demain? Vous ne vous persuadiez pas que les choses pussent tourner si mal.*

The verb is likewise in the subjunctive after the superlative relative, and frequently after an impersonal verb: as *le meilleur cortége qu'un prince puisse avoir, c'est le cortége de ses sujets.*

The subjunctive is elegantly used in elliptical phrases where the principal proposition is omitted: as *qu'il vive!* (*je souhaite qu'il*) may he live! *qu'il se soit oublié jusqu'à ce point!* (*je suis surpris qu'il*) that he should so far forget himself! *qui m'aime me suive!* (*je veux que celui qui*) whoever loves me let him follow me! *heureux l'homme qui peut, ne fût-ce que dans sa vieillesse, jouir de toute la force de sa raison!* (*quand ce ne seroit que*) happy the man that can, were it only in his old age, enjoy the whole strength of his reason!

2 x 2

1. *Is there any one* who does not *feel* that nothing is more degrading in a writer, than the pains he takes to express ordinary and common things in a singular and pompous style.

2. *Do you think* that, in forming the republic of bees, God *has not had* in view to teach kings to govern with gentleness, and subjects to obey with love?

5. You *will never be* at peace, either with yourself or with others, unless you seriously endeavour to restrain your natural impetuosity.

1. *Is degrading in*, degrader; *in*, de.
2. *Had in view*, vouloir.
5. *Be at peace*, avoir la paix; *either*, ni; *or*, ni.

REMARK. The relative pronouns *qui, que, quel, dont* and *où*, govern the subjunctive in similar circumstances.

1. *Who is the writer* that does not sometimes *experience* moments of sterility and languor?

2. *There is not in* the heart of man, a good impulse that God does not *produce*.

3. *Choose* a retreat where you *may be* quiet, a post whence you *may defend* yourself.

4. The reward the most flattering that a man *can* reap from his labours, is the esteem of an enlightened public.

5. May he live, reign, and long constitute the happiness of a nation which he loves, and by which he is adored!

6. That he should thus degrade himself, is what posterity will find very difficult to believe.

7. A man just and firm is not shaken, either by the clamours of an inconsiderate mob, or by the threats of an imperious tyrant: though * the whole world *were* to fall into ruins, he would be struck by it, but not moved.

2. *Impulse*, mouvement.
3. *May*, pouvoir.
5. (*May he*, repeated before every verb); *constitute*, faire; *which he loves*, chérir.
6. *Find difficult*, avoir de la peine; *believe*, se persuader.
7. *Is shaken*, ébranler; *inconsiderate*, insensé; *mob*, populace; *imperious*, fier; *were*, devoir; *to fall into ruins*, s'écrouler.

We cannot close this account of the conditional and the subjunctive, without making some further observations upon these two moods, as well on account of some few examples which we have left untranslated, as of those the translation of which does not perfectly agree with the models of the conjugations which we have given.

We have said the English auxiliaries *should, would, could, may* and *might,* are not always to be considered as essentially and necessarily appertaining to the conditional and subjunctive. Indeed, it seldom happens that the French tenses are the same as the English, at least in subordinate, though they may be in the principal propositions. For this reason, we earnestly recommend to the learner a strict adherence to the rules we have already given in the different sections and paragraphs of this chapter. Much depends upon that, and likewise on a clear view of the operations of the mind. For instance, *I wish you would come to-night,* cannot be translated by *je souhaite que* vous viendriez *ce soir,* because " when the verb of the principal proposition is in the present, the verb of the subordinate proposition is put in the present of the subjunctive, if we mean to express a future." Therefore, we must say *je souhaite que* vous veniez. (See Rule I.) Or, " if the first verb is in either of the conditionals, the second must be in the imperfect of the subjunctive." For which reason we must also say *je voudrois que* vous vinssiez. (See Rule II.) Now, in the first example, *que vous veniez* is marked in the conjugation of the verb by, *that you* may come, and in the second, *que vous vinssiez,* by, *that you* might come, neither of which is in the examples given.

Again, *Il n'y a personne qui le croie,* cannot be translated by *there is nobody who* may believe *it,* although *may* is the sign of the subjunctive in the model: but we mean, *there is nobody that* believes *it,* or simply, *nobody believes it.*

RELATIONS BETWEEN THE TENSES OF THE DIFFERENT MOODS.

REMARK. Our intention is not to give the relations which all the tenses bear to each other, but simply to mention some of the principal.

RELATIONS OF THE INDICATIVE.

The imperfect is accompanied by three tenses.

STANDARDS.

Je lisois $\begin{cases} quand\ vous\ écriviez. \\ quand\ vous\ avez\ écrit. \\ quand\ vous\ écrivîtes. \end{cases}$

The preterit anterior requires the preterit definite : as *quand j'eus fini, vous entrâtes.*

The pluperfect is accompanied by the preterit definite, the preterit indefinite, the preterit anterior, and the imperfect.

STANDARDS.

J'avois lu $\begin{cases} quand\ vous\ entrâtes. \\ quand\ vous\ êtes\ entré. \\ quand\ vous\ fûtes\ entré. \\ quand\ vous\ entriez. \end{cases}$

The preterit anterior indefinite is accompanied by the preterit indefinite : as *quand j'ai eu dîné, vous êtes entré.*

In conjunction with *si* for *supposé que*, the future absolute requires the present, and the future anterior the preterit indefinite.

STANDARDS.

Vous partirez, si je veux.
Il sera parti, si vous l'avez voulu.

Relations to the Conditional and of the Conditional.

In conjunction with *si* for *supposé que*, the conditional present is accompanied by the imperfect, and the first conditional past by the pluperfect, or by the second conditional past.

STANDARDS.

Vous partiriez, si je le voulois.

Vous seriez parti $\begin{cases} si\ je\ l'avois\ voulu. \\ si\ je\ l'eusse\ voulu. \end{cases}$

The tenses of the conditional present, and of the two conditionals past, are likewise accompanied by themselves.

Quand l'avare posséderoit tout l'or du monde, il ne seroit pas encore content.

Quand Alexandre auroit conquis tout l'univers, il n'auroit pas été content.

Vous fussiez parti, si je l'eusse voulu.

It has been observed, that when two verbs are joined by the conjunction *que*, the second verb is put sometimes in the indicative and sometimes in the subjunctive.

Relations of the present of the indicative to the tenses of its own mood and of the conditional.

This tense may be accompanied by all the tenses of the indicative and conditional.

On dit que
{
vous partez aujourd'hui.
vous partirez demain.
vous serez parti, quand, etc.
vous partiez hier.
vous partîtes hier.
vous êtes parti ce matin.
vous fûtes parti hier, quand, etc.
vous étiez parti hier, quand, etc.
vous partiriez aujourd'hui, si, etc.
vous seriez parti hier, si, etc.
vous fussiez parti plutôt, si, etc.
}

REMARK. The same relation subsists when the sentence is negative, except for the present absolute of the indicative, for which the present of the subjunctive is substituted. We cannot say, *on ne dit pas que vous partez aujourd'hui;* the genius of our language requires that we should say, *on ne dit pas que vous partiez aujourd'hui.*

The imperfect, the preterit definite, the preterit indefinite, and the pluperfect, are accompanied either by the imperfect or by the pluperfect.

On-disoit
On dit
On a dit   } que   vous parties aujourd'hui.
On avoit dit   vous étiez parti.

The future absolute is accompanied, like the present, by
almost all the tenses of the indicative and conditional, as
may be seen by the examples annexed to the present.

The future anterior requires the preterit indefinite; as
on aura dit que vous avez menti.

The conditional present may be accompanied by the
present, the imperfect, the preterit indefinite, the pluperfect, the future of the indicative, as well as by the three
conditionals.

On oroiroit { qu'il se trompe.
             qu'il se trompoit.
             qu'il s'est trompé.
             qu'il s'étoit trompé.
             qu'il se trompera.
             qu'il se tromperoit, si, etc.
             qu'il se seroit trompé, si, etc.
             qu'il se fût trompé, si, etc.

The first conditional past may be accompanied by the
imperfect, the pluperfect, as well as by the two other
conditionals.

On auroit cru { qu'il tomboit.
                qu'il étoit tombé.
                qu'il seroit tombé.
                qu'il fût tombé.

The second conditional past may be accompanied by the
same tenses.

Principal relations with the Subjunctive.

The present, the future absolute, and the future anterior

of the indicative are generally accompanied by the present of the subjunctive.

Il veut
Il voudra   } *que vous partiez*
Il aura voulu

The imperfect, the preterit definite, the preterit indefinite, the pluperfect, and the second conditional past may be accompanied by the imperfect of the subjunctive.

STANDARDS.

Je voulois
Je voulus
J'ai voulu   } *que vous partissiez.*
J'avois voulu
J'eusse voulu

The future anterior by the preterit of the subjunctive; as *il aura voulu qu'il soit parti.*

The conditional present is accompanied either by the imperfect, or by the pluperfect of the subjunctive.

STANDARDS.

Je voudrois que { *vous partissiez.*
                  { *vous fussiez parti.*

The first and second conditionals past by the pluperfect of the subjunctive.

STANDARDS.

J'aurois voulu
J'eusse voulu   } *que vous fussiez parti,*

etc., etc., etc., etc.

INFINITIVE.

The preposition *to* before an infinitive, is, according to circumstances, rendered either by *pour*, by *à*, or by *de*; sometimes even it is not expressed at all.

When *to* means *in order to*, it is expressed in French by *pour*; as,

He came to speak to me,	Il vint pour me parler.

As for the other two cases, there is hardly any fixed rule to distinguish whether *à* or *de* is to be used; the regimen which the preceding French verb requires after it is the only guide. Thus,

He likes to play, will be expressed by *il aime à jouer; he told me to go,* by *il me dit d'aller,* and *he preferred dying,* by *il aime mieux mourir.*

The participle present is used in English both as a substantive and an adjective, and frequently instead of the present of the infinitive.

His ruling *passion is hunting,*	Sa passion *dominante* est *la chasse.*
He is gone a-walking,	Il est allé se promener.
Prevent him from doing mischief,	Empêchez-le de faire le mal.
There is a pleasure in silencing great talkers,	Il y a plaisir à fermer la bouche aux grand parleurs.

It likewise takes almost every other preposition. In the first of the above examples it is translated by the substantive, in the second by the verbal adjective, and in the others by the present of the infinitive. But sometimes it must be expressed by the relative *qui*, with the verb in the indicative, especially when a different mode might create any ambiguity in the sense; as,

I met them riding post.	Je les ai rencontrés qui couroient la poste.

Sometimes it must be expressed by the conjunction *que*, with the verb in the indicative, or in the subjunctive, as circumstances may require: this is when the participle present is preceded by a possessive pronoun; as,

| *The fear of his coming vexed us,* | La crainte qu'il ne vint nous tourmentoit. |
| *I doubt his being faithful,* | Je doute qu'il soit fidèle, etc. |

It may be proper to observe that, in French, the preposition *en* alone is followed by the participle present. All other prepositions require the present of the infinitive.

Foreigners are apt to mistake in the use of the participle present, because they do not consider that, as it expresses an incidental proposition, it must evidently relate to the word which it restrains and modifies.

RULE. The participle present always forming a phrase incidental and subordinate to another, must necessarily relate to the subject of the principal phrase, when it is not preceded by another noun as in this sentence :

| *Je ne puis vous accompagner à la campagne, ayant des affaires qui exigent ici ma présence ;* | I cannot accompany you into the country, having some business that requires my presence here. |

The participle present *ayant* relates to the subject *je,* since the subordinate proposition, formed by *ayant,* could have no kind of relation to the principal proposition, if it could not be resolved into this, *parce que j'ai des affaires qui,* etc. But, in this sentence :

| *Combien voyons-nous de gens, qui, connaissant 'le prix du temps, le perdent mal-à-propos!* | How many people do we see, who, knowing the value of time, waste it improperly ! |

connoissant relates to the 'substantive *gens,* because this is the word which it restrains and modifies, and because the relative *qui,* placed between that substantive as the regimen, and the participle present, obviates every kind of ambiguity.

REMARKS. 1. Two participles ought never to be used together without being united by a conjunction; as,

| *C'est un homme aimant et craignant Dieu,* | He is a man loving and fearing God. |

The relative *en* ought never to be put either before a participle present, or before a gerund. We cannot say,

Je vous ai remis mon fils entre les mains, en voulant faire quelque chose de bon,

because the sense would be ambiguous: for the meaning is not,

As I wish to do something good, or, as I wish to do well, I have put my son into your hands,

but,

I have put my son into your hands, as I wish to make something of him.

We should say: *voulant en faire*, etc.

Likewise this sentence would be improper:

Le prince tempère la rigueur du pouvoir, en en partageant les fonctions,

on account of the repetition of the word *en*, used in two different senses, viz., as a preposition and a relative. Another turn must then be adopted; as,

C'est en partageant les fonctions du pouvoir, qu'un prince en tempère la rigueur.

CHAP. VI.

OF PREPOSITIONS.

The office of prepositions is to bring the two terms between which they are placed, into a state of relation. And that relation is generally expressed by their own signification; as,

Avec, sur, pendant, dans, etc.

But *à, de*, and *en* express it, either by their primitive and proper meaning, or figuratively and by extension; so that,

. in this last case, they. are merely prepositions serving to unite the two terms; whence it happens that they often express either the same relations that others do, or opposite relations. For instance, in these two sentences :

Approchez-vous du feu,	Come near the fire.
Eloignez-vous du feu,	Go from the fire.

De merely establishes a relation between the two terms, without expressing in the first the relation of approximation, or in the second the relation of distance. In order, therefore, to form a just idea of *these three prepositions*, it is of importance to consider only their primitive and proper signification.

En and *dans* have nearly the same meaning; but they differ in this, that the former is used in a more vague, the latter in a more determinate sense; as

J'étois en Angleterre, dans la province de Middlesex.

From what has just been said, it follows then that *en*, on account of its indeterminate nature, ought not to be followed by the article, except in a small number of phrases sanctioned by usage ; such are,

En la présence de Dieu; en la grand chambre du parlement ; en l'absence d'un tel; en l'année mil-huit cent dix-sept, etc.

with respect to the expressions,

En l'honneur, en l'âge, it is better to say, *à l'honneur, à l'âge.*

Avant is a preposition in this phrase:

Avant le jour,	Before day-light.

But it is an adverb in this :

N'allez pas si avant,	Do not go so forward.

Some other prepositions are likewise occasionally adverbs.

Autour and *alentour* must not be confounded; *autour* is a preposition, and *alentour* an adverb : thus,

Tous les grands étoient autour du trône,	All the grandees stood around the throne.
Le roi étoit sur son trône, et les grands étoient alentour;	The king was upon the throne, and the grandees stood round.

2 L

Avant and *auparavant* are not used indifferently. *Avant* is followed by a regimen ; as

Avant Pâques,	Before Easter.
Avant ce temps,	Before that time.

Auparavant is followed by no regimen ; as

Si vous partez, venez me voir auparavant;	If you set off, come and see me first.

Prêt à and *près de* are not the same expressions. *Prêt* is an adjective :

Je suis prêt à faire cè que vous voudrez,	I am ready to do what you please.

But *près* is a preposition :

Mon ouvrage est près d'étre fini,	My work is nearly finished.

Au travers and *à travers,* differ in this: the first is followed by the preposition *de,* the second is not ; as

Il se fit jour au travers des en- nemis,	He fought his way through the enemy.
Il se fit jour à travers les en- nemis,	

Avant denotes priority of time and order ; as

Il est arrivé avant *moi,* l'article se met avant le *nom.*

Devant is used for *en présence, vis-à-vis* ; as

Il a paru devant *le juge ; il loge* devant *l'église.*

REMARK. *Devant* is likewise a preposition marking order, and is the opposite of *après* ; as

Il a le pas devant *moi,*	He has precedence of me.
Si vous êtes pressé, courez de- vant.	If you are in a hurry, run be- fore.

THE USE OF THE ARTICLE WITH PREPOSITIONS.

Some prepositions require the article before their regimen; others do not; and others again sometimes admit, sometimes reject it.

RULE I. The following prepositions generally require the article before the noun, which they govern:

avant,	depuis,	envers,	nonobstant,	selon,
après,	devant,	excepté,	parmi,	suivant,
chez,	derrière,	hors,	pendant,	touchant,
dans,	durant,	hormis,	pour,	vers,

avant l'aurore,   chez le prince,   envers les pauvres,
après la promenade,   dans la maison,   devant l'église, etc.

There are however exceptions; as

avant terme,   avant dîner,   pour lit une paillasse,
avant midi,   après dîner,   depuis minuit, etc.

RULE II. A noun governed by the preposition *en*, is not, in general, preceded by the article; as

En ville, en campagne, en extase, en songe, en pièces, etc.

REMARK. *L'armée est entrée en campagne*, means the army has taken the field, but *Mr. N. est allé à la campagne*, means, Mr. N. is gone into the country.

RULE III. These eleven prepositions, *à, de, avec, contre, entre, malgré, outre, par, pour, sur, sans*, sometimes admit, sometimes reject the article before their regimen.
If the article is used in these phrases:

Jouer sur le *velours.*
St. Paul veut de la subordination entre la *femme et* le *mari.*
Sans les *passions, où seroit le mérite?*

It is suppressed in,

Etre sur pied; *un peu de façons ne gâte rien* entre mari *et femme.*
Vivre sans passions, *c'est vivre* sans plaisirs *et* sans peines.

REPETITION OF THE PREPOSITIONS.

RULE I. The prepositions *de, à,* and *en,* must be repeated before all the nouns which they govern; as

Voyons qui l'emportera de vous, de lui, ou de moi;   Let us see which of us will excel, you, he, or I.

2 L 2

Elle a du l'honnêteté, de la douceur, des grâces, et de l'esprit,	She has politeness, sweetness, grace, and abilities.
La loi, que Dieu a gravée au fond de mon cœur, m'instruit de tout ce que je dois à l'auteur de mon être, au prochain, à moi-même;	The law which God has deeply engraven on my heart, instructs me in every thing I owe *to* the author of my being, *to* my neighbour, and *to* myself.
En Asie, en Europe, en Afrique, et jusqu'en Amérique, on trouve le même préjugé;	In Asia, *in* Europe, *in* Africa, and even *in* America, we find the same prejudice.

RULE II. The other prepositions, especially those consisting of two syllables, are generally repeated—before nouns which have meanings totally different; but seldom before nouns that are nearly synonymous.

Rien n'est moins selon Dieu et selon le monde,	Nothing is less according to God and according to the world.
Cette action est contre l'honneur et contre toute espèce de principes;	That action is contrary to honour and to every kind of principle.

But we ought to say,

Il perd sa jeunesse dans la mollesse et la volupté,	He wastes his youth in effeminacy and pleasure.
Notre loi ne condamne personne sans l'avoir entendu et examiné,	Our laws condemn nobody without having heard and examined him.

OF THE GOVERNMENT OF PREPOSITIONS.

Some prepositions govern nouns without the help of another preposition ; as

Devant la maison,	Before the house.
Hormis son frère,	Except his brother.
Sans son épée,	Without his sword, etc.

Others require the help of the preposition *de* ; as

Près de la maison,	Near the house.
A l'insu de son frère,	Unknown to his brother.
Au-dessus du pont,	Above the bridge, etc.

These four, *jusque, par rapport, quant* and *sauf,* are followed by the preposition *à* ; as

Jusqu'au mois prochain,	Till the next month.
Quant à moi,	As for me, etc.

Practice alone can teach these different regimens.

RULE. A noun may be governed by two prepositions, provided they do not require different regimens; thus we may say with propriety,

Celui qui écrit selon les circon-stances, pour *et* contre *un parti, est un homme bien mé-prisable ;*	He who writes according to circumstances, both for and against a party, is a very contemptible man.

But it would be wrong to say,

Celui qui écrit en faveur *et* contre *un parti,* etc.

because *en faveur* requires the preposition *de.*

RULE. Prepositions which, with their regimen, express a circumstance, are generally placed as nearly as possible to the word to which that circumstance relates ; as

On voit des personnes qui, avec beaucoup d'esprit, *commettent de très-grandes fautes ;*	We see persons who, with a great deal of wit, commit very great faults.
J'ai envoyé à la poste *les lettres que vous avez écrites,*	I have sent to the post-office the letters which you have written.
Croyez-vous pouvoir ramener par la douceur *ces esprits égarés?*	Do you think you can reclaim by gentleness those mistaken people?

If we attempt to alter the place of these prepositions, we shall find that the sentences will become ambiguous.

CHAP. VII.

OF THE ADVERB.

Of the Negative ne.

Negation is expressed in French by *ne,* either alone or accompanied by *pas* or *point.* On this point the Academy has examined the four following questions :

1. Where is the place of the negatives?
2. When is *pas* to be used in preference to *point*, and *vice versâ*?
3. When may both be omitted?
4. When *ought* both to be omitted?

As this subject is of very material importance, we shall treat it upon the plan of the Academy; and agreeably to their views.

FIRST QUESTION. Where is the place of the negatives?

Ne is always prefixed to the verb; but the place of *pas* and *point* is variable.

When the verb is in the infinitive, these are placed indifferently before or after it; for we say,

Pour ne point voir, or *pour ne voir pas*.

In the other moods, except the imperative, the tenses are either simple or compound. In the simple tenses, *pas* or *point* is placed after the verb.

Il ne parle pas; ne parle-t-il pas?

In the compound tenses, it is placed between the auxiliary and the participle.

Il n'a pas parlé; n'a-t-il pas parlé?

In the imperative, it is placed after the verb.

Ne badinez pas. Ne vous en allez pas.

SECOND QUESTION. When is *pas* to be used in preference to *point*, and *vice versâ*?

Point is a stronger negative than *pas*: besides, it denotes something permanent: *il ne lit point*, means he *never* reads.

Pas denotes something accidental: *il ne lit pas*, means he does not read *now*, or he is not reading.

Point de denotes an absolute negation. To say,

Il n'a point d'esprit, is to say, he has no wit at all.

Pas de allows the liberty of a reserve. To say,

Il n'a pas d'esprit, is to say, he has nothing of what can be called wit.

Hence the Academy concludes, that *pas* is more proper,

1. Before *plus, moins, si, autant,* and other words denoting comparison; as

Milton n'est pas moins sublime qu' Homère,	Milton is not less sublime than Homer.

2. Before nouns of number; as

Il n'y a pas dix ans,	It is not ten years ago.

Point is elegantly used,

1. At the end of a sentence; as

On s'amusoit à ses dépens, et il ne s'en apercevoit point;	They were amusing themselves at his expense, and he did not perceive it.

2. In elliptical sentences; as

Je croyois avoir affaire à un honnête homme; mais point;	I thought I had to deal with an honest man: but no.

3. In answer to interrogative sentences; as

Irez-vous ce soir au parc?—point;	Shall you go this evening to the Park?—no.

The Academy also observes, that when *pas* or *point* is introduced into interrogative sentences, it is with meanings somewhat different. We make use of *point,* when we have any doubt on our minds; as

N'avez-vous point été là?	Have you not been there?

But we use *pas,* when we are persuaded. Thus,

N'avez-vous pas été là?	But you have been there, have not you?

THIRD QUESTION. When may both *pas* and *point* be omitted?

They may be suppressed,

1. After the words *cesser, oser,* and *pouvoir;* but this omission is only for the sake of elegance; as

Je ne cesse de m'en occuper,	I am incessantly attentive to it.
Je n'ose vous en parler,	I dare not speak to you about it.
Je ne puis y penser sans frémir,	I cannot think of it without shuddering.

We likewise say, but only in familiar conversation,

Ne bougez,	Do not stir.

2. In expressions of this kind;

Y a-t-il un homme' dont elle ne médise?	Is there a man that she does not slander?
Avez–vous un ami qui ne soit des miens?	Have you a friend that is not likewise mine.

FOURTH QUESTION. When ought both *pas* and *point* to be omitted?

They are omitted,

1. When the extent which we mean to give to the negative is sufficiently expressed either by the words which restrict it, by words which exclude all restriction, or lastly, by such as denote the smaller parts of a whole, and which are without article.

To exemplify the first part of this remark, we say

Je ne sors guère,	I go out but seldom,
Je ne sortirai de trois jours,	I shall not go out for three days.

To exemplify the second, we say

Je n'y vais jamais,	I never go there.
Je n'y pense plus,	I think no more of it.
Nul ne sait s'il est digne d'amour, ou de haine,	Nobody knows whether he be deserving of love, or hatred.
N'employez aucun de ces stratagèmes,	Use none of these stratagems.
Il ne plait à personne,	He pleases nobody.
Rien n'est plus charmant,	Nothing is more charming.
Je n'y pense nullement,	I do not think of it at all.

To exemplify the third, we say

Il n'y voit goutte,	He cannot see at all.
Je n'en ai cueilli brin,	I did not gather a sprig.
Il ne dit mot,	He speaks not a word.

But if to *mot* we join an adjective of number, *pas* must be added; as

Il ne dit pas un mot qui n'intéresse,	He speaks not a word but what is interesting.
Dans ce discours, il n'y a pas trois mots à reprendre;	In that speech, there are not three words that are exceptionable.

Pas is likewise used with the preposition *de ;* as

Il ne fait pas de démarche inutile,	He does not take any useless step.

REMARK. If, after the sentences we have just mentioned, either the conjunction *que*, or the relative pronouns *qui*, or *dont*, should introduce a negative sentence, then in this last *pas* and *point* are omitted; as

Je ne fais jamais d'excès que je n'en sois incommodé,	I never commit any excess, without being ill after it.
Je ne vois personne qui ne vous loue,	I see nobody but what commends you.

2. When two negatives are joined by *ni;* as

Je ne l'aime ni ne l'estime,	I neither love nor esteem him.

And when the conjunction *ni* is repeated, either in the subject, as

Ni l'or ni la grandeur ne nous rendent heureux,	Neither gold nor greatness can make us happy.

Or in the attribute; as

Il n'est ni prudent ni sage,	He is neither prudent nor wise.

Or in the regimen; as

Il n'a ni dettes ni procès,	He has neither debts nor lawsuits.

REMARK. *Pas* is preserved, when *ni* is not repeated, and when this last serves only to unite two members of a negative sentence; as

Je n'aime pas ce vain étalage d'érudition, prodiguée sans choix et sans goût, ni ce luxe de mots qui ne disent rien;	I do not like that vain display of erudition, lavished without choice and without taste, nor that pomp of words which have no meaning.

3. With the verb which follows *que*, used instead of *pourquoi*, and with *à moins que*, or *si*, used instead of it; as

Que n'êtes-vous aussi posé que votre frère?	Why are you not as sedate as your brother?
Je ne sortirai pas, à moins que vous ne veniez me prendre;	I shall not go out, unless you come to fetch me.
Je n'irai pas chez lui, s'il ne m'y engage,	I shall not go to his house, if he do not invite me.

4. With *ne—que* used instead of *seulement;* as

Une jeunesse qui se livre à ses	Youth, which abandons itself

passions, ne transmet à la vieillesse qu'un corps usé ;	to its passions, transmits to old age nothing but a worn-out body.

When before the conjunction. *que*, the word *rien* is understood ; as

Il ne fait que rire,	He does nothing but laugh.

Or when that conjunction may be changed into *sinon*, or *si ce n'est;* as

Il ne tient qu'à vous de réussir;	The success wholly depends upon you.
Trop de maîtres à la fois ne servent qu'à embrouiller l'esprit,	Too many masters at once only serve to perplex the mind.

· 5. With a verb in the preterit, preceded by the conjunction *depuis que*, or by the verb *il y a*, denoting a certain duration of time; as

Comment vous êtes-vous porté depuis que je ne vous ai vu ?	How have you been since I saw you?
Il y a trois mois que je ne vous ai vu,	I have not seen you for these three months.

But they are not omitted, when the verb is in the present; as

Comment vit-il depuis que nous ne le voyons point ?	How does he live now we do not see him.
Il y a six mois que nous ne le voyons point,	We have not seen him these six months.

6. In phrases where the conjunction *que* is preceded by the adverbs of comparison *plus, moins, mieux,* etc. or some other equivalent term; as

On méprise ceux qui parlent autrement qu'ils ne pensent,	We despise those who speak differently from what they think.
Il écrit mieux qu'il ne parle,	He writes better than he speaks.
C'est pire qu'on ne le disoit,	It is worse than was said.
C'est autre chose que je ne croyois,	It is different from what I thought.
Peu s'en faut qu'on ne m'ait trompé,	I have been very near being deceived.

· 7. In sentences united by the conjunction *que* to the

verbs *douter*, *désespérer*, *nier*, and *disconvenir*, forming a negative member of a sentence ; as

Je ne doute pas qu'il ne vienne,	I doubt not that he will come.
Ne désespérez pas que ce moyen ne vous réussisse,	Do not despair of the success of these means.
Je ne nie pas, or *je ne disconviens pas que cela ne soit ;*	I do not deny that it is so.

The Academy says, that after the last two verbs, *ne* -may be omitted ; as

Je ue nie pas, *or* je ne disconviens pas que cela soit.

8. With a verb united by the conjunction *que* to the verbs *empêcher* and *prendre garde*, meaning to take care; as

J'empêcherai bien que vous ne soyez du nombre,	I shall prevent your being of the number.
Prenez garde qu'on ne vous séduise,	Take care that they do not corrupt you.

REMARK. The Academy observes, that in the above acceptation, *prendre garde* is followed by a subjunctive; but when it means *to reflect*, the indicative is used with *pas* or *point ;* as

Prenez garde que vous ne m'entendez pas,	Mind, you do not understand what I mean.

9. With a verb united by the conjunction *que* to the verb *craindre*, and those of the same meaning, when we do not wish the thing expressed by the second verb; as

Il craint que son frère ne l'abandonne,	He is afraid his brother should forsake him.
Je crains que mon ami ne meure,	I fear my friend will die.

But *pas* is not omitted when we wish the thing expressed by the second verb ; as

Je crains que mon père n'arrive pas,	I am afraid my father will not come.

10. With the verb which follows *de peur que, de crainte que,* in similar circumstances with *craindre*. Thus, when we say,

De crainte qu'il ne perde son procès,
We wish that he may gain it; and when we say,
De crainte qu'il ne soit pas puni,
We wish that he may be punished.

REMARK. In these phrases,

Je crains que mon ami ne meure,	I am afraid my friend will die.
Vous empêchez qu'on ne chante,	You prevent them from singing.

The expression *ne* is not a negation; it is the *ne* or *quin* of the Latins introduced into the French language, as may be seen by the English translation.

11. After *savoir*, whenever it has the meaning of *pouvoir;* as.

Je ne saurois en venir à bout,	I cannot accomplish it.

When it means *être incertain*, it is best to omit *pas* and *point;* as

Je ne sais où le prendre,	I do not know where to find him.
Il ne sait ce qu'il dit,	He does not know what he says.

REMARK. But *pas* and *point* must be used when *savoir* is taken in its true meaning; as

Je ne sais pas le François,	I do not know French.

12. We also say,

Ne vous déplaise, ne vous en déplaise,	By your leave, under favour, or, let it not displease you.

Plus and *davantage* must not be used indifferently. *Plus* is followed by the preposition *de*, or the conjunction *que;* as

Il a plus de brillant que de solide,	He has more brilliancy than solidity.
Il se fie plus à ses lumières qu'à celles des autres,	He relies more upon his own knowledge than upon that of others.

Davantage is used alone and at the end of sentences; as

La science est estimable, mais la vertu l'est davantage;	Learning is estimable, but virtue is still more so.

Though *davantage* cannot be followed by the preposition *de*, it may be preceded by the pronoun *en ;* as

Je n'en dirai pas davantage,	I shall not say any more about it.

It is incorrect to use *davantage* for *le plus.* We must say,

De toutes les fleurs d'un parterre, l'anémone est celle qui me plaît le plus ;	Of all the flowers of a parterre, the anemone is that which pleases me most.

Si, aussi, tant, and *autant,* are always followed by the conjunction *que,* expressed or understood.

Si and *aussi* are joined to adjectives, adverbs, and participles ; *tant* and *autant* to substantives and verbs.

L'Angleterre n'est-pas si grande que la France,	England is not so large as France.
Il est aussi estimé qu'aimé,	He is as much esteemed as he is beloved.
Elle a autant de beauté que de vertu,	She has as much beauty as virtue.

REMARK. *Autant* may, however, be substituted for *aussi,* when it is preceded by one adjective, and followed by *que* and another adjective ; as

Il est modeste autant que sage,	He is as modest as wise.

Aussi and *autant* are used in affirmative; *si* and *tant* in negative and interrogative sentences. The two last are, however, alone to be used in affirmative sentences, when they are put for *tellement ;* as

Il est devenu si gros qu'il a de la peine à marcher,	He is become so bulky that he can hardly walk.
Il a tant couru qu'il en est hors d'haleine,	He has been running so fast that he is out of breath.

Jamais takes sometimes the preposition *à,* and *toujours* the preposition *pour ;* as

Soyez à jamais heureux,	Be for ever happy.
C'est pour toujours,	It is for ever.

2 M

CHAP. VIII.

OF GRAMMATICAL CONSTRUCTION.

GRAMMATICAL construction is the order which the genius of a language has assigned, in speech, to the different sorts of words into which it is distinguished. Construction is sometimes mistaken for syntax; but there is this difference, the latter consists in the rules which we are to observe, in order to express the relations of words one to another; whereas grammatical construction consists in the various arrangements which are allowed while we observe the rules of syntax. Now this arrangement is irrevocably fixed, not only as phrases may be interrogative, imperative, or expositive, but also as each of these kinds may be affirmative or negative.

In sentences simply interrogative, the subject is either a noun or pronoun.

If the subject be a noun, the following is the order to be observed: first, the noun, then the verb, then the corresponding personal pronoun, the adverb, if any, and the regimen in the simple tenses: in the compound tenses, the pronoun and the adverb are placed between the auxiliary and the participle; as

Les lumières sont-elles un bien pour les peuples? ont-elles jamais contribué à leur bonheur?	Are sciences an advantage to nations? Have they ever contributed to their happiness?

If the subject be a pronoun, the verb begins the series, and the other words follow in the order already pointed out; as

Vous plairez-vous toujours à médire?	Will you always take pleasure in slandering?
Aurez-vous bientôt fini?	Shall you have soon done?

N.B. When the verb is reflected, the pronoun forming the regimen begins the series; this pronoun always preserves its place before the verb, except in sentences simply imperative.

In interrogative sentences, with negation, the same order is observed; but *ne* is placed before the verb, and *pas*, or *point*, after the verb in the simple tenses, and between the auxiliary and the participle in the compound tenses; as

Votre frère ne viendra-t-il pas demain?	Will not your brother come to-morrow?
N'aurez-vous pas bientôt fini?	Shall you not have soon done?

REMARK. There are in French several other ways of interrogating.

1. With an absolute pronoun; as

Qui vous a dit cela? or, *Qui est-ce qui vous a dit cela?*	Who told you that?

2. With the demonstrative pronoun *ce;* as

Est-ce vous?	Is it you?	*Est-ce qu'il pleut?*	Does it rain?

3. With an interrogative verb; as

Pourquoi ne vient-il pas?	Why does he not come?
Comment vous trouvez-vous?	How do you find yourself?

Hence we see that the absolute pronouns and the interrogative adverbs always begin the sentence; but the demonstrative pronoun always follows the verb.

In sentences, simply imperative, the verb is always placed first, in the first and second persons; but in the third, it comes after the conjunction *que* and the noun or pronoun; as

Allons là,	Let us go there.
Venez ici,	Come here.
Qu'ils y aillent,	Let them go there.
Que Pierre aille à Londres,	Let Peter go to London.

With negation, *ne* and *pas* are placed as in interrogative sentences.

For the place of the pronouns, see p. 217.

Sentences are expositive, when we speak without either interrogating or commanding. The following is the order of the words in those which are affirmative:

the subject, the verb, the adverb, the participle, the regimen; as

Un bon prince mérite l'amour de ses sujets et l'estime de tous les peuples,	A good prince deserves the love of his subjects and the esteem of all nations.
César eût inutilement passé le Rubicon, s'il y eût eu de son temps des Fabius;	Cæsar would have crossed the Rubicon to no purpose, had there been Fabii in his time.

The negative sentences differ from this construction, only as *ne* is always placed before the verb, and *pas*, or *point*, either after the verb, or between the auxiliary and the participle; as

Un homme riche ne fait pas tou- jours le bien qu'il pourroit,	A rich man does not always do all the good he might.
Cicéron n'eût pas peut-être été un si grand orateur, si le dé- sir de s'élever aux premières dignités n'eût enflammé son âme ;	Cicero would not perhaps have been so great an orator, had not the desire of rising to the first dignities inflamed his soul.

Sentences are either simple or compound. They are simple, when they contain only one subject and one attribute; as

Vous lisez,	You read.
Vous êtes jeune,	You are young.

They are compound, when they associate several sub- jects with one attribute, or several attributes with one subject, or several attributes with several subjects, or several subjects with several attributes.

This sentence, *Pierre et Paul sont heureux,* is com- pound by having several subjects; this, *cette femme est jolie, spirituelle et sensible,* is compound by having several attributes; and this, *Pierre et Paul sont spirituels et savans,* is composed at once of several subjects and several attributes.

A sentence may be compound in various other ways; by the subject, by the verb, or by the attribute.

By the subject, when this is restricted by an incidental proposition; as

Dieu, qui est bon.

By the verb, when it is modified by some circumstances of time, order, etc.; as

Dieu, qui est bon, n'abandonne jamais.

By the attribute, when this attribute is modified by a regimen which is itself restricted; as

Dieu, qui est bon, n'abandonne jamais les hommes qui mettent sincèrement leur confiance en lui.

These simple or compound sentences may be joined to others by a conjunction; as

| Quand on aime l'étude, le temps passe sans qu'on s'en aperçoive ; | When we love study, time flies without our perceiving it. |

The two partial phrases here form but one.

RULE. When a sentence is composed of two partial phrases, joined by a conjunction, harmony and perspicuity generally require the shortest to go first.

EXAMPLES.

| Quand les passions nous quittent, nous nous flattons en vain, que c'est nous qui les quittons ; | When our passions leave us, we in vain flatter ourselves that it is we that leave them. |
| On n'est point à plaindre, quand, au défaut de plaisirs réels, on trouve le moyen de s'occuper de chimères ; | He is not to be pitied, who, for want of real pleasures, finds means to amuse himself with chimeras. |

Periods result from the union of several partial phrases, the whole of which make a complete sense. Periods, to be clear, require the shortest phrases to be placed first. The following example of this is taken from Flechier.

N'attendez pas, Messieurs,

1. Que j'ouvre un scène tragique ;

2. Que je représente ce grand homme étendu sur ses propres trophées ;

3. Que je découvre ce corps pâle et sanglant, auprès duquel fume encore la foudre qui l'a frappé ;

4. Que je fasse crier son sang comme celui d'Abel, et que j'expose à vos yeux les images de la religion et de la patrie éplorée.

2 M 3

This admirable period is composed of four members, which go on gradually increasing. It is a rule not to give more than four members to a period, and to avoid multiplying incidental sentences.

Obscurity in style is generally owing to those small phrases which divert the attention from the principal sentences, and make us lose sight of them.

The construction which we have mentioned is called direct, or regular, because the words are placed in those sentences according to the order which has been pointed out. But this order may be altered in certain cases, and then the construction is called indirect, or irregular. Now, it may be irregular, by *inversion*, by *ellipsis*, by *pleonasm*, or by *syllepsis*; these are what are called the four figures of words.

OF INVERSION.

Inversion is the transposition of a word into a place, different from that which by usage is properly assigned to it. This ought never to be done except when it introduces more perspicuity, energy, or harmony into the language; for it is a defect in construction, whenever the relation subsisting between words is not easily perceived.

There are two kinds of inversion: the one by its boldness seems to be confined to poetry: the other is frequently employed even in prose.

We shall speak here of the latter kind only.

The following inversions are authorized by custom.

The subject by which a verb is governed may with propriety be placed after it; as

Tout ce que lui promet l'amitié des Romains,	All that the friendship of the Romans promises him.

REMARK. This inversion is a rule of the art of speaking and writing, whenever the subject is modified by an incidental sentence, long enough to make us lose sight of the relation of the verb governed to the subject governing.

The noun governed by the prepositions *de* and *à* may likewise be very properly placed before the verb; as

D'une voix entrecoupée de san-glots, ils s'écrièrent ;	In a voice interrupted by sobs, they exclaimed.
A tant d'injures, qu'a-t-elle répondu ?	To so much abuse, what answer did she give?

The verb is likewise elegantly preceded by the prepositions *après, dans, par, sous, contre,* etc. with their dependencies, as well as by the conjunctions *si, quand, parce que, puisque, quoique, lorsque,* etc. as

Par la loi du corps, je tiens à ce monde qui passe;	By the law of the body, I am connected with this passing world.
Puisqu'il le veut, qu'il le fasse;	Since he wishes it, let him do it.

OF THE ELLIPSIS.

Ellipsis is the omission of a word, or even several words, which are necessary to make the construction full and complete. In order to form a good ellipsis, the mind must be able easily to supply the words omitted; as

J'accepterois les offres de Da-rius, si j'étois Alexandre;—et moi aussi, si j'étois Parme-nion :	I would accept the offers of Darius, if I were Alexander;—and so would I, if I were Parmenio.

Here the mind easily supplies the words *je les accepterois* in the second member.

The ellipsis is very common in answers to interrogative sentences; as

Quand viendrez - vous ?—de-main ;	When will you come ?—to-morrow.

that is, *je viendrai demain.*

In order to know whether an ellipsis be good, the

words that are understood must be supplied. · It is correct, whenever the construction completely express the sense denoted by the words which are supplied otherwise it is not exact.

OF THE PLEONASM.

Pleonasm, in general, is a superfluity of words: in order to constitute this figure good, it must be sanctioned by custom, which never authorizes its use, but give greater energy to language, or to express, in a clearer manner, the internal feeling with which we are affected.

Et que m'a fait *à moi* cette Troie où je cours!

Je *me* meurs. S'il ne veut pas vous le dire, je vous le dirai, *moi.*

Je l'ai vu *de mes propres yeux.*

Je l'ai entendu *de mes propres oreilles.*

A moi, in the first sentence; *me,* in the second; *moi,* in the third; *de mes propres yeux,* in the fourth; and *de mes propres oreilles,* in the fifth, are employed merely for the sake of energy, or to manifest an internal feeling. But this manner of speaking is sanctioned by custom.

REMARK. Expletives must not be mistaken for pleonasms; as

C'est une affaire, où il y va du salut de l'état;	It is an affair in which the safety of the state is concerned.

Which is better than *c'est une affaire où il va,* etc. by omitting *y,* which is in reality useless on account of *où:* but *y* here is a mode of expression from which it is not allowed to deviate.

OF THE SYLLEPSIS.

The syllepsis is a figure by which a word relates more to our meaning, than to the literal expressions, as in these :

Il est onze heures ; l'an mil sept cent quatre-vingt-dix-neuf.

When using it, the mind, merely intent upon a precise meaning, pays no attention to either the number or the gender of *heure* and *an*.
There is likewise a syllepsis in these sentences :

> Je crains qu'il ne vienne.
> J'empêcherai qu'il ne vous nuise.
> J'ai peur qu'il ne m'oublie, etc.

Full of a wish that the event may not take place, we are willing to do all we can, that nothing should prevent an obstacle to that wish. This is the cause of the introduction of the negative, which, although unnecessary to complete the sense, yet must be preserved for the idiom.

There is again a very elegant syllepsis in sentences like the following from Racine :

> Entre le *peuple* et vous, vous prendrez Dieu pour juge ;
> Vous souvenant, mon fils, que caché sous ce lin,
> Comme *eux* vous fûtes pauvre, et, comme *eux* orphelin.

The poet forgets that he has been using the word *peuple :* nothing remains in his mind but *des pauvres* and *des orphelins*, and it is with that idea of which he is full that he makes the pronoun *eux* agree. For the same reason, Bossuet and Mézengui have said :

> Quand le *peuple Hébreu* entra dans la terre promise, tout y célébroit *leurs* ancêtres.—BOSSUET.
> Moïse eut recours au Seigneur, et lui dit : que ferai-je à *ce peuple?* bientôt *ils* me lapideront.—MÉZENGUI.

Leurs and *ils* stand for *les Hébreux,*

CHAP. IX.

OF GRAMMATICAL DISCORDANCES, AMPHIBOLOGIES, AND GALLICISMS.

We have chiefly to take notice of two vicious modes of construction, which are contrary to the principles laid down in the preceding chapters; grammatical discordances, and amphibologies.

OF DISCORDANCES.

In general, there is a discordance in language, when the words which compose the various members of a sentence or period do not agree with each other, either because their construction is contrary to analogy or because they bring together dissimilar ideas, between which the mind perceives an opposition, or can see no manner of affinity. The following examples will serve to illustrate this:

Notre réputation ne dépend pas des louanges qu'on nous donne, mais des actions louables que nous faisons.

This sentence is not correct, because the first member being negative, and the second affirmative, cannot come under the government of the same verb.   It ought to be:

Notre réputation dépend, non des louanges qu'on nous donne, mais des actions, etc.	*Our reputation depends not upon the praises which are bestowed on us, but upon the praise-worthy actions which we perform.*

But the most common discordances are those which arise from the wrong use of tenses, as in this sentence:

Il regarde votre malheur comme une punition du peu de complaisance que *vous avez eue* pour lui, dans le temps qu'il vous *pria*, etc.

because the two preterits, definite and indefinite, cannot well agree together; it should be:

Que vous eûtes pour lui dans le temps qu'il vous pria.

There is discordance in this sentence :

On en ressentit autant de joie que d'une victoire complète dans une autre temps,

because the verb cannot be understood after the *que* which serves for the comparison, when that verb is to be in a different tense; it should be :

On en ressentit autant de joie qu'on en auroit ressenti, etc.

This line of Racine,

　　　Le flot, qu'il l'apporta, recule épouvanté,

is also incorrect, because the form of the present cannot associate with that of the preterit definite; it should have been : *qui l'a apporté,*

OF AMPHIBOLOGIES.

Amphibology in language is when a sentence is so constructed as to be susceptible of two different interpretations: this must be carefully avoided. As we speak only to be understood, perspicuity is the first and most essential quality of language: we should always recollect that *what is not clearly expressed in any language, is no language at all.*

Amphibologies are occasioned, 1. By the misuse of moods and tenses. 2. Of the personal pronouns, *il, le, la,* etc. 3. Of the possessive pronouns, *son, sa, ses,* etc. 4. By giving a wrong place to nouns.

EXAMPLE

Of an Amphibology of the first kind.

Qu'ai-je fait, *pour venir* accabler en ces lieux
Un héros, sur qui seul j'ai pu tourner les yeux?　RACINE.

Pour venir forms an amphibology, because we do not know whether it relates to the person who speaks, or to the person spoken to; it should have been, *pour que vous veniez.*

EXAMPLE

Of an Amphibology of the second kind.

César voulut premièrement surpasser Pompée; les grandes richesses de Crassus *lui* firent croire, qu'*il* pourroit partager la gloire de ces deux grands hommes.

This sentence is faulty in its construction, because the pronouns *il* and *lui* seem to relate to *César*, although the sense obliges us to refer them to *Crassus*.

EXAMPLE

Of an Amphibology of the third kind.

Valère alla chez Léandre; il y trouve *son* fils.

The pronoun *son* is ambiguous, because we do not know to which it relates, to *Valère* or to *Léandre*.

EXAMPLE

Of an Amphibology of the fourth kind.

J'ai envoyé les lettres, que j'ai écrites, à la poste.

A la poste, thus placed is equivocal, because we do not know whether it is meant that the letters have been *written* at the post-office, or *sent* to the post-office.

OF GALLICISMS.

We have distinguished in our "Grammaire Philosophique et Littéraire," four sorts of gallicisms: we shall only mention here those of construction.

The gallicisms of construction are, in general, irregularities and deviations from the customary rules of syntax; there are some, however, which are mere ellipses, and others which can only be attributed to the caprice of custom.

GENERAL PRINCIPLE. Every gallicism of construction which obscures the meaning of the sentence, ought to be condemned. Those only ought to be preserved which do not impair perspicuity, by introducing irregularity of construction, and which are, at the same time, sanctioned by long practice.

According to this principle, this elliptic gallicism is now rejected:

Et qu'ainsi ne soit, *meaning* ce que je vous dis est si vrai que,

because it obscures the sentence. For instance:

J'étois dans ce jardin, *et qu'ainsi ne soit*, voilà une fleur que j'y ai cueillie, *that is*, et pour preuve de cela, voilà une fleur, etc.

Molière and La Fontaine seem to have been the last great writers that have used this expression.

One of the most common gallicisms is that in which the impersonal verb *il y a*, is used for *il est, il existe*. These expressions:

Il y avoit une fois un roi;—il y a cent à parier contre un,

are gallicisms. There are two in the following sentence:

| Il n'y a pas jusqu'aux enfans, qui ne s'en mêlent; | Even children will meddle with it. |

The verb *falloir* forms a sort of gallicism with the pronoun *en*, when it is conjugated like pronominal verbs with the double pronouns, *il se;* as

Il s'en faut, il s'en falloit, etc.

It then means *to be wanting*, and when preceded by an adverb of quantity, the first pronoun is omitted; as

Peu s'en faut, tant s'en faut.

These several manners of using the verb *falloir* will be found in the following sentences:

EXAMPLES.

Il s'en faut bien qu'il soit aussi habile qu'il croit l'être,	*He is far from being so clever as he thinks.*
Peu s'en est fallu qu'il n'ait succombé dans cette entreprise,	*He was very near failing in that undertaking.*
Il ne s'en est presque rien fallu qu'il n'ait été tué,	*He was as near as possible being killed.*

2 N

Vous dites qu'il s'en faut vingt livres que la somme entière n'y soit, mais vous vous trompez, il ne peut pas s'en falloir tant;

You say it wants twenty pounds to complete the sum, but you are mistaken, it can not want so much.

Son rhume est entièrement guéri, ou peu s'en faut;

His cold is entirely well, or very near.

Que s'en est-il fallu que ces deux amis ne se soient brouillés?

How near were these two friends quarrelling?

Je ne suis pas content de votre application à l'étude, tant s'en faut;

I am not satisfied with your application to study, far from it.

Tant s'en faut que cette comédie me plaise, elle me semble au contraire détestable;

So far from this play pleasing me, I think it insufferable.

Il s'en falloit beaucoup que je vous approuvasse dans cette circonstance,

I was far from approving your conduct on that occasion.

The sentences :

Il n'est rien moins que généreux,

He is far from being generous.

Vous avez beau dire,

You may say what you please, but, etc.

A ce qu'il me semble,

By what I can see, as the matter appears to me, etc.

Nous voilà à nous lamenter,

We began to lament, here we are lamenting, crying, etc.

Qu'est-ce que de nous!

What wretched beings we are, etc. etc.

c:

are also gallicisms.

The use which is made of the preposition en, in many sentences, is likewise another source of gallicisms; some of this kind will be found in the following expressions :

A qui en avez-vous?
Où en veut-il venir?

Whom are you angry with;
What does he aim at? what would he be at?

Il lui en veut,

He has a quarrel with him, etc.

The preposition en changes also, sometimes, the significations of verbs, and then gives rise to gallicisms.

The conjunction *que* produces as great a number of gallicisms; as

C'est une terrible passion, que le jeu,	Gaming is a terrible passion.
C'est donc en vain que je travaille,	It is in vain then that I work.
Ce n'est pas trop que cela,	That is not too much.
Il n'est que d'avoir du courage,	There is nothing like having courage.

Many others will be found in the use which is made of the prepositions *à, de, dans, après,* etc. but enough has been said on this subject.

Gallicisms are of very great use in the simple style; therefore La Fontaine and Mad. de Sévigné abound in them. The middling style has not so many, and the solemn oratorical but few, and these even of a peculiar nature. Only two examples of this kind, both taken from the tragedy of Iphigenia, by Racine, will be here inserted.

> Avez-vous pu penser qu'au sang d'Agamemnon
> Achille préférât une fille sans nom,
> *Qui* de tout son destin ce qu'elle a pu comprendre,
> C'est qu'elle sort d'un sang, etc.

And

> *Je ne sais qui m'arrête* et retient mon courroux,
> *Que* par un prompt avis de tout ce qui se passe
> *Je ne coure* des dieux divulguer la menace.

In the first sentence, *qui* is the subject though without relating to any verb; and in the second, *je ne sais qui m'arrête que je ne coure,* is contrary to the rules of common construction. " But," says Vaugelas, " these extraordinary phrases, far from being vicious, possess the more beauty, as they belong to a particular kind of language."

FREE EXERCISES.

I.

MADAME DE MAINTENON TO HER BROTHER.

We can only be 1 unhappy by our own fault; this shall always be my text, and my reply to your lamentations. Recollect 2, my dear brother, the voyage to America, the misfortunes of our father, of our infancy and our youth 3; and you will bless Providence instead of murmuring against fortune. Ten years ago, we were both very far (below our present situation 4 ;) and our hopes were so feeble 5, that we limited our wishes to an (income of three thousand livres 6.) At present we have four times that sum 7, and our desires are not yet satisfied! we enjoy the happy mediocrity which you have so often extolled 8 ; let us be content. If possessions 9 come to us, let us receive them from the hand of God, but let not our views be 10 too extravagant 11. We have (every thing necessary 12) and comfortable 13 ; all the rest is avarice 14; all these desires of greatness spring from 15 a restless heart. Your debts are all paid, and you may live elegantly 16, without contracting more 17. What have you to desire? must 18 schemes 19 of wealth and ambition occasion 20 the loss of your repose and your health? read the life of St. Louis; you will see how unequal 21 the greatness of this world is to the desires of the human heart; God only can satisfy them 22. I repeat it, you are only unhappy by your own fault. Your uneasiness 23 destroys your health, which you ought to preserve, if it were 24 only because I love you. Watch 25 your temper 26 : if you can render it less splenetic 27 and less gloomy, (you will have gained a great advantage 28.) This is not the work of reflection only; exercise, amusement, and a regular life, (are necessary for the purpose 29.) You cannot think well (whilst your health is affected 30 ;) when the body is debilitated 31, the mind is without vigour. Adieu! write to me more frequently, and in a style less gloomy.

---

1 On ne être...que. 2 Songer à. 3 The misfortunes of our infancy and those of our, etc. 4 Du point où nous sommes aujourd'hui. 5 Si peu de chose. 6 Trois mille livres de rente. 7 *That sum,* en... plus. 8 *Have so often extolled,* vanter si fort, ind-2. 9 *Possessions,* biens. 10 Let us not have views. 11. Trop vaste. 12 Le nécessaire. 13 Le commode. 14 *Avarice,* cupidité. 15 *Spring from,* partir du vide de. 16 Délicieusement. 17 *Contracting more,* en faire de nouvelles. 18 *Must,* faut-il que. 19 Projet. 20 *Occasion,* coûter, sub-1. 21 *Unequal,* au-dessous de. 22 *Satisfy them,* le rassasier. 23 *Uneasiness,* inquiétude pl. 24 *If it were,* quand ce être, cond-1. 25 Travailler sur. 26 Humeur. 27 Bilieux. 28 Ce être un grand point de gagné. 29 Il y faut de. 30 Tant que vous se porter mal. 31 *Debilitated,* dans l'abattement.

II.

THE CONVERT.

AN EASTERN TALE.

Divine mercy 1 had brought a vicious man into a society of
sages, whose morals were holy and pure. He was affected by
their virtues; it was not long 2 before 3 he imitated them and
lost his old habits : he became just, sober, patient, laborious and
benevolent. His deeds nobody could deny, but they were attributed 4 to odious motives. They praised his good actions, without loving his person : they would always judge him by what
he had been, not by what he was become. This injustice filled
him with grief; he shed tears in the bosom of an ancient sage,
more just and more humane than the others. " O my son,"
said the old man to him, " thou art better than thy reputation ;
" be thankful to God for it. Happy the man who can say : my
" enemies and my rivals censure in me vices of which I am not
" guilty. What matters 5 it, if thou art good, that men perse-
" cute thee as wicked? Hast thou not, to comfort thee, the two
" best witnesses of thy actions, God and thy conscience."

SAINT-LAMBERT.

M. de Montausier has written a letter to Monseigneur upon the
taking of Philipsbourg, which very much pleases me. " Mon-
" seigneur ; I do not compliment you on the capture of Philips-
" bourg; you had a good army, bombs, cannon, and Vauban;
" neither shall I compliment you upon your valour; for that is
" an hereditary virtue in your family. But I rejoice that you
" are liberal, generous, humane, and that you know how to re-
" compense the services of those who behave well : it is for this
" that I congratulate you." SÉVIGNÉ.

III.

THE GOOD MINISTER.

AN EASTERN TALE.

The great Aaron Raschild began to suspect that his vizier
Giafar was not deserving of the confidence which he had reposed
in him. The women of Aaron, the inhabitants of Bagdad, the
courtiers, the dervises, censured the vizier with bitterness. The
calif loved Giafar ; he would not condemn him upon the clamours
of the city and the court : he visited his empire; every where
he saw the land well cultivated; the country smiling, the cottages
opulent, the useful arts honoured, and youth full of gaiety. He
visited his fortified cities and sea-ports : he saw numerous ships,

---

1 Miséricorde. 2 Ne pas tarder. 3 A inf-1. 4 On donner des motifs.
5 Importer.

2 N 2

which threateued the coasts of Africa and of Asia ; he saw warriors
disciplined and content ; these warriors, the seamen and the pea-
santry, exclaimed : " O God, pour thy blessings upon the
" faithful, by giving them a calif like Aarou, and a vizier like
" Giafar." The calif, affected by these exclamations, enters a
mosque, falls upon his knees, and cries out : " Great God, I re-
" turn thee thanks ; thou hast given me a vizier of whom my
" courtiers speak ill, and my people speak well."

SAINT-LAMBERT.

Providence conducts us with so much goodness through the different periods of our life, that we (do not perceive our progress 1.)
This loss takes place gently 2, it is imperceptible, it is the shadow
of the sun-dial whose motion we do not see. If, at twenty years
of age, we could see 3 in a mirror the face we shall have at three-
score, we (should be shocked at the contrast 4 ,) and terrified at
our own figure; but it is day by day that we advance: we are
to-day as we were yesterday, and shall be to-morrow as we are
to-day; so we go forward without perceiving it; and this is a mi-
racle of that Providence which I adore.   SÉVIGNÉ.

IV.

THE MAGNIFICENT PROSPECT.

This beautiful house was on the declivity of a hill, from whence
you beheld the sea, sometimes clear and smooth as glass, sometimes idly 1 irritated against the rocks on which it broke, bellow-
ing 2 and swelling its waves like mountains. On another side was
seen a river, in which were islands bordered with blooming limes,
and lofty poplars, which raised their proud heads to the very
clouds. The several channels, which formed those islands,
seemed sporting 3 in the plain. Some rolled their limpid waters
with rapidity : some had a peaceful and still course ; others, by
long windings, ran back again, to reascend as it were to their
source, and seemed not to have power to leave these enchanting
borders. At a distance were seen hills and mountains, which were
lost in the clouds, and formed, by their fantastic figure, as delightful a horizon (as the eye could wish to behold 4.) The neighbouring mountains were covered with verdant (vine branches 5,)
hanging in festoons; the grapes, brighter than purple, could not
conceal themselves under the leaves, and the vine 6 was over-
loaded with its fruit. The fig, the olive, the pomegranate, and
all other trees, overspread the plain, and made it one large
garden.   FÉNÉLON.

---

1 Ne le sentir quasi pas. 2 Va doucement. 3 On nous faire voir.
4· Tomber à la renverse.
  1 Follement. 2 En gémir. 3 Se jouer. 4 A souhait pour le plaisir
de. 5 Pampre, m. 6 Vigne.

Long hopes wear out 7 joy, as long maladies wear out pain.
All philosophic systems are only good when one (has no use
for them 8.)   SÉVIGNÉ.

V

A GENERAL VIEW OF NATURE.

With what magnificence does nature shine 1 upon earth! A
pure light, extending from east to west, gilds successively the
two hemispheres of this globe; an element, transparent and light,
surrounds it; a gentle fecundating heat animates, gives being 2
to the seeds of life : salubrious running streams contribute to their
preservation and growth; eminences diversified over the level
land, arrest the vapours of the air, make these springs inexhaustible and always new; immense cavities made to receive them
divide the continents. The extent of the sea is as great as that of
the earth : it is not a cold, barren element; it is a new empire,
as rich, as populous as the first. The finger of God has marked
their boundaries.

The earth, rising above the level of the sea, is secure 3 from its
eruptions : its surface, enamelled with flowers, adorned with ever-
springing verdure, peopled with thousands and thousands of species
of different animals, is a place of rest, a delightful abode, where
man, placed in order to second nature, presides over all beings.
The only one among them all, capable of knowing and worthy of
admiring, God has made him spectator of the universe, and a
witness of his wonders. The divine spark with which he is ani-
mated enables him to participate in the divine mysteries : it is by
this light that he thinks and reflects; by it he sees and reads in
the book of the universe, as in a copy of the Deity.

Nature is the exterior throne of the divine Majesty : the man
who contemplates, who studies it, rises by degrees to the interior
throne of Omnipotence. Made to adore the Creator, the vassal
of heaven, sovereign of the earth, he ennobles, peoples, enriches
it; he establishes among living beings order, subordination,
harmony; he embellishes nature herself; he cultivates, extends,
and polishes it; lops off the thistle and the briar, and multiplies
the grape and the rose.   BUFFON.

VI.

ANOTHER GENERAL VIEW OF NATURE.

Trees, shrubs, and plants are the ornaments and clothing 1 of
the earth   Nothing is so melancholy 2 as the prospect of a coun-

---

7 User.   8 N'en avoir que faire.
1 Ne briller pas.   2 Faire éclore.   3 A l'abri de.
1 Vêtement.   2 Triste.

2 N 3

try naked and bare 5, exhibiting to the eye nothing but stones,
mud, and sand.   But, vivified by nature, and clad 4 in its nup-
tial robe, amidst the course of streams and the singing of birds,
the earth presents to man, in the harmony of the three kingdoms,
a spectacle full of life, of interest and charms, the only spectacle
in the world of which his eyes and heart are never weary 5.

The more a (contemplative man's soul is fraught with sensibility 6), the more he yields to the extacies which this harmony
produces in him. A soft and deep melancholy then takes possession of his senses, and, in an intoxication of delight, he loses
himself in the immensity of that beautiful system, with which
he feels himself identified. Then, every particular object escapes
him ; he sees and feels nothing but in the whole. Some circumstance must contract his ideas and circumscribe his imagination,
before 7 he can observe by parcels that universe which he was
endeavouring to embrace.   J. J. ROUSSEAU.

VII.
CULTIVATED NATURE.

How beautiful is cultivated nature! How, by the labours of
man, how brilliant it is, and how pompously adorned!   He himself is its chief ornament, its noblest part ; by multiplying himself, he multiplies the most precious germ ; she also seems to mul-
tiply with him : by his art, he (brings forth to view 1) all that she
concealed 2 in her bosom. How many unknown treasures! What
new riches! Flowers, fruits, seeds brought to perfection, multiplied to infinity; the useful species of animals transported, pro-
pagated, increased without number ; the noxious species reduced,
confined, banished : gold, and iron more necessary than gold,
extracted from the bowels of the earth ; torrents confined 3, rivers
directed, contracted 4 ; the sea itself subjected, explored 5, crossed,
from one hemisphere to the other ; the earth accessible in every
part, and every where rendered equally cheerful and fruitful : in
the vallies, delightful meadows ; in the plains, rich pastures and
still richer harvests ; hills covered with vines and fruits ; their
summits crowned with useful trees and young forests ; deserts
changed into cities inhabited by an immense population, which,
continually circulating, spreads itself from these centres to their
extremities ; roads opened and frequented, communications established every where, as so many witnesses of the strength and
union of society : a thousand other monuments of power and glory
sufficiently demonstrate that man, possessing dominion over the
earth, has changed, renewed the whole of its surface, and that,
at all times, he shares the empire of it with nature.

3 Pelé. 4 Revêtu. 5 Se lasser. 6 Contemplateur avoir l'âme sensible. 7 Pour qu'il.
        Mettre au jour. 2 Recéler. 3 Contenu. 4 Resserré. 5 Reconnu.

VIII.
THE SAME SUBJECT CONTINUED.

However, man only reigns by right of conquest : he rather enjoys than possesses, and he can preserve only by means of continual labour. If this ceases, every thing droops, every thing declines, every thing changes and again returns 1 under the hand of nature; she reassumes her rights, erases the work of man, covers with dust and moss his most pompous monuments, destroys them in time, and leaves him nothing but the regret of having lost, through his fault, what his ancestors had conquered by their labours. Those times, in which man loses his dominion, those barbarous 2 ages, during which every thing is seen to perish, are always preceded by war, and accompanied by scarcity and depopulation. Man, who can do nothing but by number, who is strong only by union, who can be happy only by peace, is mad enough to arm himself for his misery, and to fight for his ruin. Impelled by an insatiable thirst of having, blinded by ambition still more insatiable, he renounces all the feelings of humanity, turns all his strength against himself, seeks mutual destruction, actually 3 destroys himself; and, after these periods of blood and carnage, when the smoke of glory has vanished, he contemplates with a sad eye, the earth wasted, the arts buried, nations scattered, the people weakened, his own happiness ruined, and his real power annihilated.   BUFFON.

IX.
INVOCATION TO THE GOD OF NATURE.

Almighty God! whose presence alone supports nature, and maintains the harmony of the laws of the universe : Thou, who, from the immoveable throne of the empyrean, seest the celestial spheres roll under thy feet, without shock or confusion : who, from the bosom of repose, reproducest every moment their immense movements, and alone governest, in profound peace, that infinite number of heavens and worlds; restore, restore at length tranquillity to the agitated earth! let it be silent at thy voice; let discord and war cease their proud clamours! God of goodness, author of all beings, thy paternal eye takes in 1 all the objects of the creation; but man is thy chosen being; thou hast illumined 2 his soul with a ray of thy immortal light : complete the measure of thy kindness by penetrating his heart with a ray of thy love: this divine sentiment, diffusing itself every where, will reconcile opposite natures; man will no longer dread the sight of man ; his hand will no longer wield the murderous steel 3; the devouring flames of war will no longer dry up 4 the

1 Rentrer.   2 De barbarie.   3 En effet.
1 Embrasser.   2 Eclairer.   3 Le fer..... armer sa main.   4. Tarir.

sources of population : the human species, now weakened, mu-
tilated, mowed down in the blossom, will spring anew 5 and mul-
tiply without number; nature, overwhelmed under the weight
of scourges 6, will soon re-assume, with a new life, its former
fruitfulness; and we, beneficent God, will second it, we will
cultivate it, we will contemplate it incessantly, that we may
every moment offer thee a new tribute of gratitude and admiration.   BUFFON.

X.

Happy they who are disgusted with 1 turbulent pleasures, and
know how to be contented 2 with the sweets of an innocent life!
Happy they who delight in being instructed 3, and who take a
pleasure 4 in storing their minds with knowledge! Wherever
adverse fortune may throw them, they always carry entertainment
with them ; and the disquiet which preys upon others, even in the
midst of pleasures, is unknown to those who can employ themselves in reading. Happy they who love to read, and are not like
me deprived of the ability. As these thoughts were passing in my
mind, I went into a gloomy forest, where I immediately perceived an old man holding a book in his hand. The forehead of
this sage was broad, bald, and a little wrinkled : a white beard
hung down to his girdle; his stature was tall and majestic; his
complexion still fresh and ruddy, his eyes lively and piercing,
his voice sweet, his words plain and charming. I never saw so
venerable an old man. He was a priest of Apollo, and officiated 5
in a marble temple, which the kings of Egypt had dedicated to
that God in this forest. The book which he held in his hand was
a collection of hymns in honour of the Gods. He accosted me in
a friendly manner, and we discoursed together. He related
things past so well, that they seemed present, and yet with such
brevity that his account never tired me. He foresaw the future
by his profound knowledge, which made him know men, and the
designs of which they are capable. With all this wisdom he was
cheerful and complaisant, and the sprightliest youth has not so
many graces as this man had at so advanced an age. He accordingly loved young men when they were teachable 6, and had a
taste for study and virtue.   FÉNÉLON.

XI.
THOUGHTS ON POETRY.

Wherever I went, I found that poetry was considered as the

5 Germer de nouveau. 6 Fléau.
1 Se dégoûter de. 2 Se contenter de. 3 S'instruire. 4 Se plaire.
5 Servir. 6 Docile.

(highest learning 1), and regarded with a veneration (somewhat approaching to 2) that which men would pay to angelic nature.

It yet fills me with wonder that, in almost all countries, the most ancient poets are considered as the best; whether (it be that 3) every kind of knowledge is an acquisition gradually attained, and poetry is a gift conferred at once; or that the first poetry of every nation surprised them as a novelty, and retained the credit by consent, which it received by accident at first; or whether, as the province 4 of poetry is to describe nature and passion, which are always the same, the first writers (took possession 5) of (the most striking objects for description 6), and (the most probable occurrences for fiction 7,) and left nothing to those that followed them, but transcription 8 of the same events, and new combinations 9 of the same images. Whatever be the reason, it is commonly observed, that the early writers are in possession of nature, and their followers 10 of art: that the first excel in strength and invention, and the latter in elegance and refinement.

I was desirous to add my name to this illustrious fraternity 11. I read all the poets of Persia and Arabia, and was able to repeat by memory the volumes that are suspended in the mosque of Mecca. But I soon found that no man was ever great by imitation. My desire of excellence 12 impelled 13 me to transfer 14 my attention to nature and to life 15. Nature was to be my subject, and men to be my auditors: I could never describe what I had not seen: I could not hope (to move those with delight or terror 16) whose interests and opinions I did not understand 17.

XII.

THE SAME SUBJECT CONTINUED.

Being now resolved to be a poet, I saw every thing (with a new purpose 18;) my sphere of attention was suddenly magnified: no kind of knowledge (was to be overlooked 19.) I ranged mountains and deserts for 20 images and resemblances, and (pictured upon my mind 21) every tree of the forest and flower of the valley. I observed with equal care the crags of the rock and the pinnacles of the palace. Sometimes I wandered along the mazes of the rivulet, and sometimes watched the changes of the summer-clouds. To a poet nothing can be useless. Whatever is beautiful, and

---

1 Partie la plus sublime de la littérature. 2 Qui tenoit de. 3 Cela vient de ce que. 4 But. 5 S'emparer. 6 Objets qui fournissoient les plus riches descriptions. 7 Evénemens qui prêtoient le plus à la fiction. 8 De copier. 9 Faire de nouvelles combinaisons. 10 Successeurs. 11 Famille. 12 Exceller. 13 Engager. 14 Reporter...sur. 15 Tableau de la vie. 16 Réveiller le plaisir ou la terreur dans ceux. 17 Ne connoître ni. 18 Sous un nouveau jour. 19 Je ne devois négliger. 20 Pour recueillir. 21 Pénétrer mon esprit du tableau de.

whatever·is dreadful, must be familiar to his imagination : he must (be conversant 22) with all that (is awfully vast or elegantly little 23). The plants of the garden, the animals of the wood, the minerals of the earth, and the meteors of the sky, must all concur to store his mind with inexhaustible variety ; for every idea is useful for the (enforcement or decoration 24) of moral or religious truth ; and he who knows most will have most power 25 of diversifying his scenes 26, and gratifying his; reader with remote allusions and unexpected instruction.

All the appearances of nature I was, therefore, careful to study 27,) and every country which I have surveyed has contributed something to my poetical powers.

In so wide a survey, interrupted the prince, you must surely have left much unobserved. I have lived, till now, within the circuit of these mountains, and yet cannot walk abroad without ·the sight of something which I had never beheld before or never heeded 28.

XIII.

THE SAME SUBJECT CONTINUED.

The business of a poet, said Imlac, is to examine, not the individual, but the species ; to remark general properties and (large appearances 29:) he does not number the streaks of the tulip, or describe the different shades in the verdure of the forest. He is to exhibit, in his portraits of nature, such prominent and striking features, as 30 recal the original to every mind ; and must neglect the minuter discriminations 31, which one may have remarked, and another neglected, for those characteristics 32 which are alike obvious 33 to vigilance 34 and carelessness 35.

But the knowledge of nature is only half 36 the task of a poet: he must be acquainted likewise with all the modes 37 of life. His character requires that he estimate 38 the happiness and misery of every condition : observe the power of all the passions, in all their combinations, and trace the changes 39 of the human mind, as they are modified by various institutions, and accidental influences of climate or custom ; from the sprightliness of infancy to the despondence of decrepitude. He must divest himself 40 of the prejudices of his age or country ; he must consider right and wrong 41

, 22 Bien connoître. 23 Étonne par sa grandeur, ou charme par son élégante petitesse. 24 Fortifier, ou embellir. 25 Ressources pour. 26 Tableau. 27 Etudier aveo soin toutes les, ete. 28 Remarquer. 29 Considérer les objets en grand. 50 De ees traits saillans et frappans qui·, etc. 51 Ces petits détails. 52 Pour s'appliquer à caractériser, etc., etc. 53 Frappe également. 34 Œil observateur. 35 Esprit insouciant. 36 The half of. 57 Tous les différens aspects. 38 Apprécier. 39 Suivre les vicissitudes. 40 Se dépouiller. 41 Ce qui est juste ou injuste.

in their abstracted and invariable state 42; be must disregard present laws and opinions, and rise to general and transcendental truths, which will always be the same; he must, therefore, (content himself with the slow progress of his name 43,) contemn the applause-of his own time, and commit his claims to the justice of posterity. He must write as the interpreter of nature, and the legislator of mankind, and consider himself as presiding 44 over the thoughts and manners of future generations, as a being superior to time and place.

His labour is not yet at an end: he must know many languages and many sciences; and, that his style may be worthy of his thoughts, he must, by incessant practice, familiarize himself to every delicacy of speech and grace of harmony.   S. JOHNSON.

XIV.

First follow nature, and your judgment frame
By her just standard, which is still the same:
Unerring nature, still divinely bright,
One clear, unchang'd, and universal light,
Life, force, and beauty, must to all impart;   1
At once the source, and end, and test of art.   2
Art, from that fund, each just supply provides;
Works without show, and without pomp presides;
In some fair body thus th' informing soul
With spirits feeds, with vigour fills the whole,
Each motion guides, and every nerve sustains
Itself unseen, but in th' effect remains.   3
Some, to whom heav'n in wit has been profuse,
Want as much more to turn it to its use:
For wit and judgment often are at strife,
Tho' meant each other's aid, like man and wife.   4
'Tis more to guide, than spur the muse's steed;
Restrain his fury, than provoke his speed: 5
The winged courser, like a gen'rous horse,
Shows most true mettle, when you check its course.   6

                                                          POPE.

42 Abstraction faite de ces divers préjugés.   43 Se résiguer à voir son nom percer difficilement.   44 Influer.

1 Light, clear, immutable, and universal nature, which never errs, and shines always with a divine splendour, must impart to all she does, life, force, and beauty. •

2 She is at once the source, etc.

3 So in a fair body, unseen itself, but always sensible by its effects, the soul continually acting, feeds the whole with spirits, fills it with vigour, guides every motion of it, and sustains every nerve.

4 Some to whom heaven has given wit with profusion, want as much yet to know the use they ought to make of it; for wit and judgment though made, like man and wife, to aid each other, are often in opposition.

5 It is more difficult to guide than spur the courser of the muses, and to restrain its ardour than provoke its impetuosity.

6 The winged courser is like a generous horse: the more we strive to stop it in its rapid course, the more it shows unconquerable vigour.

2 O

EXAMPLES OF PHRASES ON THE PRINCIPAL DIFFICULTIES OF THE
FRENCH LANGUAGE.

Sur les Collectifs Partitifs.	On the Collective Partitives.
La plupart des fruits verts sont d'un goût austère.	The greater part of green fruit is of a harsh taste.
La plupart des gens ne se conduisent que par intérêt.	The major part of society are guided only by interest.
La plupart du monde se trompe.	The greater part of mankind live in error.
Il méprise par philosophie les honneurs que la plupart du monde recherche.	As a true philosopher he despises those honours which mankind in general court.
Il devoit me fournir tant d'arbres, mais j'en ai rejeté la moitié qui ne valoit rien.	He was to furnish me so many trees, but I refused half of them which were good for nothing.
Un grand nombre de spectateurs ajoutoit à la beauté du spectacle.	A considerable number of spectators added to the splendor of the scene.
Toutes sortes de livres ne sont pas également bons.	Every kind of books are not equally good.
Beaucoup de personnes se sont présentées.	Many people presented themselves.
Bien des personnes se font des principes à leur fantaisie.	Many persons form principles to themselves, according to their fancy.

Sur quelques Verbes qu'on ne peut conjuguer avec Avoir, sans faire des barbarismes.	On some Verbs which cannot be conjugated with the verb Avoir, without making barbarous phrases.
Il lui est échu une succession du chef de sa femme.	An estate fell to him in right of his wife.
Il est bien déchu de son crédit.	He has lost much of his credit.
Ne sommes-nous pas convenus du prix?	Have we not agreed about the price?
N'est-il pas intervenu dans cette affaire, comme il l'avoit promis?	Did he not interfere in that affair as he had promised?
Il est survenu à l'improviste.	He came up unawares.
La neige, qui est tombée ce matin, a adouci le temps.	The snow which fell this morning has softened the weather.
Que de neige il est tombé ce matin!	How much snow has fallen this morning!
Toutes les dents lui sont tombées.	All his teeth have fallen out.
Ce propos n'est pas tombé à terre.	That remark was not allowed to escape.
Êtes-vous allé voir votre ami?	Have you been to see your friend?
Ils sont arrivés à midi, et sont repartis de suite.	They arrived at noon and set out again immediately.
Ces fleurs sont à peine écloses.	These flowers are scarcely blown.

Il est né de parens vertueux, qui n'ont rien négligé pour son éducation.

He was born of virtuous parents, who bestowed on him the best education.

Mademoiselle votre sœur est-elle rentrée?

Is your sister returned?

Madame votre mère n'est-elle pas encore venue?

Is not your mother come yet?

Sur les mots de Quantité.

On Words of Quantity.

Il a beaucoup d'esprit, mais encore plus d'amour-propre.

He has a great deal of sense, but still more vanity.

Il a assez d'argent pour ses menus plaisirs.

He has sufficient pocket-money.

Il y avoit bien du monde à l'Opéra.

There were a great many people at the Opera.

Il y avoit hier au Parc je ne sais combien de gens.

There were I do not know how many people in the Park yesterday.

Il boit autant d'eau que de vin.

He drinks as much water as wine.

Il a tant d'amis qu'il ne manquera de rien.

He has so many friends that he will want for nothing.

Personne n'y a plus d'intérét que lui.

Nobody has more interest there than he.

Il n'a pas plus d'esprit qu'il n'en faut.

He is not overburdened with sense.

Trop de loisir perd souvent la jeunesse.

Too much leisure time is frequently the destruction of youth.

J'y ai bien moins d'intérét que vous.

I am much less concerned in it than you.

Sur les Pronoms Personnels.

On the Personal Pronouns.

Sors et te retire.

Go out and retire.

Cours vite et ne t'amuse point.

Go quick and do not loiter.

Il dit aujourd'hui une chose, et demain il se démentira.

He advances a thing to-day, and will contradict himself to-morrow.

Il s'est démenti lui-méme.

He has contradicted himself.

La jeunesse est naturellement emportée; elle a besoin de quelque entrave qui la retienne.

Youth is naturally hasty, it needs some bridle to restrain it.

Il ne peut voir personne dans la prospérité sans lui porter envie.

He can see the prosperity of nobody, without envying them.

Ce que vous me dites est une énigme pour moi.

What you tell me is a perfect riddle to me.

C'est un homme extréme en tout; il aime et il hait avec fureur.

He is a man that carries every thing to excess; he is alike violent in his love and in his hatred.

Si vous n'y avez jamais été, je vous y mènerai.

If you have never been there, I will take you.

Je l'ai connu doux et modeste; il s'est bien gâté dans le commerce de ses nouveaux amis.

I knew him when he was mild and modest; he has been much corrupted by associating with his new acquaintances.

Elle n'est pas encore revenue du saisissement que lui causa cette nouvelle.

She is not yet recovered from the consternation into which that intelligence threw her.

Il menace de l'exterminer, lui et toute sa race.

He threatens to exterminate him and all his family.

Si vous n'avez que faire de ce livre-là, prêtez-le-moi.

If you have done with this book, lend it me.

Je lui avois envoyé un diamant, il l'a refusé, je le lui ai renvoyé.

I had sent him a diamond, and he refused it, but I sent him it back again.

Il apprend facilement et oublie de même.

He learns easily and forgets the same.

Je lui pardonne facilement d'avoir voulu se faire auteur; mais je ne saurois lui pardonner toutes les puérilités dont il a farci son livre.

I can easily pardon him for having attempted to turn author; but I cannot pardon him all the absurdities with which he has filled his book.

Je me plains à vous de vous-même.

I complain to you of yourself.

Si vous ne voulez pas être pour lui, au moins ne soyez pas contre.

If you will not be for him, at least do not be against him.

Quand sera-ce que vous viendrez nous voir?

When will you come to see us?

Sur soi, lui, soi-même et lui-même.

On *soi, lui, soi-même* and *lui-même.*

Quand on a pour soi le témoignage de sa conscience, on est bien fort.

The approbation of our conscience imparts great courage.

L'estime de toute la terre ne sert de rien à un homme qui n'a pas le témoignage de sa conscience pour lui.

The good opinion of the whole world is of no use to a man who has not the approbation of his own conscience.

Un homme fait mille fautes, parce qu'il ne fait point de réflexions sur lui.

A man commits a thousand faults, because he does not reflect on future consequences.

On fait mille fautes, quand on ne fait aucune réflexion sur soi.

We commit a thousand faults, when we neglect to reflect on ourselves.

Il aime mieux dire du mal de lui, que de n'en point parler.

He had rather speak ill of himself than not talk of himself at all.

L'égoïste aimera mieux dire du mal de soi, que de n'en point parler.

The egotist prefers speaking ill of himself rather than not be the subject of his own conversation.

On a souvent besoin d'un plus petit que soi.

We frequently want the assistance of one who is below ourselves.

Un prince a souvent besoin de beaucoup de gens plus petits que lui.

A prince frequently needs the assistance of many persons inferior to himself.

C'est un bon moyen de s'élever soi-même, que d'exalter ses pareils; et un homme adroit s'élève ainsi lui-même.

It is an excellent method of exalting ourselves to exalt our equals, and a man of address by this means exalts himself.

Sur les Pronoms Relatifs.

Il n'y a rien de si capable d'efféminer le courage que l'oisiveté et les delices.

Il faut empêcher que la division, qui est dans cette famille, n'éclate.

Il y a bien des évenemens que l'on suppose se passer pendant les entr'actes.

Je le trouvai qui s'habilloit.

Qui le tirera de cet embarras, le tirera d'une grande misère.

Ceux-là sont véritablement heureux, qui croient l'être.

Il n'y a que la vertu qui puisse rendre un homme heureux en cette vie.

Il n'y a règle si générale qui n'ait son exception.

C'est un orateur qui se possède et qui ne se trouble jamais.

Il n'y a pas dans le cœur humain de replis que Dieu ne connoisse.

On n'a trouvé que quelques fragmens du grand ouvrage qu'il avoit promis.

La faute, que vous avez faite, est plus importante que vous ne pensez.

Les premières démarches qu'on fait dans le monde, ont beaucoup d'influence sur le reste de la vie.

Cette farce est une des plus risibles qu'on ait encore vues.

Amassez-vous des trésors. que les vers et la rouille ne puissent point gâter, et que les voleurs ne puissent point derober.

L'incertitude où nous sommes de ce qui doit arriver, fait que nous ne saurions prendre des mesures justes.

Je m'étonne qu'il ne voie pas le danger où il est.

L'homme dont vous parlez n'est plus ici.

Celui de qui je tiens cette nouvelle ne vous est pas connu.

Celui à qui ce beau château appartient, ne l'habite presque jamais.

On the Relative Pronouns.

Nothing is so calculated to enervate the mind as idleness and pleasure.

The dissention in that family must be prevented from becoming public.

There are many events in a piece which are supposed to happen between the acts.

I found him dressing.

Whoever extricates him from this difficulty will relieve him from much distress.

Those are really happy who think themselves so.

Virtue alone can render a man happy in this life.

There is no rule so general but it admits of exceptions.

He is an orator who is master of himself, and who is never embarrassed.

There is no recess of the human heart but God perceives it.

Only some fragments of the great work he had promised have been found.

The error you have committed is of more consequence than you imagine.

The first steps we take on entering the world have considerable influence on the rest of our lives.

That farce is one of the most truly comic that ever was seen.

Lay up for yourselves treasures which neither moth nor rust can corrupt, and which thieves cannot steal.

Our uncertainty as to what shall happen, makes us incapable of properly providing against it.

I am astonished he does not see the danger he is in.

The man whom you are speaking of is not here now.

The person from whom I received the intelligence is not known to you.

The proprietor of that beautiful seat seldom resides there.

Ce sont des événemens auxquels il faut bien se soumettre.
C'est ce à quoi vous ne pensez guère.

These are events to which we must submit.
It is what you seldom think of.

Sur les Pronoms Démonstratifs.

Ne point reconnoître la divinité, c'est renoncer à toutes les lumières de la raison.
Mentir, c'est mépriser Dieu et craindre les hommes.
Il y a des épidémies morales, et ce sont les plus dangereuses.

Je crois que ce que vous dites, est bien éloigné de ce que vous pensez.
Les hommes n'aiment ordinairement que ceux qui les flattent.
Celui qui persuade à un autre de faire un crime, n'est guère moins coupable que celui qui le commet.
Penser ainsi, c'est s'aveugler soi-même.
Ce qu'on rapporte de lui est inconcevable.
Ce qui m'afflige, c'est de voir le triomphe du crime.
Connoissez-vous la jeune Emilie? c'est une enfant dont tout le monde dit du bien.
Imitez en tout votre amie; elle est douce, appliquée, honnête et compatissante.

On the Demonstrative Pronouns.

Not to acknowledge the divinity, is totally to renounce the light of reason.
To lie is to despise God and to fear man.
There are moral contagious diseases, and these are the most dangerous.
What you advance is, I think, widely different from your sentiments.
Men in general love only those who flatter them.
He who persuades another to the commission of a crime, is hardly less guilty than he who commits it.
To think in this manner is to be wilfully blind.
The reports concerning him are hardly conceivable.
What distresses me is to see guilt triumphant.
Do you know little Emily? she is a child of whom every body speaks well.
Imitate your friend in every thing; she is mild, assiduous, polite and compassionate.

Sur le Verbe *avoir* employé à l'impersonnel.

Remarque. Quand le verbe avoir s'emploie à l'impersonnel, c'est dans le sens d'être, et alors il se joint toujours avec y.
Il y a un an que je ne vous ai vu.
Y a-t-il des nouvelles?
Non, il n'y en a pas, du moins que je sache.
N'y a-t-il pas cinquante-quatre milles de Londres à Brighton?
Il y avoit déjà beaucoup de monde lorsque j'arrivai.

On the Verb *avoir*, to have, employed impersonally.

When the verb *avoir* is used impersonally, it signifies *être*, to be, and in this sense it is always accompanied by the adverb *y*.
It is a twelvemonth since I saw you.
Is there any news?
No, there is none, at least that I know.
Is not it fifty-four miles from London to Brighton?
There were already a great many people when I arrived.

Il n'y avoit hier presque personne au Parc. | There was hardly any body in the Park yesterday.

Y avoit-il de grands débats? | Were there violent debates?

N'y avoit-il pas beaucoup de curieux? | Were there not many curious people?

Je l'avois vu il y avoit à peine vingt-quatre heures. | I had seen him scarcely four-and-twenty hours before.

Il n'y avoit pas deux jours qu'il avoit dîné chez moi. | He had dined with me not two days before.

Y avoit-il si long-temps que vous ne l'aviez vu. | Was it so long since you had seen him?

Il y eut hier un bal chez M. un tel. | There was yesterday a ball at Mr. A's.

Il n'y eut pas hier de spectacle. | There was no play yesterday.

Y eut-il beaucoup de confusion et de désordre? | Was there a great deal of confusion and disorder?

N'y eut-il pas un beau feu d'artifice? | Were there not handsome fireworks?

Il y a eu aujourd'hui une foule immense à la promenade. | There was an immense crowd to-day at the public walks.

Il n'y a pas eu de bal comme on l'avoit annoncé. | There has not been any ball as had been mentioned.

Est-il vrai qu'il y a eu un duel? | Is it true that there has been a duel?

N'y a-t-il pas eu dans sa conduite un peu trop d'emportement? | Was there not rather too much hastiness in his behaviour?

Quand il y eut eu une explication, les esprits se calmèrent. | After there had been an explanation, tranquillity was restored.

N'y avoit-il pas eu un plus grand nombre de spectateurs? | Was not there a greater number of spectators?

Il y aura demain un simulacre de combat naval. | To-morrow there will be the representation of a sea-fight.

Il n'y aura aucun de vous. | There will be none of you.

Y aura-t-il une bonne récolte cette année? | Will there be a good harvest this year?

N'y aura-t-il pas quelqu'un de votre famille? | Will not there be some of your family?

A coup sûr il y aura eu bien du désordre? | There must certainly have been much disorder.

Sur cent personnes, il n'y en aura pas eu dix de satisfaites. | Out of a hundred persons there will not have been ten satisfied.

Y aura-t-il eu un bon soupé? | Will there have been a good supper?

N'y aura-t-il pas eu de mécontens? | Will there not have been some dissatisfied?

Il y auroit de la malhonnêteté dans ce procédé. | Such a step would have been ungenteel.

Il n'y auroit pas grand mal à cela. | There would be no great harm in that.

Y auroit-il quelqu'un assez hardi pour l'attaquer. | Would there be any one bold enough to attack him?

N'y auroit-il pas quelqu'un assez | Would there be nobody kind *charitable pour l'avertir de ce qu'on dit de lui?*

Il y auroit eu *de l'imprudence à cela.*

Il n'y auroit pas eu tant de mésintelligence, si l'on m'en avoit cru.

Il n'y auroit pas eu dix personnes.

Y auroit-il eu de l'inconvénient.

N'y auroit-il pas eu de jaloux pour le traverser dans ses projets?

Je ne crois pas qu'il y ait un spectacle plus magnifique.

Je désirerois qu'il y eut moins de fausseté dans le commerce de la vie.

Je n'ai pas ouï dire qu'il y ait eu hier des nouvelles du continent.

Auriez-vous cru qu'il y eût eu tant de personnes compromises dans cette affaire?

enough to acquaint him with what is said of him?

There would have been some imprudence in that.

There would not have been so great a misunderstanding had I been believed.

There would not have been ten persons.

Would there have been any inconvenience?

Would there not have been some envious person to thwart him in his designs?

I do not think there can be a more superb spectacle.

I wish there had been less duplicity in the concerns of life.

I have not heard that there was any news from the continent yesterday.

Could you have thought so many persons would have been exposed in that affair?

Phrases diverses.

Sa vie, ses actions, ses paroles, son air même et sa démarche, tout prêche, tout édifie en lui.

On craignoit qu'il n'arrivât quelque desordre dans l'assemblée, mais toutes choses s'y passèrent fort doucement.

La vigne et le lierre s'entortillent autour des ormes.

On ne disconvient point qu'il ne soit brave, mais il est un peu trop fanfaron.

Le cadet est riche, mais l'aîné l'est encore davantage.

Le ciel est couvert de nuages, et l'orage est prêt à fondre.

Après qu'il eut franchi les Alpes avec ses troupes, il entra en Italie.

La frugalité rend les corps plus sains et plus robustes.

Ce discours est peut-être un des plus beaux morceaux d'éloquence qu'il y ait jamais eu.

C'est un homme qui aime la liberté; il ne se gene pour qui que ce soit.

Promiscuous phrases.

His life, his actions, his very look and deportment, every thing in him instructs and edifies.

It was apprehended some disorder would take place in the assembly, but every thing went off very quietly.

The vine and the ivy twist round the elms.

They do not deny that he is brave, but he boasts rather too much.

The youngest is rich, but the eldest is still more so.

The sky is covered with clouds, and the storm is preparing to burst.

After having crossed the Alps with his troops, he entered Italy.

Temperance imparts an increase of health and strength to the body.

This speech is perhaps one of the finest pieces of eloquence that was ever pronounced.

He is a man fond of liberty; he will be constrained by nobody.

Il est plus haut que moi de deux doigts.
He is taller than me by two inches.

Irez-vous vous exposer à la barbarie et à l'inhospitalité de ces peuples?
Will you go and expose yourself to the barbarity and inhospitality of those nations?

À la longue, les erreurs disparoissent, et la vérité surnage.
In time errors vanish and truth survives.

Si vous le prenez avec moi sur ce ton de fierté, je serai aussi fier que vous.
If you treat me with that haughtiness, I can be as haughty as you.

C'est |un homme rigide qui ne pardonne rien ni aux autres ni à lui-même.
He is a stern character, who pardons nothing either in himself or others.

Les uns montent, les autres descendent; ainsi va la roue de la fortune.
Some mount, others descend; thus goes the wheel of fortune.

Je ne vois rien de solide dans tout ce que vous me proposez.
I see nothing certain in all you propose to me.

L'art n'a jamais rien produit de plus beau.
It is one of the finest productions of art.

Lequel est-ce des deux qui a tort?
Which of the two is in the wrong?

On aime quelquefois la trahison, mais on hait toujours les traîtres.
We sometimes love the treason, but we always hate the traitor.

Continuation.

Continuation.

L'éléphant se sert de sa trompe pour prendre et pour enlever tout ce qu'il veut.
The elephant makes use of his trunk to take and lift whatever he pleases.

Plus j'examine cette personne, plus je crois l'avoir vue quelque part.
The more I look at that person, the more I think I have seen him somewhere.

La nuit vint, de façon que je fus contraint de me retirer.
Night came on, so that I was obliged to retire.

Il faut vivre de façon qu'on ne fasse tort à personne.
We must live in such a manner as to injure nobody.

Elle sut qu'on attaquoit son mari; elle courut aussitôt tout éperdue pour le secourir.
She knew her husband was attacked, and in a state of distraction ran to his assistance.

Je trouvai ses parens tout éplorés.
I found his relations all in tears.

Cet arbre pousse ses branches toutes droites.
The branches of that tree grow quite straight.

J'en ai encore la mémoire toute fraîche.
It is still quite fresh in my memory.

Il a voulu faire voir par cet essai qu'il pouvoit réussir en quelque chose de plus grand.
He wished to shew by that attempt that he could succeed in an enterprise of more consequence.

Il fut blessé au front, et mourut de cette blessure.
He was wounded in the forehead, and died of his wound.

Ces chevaux prirent le mors aux dents et entraînèrent le carrosse.
Those horses ran away with the carriage.

C'est un homme qui compose sans chaleur ni imagination : tout ce qu'il écrit est froid et plat.

He is a man that writes without the least warmth or animation : all his productions are cold and insipid.

Ce bâtiment a plus de profondeur que de largeur.

That building is deeper than it is broad.

Cet homme est un prodige de savoir, de science, de valeur, d'esprit et de mémoire.

THan man is a prodigy of knowledge, judgment, courage, sense and memory.

Il est attaché à l'un et à l'autre, mais plus à l'un qu'à l'autre.

He is attached to both, but to one more than the other.

Ils ont bien de l'air l'un de l'autre.

They very much resemble each other.

Si l'on ruine cet homme-là, le contre-coup retombera sur vous.

If that man is ruined, his misfortune will recoil upon you.

Il seroit mort, si on ne l'eût assisté avec soin.

He would have died if he had not been kindly assisted.

Ce poème seroit parfait, si les incidens, qui le font languir, n'interrompoient la continuité de l'action.

That would be a perfect poem, if the incidents, which give a heaviness to it, did not break the connexion of the subject.

Continuation.

Continuation.

Quand je le voudrois, je ne le pourrois pas.

If I were disposed, I could not do it.

Je serai toujours votre ami, quand même vous ne le voudriez pas.

I will always be your friend, even though you should not wish it.

Quand vous auriez réussi, que vous en seroit-il revenu?

Had you even succeeded, what were you to have derived from it?

Quand on découvriroit votre démarche, on ne pourroit la blâmer.

Should the steps you have taken be discovered, they could not be blamed.

Quand vous auriez consulté quelqu'un sur votre mariage, vous n'auriez pas mieux réussi.

Had you consulted somebody about your marriage, you could not have succeeded better.

Le tonnerre et l'éclair ne sont sensibles que par la propagation du bruit et de la lumière jusqu'à l'œil et à l'oreille.

Thunder and lightning are only perceptible by the transmission of sound and light to the ear and eye.

Le langage de la prose est plus simple et moins figuré que celui des vers.

Prose language is much more simple and less figurative than poetic.

Le commencement de son discours est toujours assez sage; mais, dans la suite, à force de vouloir s'élever, il se perd dans les nues : on ne sait plus ni ce qu'on voit, ni ce qu'on entend.

The beginning of his speech is always tolerably sensible : but afterwards, by affecting the sublime, he loses himself, and we no longer understand either what we see or hear.

C'est une faute excusable dans un autre homme, mais à un homme aussi sage que lui, elle ne se peut pardonner.

This fault would be excusable in another man, but in a man of his sense it is unpardonable.

Il ne suffit pas de paroître honnête homme, il faut l'être.

It is not enough to seem an honest man, we must be so.

Il nous a reçus avec bonté, et nous a écoutés avec patience.

He received us with kindness and heard us patiently.

Tout y est si bien peint, qu'on croit voir ce qu'il a écrit.

Every thing in it is so well delineated you think you see what he describes.

On ne pense rien de vous, qui ne vous soit glorieux.

They think nothing of you but what is to your honour.

Les eaux de citernes ne sont que des eaux de pluies ramassées.

Cistern water is generally only rain water collected.

S'il n'est pas fort riche, du moins a-t-il de quoi vivre honnétement.

If he is not rich, at least he has enough to live upon respectably.

Quel quantième du mois avons-nous?

What day of the month is it?

Il lui tarde qu'il ne soit majeur, il compte les jours et les mois.

He longs to be of age, and counts the days and months.

Des qualités excellentes, jointes à de rares talens, font le parfait mérite.

Excellent qualities joined to distinguished talents constitute perfect merit.

Il a une mauvaise qualité, c'est qu'il ne sauroit garder un secret.

He has one bad quality, he cannot keep a secret.

Modèles de phrases dans lesquelles on doit faire usage de l'article.

Examples of phrases in which the article is used.

L'homme *est sujet à bien des* vicissitudes.

Man is liable to a variety of changes.

Les hommes *d'un vrai génie sont* rares.

Men of real genius are scarce.

Les hommes à imagination *sont rarement heureux.*

Men of a visionary character are seldom happy.

L'homme, *dont vous parlez, est* un de mes amis.

The man you speak of is a friend of mine.

La vie *est un mélange de biens et de maux.*

Life is a compound of good and evil.

Là perfection *en tout genre est le* but auquel on doit tendre.

Perfection in every thing ought to be our object.

La beauté, les grâces *et* l'esprit, *sont des avantages bien précieux, quand ils sont relevés par la modestie.*

Beauty, gracefulness, and wit, are valuable endowments when heightened by modesty.

Voilà des tableaux *d'une grande beauté.*

These are very beautiful pictures.

Faites-vous des principes, *dont vous ne vous écartiez jamais.*

Establish rules for yourself, and never deviate from them.

Cet arbre porte des fruits excellens.

This tree bears very excellent fruit.

Ces raisons *sont des* conjectures bien foibles.

These reasons are very idle conjectures.

Servez-vous des termes *établis par l'usage.*

Use the expressions established by custom.

On doit éviter *l'air de* l'affectation.

We ought to avoid the appearance of affectation.

Le Jupiter de *Phidias étoit d'une grande beauté.*

The Jupiter of Phidias was extremely beautiful.

Continuation des mêmes phrases. | *The same phrases continued.*

La mémoire est le trésor de l'esprit, *le fruit* de l'attention *et* de la réflexion.

Memory is the treasure of the mind, the result of attention and reflection.

J'achetai hier des gravures *précieuses et rares.*

I yesterday bought some valuable and scarce engravings.

La France *est le plus beau pays* de l'*Europe.*

France is the finest country in Europe.

L'intérêt de l'Allemagne *étoit opposé à celui* de la Russie.

The German interest was contrary to the Russian.

La longueur de l'Angleterre *du nord au sud est de* 360 *milles, et sa largeur de l'est à l'ouest est de* 300.

The length of England from north to south is 360 miles, and in breadth from east to west is 300.

Il arrive de la Chine, du Japon, *et* des Indes Orientales, *etc.*

He comes from China, Japan, and the East Indies.

Il arrive de l'Amérique, de la Barbade, de la Jamaïque, *etc.*

He comes from America, Barbadoes, Jamaica, etc.

Il vient de la Flandre *Françoise.*

He comes from French Flanders.

Il s'est établi dans la province *de Middlesex.*

He has settled in the county of Middlesex.

Des petits-maîtres *sont des êtres insupportables dans la société.*

Coxcombs are unsufferable beings in society.

C'est l'opinion des nouveaux philosophes.

It is the opinion of the new philosophers.

Elle a bien de la grâce *dans tout ce qu'elle fait.*

She does every thing most gracefully.

Cette étoffe se vend une guinée l'aune.

This stuff sells at a guinea the ell.

Ce vin coûte 70 *livres sterlings* la pièce.

This wine costs seventy pounds the hogshead.

Modèles de phrases dans lesquelles on ne doit pas faire usage de l'article.

Examples of phrases in which the Article is omitted.

Nos connoissances doivent être tireés de principes *évidens.*

Our knowledge ought to be derived from evident principles.

Cet arbre porte d'excellens fruits.

This tree produces excellent fruit.

Ces raisons sont de foibles conjectures.

These reasons are idle conjectures.

Evitez tout ce qui a un air d'affectation.

Avoid whatever bears the appearance of affectation.

Ces exemples peuvent servir de modèles.

These examples may serve as models.

Il a une grande présence d'esprit.

He has great presence of mind.

La mémoire de raison *et* d'esprit *est plus utile que les autres sortes* de mémoire.

The memory of reason and sense is more useful than any other kind of memory.

Peu de personnes *réfléchissent sur la rapidité de la vie.*

Few people reflect on the rapidity of life.

Que d'événemens *inconcevables se sont succédés les uns aux autres!*

How many inconceivable events have followed in succession!

Il y a plus d'esprit, *mais moins* de connoissances, *dans ce siècle que dans le siècle dernier.*

There's more wit, but less knowledge, in this age than in the last.

On ne vit jamais autant d'effronterie.

So much assurance never was met with.

Je pris hier beaucoup de peine *pour rien.*

I took a great deal of trouble yesterday about nothing.

Candia est une des îles les plus agréables de la Méditerranée.

Candia is one of the most agreeable islands in the Mediterranean.

Il arrive de Perse, d'Italie, d'Espagne, etc.

He comes from Persia, Italy, Spain, etc.

Il est revenu de Suisse, d'Allemagne, *etc.*

He is returned from Switzerland, Germany, etc.

Les vins de France *seront chers cette année; les vignes ont coulé.*

French wines will be dear this year; the vines have been blasted.

L'empire d'Allemagne *est composé de grands et de petits états.*

The German empire is composed of great and small states.

Les chevaux d'Angleterre *sont excellens.*

The English horses are excellent.

Après mon départ de Suisse, *je me retirai à Rome.*

After leaving Switzerland, I retired to Rome.

Continuation des mêmes phrases.

Continuation of the same phrases.

Vous trouverez ce passage page 120, livre *premier,* chapitre *dix.*

You will find this passage in page 120, first book, chapter tenth.

Il s'est retiré en Angleterre.

He has retired to England.

Il vit dans sa retraite en vrai philosophe.

He lives in his retreat like a real philosopher.

Quand il réfléchit sur sa conduite, il en eut honte.

When he reflected on his conduct, he was ashamed of it.

C'est un homme qui cherche fortune.

He is a man that seeks to make a fortune.

Il entend malice *à tout.*

He puts a malicious construction on every thing.

Ne portez envie *à personne.*

Envy nobody.

Si vous promettez, tenez parole.

If you promise, keep your word.

Dans les affaires importantes ne vous décidez jamais sans prendre conseil.

In matters of consequence never decide without advice.

Courage, soldats, *tenons ferme; la victoire est à nous.*

Cheer up, soldiers, let us continue firm; the day is our own.

Cette femme n'a ni grâce *ni* beauté.

This woman is destitute both of grace and beauty.

Monseigneur le duc de, etc. prince *du sang, alla hier à la campagne.*

The duke of, etc, a prince of the blood, went yesterday into the country.

Montrer tant de foiblesse, c'est n'être pas homme.

To shew so much weakness is not acting like a man.

Cet homme est une espèce de misanthrope, *dont les brusqueries sont quelquefois très-plaisantes.*

This man is a kind of misanthropist, whose oddities are sometimes comical.

L'ananas est une sorte de fruit *très-commun aux Antilles.*

The pine-apple is a kind of fruit very common in the Antilles.

C'est un genre de vie *qui ne me plaît point.*	It is a kind of life that is not agreeable to me,

---

Continuation des mêmes phrases.	*The same sentences continued.*
Cette dame *plaît à tout le monde par son honnêteté et sa douceur.*	This lady pleases every one by her good breeding and mildness.
Tout homme *a des défauts plus ou moins sensibles.*	Every man has defects more or less obvious.
Cette conduite *augmentoit* chaque jour *le nombre de ses amis.*	This behaviour daily increased the number of his friends.
Tous les biens nous viennent de Dieu.	Every blessing comes from God.
Vénus *étoit la déesse de la beauté, et la mère de l'amour et des grâces.*	Venus was the goddess of beauty, and the mother of love and the graces.
Selon les païens, Jupiter *étoit le premier des dieux.*	According to the Heathens, Jupiter was the first of the gods.
Apollon *étoit frère jumeau de Diane.*	Apollo was twin brother to Diana.
Rubens *a été un grand peintre.*	Rubens was a great painter.
Homère *et* Virgile *sont les deux plus grands poètes épiques.*	Homer and Virgil are the two greatest epic poets.
Londres *est la plus-belle ville que je connoisse.*	London is the finest city that I know.
L'eau de rivière *est douce, et l'eau* de mer *est salée.*	River water is sweet, and sea water is salt.
C'est un excellent poisson de mer.	It is an excellent sea-fish.
Voilà une superbe table de marbre.	There is a superb marble table.
L'eau de Seine *est celle qu'on préfère à Paris.*	The water of the Seine is preferred at Paris.
Pauvreté *n'est pas vice.*	Poverty is not a vice.
Citoyens, étrangers, grands, peuples, *se sont montrés sensibles à cette perte.*	Citizens, strangers, grandees, people, have shewn themselves sensible of this loss.

Modèles de phrases sur le pronom *Le.*	*Forms of phrases upon the pronoun* Le.
Est-ce là votre opinion? *— ne doutez point que ce ne* la *soit.*	Is that your opinion?—do not question it.
Sont-ce là vos domestiques?—*oui, ce* les *sont.*	Are those your servants?—yes, they are.
Mesdames, *êtes-vous les* étrangères *qu'on m'a annoncées?—oui, nous* les *sommes.*	Ladies, are you the strangers that have been announced to me?—yes, we are.
Madame, *êtes-vous* la malade *pour laquelle on m'a appelé?—oui, je* la *suis.*	Madam, are you the sick person, for whom I have been called?—yes, I am.
Madame, *êtes-vous* la mère de *cet enfant?—oui, je* la *suis.*	Madam, are you the mother of this child?—yes, I am.
Mesdames, *êtes-vous* contentes de *cette musique?—oui, nous les* sommes.	Ladies, are you pleased with this music?—yes, we are.

Elle est malheureuse, *et je crains bien qu'elle ne le soit toute la vie.* | She is unhappy, and I much fear she will continue so for life.

Madame, êtes-vous mère?—*oui, je le suis.* | Madam, are you a mother?—yes, I am.

Madame, êtes-vous malade? — *oui, je le suis.* | Madam, are you sick?—yes, I am.

Madame, depuis quel temps êtes-vous mariée?—*je le suis depuis un an.* | Madam, how long have you been married?—a year.

Y a-t-il long-temps que vous êtes arrivée? — *je le suis depuis quinze jours.* | Is it long since you arrived? — a fortnight.

Aristote croyoit que le monde étoit de toute éternité, mais Platon ne le croyoit pas. | Aristotle believed the world to have been from all eternity, but Plato did not.

Quoique cette femme montre plus de fermeté que les autres, elle n'est pas pour cela la *moins affligée.* | Although this woman shows more resolution than the others, she is nevertheless not the least afflicted.

Cette femme a l'art de répandre des larmes dans le-temps même qu'elle est le *moins affligée.* | This woman has the art of shedding tears, even when she is least afflicted.

Modèles de phrases sur les différentes règles du participe passé. | *Forms of phrases upon the different rules of the participle past.*

La nouvelle pièce *a-t-elle été* applaudie? | Did the new piece meet with applause?

Vos parens y seront-ils arrivés *à temps?* | Will your relations arrive there in time?

Elle s'est donné *de belles robes.* | She has given herself fine gowns.

Elles nous ont apporté *de superbes œillets.* | They have brought us beautiful pinks.

Cette ruse ne lui a pas réussi. | He has not succeeded in this stratagem.

La vie tranquille que j'ai menée *depuis dix ans, a beaucoup contribué à me faire oublier mes malheurs.* | The quiet life I have led these ten years has greatly contributed to make me forget my misfortunes.

Les lettres *que j'ai* reçues, *m'ont beaucoup* affligé. | The letters I have received have afflicted me greatly.

Que de peines *vous vous êtes* données! | What a deal of trouble you have given yourself!

Quelle tâche *vous-vous êtes* imposée! | What a task you have imposed on yourself!

C'est une satire *que j'ai* retrouvée *dans mes papiers.* | It is a satire that I have again met with in my papers.

Les lettres qu'a écrites *Pline le jeune, quelque agréables qu'elles soient, se ressentent néanmoins un peu de la décadence du goût parmi les Romains,* | The letters which the younger Pliny has written, however agreeable they may be, savour nevertheless a little of the decline of taste among the Romans.

Je ne serois pas entré avec vous dans tous ces détails de grammaire, si je ne les avois crus nécessaires. | I would not have entered into these grammatical details with you, had I not thought them necessary.

L'Egypte s'étoit rendue célèbre par la sagesse de ses lois, long-temps avant que la Grèce sortît de la barbarie.

Egypt had become celebrated for the wisdom of its laws long before Greece had emerged from barbarism.

C'est une des plus grandes mer-veilles qu'on ait vues.

It is one of the greatest wonders that has ever been seen.

L'homme de lettres, dont vous m'avez parlé, a un goût exquis.

The man of letters you spoke to me of has an excellent taste.

Vous avez très-bien instruit vos élèves.

You have instructed your pupils extremely well.

Lucrèce s'est donné la mort.

Lucretia killed herself.

La sécheresse qu'il y a eu au prin-temps a fait périr tous les fruits.

The dry weather we had in the spring has destroyed all the fruit.

Je n'ai point réussi, malgré les mesures que vous m'avez conseillé de prendre.

I have not succeeded, notwith-standing the steps you advised me to take.

Quelle aventure vous est-il ar-rivé ?

What adventures have you met with ?

Cette femme s'est proposée pour modèle à ses enfans,

This woman proposed herself as a model for her children.

Cette femme s'est proposé d'en-seigner la géographie et l'histoire à ses enfans.

This woman proposed to teach geography and history to her chil-dren.

Modèles de phrases sur les prin-cipaux rapports des modes et des temps.

Forms of phrases upon the prin-cipal relations of moods and tenses.

Je l'attendois depuis long-temps, quand il vint me joindre.

I had waited a long time for him, when he came to me.

Il sortit au moment même que j'entrois.

He was going out at the time I was entering.

Je commençois à avoir des crain-tes sur la réussite de votre affaire, lorsque j'ai reçu votre lettre.

I was beginning to be apprehen-sive of the success of your business when I received your letter.

Dès que j'eus fait quelques vi-sites indispensables, je rentrai chez moi, et je ne sortis plus.

As soon as I had paid some indis-pensable visits, I went home and did not go out afterwards.

J'avois déjà tout préparé pour mon départ, lorsque des affaires imprévues m'ont forcé à le différer de quelques jours.

I had already made every pre-paration for my departure, when some unexpected business occurred, that obliged me to defer it for some days.

Vous étiez déjà sorti, quand je me présentai chez vous.

You were already gone out when I called upon you.

J'avois déjà livré à l'impression mon ouvrage, lorsque vous me de-mandiez si je le donnerois bientôt au public.

My work had been sent to be printed when you asked me if I should soon bring it out.

Lorsque j'ai eu terminé mon af-faire, vous avez commencé la vôtre.

When my business was over you began yours.

Lorsque j'eûs déjeûné, je montai à cheval, et je fus à Londres.

When I had done breakfast, I got on horseback, and went to London.

Lorsque j'aurai lu la nouvelle pièce, je vous dirai avec franchise ce que j'en pense.

When I have read the new piece, I will candidly give you my opinion of it.

Iriez-vous à Rome si vous le pouviez?—oui, j'irois.

Would you go to Rome if it were in your power?—yes, I would.

Auriez - vous consenti à ces conditions, si on vous les avoit proposées?

Would you have agreed to these terms, had they been proposed to you?

Irez-vous demain à Londres, si vous le pouvez?—oui, j'irai.

Shall you go to London to-morrow, if you can?—yes, I shall.

Il sera sûrement parti, si vous l'avez voulu.

He will certainly have set out, if you wished it.

Vous eussiez laissé échapper une occasion si favorable, si l'on ne vous eût averti à temps.

You would have let so favourable an opportunity slip, had you not been warned in time.

Continuation des mêmes phrases.

The same phrases continued.

On dit que vous partez aujourd'hui pour Paris.

It is said that you set off to-day for Paris.

Tout le monde soutient que vous accepterez la place qu'on vous offre.

Every one maintains that you will accept of the place that is offered to you.

On soupçonne que vous aviez hier reçu cette agréable nouvelle, quand on vous rencontra.

It is suspected that you had received this agreeable intelligence when you were met yesterday.

Beaucoup de vos amis croient que vous partîtes hier pour la campagne.

Many of your friends believe that you set out yesterday for the country.

Le bruit se répand que vous avez fait une grosse perte.

There is a report that you have met with a considerable loss.

J'apprends dans l'instant que vous fussiez parti il y a trois jours, si des engagemens, que vous aviez contractés depuis long-temps, ne vous avoient retenu.

I have this moment learnt that you would have set out three days since, had not engagements, which you had formed long ago, detained you.

N'est-il pas vrai que vous partiriez aujourd'hui, si vous le pouviez?

Is it not true that you would set out to-day, if you could?

Est-il vrai que vous seriez parti depuis long-temps pour la campagne, si votre amour pour les arts ne vous avoit retenu à la ville?

Is it true that you would have set out for the country long since, had not your love for the arts detained you in town?

Je ne crois pas que vous partiez, quoique tout le monde l'assure.

I do not imagine that you will set out, although every body asserts it.

Je ne croyois pas qu'il fût sitôt de retour.

I did not believe he had gone back so soon.

Il a fallu qu'il ait eu affaire à bien des personnes.

He must have had business with a great many people.

Je doute que votre ami fût venu à bout de ses projets, s'il n'avoit pas été fortement protégé.

I doubt that your friend would have succeeded in his plans, had he not been strongly patronised.

2 F 3

Il n'est point d'homme, quelque mérite qu'il ait, qui ne fût très-mortifié, s'il savoit tout ce qu'on pense de lui.

There is not a man, whatever merit he may possess, that would not be very much mortified, were he to know every thing that is thought of him.

Vous ne vous persuadiez pas que les affaires pussent si mal tourner.

You never persuaded yourself that matters could have taken so unfortunate a turn.

Modèles de phrases sur la négative *Ne.*

Forms of phrases upon the negative Ne.

Il n'y a pas beaucoup d'argent chez les gens de lettres.

There is not much money to be found among men of letters.

Il n'y a point de ressource dans une personne qui n'a point d'esprit.

There are no resources in a person without sense.

C'est à tort que vous l'accusez de jouer; je vous assure qu'il ne joue point.

You accuse him wrongfully of gaming; I assure you he never games.

Entrez dans le salon; vous pourrez lui parler; il ne joue pas.

Go into the room, you may speak to him; he is not playing.

Si pour avoir du bien il en coûte à la probité, je n'en veux point.

I do not wish to make a fortune, if it can only be done at the expense of honesty.

Rien n'est sûr avec les capricieux: vous croyez être bien en faveur, point du tout : l'instant de la plus belle humeur est suivi de la plus fâcheuse.

Nothing is certain with capricious people : you think yourself in favour, by no means : the moment of the best humour is followed by that of the worst.

Vous ne cessez de nous répéter les mêmes choses.

You are constantly repeating the same thing to us.

Je n'aurois osé vous en parler le premier.

I should not have dared to be the first to speak to you of it.

Malgré ses protections, il n'a pu réussir dans ses projets.

With all his interest he has not been able to succeed in his plans.

Cet ouvrage seroit fort bon, n'étoit pour la négligence du style.

This work would be very good, were it not for the negligence of the style.

Y a-t-il quelqu'un dont elle ne médise.

Is there any one she does not slander?

J'ai pris tant de goût pour une vie retirée, que je ne sors presque jamais.

I have acquired so great a taste for retirement, that I seldom go abroad.

Voilà ce qui s'est passé; n'en parlez à personne.

This is what has passed; do not speak of it to any one.

Mon parti est pris; ne m'en parlez plus.

My resolution is fixed; talk to me no more of it.

N'employez aucun de ces moyens: ils sont indignes de vous.

Do not employ any one of these measures; they are unworthy of you.

Rien n'est plus joli.

Nothing is more beautiful.

Je ne dis rien que je ne pense.

I never speak but what I think.

Je ne fais jamais d'excès, que je n'en sois incommodé.

I never commit any excess without suffering by it.

Continuation des mêmes phrases.

C'est un homme pour qui je n'ai ni amour ni estime.

Il n'est ni assez prudent ni assez éclairé.

Je vous assure que je ne le fréquente ni ne le vois.

Ne *faire* que *parcourir les différentes branches des connoissances humaines sans s'arréter à aucune, c'est moins chercher à s'instruire, qu'à tuer le temps.*

Que n'*êtes-vous toujours aussi complaisant?*

Il ne le fera pas, à moins que *vous* ne *l'y engagiez.*

Il n'ira pas, si *vous* ne *l'en priez.*

Il nous a menacés de se venger; nous n'avons fait qu'*en rire.*

Trop d'insouciance ne peut que *nuire.*

Que devenez-vous? il y a trois mois que *nous* ne *vous avons vu?*

Comment vous êtes-vous porté depuis que *nous* ne *vous avons vu?*

C'est bien pire *qu'on* ne *le disoit.*

Peu s'en faut que je n'*aie donné tête baissée dans le piége.*

Dites la vérité en toute occasion; on méprise toujours ceux qui parlent autrement *qu'ils ne pensent.*

Ne *désespérez pas que la vérité* ne *se fasse jour à la longue.*

Je ne disconviens *pas que la chose* ne *soit ainsi.*

Prenez garde *qu'on* ne *vous entraîne dans quelque fausse démarche.*

*J'*empêcherai *bien qu'on* ne *vous nuise dans cette affaire.*

Il craint *qu'on* ne *le soupçonne d'avoir trempé dans ce complot.*

On lui a donné d'excellens conseils, de crainte *qu'il* ne *manquât l'occasion de faire connoître ce qu'il est en état de faire.*

J'y ai long-temps travaillé; je ne saurois *en venir à bout.*

Vous feriez mieux de vous taire; vous ne savez ce que vous *dites.*

Vous ne *sauriez me faire un plus grand plaisir.*

He is a man for whom I have neither love nor esteem.

He is neither sufficiently prudent nor enlightened.

I assure you I neither associate with him nor see him.

To go through the different branches of human knowledge only, without fixing upon any one of them, is not to seek for instruction, but to kill time.

Why are you not at all times equally complaisant?

He will not do it, unless you persuade him to it.

He will not go, if you do not request it of him.

He has threatened us with vengeance; we only laughed at him.

Too great supineness cannot but be hurtful.

What has become of you? we have not seen you these three months.

How have you been since we saw you?

It is much worse than was said.

I was near running headlong into the snare.

Tell the truth on all occasions: those who speak what they do not think are always despised.

Do not despair that truth will appear in time.

I admit that it is so.

Take care that you are not led into some false step.

I shall prevent them from doing you any harm in this business.

He is apprehensive that he is suspected of being concerned in this plot.

They have given him excellent advice, lest he should lose the opportunity of shewing what he was capable of doing.

I have been long employed about it; I cannot accomplish it.

You had better be silent; you do not know what you are saying.

You cannot do me a greater favour.

Phrases sur quelques délicatesses de la Langue Françoise.

Phrases on some delicacies of the French Language.

Irez-vous ce soir à l'opéra? — oui, j'irai.

Shall you go to the opera this evening!—yes, I shall.

Iriez-vous avec plaisir à Rome? —oui, j'irois.

Would you cheerfully go to Rome? —yes, I would.

La justice qui nous est quelquefois refusée par nos contemporains, la postérité sait nous la rendre.

Posterity knows how to do us that justice which is sometimes refused us by our contemporaries.

Cette grandeur qui vous étonne si fort, il la doit à votre nonchalance.

That greatness which so much astonishes you he owes to your indifference.

Il périt, ce héros, si cher à son pays.

That hero, so dear to his country, perished.

Je l'avois bien prévu que ce haut degré de grandeur seroit la cause de sa ruine.

I foresaw that the greatness of his elevation would be his ruin.

Citoyens, étrangers, ennemis, peuples, rois, empereurs, le plaignent et le révèrent.

Citizens, strangers, enemies, nations, kings, emperors, pity and respect him.

L'assemblée finie, chacun se retira chez soi.

The assembly being over, each returned home.

Heureux le peuple qu'un sage roi gouverne!

Happy are the people who are governed by a wise king!

Il refusa les plus grands honneurs, content de les mériter.

He refused the greatest honors, satisfied with having deserved them.

Prières, remontrances, commandemens, tout est inutile.

Entreaties, remonstrances, injunctions, all are useless.

Le vent renverse tours, cabanes, palais, églises.

The wind overturns towers. cottages, palaces, churches.

Notre réputation ne dépend pas du caprice des hommes; mais elle dépend des actions louables que nous faisons.

Our reputation does not depend on the caprice of men, but on the commendable actions we perform.

Il y a beaucoup de choses qu'il n'importe point du tout de savoir.

There are many things which it is of no consequence at all to know.

La vue de l'esprit a plus d'étendue que la vue du corps.

The eye of the mind reaches much farther than the bodily eye.

Ce qui sert à la vanité, n'est que vanité.

What promotes vanity is only vanity.

Tout ce qui n'a que le monde pour fondement, se dissipe et s'évanouit avec le monde.

All that is confined to this lower world disperses and vanishes with the world.

C'est le privilège des grands hommes de vaincre l'envie : le mérite la fait naître, le mérite la fait mourir.

It is the prerogative of great men to conquer envy : merit gives it birth, and merit destroys it.

L'amour-propre est plus habile que le plus habile homme du monde.

Self-love is more ingenious than the most ingenious man in the world.

En quittant le monde, on ne quitte le plus souvent ni les erreurs ni les folles passions du monde.

In renouncing the world we generally renounce neither the errors nor giddy passions of the world.

TREATISE

ON FRENCH VERSIFICATION.

By G. _Hamonière._

FRENCH versification is the art of making French verses
agreeably to certain rules.

These rules relate; 1, to the construction of the verses;
2, to the manner of intermingling them.

ARTICLE I.

On the Construction of French Verses.

------

§ I.

On the different kinds of Verses.

French verses are measured by the number of syllables.
Variety in the number of syllables produces various kinds
of verses.

1. Example of verses of _twelve_ syllables.

> C'est en vain qu'au Parnasse un téméraire auteur,
> Pense de l'art des vers atteindre la hauteur,
> S'il ne sent point du ciel l'influence secrète,
> Si son astre en naissant ne l'a formé poète.

French verses of twelve syllables are called Alexan-
drines, _vers Alexandrins,_ or heroic verses, _vers héroïques_
or _grand vers._

2. Example of verses of _ten_ syllables.

> Chez les amis, tout s'excuse, tout passe;
> Chez les amans, tout plait, tout est parfait;

Chez les époux, tout ennuie, tout lasse;
Le devoir nuit; chacun est ainsi fait.

3. Examples of verses of *eight* syllables.

Ne forçons pas notre talent;
Nous ne f. rions rien avec grâce;
Jamais un lourdaud, quoi qu'il fasse,
Ne sauroit passer pour galant.

4. Examples of verses of *seven* syllables.

J'avois juré d'être sage,
Mais avant peu j'en fus las;
O raison! c'est bien dommage
Que l'ennui suive tes pas.

5. Example of verses of *six* syllables.

A soi-même odieux,
Le sot de tout s'irrite,
En tous lieux il s'évite,
Et se trouve en tous lieux.

6. Examples of verses in *five* syllables.

La sombre tristesse
Toujours me poursuit;
La crainte me presse,
Le repos me fuit.

7. Example of verses of *four* syllables.

Oui, pour jamais
Chassons l'image
De la volage
Que j'adorais.

8. Example of verses of *three* syllables.

De ce vin
Le venin
Est extrême.

9. Example of verses of *two* syllables.

Quel boud
Fait chaque maison!
Je vois danser en rond
Les ormes.

10. Example of verses of *one* syllable.

Pluton dans son manoir
Noir
D'amour soupire.

The line, in each of these kinds of verse, of which the last word ends in *e* mute : as in *soupire,* or in *e* mute followed by an *s :* as in the plural of nouns, *les hommes ;* or followed by *nt,* as in the third person plural of verbs, *ils aiment,* have always a syllable more; that is to say, the lines of *twelve* syllables have *thirteen,* those of *ten* syllables have *eleven,* and so on, because the syllable in which is the *e* mute is not reckoned.

The lines so terminated are called *feminine,* and the others *masculine.*

The *e* which is followed by *nt* in the third person plural of the imperfect tense of the indicative mood, and of the conditional present, is not to be reckoned as an *e* mute, because the termination *oient* has the sound of *è* open.

Lines of five syllables and under, are seldom used but in comic pieces, or such as are intended to be set to music.

§ II.

On the Rhyme.

Rhyme is the consonance of two sounds which terminate two lines. It is indispensable in French verse. Rhyme being intended merely for the ear, it is generally to be judged from the sound rather than from the orthography. Thus, though the final syllable of two words be written differently, it is sufficient that they produce the same sound to rhyme together.

As the lines are divided into masculine and feminine lines, so is the rhyme into masculine and feminine rhymes.

It is in general only the sound of the last syllable which is considered in masculine rhymes; thus *vérité* rhymes with *fierté*; but the sound of the last syllable is not sufficient for feminine rhymes, because the hollow pronunciation of the last syllable prevents the perception of a palpable consonance. It must therefore be formed by the consonance of the sounds of the penultima. Thus *monde*, which would not rhyme with *demande*, rhymes perfectly well with *profonde*.

The masculine and feminine rhymes are divided into what the French call rich, *riches*, and sufficient, *suffisantes*, and what may be called in English *perfect* and *allowable*.

The rhyme is *rich* or *perfect*, when formed by two sounds exactly similar, and often represented by the same letters : as *impétueux* and *tortueux*, *pensée* and *insensée*.

The rhyme is *sufficient* or *allowable*, when it does not afford so exact a consonance of sound and orthography : as *main* and *seing*, *assidue* and *vue*.

In general it may be said that when a masculine rhyme is good it will be yet better by becoming feminine. For instance, if *interdit* rhymes well with *petit*, *interdite* will rhyme yet better with *petite*.

As the consonance of sounds is essential to rhyme, short syllables cannot well be made to rhyme with long ones, nor the *l* liquid with the *l* harsh.

The *e* close, the *i* and the *u*, whether alone or followed by one of the consonants *l*, *r*, *s*, *t*, *z*, cannot make good masculine rhymes, unless preceded by the same consonants or the same vowels.

It is the same with *a* in the third person singular of the preterit tense of verbs; with the sounds *ant*, *ent*, *en* and *on*, and in general with all the sounds common to a great number of words.

A word ending in *s*, *x* or *z*, can rhyme but with a word ending with one of those consonants.

The persons of verbs ending in *ent*, *ois*, *oit*, *oient* or *aient* can rhyme but with persons of verbs having the same termination.

The consonance of sound and orthography cannot authorise making the same word rhyme with itself, a simple with its compound, or even two words having the same derivation, when they are nearly synonymous.

§. III.

On the Cæsura.

The *cæsura* is a pause, or rest, which divides the line into two parts, each of which is called *hemistick*.

It is only in verses of *twelve* or *ten* syllables that the *cæsura* is found.

The *cæsura* in verses of *twelve* syllables falls immediately after the *sixth*, and divides the line into equal parts:

> Que toujours dans vos vers—le sens, coupant les mots,
> Suspende l'hémistiche,—en marque le repos.

The *cæsura*, in lines of *ten* syllables, is immediately after the *fourth*.

> A Nevers donc—chez les Visitandines,
> Vivoit naguère—un perroquet fameux.

When we say that the *cæsura*, in heroic verse, is immediately after the *sixth* syllable, and in lines of *ten* syllables
immediately after the *fourth*, we mean that there should
be a natural pause, forming an interval between the first
and second hemistick, so as to be felt in recitation without
straining or obscuring the sense of the phrase.

The *cæsura* is, therefore, vicious when the word on
which it falls, and which terminates the first hemistick,
cannot be separated in the pronunciation from the word
that immediately follows it.

It is not necessary, for the regularity of the *cæsura*, that
the sense should be absolutely completed with the *sixth* or
fourth syllable, and that there should be nothing in one
hemistick depending on, or that is the complement of, what
is in the other; it is sufficient if the complement of what
is in the other hemistick does not prevent the pause, nor
oblige to pronounce too closely upon each other the last
syllable of the first hemistick and the first syllable of the
second.

The *e* mute alone, or followed by the letters *s* or *nt*,
having but a hollow sound, can never terminate the syllable on which the *cæsura* falls. But when a word ending
n *e* mute is followed by another beginning with a vowel
with which the *e* mute is liquified, then the *cæsura* may
fall on the syllable which precedes the *e* mute, and which,
by the elision of that *e*, becomes the last of the word :

Et qui seul, sans ministre, à l'exemple des dieux,
Soutiens tout par toi-même, et vois tout par tes yeux.

The *cæsura* is not allowed to separate an adjective from
its substantive ; but if a substantive be preceded, or followed, by several adjectives, it may then be separated
from them by the *cæsura* :

Les chanoines vermeils—et brillans de santé,
S'engraissoient d'une longue—et sainte oisiveté.

All similitude of sounds must be carefully avoided at the end of each hemistick in the same line, or at the end of the first hemistick in two lines that follow each other, or at the end of a line and of the first hemistick of the preceding or ensuing line. The following are, therefore, not proper for imitation:

Aux Saumaises *futurs* préparer des *tortures.*

J'eus un frère, *Seigneur*, illustre et généreux,
Digne, par sa *valeur*, du sort le plus heureux,

Il faut pour les avoir employer *notre soin :*
Ils sont à moi *du moins* tout autant qu'à mon frère.

§. IV.

On the Junction of Vowels.

When the last syllable of a word ends in *e* mute, and the next word begins with a vowel, or *h* not aspirated, that syllable is liquified and blended in the pronunciation with the first of the word that follows it:

Dieu sait, quand il lui plaît, fai*re* éclater sa gloire,
Et son peu*ple* est toujours présent à sa mémoire.

But if the word ending in *e* mute be followed by a word beginning with a consonant, or an *h* aspirate, the *e* mute forms a syllable, and is pronounced as in the following line:

Que*lle* faus*se* pudeur à fein*dre* vous oblige?

When the *e* mute in the last syllable of a word is followed by an *s*, or by *nt*; it always forms a syllable:

Que mes prop*res* périls t'assu*rent* de ta grâce.
Que les méchants appren*nent* aujourd'hui.

Words ending in *e* mute preceded by another vowel, such as *vie, vue, proie, joie*, etc., cannot be employed with elegance in the body of a line, unless they be followed by a word beginning with a vowel with which the *e* is blended.

The following line is therefore proper.

C'est Venus toute entière à sa proie attachée.

' If the *e* mute preceded by a vowel be followed by an *s*, or by *nt*, the word can be placed only at the end of the line:

Je vois combien tes vœux sont loin de tes pensées.

The *e* mute in the middle of a word, preceded by another vowel, does not form a syllable of itself; therefore, *tuerai, crieront*, are pronounced as if written *tûrai, crîront*.

A word ending with any other vowel than *e* mute can never be placed before a word beginning with a vowel, or an *h* not aspirated.

Though the word *oui* begins and ends with a vowel, it may nevertheless be repeated in a line, or placed immediately after an interjection ending with a vowel.

The *t* final of the conjunction *et* being never pronounced, that conjunction can never be placed before a word beginning with a vowel.

We often meet, even in the best poets, with words ending with nasal letters, placed before others beginning with a vowel; but this junction of letters has in it something harsh, and should be avoided as much as possible.

§. V.

On Vowels forming or not forming Diphthongs.

Eau is only one syllable in all words in which the *e* is not accentuated; *beau, seau.*

Eo is likewise but one syllable in all words in which it is not accentuated.

Ia generally forms two syllables: *di-amant, confi-a, étudi-a.*

Some words are to be excepted; such as *diable, fiacre, bréviaire, galimathias, liard, familiarité, viande.*

Iai makes two syllables: *je confi-ai, j'étudi-ai.* Those letters form sometimes two syllables, sometimes but one, in the words *biais, biaiser.*

Iau always makes two syllables: *mi-aulen, besti-aux.*

Ie generally forms but one syllable: *fief, ciel, troisième, pièce, barrière, pitié,* etc. Are to be excepted the following words, in which *ie* forms two syllables: 1. *bri-ef, gri-ef, essenti-el, Gabri-el, matéri-el, substanti-el, kyri-elle, li-erre.* 2. Verbs of the first conjugation ending in *ier,* excepting the tenses in which the *e* is mute: as, in *j'oublierai.* 3. Substantives derived from those verbs. 4. Adjectives denoting condition, proper names denoting profession or country: as *phrygi-en, histori-en, comédi-en.* Except *chrétien.* 5. Substantives ending in *ience: expéri-ence, sci-ence.* In the words *hier* and *ancien* it is sometimes but one syllable and sometimes two.

Ieu is monosyllabical in substantives, and in the word *vieux;* it is dissyllabical in adjectives: *furi-eux, préci-eux.*

Io generally forms two syllables: *li-on, nous mari-ons, vi-olence, vi-olon.* Must be excepted the following words in which *io* is monosyllabical: 1. *Babiole, fiole, pioche.* 2. The first person plural of the imperfect tense of the indicative mood, of the conditional present, of the present and imperfect tenses of the subjunctive mood of verbs, when not preceded by an *r* and another consonant.

Oe is but one syllable in all words in which it is not accentuated.

Oi is never more than one syllable.

Oue makes two syllables, except in the word *fouet.*

Oui makes likewise two syllables, except in the word *oui.*

Ua generally forms two syllables.

Ue always forms two syllables, except in words in which the *e* is mute.

Ui makes but one syllable: *lui, construire,* etc. except in the words *ru-iner, bru-ine, pitu-ite,* and in the termination *uis.*

Uo always makes two syllables.

§. VI.

On the Running of Verses.

Verses that run into one another, that is to say, in which the sense remains imperfect at the end of one line and is completed but at the beginning of the next, are destitute of grace.

This running of the lines one into another is tolerated but in three cases: 1. When the sense is entirely suspended:

> Faut-il qu'en un moment un scrupule timide
> Perde?....mais quel bonheur nous envoie Atalide?

2. When the sense is already completed by a word betwixt a comma and a full period :

> Je ne te vante pas cette foible victoire,
> Titus. Ah plût au ciel que sans blesser ta gloire.....

3. When the sense is completed but by a word betwixt a comma and a semi-colon, or a colon: :

> Sitôt que du nectar la troupe est abreuvée,
> On dessert ; et soudain la nappe étant levée....

This running of the lines into one another is disallowed

only in lofty composition. It is allowed in comedy, in fables, and in poetry on light subjects.

§. VII.

On poetic licences, and words not to be used.

Though the French poetic language does not differ from that of prose, and though the same words are generally used, the poet is, however, allowed to make, in the construction of his phrase, certain transpositions not permitted in prose, and which contribute much to the harmony and majesty of the verses. These transpositions should always be made with judgment and taste, so as to occasion neither harshness nor obscurity :

> Celui qui met un frein à la fureur des flots,
> Sait aussi des méchans arrêter les complots.

> Ce traitement, madame, a droit de vous surprendre ;
> Mais enfin, c'est ainsi que se venge Alexandre.

French poetry allows also the use of expressions which would be improper in prose : such as, *les humains* or *les mortels* for *les hommes, forfaits* for *crimes, coursier* for *cheval, glaive* for *épée, penser* for *pensée,* ondes for *eaux, flanc* for *sein, antique* for *ancien, l'Éternel* for *Dieu, hymen* or *hyménée* for *mariage, espoir* for *espérance, Olympe* for *ciel, misère* for *calamité, labeur* for *travail, repentance* for *repentir, jadis* for *autrefois, soudain* for *aussitôt, naguère* for *il n'y a pas long-temps.*

The best French poets, *Corneille, Racine, Boileau, Molière, Lafontaine,* have sometimes allowed themselves poetic licences in which they should be imitated but with great temperance. Those licences are either in opposition to the rules of grammar or to custom.

The licences in opposition to the rules of grammar

consist in the elision of the *s* in the first person of the indicative mood in verbs of the 2d, 3d and 4th conjugations, in varying the participle active, or in varying a participle passive when it is invariable, and in making verbs active of verbs neuter; in writing *que je die* for *que je dise*, *grâces à* for *grâce à*, *mêmes* for *même*, *en* for *dans*, *dont* for *avec lequel*, *eux-même* for *eux-mêmes*, *où* for *auquel*, *est* for *sont*.

EXAMPLES.

En les blâmant enfin, j'ai dit ce que je *croi*,
Et tel qui m'en reprend, en pense autant que moi.

BOILEAU.

Et les petits en même temps,
Voletans, se *culbutans*,
Délogèrent tous sans trompette.

LAFONTAINE.

Le seul amour de Rome a sa main *animée*.
.... les misères
Que durant notre enfance ont *enduré* nos pères.

CORNEILLE.

Ce n'étoit pas jadis sur ce ton ridicule
Qu'amour dictoit les vers que *soupiroit* Tibulle.
Je ne prends point plaisir à *croître* ma misère.

BOILEAU.

Mais quoique je craignisse, il faut *que je le die*,
Je n'en avois prévu que la moindre partie.
Grâces au ciel, nos mains ne sont point criminelles.

RACINE.

Ici dispensez-moi du récit des blasphèmes
Qu'ils ont vomi tous deux contre Jupiter *mêmes*.

CORNEILLE.

The licences in opposition to custom consist in writing *encor* for *encore*, *certe* for *certes*, etc.

In poetry, and particularly in lofty poetry, all words that are unpleasant to the ear should be carefully avoided, whether it be because they have some similitude of sound with other words in the same line, or because they are too mean, or too prosaic : as *ceux-ci, c'est pourquoi, parce que, ainsi, car, en effet, afin que,* etc.

   Il est un heureux choix de mots harmonieux.
   Fuyez des mauvais sons le concours odieux.
   Le vers le mieux rempli, la plus noble pensée,
   Ne peut plaire à l'esprit quand l'oreille est blessée.

Taste and discernment, aided by an attentive reading of the best poets, will teach better than all the rules that can be given, the proper use and choice of words; for an able poet will sometimes make   happy use of a word which seems to be excluded from poetic language.

ARTICLE II.

On the intermingling of Verses.

The intermingling of verses may be considered with respect to measure and with respect to rhyme.

The measure is arbitrary in poems on light subjects, and lyric poetry; but it is determined in serious pieces which are generally written in verses of *twelve* or *ten* syllables. Epic poem, tragedy, and noble comedy are written only in verses of *twelve* syllables. Didactic and descriptive poems, epistles, satires, elegies, and eclogues, are written in verses of *twelve* or *ten* syllables.

In all French poetical writings the masculine rhymes are mixed with the feminine.

According to the different manners in which the rhymes may be mixed, they are divided into *following* or *close* rhymes, *rimes suivies*, or into *intermingled* rhymes, *rimes croisées* ou *entremêlées.*

The rhymes are called *following* or *close*, when, after two masculine rhymes, come two feminine, then two masculine, and so on, as in the following lines.

> Dans le réduit obscur d'une alcove enfoncée,
> S'élève un lit de plume à grands frais amassée,
> Quatre rideaux pompeux, par un double contour,
> En défendent l'entrée à la clarté du jour ;
> Là, parmi les douceurs d'un tranquille silence,
> Règne sur le duvet une heureuse indolence.
> C'est là que le prélat, muni d'un déjeuner,
> Dormoit d'un léger somme attendant le dîner.

The rhymes are called *intermingled* when a masculine rhyme is separated from that which corresponds with it, by one or two feminine rhymes, and reciprocally, as in the following verses.

> Fortune dont la main couronne
> Les forfaits le plus inouis,
> Du faux éclat qui t'environne.
> Serons-nous toujours éblouis?
> Jusques à quand, trompeuse idole,
> D'un culte honteux et frivole
> Honorerons-nous tes autels?
> Verra-t-on toujours tes caprices
> Consacrés par les sacrifices
> Et par l'hommage des mortels?

Following or *close* rhymes are seldom used but in verses of twelve and ten syllables, and consequently but in serious and long poems.

The fault chiefly to be avoided in following rhymes is ending four masculine lines with the same rhyme, when they are separated but by two feminine lines; or four feminine, when separated but by two masculine.

Similitude of sound in masculine and feminine rhymes which follow each other, produces also an effect unpleasant to the ear, and which should be avoided.

Intermingled rhymes are used in all kinds of verse, in stanzas and irregular verses; in a word, in lyric poetry, in pieces on light subjects, and those intended to be set to music.

§. I.

On Stanzas.

Stanzas are a certain number of lines at the end of which the sense is finished and complete.

A stanza may be composed of a greater or lesser number of lines; there should not be less than *four*, and there are seldom more than *ten*.

When all the stanzas of a poem are of an equal number of lines, having the same mixture of rhymes, and the number of syllables in each line is equally distributed, they are called *regular stanzas*. They are on the contrary called *irregular* when they differ from each other, either by the intermingling of the rhymes or by the number of syllables in each line.

It is necessary that stanzas written on the same subject should begin and end with the same kind of rhyme; that is to say, that if the first stanza begin with a masculine rhyme and end with a feminine, the second must likewise begin with a masculine rhyme and end with a feminine, and the same with the rest; whence it results, that when a stanza begins and ends with the same kind of rhyme, a feminine rhyme for instance, the one which immediately follows beginning likewise with a feminine rhyme, two different rhymes of the same kind are thus found together. The last line of a stanza should never rhyme with the first of the next stanza.

Stanzas considered with respect to the number of lines of which they are composed, may be divided into stanzas of an even number of lines and stanzas of an odd number of lines (*stances de nombre pair, stances de nombre impair*).

. As the intermingling of verses with respect to the number of syllables is arbitrary in stanzas, the rules we are going to lay down relate to the intermingling of the rhymes.

Stanzas of four *lines.*

In quatrains, or stanzas of four lines, the lines may be intermingled two ways:

> Auprès d'une féconde source
> D'où coulent cent petits ruisseaux,
> L'amour, fatigué de sa course,
> Dormoit sur un lit de roseaux.

> L'univers te dut la naissance,
> Feu créateur, céleste amour !
> Le plaisir te révèle au jour,
> Et la mort n'est que ton absence.

Stanzas of six *lines.*

The stanza of six lines is nothing more than a quatrain, to which are added two verses that rhyme together.

These two lines are generally placed at the beginning; then there should be a slight pause after the third line: sometimes they are placed at the end, and there is no pause after the third line. The intermingling of the rhymes in the four other lines is the same as in the quatrain.

Renonçons au stérile appui
Des grands qu'on adore aujourd'hui :
Ne fondons point sur eux une espérance folle :
Leur pompe, indigne de nos vœux,
N'est qu'un simulacre frivole,
Et les solides biens ne dépendent point d'eux.

Seigneur, dans ton temple adorable
Quel mortel est digne d'entrer ?
Qui pourra, grand Dieu, pénétrer
Dans ce séjour impénétrable,
Où tes saints inclinés, d'un œil respectueux,
Contemplent de ton front l'éclat majestueux.

Stanzas of eight *lines.*

Stanzas of eight lines are in general only two quatrains
united. There should be a pause after the first quatrain.

Dans l'aurore de la vie,
Les jeux font tous nos plaisirs :
A cette heureuse folie
Succèdent d'autres désirs :
Bacchus, dans notre vieillesse
Fait oublier les amours :
La mort vient, le charme cesse,
Et nous dormons pour toujours.

In stanzas of eight lines the rhymes may also be so
arranged as to begin or end with two lines that rhyme
together, while three of the remaining six have one rhyme,
and the other three another.

Stanzas of ten *lines.*

Stanzas of ten lines are, properly speaking, but a quatrain
and sextain united, in each of which the rhymes are intermingled as we have just said. There should be a pause
after the fourth line and after the seventh.

Ce n'est pas d'un amas funeste
De massacres et de débris
Qu'une vertu pure et céleste
Tire son véritable prix :
Un héros qui de la victoire
Emprunte son unique gloire,
N'est héros que quelques momens :
Et pour l'être toute sa vie
Il doit opposer à l'envie
De plus paisibles monumens.

RULES FOR STANZAS HAVING AN ODD NUMBER OF LINES.

These stanzas must necessarily have three lines that rhyme together. They must all three be separated by different rhymes, or at least one of them must be separated from the other two.

Stanzas of five lines.

In these stanzas the only rules to be observed are those we have just given for stanzas of an odd number of lines.

O rives du Jourdain ! ô champs aimés des cieux !
Sacrés monts, fertiles vallées,
Par cent miracles signalées,
Du doux pays de nos aïeux
Serons-nous toujours exilées.

Stanzas of seven lines.

Stanzas of seven lines begin with a quatrain, at the end of which there is a pause.

L'hypocrite en fraude fertile,
Dès l'enfance est pétri de fard ;
Il sait colorer avec art

. Le fiel que sa bouche distille;
Et la morsure du serpent
Est moins aiguë et moins subtile .
Que le venin caché que sa langue répand.

Stanzas of nine lines.

The first part is a quatrain, ending with a pause, and the latter part a stanza of five lines.

Offrez, à l'exemple des anges,
A ce Dieu, votre unique appui,
Un sacrifice de louanges,
Le seul qui soit digne de lui.
Chantez d'une voix ferme et sûre
De cet auteur de la nature
Les bienfaits toujours naissaṇs:
Mais sachez qu'une main impure
Peut souiller le plus pur encens.

Intermingled rhymes were formerly used in several kinds of little pieces, which are to be found in the ancient poets, such as the *sonnet*, the *rondeau*, simple and redoubled, the *triolet*, the *ballad*, the *chant-royal*, the *lai*, the *virelai* and the *villanelle*. These little pieces had rules for the intermingling of the rhymes, but as they are now entirely out of use, we will not speak of them.

§ II.

On irregular verses.

We call irregular verses, *vers libres*, those which have no uniformity either with respect to the number of the syllables or the intermingling of the rhymes, and which are not divided into stanzas; that is to say, that in irregular verse the rhymes may be intermingled agreeably to the will of the writer, who may give to each line the

CHAPTER II.

CHAPTER III.

CHAPTER IV.

CHAPTER V.

CHAPTER VI.

CHAPTER VII.

CHAPTER VIII.

CHAPTER IX.

PART II.

THE SYNTAX, OR WORDS CONSIDERED IN THEIR CONSTRUCTION.

CHAPTER I.

· F I N I S.

OUVRAGES publiés par M. HAMONIÈRE, *qui se trouvent à Paris, chez* THÉOPHILE BARROIS *fils, Libraire pour les Langues étrangères vivantes, quai Voltaire, n.° 11.*

LE NOUVEAU GUIDE DE LA CONVERSATION, EN ANGLAIS ET EN FRANÇAIS, contenant un Vocabulaire, des Dialogues et des Idiotismes; par G. HAMONIÈRE, Paris, 1 vol. in-12, sur beau papier, demi-reliure, 3 fr.

NOUVEAU DICTIONNAIRE DE POCHE FRANÇAIS-ANGLAIS ET ANGLAIS-FRANÇAIS, contenant tous les mots des deux langues dont l'usage est autorisé; dans lequel on a inséré les termes de marine et d'art militaire, les prétérits et les participes passés de tous les verbes anglais irréguliers, et où l'on a marqué l'accent de tous les mots anglais, pour en faciliter la prononciation : le tout suivi d'un Dictionnaire géographique; par G. HAMONIÈRE. Paris, 1816; 2 vol. in-16, imprimés sur papier vélin superfin, reliés en un volume, 7 fr.

LETTRES DE LADY MARIE WORTLEY MONTAGU, écrites pendant ses voyages en Europe, en Asie et en Afrique; nouvelle édition, augmentée de beaucoup de lettres qui ne se trouvent pas dans les précédentes : traduction française, par G. HAMONIÈRE, avec le texte en regard. Paris, 1816, 2 vol. in-12, brochés, 6 fr.

GRAMMAIRE ANGLAISE simplifiée et réduite à vingt-une leçons, par VERGANI; cinquième édition, augmentée par G. HAMONIÈRE. Paris, 1817; 1 vol. in-12, cartonné, 2 fr. 50 c.

NOUVELLE GRAMMAIRE ESPAGNOLE raisonnée, par JOSSE; nouvelle édition, revue, corrigée et augmentée d'un traité de versification espagnole, par G. HAMONIÈRE. Paris, 1818, 2 vol. in-12, br. 5 f.

LE NOUVEAU GUIDE DE LA CONVERSATION, EN ESPAGNOL ET EN FRANÇAIS, contenant un Vocabulaire, des Dialogues et des Idiotismes; par G. HAMONIÈRE. Paris, 1815, 1 vol. in-8°, papier vélin, broché, 4 fr.

LE NOUVEAU GUIDE DE LA CONVERSATION, EN PORTUGAIS ET EN FRANÇAIS, contenant un Vocabulaire, des Dialogues et des Idiotismes, et suivi d'un Tableau comparatif des monnaies, poids et mesures de France, de Portugal et du Brésil; par G. HAMONIÈRE. Paris, 1817; 1 vol. in-18, demi-reliure; 3 f. 50 c.

RECUEIL DE MORCEAUX EN PROSE EXTRAITS DES MEILLEURS AUTEURS PORTUGAIS ET FRANÇAIS, en portugais et en français; par G. HAMONIÈRE. Paris, 1818, 1 vol. in-12, broché, 3 fr.

GRAMMAIRE RUSSE, avec un appendice, contenant des remarques sur la langue slavonne et une très-belle planche gravée offrant un modèle d'écriture russe; par G. HAMONIÈRE. Paris, Imprimerie royale, 1817, 1 vol. in-8°, broché, 7 f. 50 c.

DIALOGUES RUSSES ET FRANÇAIS A L'USAGE DES DEUX NATIONS, suivis d'un Recueil de phrases familières et de proverbes; par G. HAMONIÈRE. Paris, Imprimerie royale, 1816; 1 vol. in-8°, broché, 4 fr.

VOCABULAIRE FRANÇAIS ET RUSSE, précédé d'un Alphabet et d'un Traité de prononciation russes, et suivi d'un tableau comparatif des monnaies, poids et mesures de France et de Russie; par G. HAMONIÈRE. Paris, Imprimerie royale, 1815; 1 vol. in-8°, papier vélin, broché, 4 fr. 50 c.

GRAMMAIRE FRANÇAISE A L'USAGE DES RUSSES, nouvelle édition, revue, corrigée et augmentée par G. HAMONIÈRE. Paris, Imprimerie royale, 1816; 1 vol. in-8°, papier vélin, broché, 5 fr.

Lightning Source UK Ltd.
Milton Keynes UK
UKHW012246031118
331733UK00005B/993/P